## Acknowledgements

*My sincerest thanks to the enthusiastic, insightful support of Michel and Brenda.
Thank you very much to all of the diligent and unselfish work of the owners, staff and
tireless contributors and editors of Wikipedia.org upon which the
material in this book relies heavily for efficacious documentary support of
many of the footnoted items sited in the text of the transcripts and comments
from Matilda O'Donnell MacElroy.*

## Disclaimer

*As far as the Editor of the book, "Alien Interview" is concerned, and for all practical
purposes, the content of the book is a work of fiction. The Editor makes no claim to
the factuality of the content, and in fact, cannot prove that the alleged author
actually ever existed. Although some of the dates, locations, persons and incidents
described may be factual or based on fact, there is no evidence to authenticate that
equally as many may be subjective contrivances of the author.*

*All of the information, notes and transcripts received by the Editor are contained in
their complete, original form, as represented in the book. The Editor is no longer in
possession of any original documents or copies of original documents from the
author, i.e. Mrs. MacElroy.*

*Some material contained in the book may have similarities to Earth philosophies as
the variety of these are too numerous to list, and bear too many fundamental
similarities to be easily differentiated. Although the book discusses the origins of the
universe, the time track of the physical universe, paranormal activities of immortal
and/or extraterrestrial beings, "aliens" or "gods", it is in no way the intention of the
Editor to represent, endorse, forward or assume the viewpoint of the author, any
political doctrine, economic vested interest, scientific hypothesis, religious practice
or philosophy, whether terrestrial or extraterrestrial.*

*The notes and transcripts contained in the book, are solely and only based on the
representations and documents provided by the author, the late Matilda O'Donnell
MacElroy, unless otherwise specifically annotated by Footnotes in The Appendix of
the book.*

*The Editor is not responsible for any assumptions, inferences or conclusions made
by the reader based on the material is this book, which are solely and only the
responsibility of the reader.*

*What is true for you, is true for you.*

Lawrence R. Spencer -- Editor

# Table Of Contents

# Foreword:

"We ask, as Fools who know not Our Own Spirit:

Where are the hidden traces left by The Gods?"

-- Rig Veda --
book i, stanza 164, lines 5 a & b

# Preamble

What greater brutality can be inflicted on anyone than to erase or
deny the spiritual awareness, identity,
ability, and memory that is the essence of oneself?

-- Lawrence R. Spencer --
2008

# Dedication

This book is dedicated to all Immortal Spiritual Beings, whether they are aware of themselves as such, or not. It is especially dedicated to the wisdom, courage and integrity of those Greater Beings, who in various incarnations at various times during the past, in the present and into the future, enkindle and carry the Flame of Truth into the darkest corners of the universe.

This dedication is not only to the philosophical teachings and technologies developed by these beings, but to the demonstrated and documented courage to apply their philosophy in the face of overwhelming ignorance, overt hostility and aggressive suppression by lesser beings and by the self-serving vested interests of inter-galactic and planetary political, economic, and religious institutions.

Though relatively few in number, the profound wisdom and heroic dedication of such beings, and those who share their quest, have been the only effective deterrent to spiritual slavery. Freedom, Communication, Creativity ,Trust and Truth for all Immortal Spiritual Beings in this universe is their legacy. The Good Examples set by them is our sanctuary and sustenance. Personal, diligent application of their teachings is our weapon against the dwindling spiral of chaos and oblivion that is the material universe.

-- Lawrence R. Spencer --

# Editorial Guidelines Used In This Book

I have tried not to edit the material I received from Mrs. MacElroy except to the degree necessary to make a logical sequence of the material she mailed to me. Wherever possible I have quoted or transcribed her original written notes verbatim.

In some instances I have taken editorial liberty to add other information, or supplementary commentary which I feel will add useful definitions, or clarification to the information given in the official transcripts, or to her remarks or observations. These appear as a numbered "(Footnote)" in the **Appendix** at the end of the book. All footnote references, where possible, are **copied verbatim** from the free internet encyclopedia website **www.wikipedia.org.** If information was not available through Wikipedia.org, I used the popular internet search engine **www.google.com** to find a website reference that seemed most appropriate to the subject matter.

Mrs. MacElroy did not make a notation of dates in most of the documents, so I am not certain that the sequence of material matches the actual sequence of events, or sequence of the interviews, except as noted on the official transcripts themselves.

Since it has been 60 years since the date of the interviews, and considering the age of Mrs. MacElroy before her death, I reasoned that she did not necessarily have an acute recollection of exact names, dates and times, except as recorded in the transcripts of July 8th through August 12th, 1947.

The material in this book is organized into three different types. The following notations will be used to designate where these appear in this book:

1) (MATILDA O'DONNELL MACELROY PERSONAL NOTES)
(TYPE FONT: Times Roman, 12 point)

2) (OFFICIAL TRANSCRIPT OF INTERVIEW)
(Courier New, 12 point)

3) **1 (Footnote)**
(TYPE FONT: Arial, 10 point, Bold)

**-- The Editor**

# Definitions

Vested Interest:

- a survival or non-survival plan or agenda which has been "clothed" to make it seem like something other than what it actually is.

- any person, group or entity which prevents or controls communication to serve their own purposes, (plans or agenda).

-- Reference: Page 37, *The Oz Factors*, by Lawrence R. Spencer.

Mystery:

- an enigma or problem involving paradox or apparent contradiction

- profound, inexplicable, or secretive quality or character

-- Reference: www.merriam-webster.com

# Introduction:

# The Mystery of UFOs and Extraterrestrials

If you have studied UFO phenomena at all, you are already familiar with the infamous Orson Welles radio broadcast of "War of the Worlds, And The Invasion from Mars" [1] (Footnote) on Oct. 30, 1938. This fictitious radio dramatization of an invasion of Earth by "aliens" incited a global UFO and extraterrestrial hysteria long before the UFO crash near Roswell, N.M. in 1947.

During the past 60 years, since the alleged Roswell crash, there have been tens of thousands of reported UFO sightings. A global hysteria has emerged from "evidence" of what is presumed to be extraterrestrial phenomenon. Concurrently, the unrelenting denial of this phenomenon by the U.S. government has precipitated an uninterrupted flurry of accusations, counter-accusations, cover-up conspiracy theories, lunatic fringe speculations, "scientific investigations", etc., etc., ad nauseam, and a growing multitude of similar alleged "close encounters".

My first thought when I received the package of documents from Mrs. MacElroy was: "This is just another set of Majestic-12 documents". [2] (Footnote) I am referring to a "mysterious package" reportedly received by mail in 1984 shortly after the death of the last surviving member of the so-called "Majestic-12" committee, alleged to have been organized by President Harry Truman shortly after the Roswell incident in 1947.

There are several similarities to the "Majestic-12" documents and the package I received from Mrs. MacElroy. In the case of the former, an envelope was sent from an anonymous sender with no return address. It contained an undeveloped roll of film. That's all. On the roll of film were photos of documents that were assumed to be authentic by the recipient and his colleagues whose vested interest, i.e. livelihood, depend heavily on attracting public notice and credibility to themselves as "leading authorities" on the subject of UFO phenomena. They have worked relentlessly since then to discover "proof" that the documents are authentic. Of course, government agencies deny everything alleged in the documents and anything having to do with the subject of extraterrestrials in general.

In addition, the subject has become so thoroughly overwhelmed with obvious false reports, discredited sources, hearsay, manufactured falsehoods, misunderstandings, missing information, added inapplicable information and a myriad of other conflicting complexities which have made the subject laughable or unapproachable as a science. This may be intentional, or simply a reflection of the general chaos and barbarism that is Humanity.

As for government denials and cover-ups, the events of September 11, 2001, have made it abundantly apparent to me that the U.S. government has destroyed any vestige of trust the American people and the world may have harbored, even through the Vietnam war, Watergate, and many similar betrayals, in the "honesty" of the American government, military and intelligence community, by blatantly lying to it's own people about almost anything and everything.

In spite of vast numbers of "UFO sightings", innumerable reports of "alien abductions", and "close encounters" with extraterrestrials that pervade nearly all of prehistoric and recorded human history I found only one underlying, unifying, undisputable, axiomatic common denominator that permeates all of this data:

Assuming that subjective reality, or beliefs, of individuals is acceptable evidence, there has been no universally agreed upon "proof" that UFOs and / or extraterrestrial life forms exist whether based on government admission , physical evidence, circumstantial or subjective data.

There are several deductions I can infer from the lack of agreement, government admission or physical evidence that such things are real that, if verified, may lead to a workable solution to this mystery:

### deduction:
In spite of an enormous collection of subjective, circumstantial and objective "evidence" of extraterrestrial activity on and around Earth, the existence, intentions and the activities of extraterrestrials remain hidden and mysterious.

### deduction:
Universally agreed upon proof of extraterrestrial life based on subjective data, government admission, physical and circumstantial evidence are subject to conflicting vested interests, which has made such proof unattainable.

Collectively, these deductions beg the obvious question:
*If extraterrestrials life forms exist, why is there no consistent, forthright , open, interactive communication between Mankind and Extraterrestrials?*

Fortunately, subjective reality does not require evidence or "proof". Therefore, I decided to publish this book in order to pass along a subjective communication I received from Mrs. MacElroy to other people who may be interested in it.

Personally, I am not assuming that anything I received from Mrs. MacElroy is in any way authentic, with the exception of the envelope and the paper inside the envelope. I cannot substantiate any of it. Indeed, I can't truly verify that there was ever such a person as Mrs. MacElroy other than a voice I heard over the phone in 1998. The voice could have been anyone. Personally, I do not have a vested interest in UFO research. Yes, I've written a few books about immortal spiritual beings -- because I'm interested in the subject. But I haven't sold enough of those books to pay for the time it took to write them. It is a hobby. I earn my living as a small business consultant.

It is not my intention to justify, explain, or remedy any disability to perceive or understand the mysteries of extraterrestrial existence, UFOs, governments agendas or spiritual abilities. Nor is it intended to educate, persuade, or promote to anyone that any of these phenomena exist. Furthermore, what I may or may not think about any of this is irrelevant.

Moreover, I have burned all of the original documents, including the envelope I received from Mrs. MacElroy. I do not want to spend the rest of my life being hounded by UFO researchers, government agents, grocery store tabloids reporters, UFO advocates and de-bunkers alike, or anyone else. Any "proofs" or attempts to authenticate the assertion that Mrs. MacElroy actually interviewed an alien in 1947 will have to be done by others.

Ripley says, "Believe It, or Not". [3] (Footnote)

I say, "What's true for you, is true for you".

Lawrence R. Spencer
Editor

# About The Source Of Material In This Book

The content of this book is primarily excerpted from the letter, interview transcripts and personal notes I received from the late Matilda O'Donnell MacElroy. Her letter to me asserts that this material is based on her recollection of communication with an alien being, who "spoke" with her telepathically. During July and August of 1947 she interviewed an extraterrestrial being who she identifies as "Airl", and whom she claims was and continues to be an officer, pilot and engineer who was recovered from a flying saucer that crashed near Roswell, New Mexico on July 8th, 1947.

Obviously, anyone reading anything about this most famous, or infamous, of all "flying saucer" or "alien encounter" events must necessarily be highly suspicious regarding 1) the authenticity of the report and 2) the credibility of the source of information, especially when it appears for the first time sixty years after the alleged event!

I received the aforementioned letter from Mrs. MacElroy on September 14th, 2007, together with a package of documents. The package contained three types of documents:

1) handwritten notes in cursive on ordinary, lined, 8 1/2" X 11"school notebook paper, which I assume had been written personally by Mrs. MacElroy.

2) notes typed on a manual typewriter on plain, white 20 lb. bond paper, which I am assume were prepared personally by her. At least both had the appearance of having been written in the same handwriting, and / or typed on the same typewriter consistently throughout. The writing in the notes I received also appeared to be the same as the writing on the address and return address of the manila envelope I received from Navan, Ireland, which was postmarked on 3 September, 2007. Since I am not a forensic expert, or handwriting analyst, my opinion in these matter is not a professionally qualified judgment.

3) many pages of typewritten transcriptions of her interview with the alien. These were obviously typed on a different typewriter. These pages were typed on a different type of paper and showed apparent signs of age and repeated handling.

None of these notes were assembled in any particular order, or by date, except where indicated by a sentence or paragraph of preamble or explanation by her, or by extrapolation from the context of the pages.

Voltaire [4] (Footnote) is quoted as having said: "History is a Mississippi of lies".

According to the comments made by the alien in the interview transcripts supplied by Mrs. MacElroy, the fundamental lesson of history is that many, many gods have become men, but very few men, if any, have returned to being a god again.

According to the alien being -- "Airl" -- if anything he / she / it supposedly communicated can be trusted -- and if the "translation" or interpretation of this alleged communication is accurate, the history of this universe is a "River of Lies" down which the might and freedom of all-powerful, god-like, immortal spiritual beings ended and was lost in a Sea of Matter and Mortality.

Furthermore, according to the very direct and undiplomatic statements made -- which seem to express the "personal opinion" of the alien -- if one were traveling the far reaches of the universe in search of a place called "Hell", it would be an accurate description of Earth and the inhabitants in its current condition.

To further compound, complicate and magnify the "incredible" source of the "interview transcriptions" I received from Mrs. MacElroy is the fact that they are:

1) based almost entirely on "telepathic communication" between the alien and Mrs. MacElroy.

2) many of these interviews discuss "paranormal" activities of "immortal spiritual beings".

Of course, most "scientific authorities" are unwilling to acknowledge or perceive spiritual phenomena of any kind.

The dictionary definition of the word *paranormal* is:

adjective:

1. cannot be explained by scientific methods
2. supernatural, or seemingly outside "normal" sensory channels

By definition, people who use the word "paranormal" are 1) not able to explain spiritual phenomena and 2) spiritual phenomena are outside of their normal sensory channels.

**In short, scientists suffer from the inability and/or unwillingness to perceive and/or explain spiritual activities. Therefore, the discussion of**

**spiritual activities or spiritual universes in this book are expected to be understood only by those who can and will perceive such things.**

According to the time spans related by the alien in several of the interviews, there are a number of compelling and heretofore unknown reasons that suggest the possibility that many extraordinary miscalculations have been made by Earth scientists regarding the origins and antiquity of the universe, Earth, life forms and events. Of course, these may or may not be accurate either, as time and its ugly step-child, history, are largely subjective.

However, it can be observed that, by contrast with interstellar or "macrocosmic time", the historical perspective of residents of Earth is limited to a relatively microscopic period of time, compared to what are considered to be "recent events" in the chronology of a space travel civilization, much less the entire time span of the universe.

The geological record of Earth is reckoned, by the best guesses of scientists, to be only about 4 billion years. The antiquity of homo sapiens in the archaeology textbooks is estimated at only a few million years, at most. Even the entire biological spectrum is considered to have existed on this planet for only a few hundred million years. And, by and large, the personal memory of individual beings on this planet is limited to only one lifetime.

All other dates, events, or interpretations of events cited in this book are from terrestrial sources, which are purely subjective observations, conjectures, or inventions of human beings, including those of the author, and must therefore be credited or disregarded by the reader accordingly, considering the penchant of Earth inhabitants to myopia, egocentricity, and general ignorance of the several universes in which we dwell.

This book is intended to be an informal presentation of information provided to me, sixty years after the fact, of a series of interviews between an alien space craft officer, pilot & engineer and an Army Air Force surgical nurse.

# Matilda O'Donnell MacElroy

## Biographical Information

Since I have never met Mrs. MacElroy in person, and spoke with her over the phone only once for about 20 minutes, I can not vouch personally for her as a credible source of information. In fact, I cannot factually substantiate that such a person actually existed, accept that I did speak with her on the phone and I received handwritten material in the mail which was sent from a physical address in Ireland.

I spoke to her on the phone in 1998. At the time of our brief phone interview, Mrs. MacElroy lived on Scotty Pride Drive in Glasgow, Montana. I know this because I mailed a copy of my book, *The Oz Factors*, to her as a gift after it was published in 1999. I am sure she received the book, because she refers to it by name in the letter I received from Ireland, and says that she read it.

I did a little research on the internet about Glasgow, Montana for my own interest. Glasgow was founded in 1887 as a railroad town that became popular during the 1930s because President FDR requested that Fort Peck Dam be constructed there which became a huge source of employment for the Glasgow area. In the 1960s the population flourished up to 12,000 because of Glasgow Air Force Base (SAC), which was used during the Vietnam conflict and the earlier part of the 'Cold War'. The base was deactivated and closed in 1969.

When I talked to Mrs. MacElroy on the phone she mentioned that she had been relocated there by the U.S. Air Force after her service was completed, and that's where she met her husband, who was an engineer. I don't think she mentioned his first name. However, he worked on building the Fort Peck Dam, which created the massive Fort Peck Lake. Although the dam was finished in 1940, he was a great fisherman and outdoorsman, so he stayed in the area. I gathered that the Irish heritage of the place had something to do with it, but didn't pursue that point with her. I haven't been able to find any record of a "MacElroy" who worked at the dam, but the personnel records from that period are virtually non-existent as far as I can determine.

I contacted her during my research for *The Oz Factors* book because I was led to believe, through a very circuitous line of investigation, that this woman was suspected of having been involved with alien contact at Area 51, or the Roswell crash site, or something similar.

Through a sequence of circumstantial inferences and accidental referrals, I actually found a number in the phone book and called just on the chance that there might really be such a person.

Needless to say, when I called her she was less than forthcoming in her response to my questions. However, I think she was impressed by my genuine and innocent sincerity to get information for my book, and realized that I had no nefarious or financially motivated purposes or reason to exploit her in any way. Nonetheless, she did not give me any useful information at that time, except to say that she had been in the Army and was stationed in New Mexico in 1947.

She could not discuss anything whatsoever about any kind of incident, as her life depended on remaining silent. Although this piqued my interest even more, it was futile to try to push her any further, so I gave up and forgot about her until last September, when I got the package from Ireland.

I tried to contact her in Ireland at the return address on the package, but received no reply from her, nor have I been able to find anyone in Meath County, Ireland who was acquainted with either of them except the landlady from whom they rented a room for a few weeks before their deaths, which seemed to have occurred simultaneously, although I have no real evidence of this.

However, the post mark of the envelope she sent to me was stamped at the post office in Navan, Co. Meath, Ireland on the date cited above. Since there is an actual residence (according to *Google Maps*) at the return address shown on the envelope, I wrote to the address and was advised by the home owner that both Mrs. MacElroy and her husband, whose name turns out to have been "Paul", were both recently deceased. She said that the cremated remains of Mrs. MacElroy and her husband were interred at Saint Finian Cemetery on Athboy Road.

Subsequently, I have not been able to find any record of her under the maiden name of O'Donnell, nor have I had any success at discovering any personal friend, family member or document to confirm her birth, medical education, or military record, marriage or death, with the exception of her landlady in Ireland (who is not a relative) just before her death. I suspect that this is the false identity given to her by the military when she left Roswell, as mentioned in her notes.

In either case, it seems likely that her identity and all evidence of her has been expunged from the public record. I understand that certain government agencies are adept at covering up evidence, or making records (and people) disappear. It seems likely that this has been done in her case, due to the highly sensitive nature of the Roswell incident and consistent with the rest of the alleged "cover up".

Inasmuch as I do not have any further information to verify or substantiate that any of the notes of these "interviews" sent to me by Mrs. MacElroy are in any way factual, other than what I have already mentioned, let the reader beware, and take heed accordingly!

# The Letter from Mrs. MacElroy

August 12, 2007

Dear Lawrence,

I am typing this letter to you on my old Underwood typewriter [5] **(Footnote)** that I bought after I was discharged from the Army. Somehow it seems like a fitting contrast to the subject of this letter and the documents you will find enclosed in this envelope.

The last time I spoke to you was about eight years ago. During your brief telephone interview with me you asked me to assist you with the research for "The Oz Factors" book you were writing because you suspected that I might know something that would help your investigation into the possibility that extraterrestrial beings may have influenced the history of Earth. When we spoke, I told you that I did not have any information that I could share with you about anything.

Since then I have read your book and found it very interesting and compelling. You are obviously a man who has done his homework, and who could understand my own experiences. I've been thinking a lot about your allusion to the old philosopher whom you paraphrased in our phone conversation: "with great power, comes great responsibility". Although I don't think power is pertinent in my life or to my reasons for sending you the enclosed documents, you certainly did get me thinking about my responsibility.

I have reconsidered my position, for a variety of reasons, not the least of which is my realization that you were right. I do have a responsibility to myself, at least. I can not possibly tell you the personal Hell [6] **(Footnote)** of ethical irresolution and spiritual ambivalence I have endured since 1947. I do not want to keep playing the game of "maybe I should have, or maybe I shouldn't have", through the rest of Eternity!

Many men have been killed to extinguish the possibility
of revealing the knowledge I have helped to withhold
from society, until now. Only a small handful of people
on Earth have seen and heard what I have had the burden
of keeping secret for sixty years. All those years I
thought that I had been entrusted with a great deal of
confidence by the "powers that be" in our government,
although I have often felt that power is greatly
misguided, to "protect" Mankind from the certain
knowledge that, not only do intelligent extraterrestrial
life forms exist, but that they have and continue to
aggressively monitor and invade the lives of everyone on
Earth every day.

Therefore, I think the time has come to pass along my
secret knowledge to someone I think will understand it.
I don't think it would be responsible of me to take the
knowledge I have into the silent afterlife, beyond reach
or recognition. I think there is a greater good to be
served than protecting the "vested interests" for whom
this information is considered a matter of "national
security", whatever that means, and is therefore
justification for making it "TOP SECRET". [7] **(Footnote)**

Also, I am now 83 years old. I have decided to leave
this body, which has outlasted its usefulness to me,
using a painless method of self-administered euthanasia. [8]
**(Footnote)** I have a very few months to live, and nothing to
fear or lose.

So, I have moved away from Montana, where my husband and
I lived for most of my life, to spend our remaining days
in a lovely rented upstairs bedroom in a house in the
homeland of my husband's family in County Meath,
Ireland. [9] **(Footnote)**

I will die not far from "The Great Mound" at Knowth
[10] **(Footnote)** and Dowth, the "Fairy Mound of Darkness". These
are sacred "cairns" or massive stone structures that
were erected about 3,700 BCE and engraved with
indecipherable hieroglyphs -- about the same time as
pyramids and other inexplicable stone monuments were
being built all over the Earth.

I am also not far from "The Hill of Tara", [11] **(Footnote)** that
was once the ancient seat of power in Ireland where 142
kings are said to have reigned in prehistoric and

historic times. In ancient Irish religion and mythology this was the sacred place of dwelling for the "gods" and was the entrance to the "other world".

Saint Patrick came to Tara to conquer the ancient religion of the pagans. He may have suppressed the religious practices in the area, but he certainly did not have any impact on the "gods" who brought these civilizations to Earth, as you will discover when you read the documents enclosed. Therefore, this is a fitting location for my departure from this unholy world and final release from the burdens of this life.

The crystal clear perspective of hindsight has revealed a higher purpose to me: assisting the survival of the planet, all living beings and life forms in our galaxy!

The status quo of our government establishment has been to "protect the people" from knowledge of such matters. In fact, the only protection afforded by ignorance and secrecy is to hide the private agenda of those in power to enslave others. And, by doing so, to disarm every perceived enemy, and ally, through superstition and stupidity.

Therefore, I have enclosed the original and only existing copies of my personal notes and reflections on a matter which I have kept hidden from everyone, even my own family. I have also enclosed my copies of typed transcripts created by the stenographer who transcribed all of my interviews with the alien saucer pilot after each interview was finished. I do not have any copies of the tape recordings that were made of my interview reports. No one, until now, knows that I was able to secretly retain copies of the official interview transcripts.

Now I am entrusting these documents to your discretion to impart to the world in any form or manner you see fit. My only request is that you do so in a way that will not threaten your own life or well being, if possible. If you were to incorporate these notes of my experiences into a work of fiction, such as a novel, the factual nature of the material could be easily dismissed or discredited by any agency for whom "national security" is used as a personal shield against scrutiny and justice.

In so doing, you could "disavow any knowledge" of their true origin, and claim that it is a fictitious work of your imagination. Whoever said that "truth is stranger than fiction" was "right as rain". For most people all of this will be "unbelievable". Unfortunately, beliefs are not a reliable criteria for reality.

Also, I am sure that if you were to show these notes to anyone that would prefer physical, economic or spiritual slavery over freedom, the subject matter contained in them would seem quite objectionable. If you attempted to publish the documents as a matter of factual reporting in a newspaper or on the evening TV news they would be rejected out of hand as the work of a kook. The very nature of these documents make them unbelievable, and therefore discreditable. Conversely, the release of this information is potentially catastrophic for certain political, religious and economic vested interests.

These documents contain information which is quite relevant to your interest and investigations into alien encounters and paranormal experience. To use your analogy in "The Oz Factors" book, I can honestly say that the few factual reports that have been made by others about "alien" influences are only a gentle breeze in the eye of an Apocalyptic Hurricane swirling around Earth. There really are wizards and wicked witches and flying monkeys in this universe!

This information, which has been suspected and/or speculated upon by so many for so long, has been constantly denied by mainstream media, academia, and the Military-Industrial Complex [12] **(Footnote)** that President Eisenhower warned us about in his farewell address.

As you know in July, 1947, the Roswell Army Air Field (RAAF) [13] **(Footnote)** issued a press release stating that personnel from the field's 509th Bomb Group had recovered a crashed "flying disc" from a ranch near Roswell, New Mexico, sparking intense media interest. [14] **(Footnote)**

Later the same day, the Commanding General of the Eighth Air Force [16] **(Footnote)** stated that Major Jesse Marcel, who was involved with the original recovery of the debris, had recovered only the tattered remnants of a weather balloon. The true facts of the incident have been suppressed by the United States government since then.

You may not know that I was enlisted in the U.S. Women's Army Air Force(WAC) [16] **(Footnote)** Medical Corp which was a part of the US Army back then. I was assigned to the 509th Bomb Group as a Flight Nurse [17] **(Footnote)** at the time of the incident.

When the news that there had been a crash was received at the base, I was asked to accompany Mr. Cavitt, the Counter Intelligence Officer, [18] **(Footnote)** to the crash site as the driver of his vehicle, and to render any needed emergency medical assistance to any survivors, if necessary. [19] **(Footnote)** Therefore, I briefly witnessed the wreckage of an alien space craft, as well as the remains of the several alien personnel aboard the craft who were already dead.

When we arrived I learned that one of the personnel on board the craft had survived the crash, and was conscious, and apparently uninjured. The conscious alien was similar in appearance, but not the same as, the others. [20] **(Footnote)**

None of the other personnel present could communicate with the survivor, as the being did not communicate verbally or by any recognizable signs. However, while I examined the "patient" for injuries I immediately detected and understood that the alien being was attempting to communicate with me by "mental images", or "telepathic thought", [21] **(Footnote)** which projected directly from the mind of the being.

I immediately reported this phenomenon to Mr. Cavitt. As no other person present could perceive these thoughts, and the alien seemed able and willing to communicate with me, it was decided, after a brief consultation with a senior officer, that I would accompany the surviving alien back to the base.

This was partly due to the fact that I was a nurse, and could attend to the physical needs of the alien, as well as serve as a non-threatening communicator and companion. After all, I was the only woman at the site and the only one who was not armed. I was thereafter assigned permanently to serve as a "companion" of the alien at all times. [22] **(Footnote)**

My duty was to communicate with and interview the alien and to make a complete report of all that I discovered to command authorities. Subsequently, I was supplied with specific lists of questions provided to me by military and non-military personnel, which I was to "interpret" for the alien, and record the responses to the questions provided.

I also accompanied the alien at all times during medical testing and the many other examinations to which the alien was subjected by staff from numerous government agencies.

I was given a promotion in rank to Senior Master Sergeant to improve my security rating, and to increase my pay grade from $54.00 a month to $138.00 a month, for this very unusual assignment. I performed these duties from July 7th through August,1947,at which time the alien "died" or departed the "body", as you will read about in my notes.

Although I was never left entirely alone with the alien, as there were always military personnel, intelligence agency people and a variety of other officials present from time to time, I did have uninterrupted access to and communication with the alien being for nearly six weeks.

Hereinafter is an overview and summary of my personal recollections of "conversations" with the alien craft pilot, whom I came to know by the identity of "Airl".

I feel that it is my duty at this time, in the best interest of the citizens of Earth, to reveal what I have learned from my interaction with "Airl" during those six weeks, on the anniversary of her "death" or departure sixty years ago.

Although I served as a nurse in the Army Air Force, I am not a pilot or technician. Further, I did not have any direct contact with the space craft or other materials recovered from the crash site at that time, or thereafter. To that degree it must be taken into consideration that my understanding of the communications I had with " Airl" are based on my own subjective ability to interpret the meaning of the thoughts and mental images I was able to perceive.

Our communication did not consist of "spoken language", in the conventional sense. Indeed, the "body" of the alien had no "mouth" through which to speak. Our communication was by telepathy. At first, I could not understand Airl very clearly. I could perceive images, emotions and impressions, but it was difficult for me to express these verbally. Once Airl learned the English language, she was able to focus her thoughts more precisely using symbols and meanings of words I could understand. Learning the English language was done as a favor to me. It was more for my own benefit than hers.

By the end of our interview sessions, and increasingly since then, I have become more comfortable with telepathic communication. I have become more adept at understanding Airl's thoughts as though they are my own. Somehow, her thoughts become my thoughts. Her emotions are my emotions. However, this is limited by her willingness and intention to share her own, personal universe with me. She is able to be selective about what communication I am allowed to receive from her. Likewise, her experience, training, education, relationships and purposes are uniquely her own.

The Domain is a race or civilization of which Airl, the alien I interviewed, is an officer, pilot and engineer serving in The Domain Expeditionary Force. The symbol represents the origin and unlimited boundary of the known universe, united and integrated into a vast civilization under the control of The Domain.

Airl is currently stationed at a base in the asteroid belt which she refers to as a "space station" in the solar system of Earth. First and foremost, Airl is herself. Secondarily, she voluntarily serves as an Officer, Pilot and Engineer in The Domain Expeditionary Force. In that capacity she has duties and responsibilities, but she is at leave to come and go as she pleases also.

Please accept this material and make it known to as many people as possible. I repeat that it is not my intention to endanger your life with the possession of this material, nor do I really expect you to believe any of it either. However, I do sense that you can appreciate the value that such knowledge may have to

those who are willing and able to face the reality of
it.

Mankind needs to know the answers to questions which are
contained in these documents.  Who are we?  Where did we
come from?  What is our purpose on Earth? Is Mankind
alone in the universe?  If there is intelligent life
elsewhere why have they not contacted us?

It is vital that people understand the devastating
consequences to our spiritual and physical survival if
we fail to take effective action to undo the long-
standing and pervasive effects of alien intervention on
Earth.

Perhaps the information in these documents will serve as
a stepping stone to a better future for Mankind. I hope
that you can be more clever, creative and courageous in
the distribution of this information than I have been.

May The Gods Bless You and Keep You.

Mrs. Matilda O'Donnell MacElroy
Senior Master Sergeant
Women's Army Air Force Medical Corp, Retired
100 Troytown Heights
Navan, Meath
Co. Meath, Ireland

# Chapter One

# My First Interview With The Alien

(MATILDA O'DONNELL MACELROY PERSONAL NOTE)

"By the time the alien had been returned to the base I had already spent several hours with her. As I mentioned, Mr. Cavitt told me to stay with the alien, since I was the only person among us who could understand her communication. I could not understand my ability to "communicate" with the being. I had never before that time experienced telepathic communication with anyone.

The non-verbal communication I experienced was like the understanding you might have when a child or a dog is trying to get you to understand something, but much, much more direct and powerful! Even though there were no "words" spoken, or signs made, the intention of the thoughts were unmistakable to me. I realized later that, although I received the thought, I did not necessarily interpret its meaning exactly.

I think that the alien being was not willing to discuss technical matters, due to the nature of her position as an officer and pilot with the duty to maintain the security and confidentiality required by her own "unit" or organization. Any soldier who is captured by the "enemy" in the line of duty has a responsibility to withhold vital information, even in the face of interrogation or torture, of course.

But, in spite of that, I have always felt that the alien being was not really trying to hide anything from me. I just never got that feeling. Her communication always seemed honest and sincere to me. But, I suppose you can never know for sure. I definitely feel that I shared a unique "bond" with the alien. It was a kind of "trust" or empathy that you have with a patient, or a child. I think this is because the alien could understand that I was really interested in "her" and had no harmful intention, nor would I allow any harm to come to her, if I could prevent it. This was true too.

I refer to the alien as "her". Actually, the being was not sexual in any way, either physiologically or psychologically. "She" did have a rather strong, feminine presence and demeanor. However, in terms of physiology, the being was "asexual" and had no internal or external reproductive organs. Her body was more like the body of a "doll" or "robot". There were no internal "organs", as the body was not constructed of biological cells. It did have a kind of "circuit" system or electrical nervous system that ran throughout the body, but I could not understand how it worked.

In stature and appearance the body was quite short and petite. About 40 inches tall. The head was disproportionately large, relative to arms, legs and torso, which where thin. There were three "fingers" on each of two" hands" and "feet" which were somewhat prehensile. [23] (Footnote) The head had no operational "nose" or "mouth" or "ears". I understood that a space officer does not need these as space has no atmosphere to conduct sound. Therefore, sound related sensory organs are not built into the body. Nor does the body need to consume food, hence, the absence of a mouth.

The eyes were quite large. I was never able to determine the exact degree of visual acuity of which the eyes were capable, but I observed that her sense of sight must have been extremely acute. I think the lenses of the eyes, which were very dark and opaque, may also have been able to detect waves or particles beyond the visual spectrum of light. [24] (Footnote) I suspect that this may have included the full range of the electromagnetic spectrum, [25] (Footnote) or more, but I do not know this for sure.

When the being looked at me her gaze seemed to penetrate right through me, as though she had "x-ray vision". [26] (Footnote) I found this a little embarrassing, at first, until I realized that she had no sexual intentions. In fact, I don't think she ever even had the thought that I was male or female.

It became very obvious after a short time with the being that her body did not require oxygen, food or water or any other external source of nutrition or energy. As I learned later, this being supplied her own "energy", which animated and operated the body. It seemed a little bit eerie at first, but I got used to the idea. It's really a very, very simple body. There is not much to it, compared to our own bodies.

Airl explained to me that it was not mechanical, like a robot, nor was it biological. It is animated directly by her as a spiritual being. Technically, from a medical standpoint, I would say that Airl's body could not even be called "alive". Her "doll" body is not a biological life form, [27] (Footnote) with cells, and so forth.

It had a smooth skin, or covering which was gray in color. The body was highly tolerant to changes in temperature, atmospheric conditions, and pressure. The limbs were quite frail, without musculature. In space there is no gravity, [28] (Footnote) so very little muscle strength is needed. The body was used almost entirely on space craft or in low, or no-gravity environments. Since Earth has a heavy gravity, the body was not able to walk around very well as the legs were not really suited to that purpose. The feet and hands were quite flexible and agile however.

Overnight, before my first interview with the alien, the area had been transformed into a buzzing hive of activity. There were a dozen men working on setting up lights and camera equipment. A motion picture camera and microphone and a tape recorder were also set up in the "interview room". (I don't understand why a microphone was needed, since there was no verbal communication possible with the alien.) There was also a stenographer [29] **(Footnote)** and several people busily typing on typewriters.

I was informed that an expert foreign language interpreter and a "code breaking" team had been flown to the base during the night to assist with my efforts to communicate with the alien. There were also several medical personnel -- specialists in various fields -- to examine the alien. And, a professor of psychology was there to help formulate questions and "interpret" the answers. As I was just a nurse, I was not considered to be a "qualified" interpreter, even though I was the only one there who could understand anything the alien was thinking!

There were many subsequent conversations between us. Each "interview" resulted in an exponential increase in understanding between us, as I will discuss later on in my notes. This is the first transcript with the answers to a list of questions provided to me by the intelligence officer at the base which I debriefed to the stenographer immediately following the interview."

(OFFICIAL TRANSCRIPT OF INTERVIEW)

TOP SECRET

Official Transcript of the U.S. Army Air Force
Roswell Army Air Field, 509th Bomb Group
SUBJECT: ALIEN INTERVIEW, 9. 7. 1947

"QUESTION - "Are you injured?"

ANSWER -

NO

QUESTION - "What medical assistance do you require?"

ANSWER -

NONE

QUESTION - "Do need food or water or other sustenance?"

ANSWER -

NO

QUESTION - "Do you have any special environmental needs, such as air temperature, atmospheric chemical content, air pressure, or waste elimination?"

ANSWER -

NO.  I AM NOT A BIOLOGICAL BEING.

QUESTION - "Does your body or space craft carry any germs or contamination that may be harmful to humans or other Earth life forms?"

ANSWER -

NO GERMS IN SPACE.

QUESTION - "Does your government know you are here?"

ANSWER -

NOT AT THIS TIME

QUESTION - "Are others of your kind going to come looking for you?"

ANSWER -

YES

QUESTION - "What is the weapons capability of your people?"

ANSWER -

VERY DESTRUCTIVE.

I did not understand the exact nature of the kind of arms or weapons that they might have, but I did not feel that there was any malevolent intention in her reply, just a statement of fact.

QUESTION - "Why did your space craft crash?"

ANSWER -

IT WAS STRUCK BY AN ELECTRICAL DISCHARGE FROM THE ATMOSPHERE WHICH CAUSED US TO LOSE CONTROL.

QUESTION - "Why was your space craft in this area?"

ANSWER -

INVESTIGATION OF "BURNING CLOUDS" / RADIATION /
EXPLOSIONS [30] (Footnote)

QUESTION - "How does your space craft fly?"

ANSWER -

IT IS CONTROLLED THROUGH "MIND". RESPONDS TO
"THOUGHT COMMANDS".

"Mind" or "thought command" are the only English
language words I can think of to describe the
thought. Their bodies, and I think, the space craft,
are connected directly to them through some kind of
electrical "nervous system" that they control with
their own thoughts.

QUESTION - "How do your people communicate with each
other?"

ANSWER -

THROUGH MIND /THOUGHT.

The words "mind" and "thought" combined together are
the closest English language words I can think of to
describe the idea at this time. However, it was very
obvious to me that they communicate directly from the
mind, just as she is communicating with me.

QUESTION - "Do you have a written language or symbols
for communication?"

ANSWER -

YES

QUESTION - "What planet are you from?"

ANSWER -

THE HOME /   BIRTHPLACE WORLD OF THE DOMAIN

31

Since I am not an astronomer, I have no way of
thinking in terms of stars, galaxies, constellations
and directions in space. The impression I received
was of a planet in the center of a huge cluster of
galaxies that is to her like "home", or "birthplace".
The word "domain" is the closest word I can think of
to describe her concept, images and thoughts about
where she is from. It could as easily be called the
"territory" or the "realm". However, I am sure that
it was not just a planet or a solar system or a
cluster of stars, but an enormous number of galaxies!

QUESTION - "Will your government send representatives
to meet with our leaders?"

ANSWER -

NO

QUESTION - "What are your intentions concerning
Earth?"

ANSWER -

PRESERVE / PROTECT PROPERTY OF THE DOMAIN

QUESTION - "What have you learned about Earth
governments and military installations?"

ANSWER -

POOR / SMALL. DESTROY PLANET.

QUESTION - "Why haven't your people made your
existence known to the people of Earth?"

ANSWER -

WATCH / OBSERVE. NO CONTACT.

I got the impression that contact with people on
Earth was not permitted, but I could not think of a
word or idea that communicated the impression I got
exactly. They are just observing us.

QUESTION - "Have your people visited Earth previously?"

ANSWER -

PERIODIC / REPEATING OBSERVATIONS.

QUESTION - "How long have you known about Earth?"

ANSWER -

LONG BEFORE HUMANS.

I am not sure if the word "prehistoric" would be more accurate, but it was definitely a very long period of time before human beings evolved.

QUESTION - "What do you know about the history of civilization on Earth?"

ANSWER -

SMALL INTEREST / ATTENTION.  SMALL TIME.

The answer to this question seemed very vague to me. However, I perceived that her interest in Earth history is not very strong or that she did not pay much attention to it.  Or, maybe, ... I don't know. I didn't really get an answer to the question.

QUESTION - "Can you describe your home world to us?"

ANSWER -

PLACE OF CIVILIZATION / CULTURE  /  HISTORY.  LARGE PLANET.  WEALTH  /  RESOURCES ALWAYS.  ORDER.  POWER. KNOWLEDGE / WISDOM.  TWO STARS.  THREE MOONS.

QUESTION - "What is the state of development of your civilization?"

ANSWER -

ANCIENT.  TRILLIONS OF YEARS.  ALWAYS.  ABOVE ALL OTHERS.  PLAN.  SCHEDULE.  PROGRESS.  WIN.  HIGH GOALS / IDEAS.

I use the number "trillions" [31] **(Footnote)** because I am
sure that the meaning was a number larger than many
billions.  The idea of the length of time she
communicated is beyond me.   It's really closer to
the idea of "infinity" in terms of Earth years.

QUESTION - "Do you believe in God?"

ANSWER -

WE THINK.  IT IS.  MAKE IT CONTINUE.  ALWAYS.

I am sure that the alien being does not understand
the concept of "god" or "worship" as we do.  I assume
that the people in her civilization were all
atheists.   My impression was that they think very
highly of themselves and are very  prideful indeed!

QUESTION - "What type of society do you have?"

ANSWER -

ORDER.  POWER.  FUTURE ALWAYS.  CONTROL.  GROW.

These are the closest words I could use to describe
the idea she had about her own society or
civilization.  Her "emotion" when communicating her
response to this question became very intense, very
bright and emphatic!  Her thought was filled with an
emotion that gave me a feeling of jubilation or joy.
But, it made me very nervous also.

QUESTION - "Are there other intelligent life forms
besides yourself in the universe?"

ANSWER -

EVERYWHERE.  WE ARE GREATEST  /  HIGHEST OF ALL.

Due to her small stature, I am sure that she did not
mean "tallest" or "biggest".  Again, her prideful
"nature" showed through in the feeling I received
from her."

(MATILDA O'DONNELL MACELROY PERSONAL NOTE)

"This was the conclusion of the first interview. When the answers to the first list of questions were typed and given to the people who were waiting for them, they were very excited that I was able to get the alien to say anything!

However, after they finished reading my answers they were disappointed that I could not understand more clearly. Now they had a lot of new questions because of the answers I received to the first list of questions.

An officer told me to await further instructions. I waited for several hours in the adjoining office. I was not allowed to continue my "interview" with the alien. However, I was always well treated and allowed to eat and sleep and use the restroom facilities whenever I wanted.

Eventually, a new list of questions was written for me to ask the alien. I gathered that quite a few other agents, government and military officials had arrived at the base by this time. They told me that several other people would be in the room with me during the next interview so they could prompt me to ask for more details during the interview. However, when I attempted to conduct the interview with these people in the room, I received no thoughts, emotions or any other perceptible communication from the alien. Nothing. The alien just sat in a chair without moving.

We all left the interview room. The intelligence agent became very agitated about this. He accused me of lying or making up the answers to the first questions. I insisted that my answers were honest, and as accurate as I could make them!

Later that day, it was decided that several other people would attempt to ask questions of the alien. However, in spite of several attempts by different "experts", no one else was ever able to get any communication at all from the alien.

Over the next several days a psychic research scientist from back East was flown to the base to interview the alien. Her name was Gertrude something or other. I don't recall the last name. [32] **(Footnote)** On another occasion an Indian clairvoyant named Krishnamurti [33] **(Footnote)** came to the base to try to communicate with the alien . Neither one was successful at getting the alien to communicate anything. I was personally not able to communicate telepathically with either of these people either, although I did think that Mr. Krishnamurti was a very kind and intelligent gentleman.

Finally, it was decided that I should be left with the alien by myself to see if I could get any answers."

35

# Chapter Two

# My Second Interview

"In the next interview I was told to ask the alien only one question."

## TOP SECRET

Official Transcript of the U.S. Army Air Force
Roswell Army Air Field, 509th Bomb Group
SUBJECT: ALIEN INTERVIEW, 10. 7. 1947


"QUESTION -  "Why have you stopped communicating?"

ANSWER -

NO STOP. OTHERS.  HIDDEN / COVERED.  SECRET FEAR.

The alien can not communicate with them because they
were afraid of her, or do not trust her.  And, it is
clear to me that the alien is very  aware that some
people have secret intentions toward her and are hiding
their real thoughts.  It is equally obvious to me that
the alien does not have even a tiny bit of fear of us,
or anything else, for that matter!"

**(MATILDA O'DONNELL MACELROY PERSONAL NOTE)**

"I pondered the words I chose to convey the meaning of the aliens thoughts very carefully before reporting to the stenographer and the people who were waiting anxiously in the other room.

Personally, I never suffered any fear or misapprehension about the alien whatsoever. I was very, very curious and excited to learn anything and everything I could about her and from her. However, like the alien, I did not have much trust or confidence in the agents or "authorities" who were controlling my interviews. I had no idea what their intentions toward her might be. However, I am sure that the military officers were very, very nervous about having an alien space craft and pilot on their hands!

At that moment, my greatest worry was how to more clearly understand the thoughts and ideas of the alien. I think that I was doing pretty well as a telepathic "receiver", but not as good as telepathic "sender".

I wanted desperately to figure out a better way to communicate with the alien in a way that would enable the growing legion of government officials to understand her more directly, without having to rely on my interpretation of her thoughts. I did not feel very well qualified to act as an interpreter, yet I was the only person with whom the alien would communicate, so it was up to me to get the job done.

I was also becoming acutely aware that this was probably the biggest "news event" in the history of Earth, and that I should be proud to have any part in it. Of course by that time the entire incident had been officially denied in the press and a cover-up of immense proportions by the military and the "powers that be" [34] **(Footnote)** had already begun.

However, I was beginning to feel the pressure of the responsibility for being the first person on Earth, as far as I knew, to communicate with an extraterrestrial life form! I think I know how Columbus [35] **(Footnote)** must have felt when he discovered a "new world" the size of a continent on one small planet. But, I was about to discover an entirely new, unexplored universe! [36] **(Footnote)**

While I waited for my next instructions from my superiors I went to my quarters, under escort of several heavily armed MPs. Several other men dressed in black suits and ties accompanied me also. They were still there when I got up in the morning. After breakfast, which was brought to me in my own quarters, they escorted me back to the office at the base that was used for the interview."

# Chapter Three

## My Third Interview

(MATILDA O'DONNELL MACELROY PERSONAL NOTE)

"The third interview, and all subsequent interviews that I had with the alien were observed and recorded, as I mentioned above, by dozens of other people. Although they were not physically present, a special room had been constructed with a window of one-way glass through which the interview could be observed from an adjoining room, without intruding on the alien.

The alien had been moved into the newly constructed room and was seated in an ordinary overstuffed living room chair covered with a flowery fabric. I'm sure that someone had been sent into town to buy a chair from the nearest available furniture store. The alien's body was about the same size as a very thin 5 year old child, so she was dwarfed by the chair.

Since her body was not biological it didn't need any food, air or heat, and apparently, she didn't sleep either. There were no eyelids, or eyebrows above her eyes, so the eyes didn't close. I don't think anyone could tell whether she was sleeping or awake as long as she was sitting upright in the chair. Unless she moved her body or gestured with her hand, it would be hard to tell whether she was even alive or not, unless you could perceive her thoughts.

Eventually I learned that the alien was not identified by her body, but by her "personality", so to speak. She was known by her fellow aliens as "Airl". This is the closest word I can use to describe the name using the English alphabet. I sensed that she preferred the feminine gender. I think we shared a natural, female empathy and nurturing attitude toward life and each other. I am sure she did not feel comfortable with the combative, aggressive, domineering attitude of the male officers and agents, each of whom was more concerned with their own personal self-importance and power than with discovering the secrets of the universe!

When I entered the room, she was very pleased to see me. I felt a very genuine sense of recognition, relief and a "warm" feeling from her. It was like the eager excitement and unconditional, platonic affection one feels from a dog or child, yet with a calm and reserved control. I must say that I was surprised that I felt the same sort of affection for the alien being, especially since we had spent so little time with each other. I was pleased that I was able to continue my interviews with her in spite of all the attention it was getting from the stream of government and military people arriving at the base.

It was very obvious that the people who wrote the next series of questions for me wanted to learn how to communicate with the alien themselves, without having to go through me.

Here are the answers to the new list of questions:"

TOP SECRET

Official Transcript of the U.S. Army Air Force
Roswell Army Air Field, 509th Bomb Group
SUBJECT: ALIEN INTERVIEW, 11. 7. 1947

"QUESTION - Can you read or write any Earth languages?

ANSWER -

NO.

QUESTION - Do you understand numbers or mathematics?

ANSWER -

YES.  I AM OFFICER / PILOT / ENGINEER

QUESTION - Can you write or draw symbols or pictures that we may be able to translate into our own language?

ANSWER -

UNCERTAIN

QUESTION - Are there any other signs or means of communication you can use to help us understand your thoughts more clearly?

ANSWER -

NO."

"I was very sure that this was not true. But, I understood clearly that Airl was not willing to communicate in writing or drawing or sign language. My feeling was that she was following orders, like any soldier who has been captured, not to reveal any information that might be useful to an enemy, even under torture. She was only able and willing to reveal non-confidential, or personal information, or "name, rank and serial number"."

(OFFICIAL TRANSCRIPT OF INTERVIEW)

TOP SECRET

Official Transcript of the U.S. Army Air Force
Roswell Army Air Field, 509th Bomb Group
SUBJECT: ALIEN INTERVIEW, 11. 7. 1947, 2nd Session

"QUESTION - Can you show us on a map of the stars which is the star of your home planet? [37] (Footnote)

ANSWER -

NO.

This is not because she does not know the directions from Earth to her home planet. She was unwilling to reveal the location. It was also due to the fact that the star system of her home planet does not exist on any star map on Earth. It is too far away.

QUESTION - How long will it take your people to locate you here?

ANSWER -

UNKNOWN.

QUESTION - How long would it take your people to travel here to rescue you?

ANSWER -

MINUTES OR HOURS.

QUESTION - How can we make them understand that we do not intend to harm you?

ANSWER -

INTENTIONS ARE CLEAR.  SEE IN YOUR MIND / IMAGES / FEELINGS.

QUESTION -  If you are not a biological entity, why do you refer to yourself as feminine?

ANSWER -

I AM A CREATOR.  MOTHER.  SOURCE."

### (MATILDA O'DONNELL MACELROY PERSONAL NOTE)

"These questions took me only a few minutes to complete. I realized then that we may be in for some serious trouble if the alien was not willing to cooperate, or reveal any information that the military or intelligence agencies or scientists considered to be useful to them.

I was also sure that the alien was _very_ certain of the actual intentions of the people who wrote these questions, as she could "read their minds" just as easily as she could read my thoughts and communicate with me telepathically. Because of these intentions, she was unwilling and unable to cooperate with any of them in any way, under any circumstances. I am equally sure that since she was not a biological life form, that there was no kind of torture or coercion that would change her mind!"

# Chapter Four

# The Language Barrier

"After I explained what I thought were the reasons for the "no answer" answer to the intelligence agents, there was a great deal of upset and turmoil. A very heated discussion took place between some of the intelligence officers, military officials, psychologist and the language interpreters. This lasted for several hours. It was finally decided that I should be allowed to continue to interview the alien, provided I could get a satisfactory answer from her to the following question:"

(OFFICIAL TRANSCRIPT OF INTERVIEW)

TOP SECRET

Official Transcript of the U.S. Army Air Force
Roswell Army Air Field, 509th Bomb Group
SUBJECT: ALIEN INTERVIEW, 11. 7. 1947, 3rd Session

"QUESTION - "What assurance or proof do you require from us that will make you feel safe enough to answer our questions."

ANSWER -

ONLY SHE SPEAKS. ONLY SHE HEARS. ONLY SHE QUESTIONS. NO OTHERS. MUST LEARN / KNOW / UNDERSTAND."

(MATILDA O'DONNELL MACELROY PERSONAL NOTE)

"When I returned from the interview room to report the alien response to this question I received a grim and skeptical reception from the assembled intelligence agents and military personnel. They could not understand what the alien meant by this.

I admitted that I couldn't really understand what she meant either, but I was doing the best I could to articulate her telepathic intentions. I told the officials that perhaps the communication problem had to do with my inability to understand the telepathic language of the alien clearly enough to be satisfactory.

I was so discouraged at that point I almost felt like giving up!

And now, there was even more arguments than before! I was sure I was going to be removed from my position, in spite of the fact that the alien refused to communicate with anyone else, or that no one else had been found who could communicate with her.

Fortunately, a very clever fellow named John Newble, who was a Japanese language specialist from the Navy, [38] **(Footnote)** had an explanation and a solution to the problem. He explained that, first, the problem had very little to do with the inability of the alien to communicate. It had more to do with her <u>unwillingness</u> to communicate with anyone other than myself. Second, in order for any clear, comprehensive communication to happen, both parties needed to understand and communicate through a common language.

Words and symbols in language convey very precise concepts and meanings. He said that the Japanese people have a lot of homonyms [39] **(Footnote)** in their language which cause a lot of confusion in day to day communication. They solve this problem by using standard Chinese characters [40] **(Footnote)** to write down the exact meanings of the word they are using. This clears up the matter for them.

Without a defined nomenclature communication was not possible beyond the rudimentary understanding between men and dogs, or between two small children. The lack of a common vocabulary of clearly defined words that all parties can use fluently, was the limiting factor in communication between all people, groups, or nations.

Therefore, he suggested that there were only two choices. I had to learn to speak the language of the alien, or the alien had to learn to speak English. Factually only one choice was possible: that I persuade Airl to learn English, and that I teach it to her with the guidance of the language specialist. No one had any objection to trying this approach, as there were no other suggestions.

The language specialists suggested that I take several children's books, and a basic reading primer, and grammar text with me into the interview room. The plan was that I would sit next to the alien and read aloud to her from the books, while pointing to the text I was reading with my finger so that she could follow along.

The theory was that the alien could eventually be taught to read, just as a child is taught to read by word and sound association with the written word, as well as instruction in fundamental grammar. They also assumed, I think, that if the alien was intelligent enough to communicate with me telepathically, and fly a space craft across the galaxy, that she could probably learn to speak a language as quickly as a 5 year old, or faster!

I returned to the interview room and proposed this idea to Airl. She did not object to learning the language, although she did not make any commitment to answer questions either. No one else had a better idea, so we went ahead."

# Chapter Five

# Reading Lessons

(MATILDA O'DONNELL MACELROY PERSONAL NOTE)

"I began the reading lessons with the first pages of a school book that had been used to teach pioneer children in the 1800's on the frontiers of America. It is called "McGuffey's Eclectic Reader, Primer Through Sixth". [41] (Footnote)

Since I am a nurse, and not a teacher, the language expert who gave me the books also gave me an extensive briefing -- a course that took an entire day -- on how to use the books to teach the alien. He said the reason he chose these particular books was because the original 1836 version of these books were used for three-quarters of a century to teach about four-fifths of all American school children how to read. No other books ever had so much influence over American children for so long.

McGuffey's educational course begins in "The Primer" by presenting the letters of the alphabet to be memorized, in sequence. Children were then taught, step by step, to use the building blocks of the language to form and pronounce words, using the phonics method [42] (Footnote) which involves teaching children to connect sounds with letters. Each lesson begins with a study of words used in the reading exercise and with markings to show the correct pronunciation for each word.

I discovered that the stories in the "First and Second Readers" picture children in their relationship with family members, teachers, friends, and animals. The "Third, Fourth, Fifth and Sixth Readers" expanded on those ideas. One of the stories I remember was "The Widow and the Merchant". It's kind of a morality tale about a merchant who befriends a widow in need. Later, when the widow proves herself to be honest, the merchant gives her a nice gift. The books do not necessarily teach you to believe that charity is expected only of wealthy people though. We all know that generosity is a virtue that should be practiced by everyone.

All of the stories were very wholesome and they gave very good explanations to illustrate virtues like honesty, charity, thrift, hard work, courage, patriotism, reverence for God, and respect for parents. Personally, I would recommend this book to anyone!

I also discovered that the vocabulary used in the book was very advanced compared to the relatively limited number of words people use commonly in our modern age. I think we have lost a lot of our own language since our Founding Fathers wrote the Declaration of Independence over 200 years ago!

As instructed, I sat next to Airl in the interview room reading aloud to her from each successive book in the series of McGuffey's Readers. Each of the books had excellent, simple illustrations of the stories and subjects being taught, although they are very outdated by today's standards. Nonetheless, Airl seemed to understand and absorb every letter, sound, syllable and meaning as we progressed. We continued this process for 14 hours a day for 3 consecutive days without interruption, except for a few meals and rest breaks on my part.

Airl did not take breaks for anything. She did not sleep. Instead she remained sitting in the overstuffed chair in the interview room, reviewing the lessons we had already covered. When I returned each morning to begin where we'd left off, she had already memorized the previous lessons and was well into the next pages. This pattern continued to accelerate until it became pointless for me to continue reading to her.

Although Airl did not have a mouth to speak with, she was now able to "think" at me in English. At the end of these lessons, Airl was able to read and study by herself. I showed her how to use a dictionary to look up new words she encountered. Airl consulted the dictionary continually after that. From then on my job was acting as a courier for her, requesting that reference books be brought to her in a steady stream.

Next, Mr. Newble brought in a set of the *Encyclopedia Britannica*. [43] **(Footnote)** Airl especially enjoyed this because it had a lot of pictures. After that, she requested many more picture books and reference books with photographs and drawings because it was much easier to understand the meaning if she could see a picture of the thing she was studying.

Over the next six days books were brought in from libraries all over the country, I presume, because it wasn't more than a few more days before she had read through several hundred of them! She studied every subject I could imagine, and many other very technical things I never wanted to know anything about, like astronomy, metallurgy, engineering, mathematics, various technical manuals, and so forth.

Later she began to read fiction books, novels, poetry and the classics of literature. Airl also asked to read a great many books on subjects in the humanities, especially history. I think she must have read at least 50 books about human history and archaeology. Of course, I made sure that she received a copy of the Holy Bible also, which she read from cover to cover without comment or questions.

Although I continued to stay with Airl for 12 to 14 hours each day, most of that time during the following week had been spent without much communication between us, except for an occasional question she asked me. The questions were usually meant to give her a sense of context or to clarify something in the books she was reading. Oddly, Airl told me that her favorite books are "Alice's Adventures in Wonderland" [44] **(Footnote)**, "Don Quixote de la Mancha" [45] **(Footnote)** and "One Thousand and One Nights" [46] **(Footnote)**. She said the authors of these stories showed that it is more important to have great spirit and imagination than great skill or power.

I could not answer a lot of her questions, so I consulted with the people in the outer room for answers. Most of these had to do with technical and scientific things. A few of her questions were about the humanities. The depth of complex understanding and subtlety of her questions showed that she had a very penetrating intellect.

Personally, I think she had already known a lot more about the culture and history of Earth than she was willing to admit when we started. I would soon discover how much more."

# Chapter Six

# My Education Begins

(MATILDA O'DONNELL MACELROY PERSONAL NOTE)

"By the 15th day after "rescuing" Airl from the crash site, I was able to communicate fluidly and effortlessly with her in English. She had absorbed so much written material by this time that her academic education far exceeded my own. Although I graduated from high school in Los Angeles in 1940 and attended college for four years of premedical and nursing training, the variety of my own reading had been fairly limited.

I had not studied most of the subjects to which Airl had now been exposed, especially considering her acute understanding, very intense study habits and a nearly photographic memory! She was able to recall long passages from books she read. She was especially fond of sections of her favorite stories from classic literature like *The Adventures of Huckleberry Finn* [47] **(Footnote)**, tales from *Gulliver's Travels* [48] **(Footnote)** and *Peter Pan* [49] **(Footnote)** and *The Legend of Sleepy Hollow* [50] **(Footnote)**.

By this time Airl had become the teacher, and I was the student. I was about to learn what men of Earth do not know and have no way of knowing!

The throng of scientists and agents who observed us through the one-way glass [51] **(Footnote)** of our interview room, whom Airl and I now referred to as "the gallery", were growing increasingly impatient to ask her questions. But Airl continued to refuse to allow any questions to be asked of her by anyone other than myself, even vicariously through me as an interpreter, or in writing.

On the afternoon of the 16th day Airl and I sat next to each other as she read. She closed the last page of a book she was reading and placed it aside. I was about to hand her the next book from a large pile waiting to be read, when she turned and said or "thought" to me, "I am ready to speak now". At first I was a little confused by the remark. I gestured for her to continue and she began to teach me my first lesson."

(OFFICIAL TRANSCRIPT OF INTERVIEW)

TOP SECRET

Official Transcript of the U.S. Army Air Force
Roswell Army Air Field, 509th Bomb Group
SUBJECT: ALIEN INTERVIEW, 24. 7. 1947, 1st Session

"What would you like to say, Airl?", I asked.

"I have been a part of the Domain Expeditionary Force in
this sector of space for several thousand years.
However, I have not personally had intimate contact with
beings on Earth since 5,965 BCE. It is not my primary
function to interact with inhabitants of planets within
The Domain. I am an Officer, Pilot and Engineer, with
many duties to perform. Nonetheless, although I am
fluent in 347 other languages within The Domain, I have
not been exposed to your English language.

The last Earth language with which I was conversant was
the Sanskrit language of the Vedic Hymns. [52] **(Footnote)** At
that time I was a member of a mission sent to
investigate the loss of a Domain base located in the
Himalaya Mountains. An entire battalion of officers,
pilots, communications and administrative personnel
disappeared and the base destroyed.

Several million years ago I was trained and served as an
Investigation, Data Evaluation and Program Development
Officer for The Domain. Because I was experienced in
that technology, I was sent to Earth as part of the
search team. One of my duties involved interrogation of
the human population that inhabited the adjoining area
at that time. [53] **(Footnote)** Many of the people in that region
reported sighting "vimanas" or space craft in the area. [54]
**(Footnote)**

Following the logical extension of evidence, testimony,
observation, as well as the absence of certain evidence,
I led my team to the discovery that there were still
"Old Empire" ships and well-hidden "Old Empire"
installations in this solar system of which we had been
completely unaware.

You and I were unable to communicate in your language
because I, personally, have not been exposed to your
language. However, now that I have scanned the books and
material you provided me this data has been relayed to
our space station in this region and processed by our
communications officer through our computers. It has
been translated into my own language and relayed back to
me in a context that I can think with. I have also
received additional information from the files stored in

49

our computers about the English language and Domain records concerning Earth civilization." [55] **(Footnote)**

"Now I am prepared to give you certain information that I feel will be of great value to you. I will tell you the truth. Although truth is relative to all other truth, I wish to share with you as honestly and accurately as possible, truth as I see it, within the boundaries of my integrity to myself, to my race and without violating my obligations to the organization I serve and have sworn to uphold and protect".

"OK", I thought. "Will you answer questions from the gallery now?"

"No. I will not answer questions. I will provide information to you that I think will be beneficial to the well-being of the immortal spiritual beings who comprise humanity, and that will foster the survival of all the myriad life forms and the environment of Earth, as it is a part of my mission to ensure the preservation of Earth.

"Personally, it is my conviction that all sentient beings are immortal spiritual beings. This includes human beings. For the sake of accuracy and simplicity I will use a made-up word: "IS-BE". Because the primary nature of an immortal being is that they live in a timeless state of "is", and the only reason for their existence is that they decide to "be".

No matter how lowly their station in a society, every IS-BE deserves the respect and treatment that I myself would like to receive from others. Each person on Earth continues to be an IS-BE whether they are aware of the fact or not."

### (MATILDA O'DONNELL MACELROY PERSONAL NOTE)

(I will never forget this conversation. Her tone was very matter-of-fact and emotionless. However, for the first time, I sensed the presence of a warm and real "personality" in Airl. Her reference to "immortal spiritual beings" struck me like a flash of light in a dark room. I had never before considered that a human being could be an immortal being.

I thought that status or power was reserved solely for The Father, The Son, and The Holy Ghost. And, because I am a devout Catholic and subject to the word of The

Lord Jesus, and The Holy Father, I have never thought of a woman as an immortal spiritual being either -- not even the Holy Mother Mary. Yet, when Airl thought that thought, I became vividly aware for the very first time that she, personally, was an immortal spiritual being, and so are we all!

Airl said that she sensed that I was confused about the idea. She said she would demonstrate to me that I am also an immortal spiritual being. She said, "Be above your body!" Immediately, I realized that I was "outside" of my body, looking down from the ceiling at the top of my body's head! [56] (Footnote) I was also able to see the room around me, including Airl's body sitting in the chair next to my own body. After a moment, I realized the simple, but shocking, reality, that "I" am not a body.

In that moment a black veil lifted and for the first time in my life, and for a very long time into the past, I realized that I am not "my soul", but that "I" am "me" -- a spiritual being. This was an unexplainable epiphany, but one that fills me with a joy and relief I cannot recall having experienced ever before. As for the "immortal" part, I do not understand her meaning, as I have always been taught that I am not immortal -- a spirit, perhaps -- but certainly not immortal!

After a moment -- I'm not sure how long -- Airl asked me if I had a better understanding of the idea. Suddenly, I was back inside my body again, and said out loud, "Yes! I see what you mean!".

I was so taken aback by the experience that I had to get up from my chair and walk around the room for a few minutes. I made an excuse that I needed to get a drink of water, and go to the restroom, which I did. In the restroom I looked at my "self" in the mirror. I used the toilet, refreshed my make-up, and straightened my uniform. After 10 or 15 minutes I felt more "normal" again and returned to the interview room.

After that I felt as though I was no longer just an interpreter for Airl. I felt as though I was a "kindred spirit". I felt like I was safe, at home, with a trusted friend or family member, as close as any I have ever had. Airl sensed and understood my confusion about the concept of "personal immortality". She began her first "lesson" with me by explaining this to me."

(OFFICIAL TRANSCRIPT OF INTERVIEW CONTINUED)

"Airl told me her reasons for coming to Earth and for being in the area of the 509th Bomber Squadron. [57] (Footnote) She was sent by her superior officers to investigate the explosions of nuclear weapons which have been tested in New Mexico. [58] (Footnote) Her superiors ordered her to gather information from the atmosphere that could be used to determine the extent of radiation [59] (Footnote) and potential harm this might cause to the environment. During her

51

mission, the space craft was struck by a lighting
[60] (Footnote), which caused her to lose control and crash.

The space craft is operated by IS-BEs who use "doll
bodies" in much the same way that an actor wears a mask
and costume. It is a like a mechanical tool through
which to operate in the physical world. She, as well as
all of the other IS-BEs of the officer class and their
superiors, inhabit these "doll bodies" when they are on
duty in space. When they are not on duty, they "leave"
the body and operate, think, communicate, travel, and
exist without the use of a body.

The bodies are constructed of synthetic materials,
including a very sensitive electrical nervous system, to
which each IS-BE adjusts themselves or "tune in" to an
electronic wavelength [61] (Footnote) that is matched uniquely
to the wavelength or frequency emitted by each IS-BE.
Each IS-BE is capable of creating a unique wave
frequency which identifies them, much like a radio
signal frequency. This serves, in part, as
identification like a finger print. The doll body acts
like a radio receiver for the IS-BE. No two frequencies
or doll bodies are exactly the same.

The bodies of each IS-BE crew member are likewise tuned
into and connected to the "nervous system" built into
the space craft. The space craft is built in much the
same way as the doll body. It is adjusted specifically
to the frequency of each IS-BE crew member. Therefore,
the craft can be operated by the "thoughts" or energy
emitted by the IS-BE. It is really a very simple,
direct control system. So, there are no complicated
controls or navigation equipment on board the space
craft. They operate as an extension of the IS-BE.

When the lightning bolt struck the space craft this
caused a short circuit and consequently "disconnected"
them from the control of the ship momentarily which
resulted in the crash.

Airl was, and still is, an officer, pilot and engineer
in an expeditionary force which is part of a space opera
[62] (Footnote) civilization which refers to itself as "The
Domain". This civilization controls a vast number of
galaxies, stars, planets, moons and asteroids throughout
an area of space that is approximately one-fourth of the

entire physical universe!  The continuing mission of her
organization is to "Secure, control and expand the
territory and resources of The Domain".

Airl pointed out that their own activities were very
similar in many ways to the European explorers who
"discovered" and "claimed" the New World for The Holy
Father, The Pope [63] **(Footnote)** and for the kings of Spain,
Portugal and later, Holland, England, France and so
forth. Europe benefited from the property "acquired"
from the native inhabitants.  However, the native
inhabitants were never consulted with or asked for their
permission to become a part of the "domain" of European
nations and the soldiers and priests they sent to
acquire territory and wealth in order to advance their
interests.

Airl said she read in a history book that the Spanish
king regretted the brutal treatment of the native
inhabitants by his soldiers.  He feared retribution from
the gods he worshipped, as described in the various
testaments of the Bible.  He asked the Pope to prepare a
statement called "The Requirement" [64] **(Footnote)** which was
supposed to be read to each of the newly encountered
native inhabitants.

The king hoped that the statement, whether it was
accepted or rejected by the natives, would absolve the
King of all responsibility for the resulting slaughter
and enslavement of these people.  He used this statement
as justification to confiscate their lands and
possessions by his soldiers and the Pope's priests.
Apparently, the Pope, personally, did not have any
feelings of guilt or responsibility in the matter.

Airl thought that such actions were those of a coward
and that it is no surprise that the territory of Spain
was diminished so quickly.  Only a few years later the
king was dead and his empire had been assimilated by
other nations.

Airl said that this sort of  behavior does not occur in
The Domain.  Their leaders assume full responsibility
for the actions of The Domain, and would not denigrate
themselves in this fashion.  Nor do they fear any gods
or have any regret for their actions. This idea

reinforces my earlier suggestion that Airl and her
people are probably atheists.

In the case of the acquisition of Earth by The Domain,
the rulers of The Domain have chosen not to openly
reveal this intention to the "native inhabitants" of
Earth until a later time when it may, or may not, suit
their interests to reveal themselves.  For the present
time, it is not strategically necessary to make the
presence of The Domain Expeditionary Force known to
Mankind.  In fact, until now, it has been very
aggressively hidden, for reasons that will be revealed
later.

The asteroid belt near Earth is a very small, but
important location for The Domain in this part of space.
Actually, some of the objects in our solar system are
very valuable for use as low-gravity "space stations".
They are interested primarily in the low gravity
satellites in this solar system which consists mainly of
the side of the moon facing away from Earth [65] **(Footnote)** and
the asteroid belt, which was a planet that was destroyed
billions of years ago, and to a lesser degree, Mars and
Venus.  Doom structures synthesized from gypsum [66] **(Footnote)**
or underground bases covered by electromagnetic force
screens [67] **(Footnote)** are easily constructed to house the
Domain forces.

Once an area of space is acquired by The Domain and
becomes a part of the territory under its control, it is
treated as the "property" of The Domain.  The space
station near the planet Earth is important only because
it lay along a path of The Domain expansion route toward
the center of the Milky Way galaxy and beyond.  Of
course, everyone in The Domain is aware of this --
except for the people of Earth."

# Chapter Seven

# A Lesson In Ancient History

(MATILDA O'DONNELL MACELROY PERSONAL NOTE)

"My instruction with Airl continued through the night until dawn of the next morning. I must say that I was fascinated, skeptical, shocked, alarmed, dismayed and disgruntled by the "lesson" I was getting from Airl. I could never have imagined any of what she was telling me -- not even in my wildest dreams and nightmares!

The next afternoon, after I had slept, showered and eaten, I was debriefed about my interview session the previous evening by members of the gallery who recorded my account of what Airl told me. There was a stenographer present for this session, as usual, to whom I debriefed after each interview, and there were also 6 or 7 men who asked for clarification of my statements. As always, there was constant pressure applied to me to use my influence with Airl to persuade her to answer specific questions prompted by members of the gallery. I did my best to reassure everyone that I would give my very best efforts to do so.

Nevertheless, only three things happened every day thereafter:

1) Airl resolutely refused to answer any questions that she sensed had been posed by or suggested to me by the gallery.

2) Airl continued to "instruct" me in subject matter of her own choice.

3) Every evening after my interview with, or instruction from Airl, she would give me a new list of subject matter about which she wanted more information. Each evening I presented this list to the gallery. The next day Airl received a large stack of books, magazines, articles, and so forth. She would study all of these during the night while I slept. This pattern repeated every day during the remainder of the time I spent with her.

The subject matter of my next interview, or lesson, from Airl continued with a brief history of Earth, our solar system and nearby space, from the perspective of The Domain."

(OFFICIAL TRANSCRIPT OF INTERVIEW)

TOP SECRET

Official Transcript of the U.S. Army Air Force

Roswell Army Air Field, 509th Bomb Group
SUBJECT: ALIEN INTERVIEW, 25. 7. 1947, 1st Session

"Before you can understand the subject of history, you
must first understand the subject of time. Time is
simply an arbitrary measurement of the motion of objects
through space.

Space is not linear. Space is determined by the point
of view of an IS-BE when viewing an object. The
distance between an IS-BE and the object being viewed is
called "space".

Objects, or energy masses, in space do not necessarily
move in a linear fashion. In this universe, objects
tend to move randomly or in a curving or cyclical
pattern, or as determined by agreed upon rules.

History is not only a linear record of events, as many
authors of Earth history books imply, because it is not
a string that can be stretched out and marked like a
measuring tool. History is a subjective observation of
the movement of objects through space, recorded from the
point of view of a survivor, rather than of those who
succumbed. Events occur interactively and concurrently,
just as the biological body has a heart that pumps
blood, while the lungs provide oxygen to the cells,
which reproduce, using energy from the sun and chemicals
from plants, at the same time as the liver strains toxic
wastes from the blood, and eliminates them through the
bladder and the bowels.

All of these interactions are concurrent and
simultaneous. Although time runs consecutively, events
do not happen in an independent, linear stream. In
order to view and understand the history or reality of
the past, one must view all events as part of an
interactive whole. Time can also be sensed as a
vibration which is uniform throughout the entire
physical universe.

Airl explained that IS-BEs have been around since before
the beginning of the universe. The reason they are
called "immortal", is because a "spirit" is not born and
cannot die, but exists in a personally postulated
perception of "is - will be". She was careful to explain

that every spirit is not the same. Each is completely unique in identity, power, awareness and ability.

The difference between an IS-BE like Airl and most of the IS-BEs inhabiting bodies on Earth, is that Airl can enter and depart from her "doll" at will. She can perceive at selective depths through matter. Airl and other officers of The Domain can communicate telepathically. Since an IS-BE is not a physical universe entity it has no location in space or time. An IS-BE is literally, "immaterial". They can span great distances of space instantly.

They can experience sensations, more intensely than a biological body, without the use of physical sensory mechanisms. An IS-BE can exclude pain from their perception. Airl can also remember her "identity", so to speak, all the way back into the dim mists of time, for trillions of years!

She says that the existing collection of suns in this immediate vicinity of the universe have been burning for the last 200 trillion years. The age of the physical universe is nearly infinitely old, but probably at least four quadrillion [68] **(Footnote)** years since its earliest beginnings.

Time is a difficult factor to measure as it depends on the subjective memory of IS-BEs and there has been no uniform record of events throughout the physical universe since it began. As on Earth, there are many different time measurement systems, defined by various cultures, which use cycles of motion, and points of origin to establish age and duration. [69] **(Footnote)**

The physical universe itself is formed from the convergence and amalgamation of many other individual universes [70] **(Footnote)**, each one of which were created by an IS-BE or group of IS-BEs. The collision of these illusory universes commingled and coalesced and were solidified to form a mutually created universe. Because it is agreed that energy and forms can be created, but not destroyed, [71] **(Footnote)** this creative process has continued to form an ever-expanding universe of nearly infinite physical proportions.

Before the formation of the physical universe there was a vast period during which universes were not solid, but wholly illusionary. You might say that the universe was a universe of magical illusions which were made to appear and vanish at the will of the magician. In every case, the "magician" was one or more IS-BEs. Many IS-BEs on Earth can still recall vague images from that period. Tales of magic, sorcery and enchantment, fairy tales and mythology speak of such things, [72] **(Footnote)** although in very crude terms.

Each IS-BE entered into the physical universe when they lost their own, "home" universe. That is, when an IS-BE's "home" universe was overwhelmed by the physical universe, or when the IS-BE joined with other IS-BEs to create or conquer the physical universe.

On Earth, the ability to determine when an IS-BE entered the physical universe is difficult for two reasons: 1) the memory of IS-BEs on Earth have been erased, and 2) IS-BEs arrival or invasion into the physical universe took place at different times, some 60 trillion years ago, and others only 3 trillion. Every once in a short while, a few million years, an area or planet will be taken over by another group of IS-BEs entering into the area.

Sometimes they will capture other IS-BEs as slaves. [73] **(Footnote)** They will be forced to inhabit bodies to perform menial, or manual work -- especially mining mineral ores on heavy-gravity planets, such as Earth.

Airl says that she has been a member of The Domain Expeditionary Force for more than 625 million years, when she became a pilot for a biological survey mission which included occasional visits to Earth. She can remember her entire career there, and for a very long time before that.

She told me that Earth scientists do not have an accurate measuring system to gauge the age of matter. They assume that because certain types of materials seem to deteriorate rather quickly, such as organic or carbon-based matter, that there is a deterioration of matter. It is not accurate to measure the age of stone, based on the measurement of the age of wood or bone. This is a fundamental error. Factually, matter does not

deteriorate.  It cannot be destroyed.  Matter may be
altered in form, but it is never truly destroyed.

The Domain has conducted a periodic survey of the
galaxies in this sector of the universe since it
developed space travel technologies about 80 trillion
years ago.  A review of changes in the complexion of
Earth reveal that mountain ranges rise and fall,
continents change location, the poles of the planet
shift, ice caps come and go, oceans appear and
disappear, rivers, valleys and canyons change.  In all
cases, the matter is the same.  It is always the same
sand.  Every form and substance is made of the same
basic material, which never deteriorates.

### (MATILDA O'DONNELL MACELROY PERSONAL NOTE)

("I cannot even begin to imagine how advanced a civilization may have become,
technically, and mentally, after trillions of years!  Just think of how advanced our
own country has become, compared to only 150 years.  Only a few generations ago
transportation was on foot, horseback or boat, reading was done by candlelight,
heating and cooking were done over a fireplace, and there wasn't any indoor
plumbing!")

### (OFFICIAL TRANSCRIPT OF INTERVIEW)

"Airl described the abilities of an IS-BE officer of The
Domain to me, and she demonstrated one to me when she
contacted -- telepathically -- a communications officer
of The Domain who is stationed in the asteroid belt.
[74] (Footnote)

The asteroid belt is composed of thousands of broken up
pieces of a planet that once existed between Mars and
Jupiter.  It serves as a good low-gravity jumping off
point for incoming space craft traveling toward the
center of our galaxy.

She requested that this officer consult information
stored in the "files" of The Domain, concerning the
history of Earth.  She asked the communications officer
to "feed" this information to Airl.  The communications
officer immediately complied with the request.  Based on
the information stored in the files of The Domain, Airl
was able to give me a brief overview or "history
lesson".  This is what Airl told me that The Domain had
observed about the history of Earth:

She told me that The Domain Expeditionary Force first
entered into the Milky Way galaxy very recently -- only
about 10,000 years ago. Their first action was to
conquer the home planets of the "Old Empire" (this is
not the official name, but a nick-name given to the
conquered civilization by The Domain Forces) that served
as the seat of central government for this galaxy, and
other adjoining regions of space. These planets are
located in the star systems in the tail of the Big
Dipper constellation. [75] **(Footnote)** She did not mention which
stars, exactly.

About 1,500 years later The Domain began the
installation bases for their own forces along the path
of invasion which leads toward the center of this galaxy
and beyond. About 8,200 years ago The Domain forces set
up a base on Earth in the Himalaya Mountains near the
border of modern Pakistan and Afghanistan. This was a
base for a battalion of The Domain Expeditionary Force,
which included about 3,000 members.

They set up a base under or inside the top of a
mountain. The mountain top was drilled into and made
hollow to create an area large enough to house the ships
and personnel of that force. An electronic illusion of
the mountain top was then created to hide the base by
projecting a false image from inside the mountain
against a "force screen". The ships could then enter
and exit through the force screen, yet remain unseen by
homo sapiens.

Shortly after they settled there the base was surprised
by an attack from a remnant of the military forces of
the "Old Empire". Unbeknownst to The Domain, a hidden,
underground base on Mars, operated by the "Old Empire",
had existed for a very long time. The Domain base was
wiped out by a military attack from the Mars base and
the IS-BEs of The Domain Expeditionary Force were
captured.

You can imagine that The Domain was very upset about
losing such a large force of officers and crew, so they
sent other crews to Earth to look for them. Those crews
were also attacked. The captured IS-BEs from The Domain
Forces were handled in the same fashion as all other IS-
BEs who have been sent to Earth. They were each given
amnesia, had their memories replaced with false pictures

and hypnotic commands and sent to Earth to inhabit biological bodies. They are still a part of the human population today.

After a very persistent and extensive investigation into the loss of their crews, The Domain discovered that "Old Empire" has been operating a very extensive, and very carefully hidden, base of operations in this part of the galaxy for millions of years. No one knows exactly how long. Eventually, the space craft of the "Old Empire" forces and The Domain engaged each other in open combat in the space of the solar system.

According to Airl, there was a running battle between the "Old Empire" forces and The Domain until about 1235 AD, when The Domain forces finally destroyed the last of the space craft of the "Old Empire" force in this area. The Domain Expeditionary Force lost many of its own ships in this area during that time also.

About 1,000 years later the "Old Empire" base was discovered by accident in the spring of 1914 AD. The discovery was made when the body of the Archduke of Austria, [76] (Footnote) was "taken over" by an officer of The Domain Expeditionary Force. This officer, who was stationed in the asteroid belt, was sent to Earth on a routine mission to gather reconnaissance.

The purpose of this "take over" was to use the body as a "disguise" through which to infiltrate human society in order to gather information about current events on Earth. The officer, as an IS-BE, having greater power than the being inhabiting the body of the Archduke, simply "pushed" the being out and took over control of the body.

However, this officer did not realize how much the Hapsburgs were hated by feuding factions in the country, so he was caught off guard when the body of the Archduke was assassinated by a Bosnian student. The officer, or IS-BE, was suddenly "knocked out" of the body when it was shot by the assassin. Disoriented, the IS-BE inadvertently penetrated one of the "amnesia force screens" and was captured.

Eventually The Domain discovered that a wide area of space is monitored by an "electronic force field"

[77] (Footnote) which controls all of the IS-BEs in this end of the galaxy, including Earth. The electronic force screen is designed to detect IS-BEs and prevent them from leaving the area.

If any IS-BE attempts to penetrate the force screen, it "captures" them in a kind of "electronic net". The result is that the captured IS-BE is subjected to a very severe "brainwashing" treatment which erases the memory of the IS-BE. This process uses a tremendous electrical shock, just like Earth psychiatrists use "electric shock therapy" to erase the memory and personality of a "patient" and to make them more "cooperative". [78] (Footnote)

On Earth this "therapy" uses only a few hundred volts of electricity. However, the electrical voltage [79] (Footnote) used by the "Old Empire" operation against IS-BEs is on the order of magnitude of billions of volts! This tremendous shock completely wipes out all the memory of the IS-BE. The memory erasure is not just for one life or one body. It wipes out all of the accumulated experiences of a nearly infinite past, as well as the identity of the IS-BE!

The shock is intended to make it impossible for the IS-BE to remember who they are, where they came from, their knowledge or skills, their memory of the past, and ability to function as a spiritual entity. They are overwhelmed into becoming a mindless, robotic non-entity.

After the shock a series of post hypnotic suggestions [80] (Footnote) are used to install false memories, and a false time orientation in each IS-BE. This includes the command to "return" to the base after the body dies, so that the same kind of shock and hypnosis can be done again, and again, again -- forever. The hypnotic command also tells the "patient" to forget to remember.

What The Domain learned from the experience of this officer is that the "Old Empire" has been using Earth as a "prison planet" for a very long time -- exactly how long is unknown -- perhaps millions of years.

So, when the body of the IS-BE dies they depart from the body. They are detected by the "force screen", they are captured and "ordered" by hypnotic command to "return

to the light". The idea of "heaven" and the "afterlife"
are part of the hypnotic suggestion -- a part of the
treachery that makes the whole mechanism work.

After the IS-BE has been shocked and hypnotized to erase
the memory of the life just lived, the IS-BE is
immediately "commanded", hypnotically, to "report" back
to Earth, as though they were on a secret mission, to
inhabit a new body. Each IS-BE is told that they have a
special purpose for being on Earth. But, of course
there is no purpose for being in a prison -- at least
not for the prisoner.

Any undesirable IS-BEs who are sentenced to Earth were
classified as "untouchable" [81] **(Footnote)** by the "Old Empire".
This included anyone that the "Old Empire" judged to be
criminals who are too vicious to be reformed or subdued,
as well as other criminals such as sexual perverts, or
beings unwilling to do any productive work.

An "untouchable" classification of IS-BEs also includes
a wide variety of "political prisoners" [82] **(Footnote)**. This
includes IS-BEs who are considered to be noncompliant
"free thinkers" or "revolutionaries" who make trouble
for the governments of the various planets of the "Old
Empire". Of course, anyone with a previous military
record against the "Old Empire" is also shipped off to
Earth.

A list of "untouchables" include artists, painters,
singers, musicians, writers, actors, and performers of
every kind. For this reason Earth has more artists per
capita than any other planet in the "Old Empire".

"Untouchables" also include intellectuals, inventors and
geniuses in almost every field. Since everything the
"Old Empire" considers valuable has long since been
invented or created over the last few trillion years,
they have no further use for such beings. This includes
skilled managers also, which are not needed in a society
of obedient, robotic citizens.

Anyone who is not willing or able to submit to mindless
economic, political and religious servitude as a tax-
paying worker in the class system of the "Old Empire"
are "untouchable" and sentenced to receive memory wipe-
out and permanent imprisonment on Earth.

The net result is that an IS-BE is unable to escape because they can't remember who they are, where they came from, where they are. They have been hypnotized to think they are someone, something, sometime, and somewhere other than where they really are.

The Domain officer who was "assassinated" while in the body of Archduke of Austria was, likewise, captured by the "Old Empire" force. Because this particular officer was a high powered IS-BE, compared to most, he was taken away to a secret "Old Empire" base under the surface of the planet Mars. They put him into a special electronic prison cell and held him there.

Fortunately, this Domain officer was able to escape from the underground base after 27 years in captivity. When he escaped from the "Old Empire" base, he returned immediately to his own base in the asteroid belt. His commanding officer ordered that a battle cruiser be dispatched [83] **(Footnote)** to the coordinates of the base provided by this officer and to destroy that base completely. This "Old Empire" base was located a few hundred miles north of the equator on Mars in the Cydonia region. [84] **(Footnote)**

Although the military base of the "Old Empire" was destroyed, unfortunately, much of the vast machinery of the IS-BE force screens, the electroshock / amnesia / hypnosis machinery continues to function in other undiscovered locations right up to the present moment. The main base or control center for this "mind control prison" [85] **(Footnote)** operation has never been found. So, the influences of this base, or bases, are still in effect.

The Domain has observed that since the "Old Empire" space forces were destroyed there is no one left to actively prevent other planetary systems from bringing their own "untouchable" IS-BEs to Earth from all over this galaxy, and from other galaxies nearby. Therefore, Earth has become a universal dumping ground for this entire region of space.

This, in part, explains the very unusual mix of races, cultures, languages, moral codes, religious and political influences among the IS-BE population on Earth. The number and variety of heterogeneous societies on Earth are extremely unusual on a normal

64

planet. Most "Sun Type 12, Class 7" planets are
inhabited by only one humanoid body type or race, if
any.

In addition, most of the ancient civilizations of Earth,
and many of the events of Earth have been heavily
influenced by the hidden, hypnotic operation of the "Old
Empire" base. So far, no one has figured out exactly
where and how this operation is run, or by whom because
it is so heavily protected by screens and traps.

Furthermore, there has been no operation undertaken to
seek out, discover and destroy the vast and ancient
network of electronics machinery that create the IS-BE
force screens at this end of the galaxy. Until this has
been done, we are not able to prevent or interrupt the
electric shock operation, hypnosis and remote thought
control [86] **(Footnote)** of the "Old Empire" prison planet.

Of course all of the crew members of The Domain
Expeditionary Force now remain aware of this phenomena
at all times while operating in this solar system space
so as to prevent detection and the capture by "Old
Empire" traps."

# Chapter Eight

# A Lesson In Recent History

(MATILDA O'DONNELL MACELROY PERSONAL NOTE)

"This interview taught me a history lesson I will never read in any text book written on Earth! The Domain has a much different view of events than we do."

(OFFICIAL TRANSCRIPT OF INTERVIEW)

TOP SECRET

Official Transcript of the U.S. Army Air Force
Roswell Army Air Field, 509th Bomb Group
SUBJECT: ALIEN INTERVIEW, 26. 7. 1947, 1st Session

"The Domain Expeditionary Force has observed a
resurgence in science and culture of the Western world
since 1150 AD when the remaining remnants of the space
fleet of the "Old Empire" in this solar system were
destroyed.  The influence of the remote control [87] **(Footnote)**
hypnosis operation diminished slightly after that time,
but still remains largely in force.

Apparently a small amount of damage was done to the "Old
Empire" remote mind control [88] **(Footnote)** operation which
resulted in a small decrease in the power of this
mechanism.  As a result, some memory of technologies
that IS-BEs already knew before they came to Earth
started to be remembered.  Thereafter the oppression of
knowledge that is called the "Dark Ages" [89] **(Footnote)** in
Europe began to diminish after that time.

Since then knowledge of the basic laws of physics [90]
**(Footnote)** and electricity [91] **(Footnote)** have revolutionized Earth
culture virtually overnight.  The ability to remember
technology by many of the geniuses in the IS-BE
population of Earth was partially restored, when not so
actively suppressed as it was before 1150 AD.  Sir Isaac
Newton, [92] **(Footnote)** is one of the best examples of this.  In
only a few decades he single-handedly reinvented several

66

major and fundamental scientific and mathematical disciplines.

The men who "remembered" these sciences already knew them before they were sent to Earth. Ordinarily, no one would ever observe or discover as much about science and mathematics in a single life-time, or even in a few hundred life-times. These subjects have taken civilizations billions and billions of years to create!

IS-BEs on Earth have only just begun to remember small fragments of all the technologies that exist throughout the universe. Theoretically, if the amnesia mechanisms being used against Earth could be broken entirely, IS-BEs would regain all of their memory!

Unfortunately, similar advances have not been seen in the humanities as the IS-BEs of Earth continue to behave very badly toward each other. This behavior, however, is heavily influenced by the "hypnotic commands" given to each IS-BE between lifetimes. [93] **(Footnote)**

And, the very unusual combination of "inmates" on Earth - criminals, perverts, artists, revolutionaries and geniuses - is the cause of a very restive and tumultuous environment. The purpose of the prison planet is to keep IS-BEs on Earth, forever. Promoting ignorance, superstition, and war between IS-BEs helps to keep the prison population crippled and trapped behind "the wall" of electronic force screens.

IS-BEs have been dumped on Earth from all over the galaxy, adjoining galaxies, and from planetary systems all over the "Old Empire", like Sirius, Aldebaron, the Pleiades, Orion, Draconis, and countless others. There are IS-BEs on Earth from unnamed races, civilizations, cultural backgrounds, and planetary environments. Each of the various IS-BE populations have their own languages, belief systems, moral values, religious beliefs, training and unknown and untold histories.

These IS-BEs are mixed together with earlier inhabitants of Earth who came from another star system more than 400,000 years ago to establish the civilizations of Atlanta [94] **(Footnote)** and Lemuria [95] **(Footnote)**. Those civilizations vanished beneath the tidal waves caused by a planetary "polar shift", [96] **(Footnote)** many thousands of years before

67

the current "prison" population started to arrive.
Apparently, the IS-BEs from those star systems were the
source of the original, oriental races of Earth,
beginning in Australia.

On the other hand, the civilizations set up on Earth by
the "Old Empire" prison system were very different from
the civilization of the "Old Empire" itself, which is an
electronic space opera, atomic powered conglomeration of
earlier civilizations that were conquered with nuclear
weapons and colonized by IS-BEs from another galaxy.

The bureaucracy that controlled the former "Old Empire"
was from an ancient space opera society, run by a
totalitarian [97] **(Footnote)** confederation of planetary
governments, regulated by a brutal social, economic, and
political hierarchy, [98] **(Footnote)** with a royal monarch as its
figurehead. [99] **(Footnote)**

This type of government emerges with regularity on
planets where the citizens abandon personal
responsibility for autonomous, self-regulation. They
frequently lose their freedom to demented IS-BEs who
suffer from an overwhelming paranoia that every other
IS-BE is their enemy who must be controlled or
destroyed. Their closest friends and allies, whom they
espouse to love and cherish, are literally "loved to
death" by them.

Because such IS-BEs exist, The Domain has learned that
freedom must be won and maintained through eternal
vigilance and the ability to use defensive force to
maintain it. As a result, The Domain has already
conquered the governing planet of the "Old Empire". The
civilization of The Domain, although considerably
younger and smaller in size, is already more powerful,
better organized, and united by an egalitarian esprit de
corps [100] **(Footnote)** never known in the history of the "Old
Empire".

The recently despoiled German totalitarian state on
Earth was similar to the "Old Empire", but not nearly as
brutal, and about ten thousand times less powerful.
Many of the IS-BEs on Earth are here because they are
violently opposed to totalitarian government, [101] **(Footnote)** or
because they were so psychotically vicious that they
could not be controlled by "Old Empire" government.

Consequently, the population of Earth is
disproportionately comprised of a very high percentage
of such beings. The conflicting cultural and ethical
moral codes of the IS-BEs on Earth is unusual in the
extreme.

The Domain conquest of the central "Old Empire" planets
was fought with electronic cannon. [102] **(Footnote)** The citizens
of the planets forming the core of government for the
"Old Empire" are a filthy, degraded, slave society of
mindless, tax-paying workers, who practice cannibalism.
Violent automotive race tracks and bloody, Roman circus
type entertainments are their only amusements.

Regardless of any reasonable justification we may have
had for using atomic weapons to vanquish the planets of
the "Old Empire", The Domain is careful not to ruin the
resources of those planets by using weapons of crude,
radioactive force.

The government of the "Old Empire", before being
supplanted by The Domain, was comprised of beings who
possessed a very craven intelligence, very much like the
Axis powers [103] **(Footnote)** during your recent world war.
Those beings manifested precisely the same behavior as
the galactic government that exiled them to eternal
imprisonment on Earth. They were a gruesome reminder of
the ageless maxim that an IS-BE will often manifest the
treatment they have received from others. Kindness
fosters kindness. Cruelty begets cruelty. One must be
able and willing to use force, tempered with
intelligence, to prevent harm to the innocent. However,
extraordinary understanding, self-discipline and courage
are required to effectively prevent brutality, without
being overwhelmed by the malice that motivated the
brutality.

Only a demonic, self-serving government would employ a
"logic" or "science" to conceive that an "ultimate
solution" to any problem is to murder and permanently
erase the memory of every artist, genius, skilled
manager, and inventor, and cast them into a planetary
prison together with political opponents, killers,
thieves, perverts, and disabled beings of an entire
galaxy!

Once the IS-BEs expelled from the "Old Empire" arrived
on Earth, they were given amnesia, and hypnotically
tricked into thinking that something else had happened
to them.  The next step was to implant the IS-BEs into
biological bodies on Earth.  The bodies became the human
populations of "false civilizations" which were designed
and installed in the minds of IS-BEs to look completely
unlike the "Old Empire".

All of the IS-BEs of India, Egypt, Babylon, Greece,
Rome, and Medieval Europe were guided to pattern and
build the cultural elements of these societies based on
standard patterns developed by the IS-BEs of many
earlier, similar civilizations on "Sun Type 12, Class 7"
planets that have existed for trillions of years
throughout the universe.

In the earliest times the IS-BEs sent to prison Earth
lived in India.  They gradually spread into Mesopotamia,
Egypt, Mesoamerica, Achaea, Greece, Rome, Medieval
Europe, and to the New World.  They were hypnotically
"commanded" to follow the pattern of a given
civilization by the "Old Empire" prison operators.  This
is an effective mechanism to disguise the actual time
and location from the IS-BEs imprisoned on Earth.  The
languages, costumes and culture of each false
civilization are intended to reinforce amnesia because
they do not remind the IS-BEs on Earth of the original
"Old Empire" planets from which they were deported.

On the very far back-track of time these types of
civilizations tended to repeat themselves over and over
because the IS-BEs who created them become familiar with
certain patterns and styles, and stayed with them.  It
is a lot of work to invent an entire civilization,
complete with culture, architecture, language, customs,
mathematics, moral values, and so forth.  It is much
easier to replicate a copy based on a familiar and
successful pattern.

A "Sun Type 12, Class 7" planet is the designation given
to a planet inhabited by carbon-oxygen based life forms.
The class of the planet is based on the size and
radiation intensity of the star, the distance of the
planetary orbit from the star, and the size, density,
gravity, and chemical composition of the planet.
Likewise, flora and fauna are designated and identified

according to the star type and class of planet they
inhabit.

On the average, the percentage of planets in the
physical universe with a breathable atmosphere is
relatively small.  Most planets do not have an
atmosphere upon which life-forms "feed", as on Earth,
where the chemical composition of the atmosphere
provides nutrition to plants, and other organisms, which
in turn support other life forms.

When the Domain Force brought the Vedic Hymns [104] **(Footnote)**
to the Himalayas region 8,200 years ago, some human
societies already existed.  The Aryan people invaded and
conquered India [105] **(Footnote)**, bringing the Vedic Hymns [106]
**(Footnote)** to the area.

The Vedas were learned by them, memorized and carried
forward verbally for 7,000 years before being committed
to written form.  During that span of time one of the
officers of The Domain Expeditionary Force was
incarnated on Earth as "Vishnu" [107] **(Footnote)**.  He is
described many times in the Rig-Veda.  He is still
considered to be a god by the Hindus.  Vishnu fought in
the religious wars against the "Old Empire" forces.  He
is a very able and aggressive IS-BE as well as a highly
effective officer, who has since been reassigned to
other duties in The Domain.

This entire episode was orchestrated as an attack and
revolt against the Egyptian pantheon installed by "Old
Empire" administrators.  The conflict was intended to
help free humankind from implanted elements of the false
civilization that focused attention on many "gods" and
superstitious ritual worship demanded by the priests who
"managed" them.  It is all part of the mental
manipulation by the "Old Empire" to hide their criminal
actions against the IS-BEs on Earth.

A priesthood, or prison guards, were used to help
reinforce the idea that an individual is only a
biological body and is not an Immortal Spiritual Being.
The individual has no identity.  The individuals have no
past lives. [108] **(Footnote)** The individual has no power.  Only
the gods have power.  And, the gods are a contrivance of
the priests who intercede between men and the gods they
serve.  Men are slaves to the dictates of the priests

who threaten eternal spiritual punishment if men do not
obey them.

What else would one expect on a prison planet where all
prisoners have amnesia, and the priests themselves are
prisoners?  The intervention of The Domain Force on
Earth has not been entirely successful due to the secret
mind-control operation of the "Old Empire" that still
continues to operate.

A battle was waged between the "Old Empire" forces and
The Domain through religious conquest.  Between 1500 BCE
and about 1200 BCE, The Domain Forces attempted to teach
the concept of an individual, Immortal Spiritual Being,
to several influential beings on Earth.

One such instance resulted in a very tragic
misunderstanding, misinterpretation and misapplication
of the concept.  The idea was perverted and applied to
mean that there is only one IS-BE, instead of the truth
that everyone is an IS-BE!  Obviously, this was a gross
incomprehension and an utter unwillingness to take
responsibility for one's own power.

The "Old Empire" priests managed to corrupt the concept
of individual immortality into the idea that there is
only one, all-powerful IS-BE, and that no one else is or
is allowed to be an IS-BE.  Obviously, this is the work
of the "Old Empire" amnesia operation.

It is easy to teach this altered notion to beings who do
not want to be responsible for their own lives.  Slaves
are such beings.  As long as one chooses to assign
responsibility for creation, existence and personal
accountability for one's own thoughts and actions to
others, one is a slave.

As a result, the concept of a single monotheistic "god"
resulted and was promoted by many self-proclaimed
prophets, such as the Jewish slave leader -- Moses --
[109] **(Footnote)** who grew up in the household of the Pharaoh
Amenhotep III [110] **(Footnote)** and his son, Akhenaten [111] **(Footnote)**
and his wife Nefertiti, [112] **(Footnote)** as well as his son
Tutankhamen. [113] **(Footnote)**

The attempt to teach certain beings on Earth the truth
that they are, themselves, IS-BEs, was part of a plan to

overthrow the fictional, metaphorical, anthropomorphic panoply of gods created by the "Old Empire" mystery cult called "The Brothers of The Serpent" [114] **(Footnote)** known in Egypt as the Priests of Amun. [115] **(Footnote)** They were a very ancient, secret society within the "Old Empire".

The Pharaoh Akhenaten was not a very intelligent being, and was heavily influenced by his personal ambition for self-glorification. He altered the concept of the individual spiritual being and embodied the concept in the sun god, Aten. His pitiful existence was soon ended. He was assassinated by Maya and Parennefer, two of the Priests of Amun, or "Amen", which the Christians still say, who represented the interests of the "Old Empire" forces.

The idea of "One God" was perpetuated by the Hebrew leader Moses [116] **(Footnote)** while he was in Egypt. He left Egypt with his adopted people, the Jewish slaves. While they were crossing the desert, Moses was intercepted by an operative of the "Old Empire" near Mt. Sinai. Moses was tricked into believing that this operative was "the" One God through the use of hypnotic commands, as well as technical and aesthetic tricks which are commonly used by the "Old Empire" to trap IS-BEs. Thereafter, the Jewish slaves, who trusted the word of Moses implicitly, have worshiped a single god they call "Yaweh". [117] **(Footnote).**

The name "Yaweh" means "anonymous", as the IS-BE who "worked with" Moses could not use an actual name or anything that would identify himself, or blow the cover of the amnesia / prison operation. The last thing the covert amnesia / hypnosis / prison system wants to do is to reveal themselves openly to the IS-BEs on Earth. They feel that this would restore the inmates memories!

This is the reason that all traces of physical encounters between operatives of space civilizations and humans is very carefully hidden, disguised, covered-up, denied or misdirected.

This "Old Empire" operative contacted Moses on a desert mountain top and delivered the "Ten Hypnotic Commands" to him. These commands are very forcefully worded, and compel an IS-BE into utter subservience to the will of the operator. These hypnotic commands are still in

effect and influence the thought patterns of millions of
IS-BEs thousands of years later!

Incidentally, we later discovered that the so-called
"Yaweh" also wrote, programmed and encoded the text of
the Torah, which when it is read literally, or in its
decoded, [118] (Footnote) form, will provide a great deal more
false information to those who read it.

Ultimately, the Vedic Hymns became the source of nearly
all of Eastern the religions and were the philosophical
source of the ideas common to Buddha [119] (Footnote), Laozi
[120] (Footnote), Zoroaster [121] (Footnote), and other philosophers.
The civilizing influences of these philosophies
eventually replaced the brutal idolatry of the "Old
Empire" religions and were the true genesis of kindness
and compassion.

You asked me earlier why The Domain, and other space
civilizations do not land on Earth or make their
presence known.  Land on Earth?  Do you think we are
crazy or want to be crazy?  It takes a very brave IS-BE
to come down through the atmosphere and land on Earth,
because this is a prison planet, with a very
uncontrolled, psychotic population.  And, no IS-BE is
entirely proof against the risk of entrapment, as with
the  members of The Domain Expeditionary Force who were
captured in the Himalayas 8,200 years ago.

No one knows what IS-BEs on Earth are going to do.  We
are not scheduled to invest the resources of The Domain
to take total control of all the space surrounding the
area at this time.  This will occur in the not-too-
distant future -- about 5,000 Earth years -- according
to the time schedule of The Domain.  At this time we do
not prevent transports from other planetary systems or
galaxies from continuing to drop IS-BEs into the amnesia
force screen area. Eventually, this will change.

In addition, Earth, inherently, is a highly unstable
planet. It is not suitable for settlement or permanent
habitation for any sustainable civilization.  This is
part of the reason why it is being used as a prison
planet.  No one else would seriously consider living
here for a variety of simple and compelling reasons:

74

1) The continental land masses of Earth are floating on a sea of molten lava beneath the surface which causes the land masses to crack, crumble and drift continually. [122] (Footnote)

2) Because of the liquid nature of the core, the planet is largely volcanic and subject to earthquakes and volcanic explosions.

3) The magnetic poles of the planet shift radically about once every 20,000 years. [123] (Footnote) This causes a greater or lesser degree of devastation as a result of tidal waves, and climatic changes.

4) Earth is very distant from the center of the galaxy and from any other significant galactic civilization. This isolation makes it unsuitable for use, except as a "pit stop" or jumping off point along the way between galaxies. The moon and asteroids are far more suitable for this purpose because they do not have any significant gravity.

5) Earth is a heavy gravity planet, with heavy metallic soil and a dense atmosphere. This makes it treacherous for navigational purposes. That fact that I am in this room, as the result of an in flight accident, in spite of the technology of my craft and my extensive expertise as a pilot, are proof of these facts.

6) There are approximately sixty billion Earth-like (Sun Type 12, Class 7) planets in the Milky Way galaxy alone, not to mention the vast expanses of The Domain, and the territories we will claim in the future. It is difficult to stretch our resources to do much more than a periodic reconnaissance of Earth. Especially when there are no immediate advantages to invest resources here.

7) On Earth most beings are not aware that they are IS-BEs, or that there are spirits of any kind. Many other beings are aware of this, but nearly everyone has a very limited understanding of themselves as an IS-BE.

One of the reasons for this is that IS-BEs have been waging war against each other since the beginning of time. The purpose of these wars have always been to establish domination by one IS-BE or group of IS-BEs over another.  Since an IS-BE cannot be "killed", the objective has been to capture and immobilize IS-BEs. This has been done in an nearly unlimited variety of ways.  The most basic method to capture and immobilize an IS-BE is through the use of various kinds of "traps".

IS-BE traps have been made and put in place by many invading societies, such as the one that established the "Old Empire", beginning about sixty-four trillion years ago.  Traps are often set up in the "territory" of the IS-BEs being attacked.  Usually a trap is set with the electronic wave of "beauty" to attract the interest and attention of the IS-BE.  When the IS-BE moves toward the source of the aesthetic wave, such as a beautiful building or beautiful music, the trap is activated by the energy put out by the IS-BE.

One of the most common trap mechanism uses the IS-BE's own thought energy output when the IS-BE tries to attack or fight back against the trap.  The trap is activated and energized by the IS-BE's own thought energy. The harder the IS-BE fights against the trap, the more it pulls the IBS toward it and keeps them "stuck" in the trap.

Throughout the entire history of this physical universe, vast areas of space have been taken over and colonized by IS-BE societies who invade and take over new areas of space in this fashion.  In the past, these invasions have always shared common elements:

1) the overwhelming use of force of arms, usually with nuclear or electronic weapons.

2) mind control of the IS-BEs in the invaded area through the use of electroshock, drugs, hypnosis, erasure of memory and the implantation of false memory or false information intended to subjugate and enslave the local IS-BE population.

3) takeover of natural resources by the invading IS-BEs.

4) political, economic and social slavery of the local population.

These activities continue in present time.  All of the IS-BEs on Earth have been members of one or more of

76

these activities in the past, both as an invader, or as part of the population being invaded. There are no "saints" in this universe. Very few have avoided or been exempted from warfare between IS-BEs.

IS-BEs on Earth are still the victims of this activity at this very moment. The between-lives amnesia administered to IS-BEs is one of the mechanisms of an elaborate system of "Old Empire" IS-BE traps, that prevent an IS-BE from escaping.

This operation is managed by an illicit, renegade secret police [124] **(Footnote)** force of the "Old Empire", using false provocation operations to disguise their activities [125] **(Footnote)** in order to prevent detection by their own government, The Domain and by the victims of their activities. They are mind-control methods developed by government psychiatrists. [126] **(Footnote)**

Earth is a "ghetto" [127] **(Footnote)** planet. It is the result of an intergalactic "Holocaust". [128] **(Footnote)** IS-BEs have been sentenced to Earth either because:

1) They are too viciously insane or perverse to function as part of any civilization, no matter how degraded or corrupt.

2) Or, they are a revolutionary threat to the social, economic and political caste system that has been so carefully built and brutally enforced in the "Old Empire". Biological bodies are specifically designed and designated as the lowest order of entity in the "Old Empire" caste system. When an IS-BE is sent to Earth, and then tricked or coerced into operating in a biological body, they are actually in a prison, inside a prison.

3) In an effort to permanently and irreversibly rid the "Old Empire" of such "untouchables", the eternal identity, memory, and abilities of every IS-BE is forcefully erased. This "final solution" [129] **(Footnote)** was conceived and carried out by the psychopathic criminals who are controlled by the "Old Empire".

The mass extermination of "untouchables" and prison camps created by Germany during World War II were recently revealed. Likewise, the IS-BEs of Earth are the

77

victims of spiritual eradication and eternal slavery inside frail, biological bodies, inspired by the same kind of craven hatred in the "Old Empire".

The kind and creative inmates of Earth are continuously tortured by butchers and lunatics who are controlled by the "Old Empire" prison operators. The so-called "civilizations" of Earth, from the age of useless pyramids to the age of nuclear holocaust, have been a colossal waste of natural resources, a perverted use of intelligence, and an overt oppression of the spiritual essence of every single IS-BE on the planet.

If The Domain sent ships to every corner of the universe in search of "Hell", their quest could end on Earth. What greater brutality can be inflicted on anyone than to erase the spiritual awareness, identity, ability, and memory that is the essence of oneself?

The Domain has, as yet, been unable to rescue the 3,000 IS-BEs of the Expeditionary Force Battalion either. They are forced to inhabit biological bodies on Earth. We have been able to recognize and track most of them for the past 8,000 years. However, our attempts to communicate with them are usually futile, as they are unable to remember their true identity.

The majority of lost members of The Domain force have followed the general progression of Western civilization from India, into the Middle East, then to Chaldea, and Babylon, into Egypt, through Achaia, Greece, Rome, into Europe, to the Western Hemisphere, and then all around the world.

The members of the lost Battalion and many other IS-BEs on Earth, could be valuable citizens of The Domain, not including those who are vicious criminals or perverts. Unfortunately, there has been no workable method conceived to emancipate the IS-BEs from Earth.

Therefore, as a matter of common logic, as well as the official policy of The Domain, it is safer and more sensible to avoid contact with the IS-BE population of Earth until such time as the proper resources can be allocated to locate and destroy the "Old Empire" force screen and amnesia machinery and develop a therapy to restore the memory of an IS-BE."

# Chapter Nine

# A Time Line of Events

(MATILDA O'DONNELL MACELROY PERSONAL NOTE)

"For this interview I took written notes because Airl gave me a lot of dates and names that I couldn't possibly remember without writing them down. I didn't usually take notes, but during this lesson I thought it was important to get the information exactly as she gave it to me. However, I discovered that my note taking made it much more difficult for me to focus on receiving the communication from Airl. I was sometimes so distracted by my own writing that I lost the train of her thought, so I had to ask her to "repeat" herself several times.

Airl continued to stay in communication with the Communications Officer on the asteroid belt space station, from which she received much of this information. Since Airl was an officer / pilot / engineer of The Domain, and not a historian, she had to get this information from records of reconnaissance missions conducted by other officers of The Domain Expeditionary Force."

(OFFICIAL TRANSCRIPT OF INTERVIEW)

TOP SECRET

Official Transcript of the U.S. Army Air Force
Roswell Army Air Field, 509th Bomb Group
SUBJECT: ALIEN INTERVIEW, 27. 7. 1947, 1st Session

"The actual history of Earth is very bizarre. It is so nonsensical that is it is incredible to anyone on Earth who attempts to investigate it. A myriad of vital information is missing from it. A huge conglomeration of non sequitur relics and mythology has been arbitrarily introduced into it. The volatile nature of the Earth itself cyclically covers, drowns, mixes and shreds physical evidence.

These factors, combined with amnesia and post-hypnotic suggestions, false facades and covert manipulation make a reconstruction of the factual origins and history of Earth civilizations virtually indecipherable. Any investigator, no matter how brilliant, is doomed to wallow in a quagmire of inconclusive assumptions, unworkable hypotheses, and perpetual mystery.

Since The Domain does not suffer these afflictions, having the advantage of memory, longevity and an exterior point of view, I will add some clarification to your fragmentary knowledge of the history of Earth.

These are some of the dates and events that are not mentioned in Earth history textbooks. These dates are significant because they provide some information concerning the influences of the "Old Empire" and of The Domain on Earth.

Although I have attended several briefings by our mission control personnel on the general background of Earth within the past few hundred years, I will rely principally on data gathered from records captured after our invasion of the "Old Empire" planetary headquarters. Since that time The Domain Expeditionary Force has tracked the general progress of events on Earth.

As I mentioned, in some cases The Domain has chosen to intervene in certain affairs on Earth in order to ensure the success of our long term expansion plans. Although The Domain has no interest in Earth, per se, or in the population of IS-BEs on this planet, it does serve our interests to ensure that the resources of Earth are not destroyed or spoiled. To that end, certain officers of The Domain have been sent to Earth on reconnaissance missions from time to time to gather information.

However, the following dates and events have been extrapolated from the accumulated information in the data files of The Domain -- at least those that are accessible to me through the space station communications center.

208,000 BCE --

The establishment of the "Old Empire", whose headquarters were located near one of the "tail stars" in the Ursa Major (Big Dipper) Constellation [130] **(Footnote)** of this galaxy. The "Old Empire" invasion force conquered the area with nuclear weapons sometime earlier. After the radioactivity [131] **(Footnote)** subsided and the clean-up and restoration were completed, it received the immigration of beings from another galaxy into this galaxy. Those beings set up a society that kept going until about 10,000 years ago when it was superseded by The Domain.

Very recently Earth civilization has come to resemble aspects of that civilization, now that it has fallen out of its immediate control. In particular, the appearance and technology of transportation such as planes, trains, ships, fire engines, and automobiles, as well as what you consider to be "modern" or "futuristic" architecture, which emulate the design of buildings in the major cities of the "Old Empire".

Before 75,000 BCE --

The Domain records contain very little information about the civilizations on the continental land masses of Atlanta [132] **(Footnote)** and Lemur [133] **(Footnote),** except to note that they did coexist on Earth at more or less the same time. Apparently, both civilizations were founded by remnants of electronic, space opera cultures who fled from their native planetary systems to escape political or religious persecution.

The Domain knows that a long-standing edict of the "Old Empire" prohibits unauthorized colonization of planets. Therefore, it is possible that their destruction was caused by police or military forces who pursued the colonists as criminals and destroyed them. Although this seems a likely supposition, no conclusive evidence exists that explains the complete destruction and disappearance of two entire electronic civilizations.

Another possibility is that a massive submarine volcanic eruption in the region of Lake Toba, in Sumatra [134] **(Footnote)** and Mt. Krakatoa [135] **(Footnote)** in Java caused the destruction of Lemur. The flood waters caused by the eruption overwhelmed all the land masses, including the highest mountains. Survivors of the destruction of the civilization, the Lemurians, are the earliest ancestors of the Chinese. Australia and the ocean areas to the north were the center of the Lemurian civilization and are the source of Oriental races. Both civilizations possessed electronics, flight and similar technologies of space opera cultures.

Apparently, the volcanic eruption expelled such a significant mass of molten rock that the resulting vacuum beneath the crust of Earth caused great areas of the land masses to sink below the oceans. The continental areas occupied by both civilizations were covered with volcanic matter, and then submerged, leaving very little evidence that they ever existed except for legends of a global flood which prevail in every culture of the Earth, and for survivors who are the genus of oriental races and cultures.

That kind of colossal volcanic explosion [136] **(Footnote)** fills the stratosphere with toxic gases which are carried around the whole planet. The usual refuse of these volcanic eruptions can easily cause a rain that lasts for "40 days and 40 nights" due to atmospheric pollution as well as an extensive period during which radiation from the sun is deflected back into space, and cause global cooling. [137] **(Footnote)** Certainly such an event would cause an ice age, extinctions of life forms and many other relatively long-term changes lasting thousands of years.

Due to the myriad types of naturally occurring global cataclysmic events which are indigenous to Earth, it is not a suitable planet for habitation by IS-BEs. In addition there have been occasional global cataclysms caused by IS-BEs such as the one that destroyed the dinosaurs [138] **(Footnote)** more than 70 million years ago. That destruction was caused by intergalactic warfare during which time Earth, and many other neighboring moons and planets, were bombarded by atomic weapons. Atomic explosions cause atmospheric fallout much like that of volcanic eruptions. [139] **(Footnote)** Most of the planets in this sector of the galaxy have been uninhabitable deserts since then.

Earth is undesirable for many other reasons: heavy gravity and dense atmosphere, floods, earthquakes, volcanoes, polar shifts, continental drift, meteor impacts, atmospheric and climatic changes, to name a few. What kind of lasting civilization could any sophisticated culture propose to develop in such an environment?

In addition, Earth is a small planet of a "rim star" of a galaxy. This makes Earth very isolated geographically from the more concentrated planetary civilizations which exist toward the center of the galaxy. These obvious

facts have made Earth suitable for use only as a
zoological or botanical garden, or for its current use
as a prison -- but not much else.

Before 30,000 BCE --

Earth started being used as a dumping ground and prison
for IS-BEs who were judged "untouchable", meaning
criminal or non-conformists.  IS-BEs were captured,
encapsulated in electronic traps and transported to
Earth from various parts of the "Old Empire".
Underground "amnesia stations" were set up on Mars and
on Earth in the Rwenzori Mountains [140] **(Footnote)** in Africa, in
the Pyrenees Mountains [141] **(Footnote)** of Portugal, and in
steppes of Mongolia. [142] **(Footnote)**

These electronic monitoring points create force screens
designed to detect and capture IS-BEs, when the IS-BE
departs the body at death.  IS-BEs are brainwashed using
extreme electronic force in order to maintain Earth's
population in state of perpetual amnesia.  Further
population controls are installed through the use of
long range electronic thought control mechanisms.
These stations are still in operation and they are
extremely difficult to attack or destroy, even for The
Domain, which will not maintain a significant military
force in this area until a later date.

The pyramid civilizations were intentionally created as
part of the IS-BE prison system on Earth.  The pyramid
is alleged to be the symbol for "wisdom".  However, the
"wisdom" of the "Old Empire" on planet Earth is intended
to operate as part of the elaborate amnesia "trap"
consisting of MASS, MEANING and MYSTERY.  These are
opposite to the qualities of an Immortal Spiritual Being
which have no mass, or meaning.  An IS-BE "is" solely
because it thinks that it "is".

MASS represents the physical universe, including objects
such as stars, planets, gases, liquids, energy particles
and tea cups.  The Pyramids were very, very solid
objects, as were all of the structures created by the
"Old Empire".  Heavy, massive, dense, solid objects
create the illusion of eternity.  Dead bodies wrapped in
linen, soaked in resin, placed inside engraved golden
coffins and entombed with Earthly possessions amid
cryptic symbols create an illusion of eternal life.

However, dense, heavy physical universe symbols are the
exact opposite of an IS-BE. An IS-BE has no mass or
time. Objects do not endure forever. An IS-BE "is"
forever.

MEANING: False meanings prevent knowledge of the truth.
The pyramid cultures of Earth are a fabricated illusion.
They are nothing more than "false civilizations"
contrived by the "Old Empire" mystery cult called the
Brothers of the Serpent. False meanings were invented
to create the illusion of a false society to further
reinforce the amnesia mechanism among the intimates in
the Earth prison system.

MYSTERY is built of lies and half-truths. Lies cause
persistence because they alter facts which are comprised
of exact dates, places and events. When truth is known,
a lie no longer persists. If the exact truth is
revealed, it is no longer a mystery.

All of the pyramid civilizations of Earth were carefully
contrived of layer upon layer of lies, skillfully
combined with a few truths. The priest cult of the "Old
Empire" combined sophisticated mathematics and space
opera technology, with theatrical metaphors and
symbolism. All of these are complete fabrications of
truth, baited with the allure of aesthetics and mystery.

The intricate rituals, astronomical alignments, secret
rites, massive monuments, marvelous architecture,
artistically rendered hieroglyphs and man-animal "gods"
were designed to create a unsolvable mystery for the IS-
BE prison population on Earth. The mystery diverts
attention away from the truth that IS-BEs have been
captured, given amnesia and imprisoned on a planet far,
far away from their home.

The truth is that every single IS-BE on Earth came to
Earth from some other planetary system. Not one person
on Earth is a "native" inhabitant. Human beings did not
"evolve" on Earth.

In the past, Egyptian society was run by the prison
administrators or priests, who, in turn, manipulated a
Pharaoh, controlled the treasury and kept the inmate
population enslaved physically and spiritually. In
modern times, the priests have changed, but the function

is the same.  However, now the priests are prisoners
too.

Mystery reinforces the walls of the prison.  The "Old
Empire" feared that the IS-BEs on Earth might regain
their memory.  Therefore, one of the primary functions
of The "Old Empire" priesthood is to prevent IS-BEs on
Earth from remembering who they really are, how they
came to Earth, where they came from.

The "Old Empire" operators of the prison system, and
their superiors, do not want IS-BEs to remember who
murdered them, captured them, stole all of their
possessions, sent them to Earth, gave them amnesia and
condemned them to eternal imprisonment!

Imagine what might happen if all of the inmates in the
prison suddenly remembered that they have the right to
be free!  What if they suddenly realized that they have
been falsely imprisoned and rise up as one against the
guards?

They are afraid to reveal anything that looks like the
civilization of the inmates home planets.  A body, a
piece of clothing, a symbol, a space ship, an advanced
electronics device, or any other remnant of civilization
from a home planet could "remind" a being and rekindle
his memory.

Sophisticated technologies of entrapment and
enslavement,  which were developed over millions of
years in the "Old Empire", have been applied to the IS-
BEs on Earth with the intention to create a false facade
for the prison.  These facades were installed on Earth
in totality, all at once.  Every piece is a fully
integrated part of the prison system.

This includes a religion of mumbo-jumbo double-speak.
Every pyramid civilization uses this as part of a
control mechanism  to keep the population enslaved by
force, by fear and by ignorance. The indecipherable
muddle of irrelevant information, geometric designs,
mathematical calculation, astronomical alignments, are
part of a false spirituality based on solid objects,
rather than immortal spirits, in order to confuse and
disorient the IS-BEs on Earth.

When the body of a person died they were buried with
their Earthly possessions, including their former body
wrapped in linen, to sustain their "soul" or "Ka" after
death.  An IS-BE does not "have" as soul.  An IS-BE is a
soul.

On the home planet of an IS-BE their material
possessions were not lost, stolen or forgotten when the
being died or left the body.  An IS-BE could return and
claim the possessions.  However, if the IS-BE has
amnesia, they will not remember that they had any
possession.  So, governments, insurance companies,
bankers, family members and other vultures can pick
their possessions clean without fear of retribution from
the deceased. [143] **(Footnote)**

The only reason for these false meanings is to instill
the idea that an IS-BE is NOT a spirit, but a physical
object!  This is a lie.  It is a trap for an IS-BE.

Countless people have spent endless hours attempting to
solve the jig-saw puzzle of Egypt and other "Old Empire"
civilizations. They are puzzles made of pieces that do
not fit.  A question states its own answer.  What is the
mystery of Egypt and other pyramid cultures?  Mystery!

circa 15,000 BCE --

The "Old Empire" forces supervised the construction of a
hydraulic mining operation in the Andes Mountains in
present day Bolivia near Lake Titicaca (Lake of Tin
Stones) at Tiahuanaco [144] **(Footnote)** including construction of
the massive stone complex of carved stone buildings
known as Kalasasaya and its "Gate of the Sun" at an
elevation of nearly 14,000 feet.

11,600 BCE --

The Polar Axis of Earth shifted [145] **(Footnote)** to a sea area.
The last Ice Age came to an end abruptly as the polar
ice caps melted and the level of the ocean rose to
submerge large sections of the land masses of Earth.
The last remaining vestiges of Atlantis and Lemuria were
covered by water. Massive extinctions of animals
occurred in the Americas, Australia and the Artic
Regions due to the shift of the poles.

10,450 BCE --

Plans were made by the "Old Empire" IS-BE called Thoth
for construction of a Great Pyramid of Giza. The 4 "air
shafts" of the pyramid point precisely to key stars in
the "Old Empire" as seen from Giza in this year. The
alignment of the Pyramids of Giza on the ground matches
perfectly the alignment of the constellation of Orion as
seen in the sky from Giza relative to the Nile as the
earthly representation of the Milky Way in the sky. [146]
**(Footnote)**

10,400 BCE --

According to the Earth historian, Herodotus, records
from the ruined civilization of Atlantis, containing
electronic technology and other technology of that
society, were buried in a vault beneath the paws of The
Sphinx. The Greek historian wrote that he was told this
by some of his friends who were Priests of Anu, the
Sumerian god, at the Egyptian city of Heliopolis.
However, it is highly unlikely that any traces of an
electronic civilization would be allowed to be left
intact on Earth by the "Old Empire" prison system
administrators. [147] **(Footnote).**

8,212 BCE --

The Veda or Vedic hymns are a set of religious hymns
that were introduced into the societies of Earth. They
came forward in spoken tradition, memorized, from
generation to generation. "The Hymn to the Dawn Child''
includes an idea called the "cycle of the physical
universe": the creation, growth, conservation, decay and
death or destruction of energy and matter in a space.
These cycles produce time. The same set of hymns
describes the "theory of evolution". Here is a
tremendous body of knowledge which contains a great deal
of spiritual truth. Unfortunately, it has been
incorrectly evaluated by humans and altered with lies
and reversals of fact by priests which are a booby trap
to prevent anyone from using the wisdom to discover a
way to escape from the prison planet.

8,050 BCE --

Destruction of the "Old Empire" home planet government
in this galaxy. This was the end of the "Old Empire" as

a political entity in the galaxy. However, the vast size of the "Old Empire" will take many thousands of years for The Domain to conquer completely. The inertia of the political, economic and cultural systems of the "Old Empire" will remain in place for some time to come.

However, remnants of the "Old Empire" space fleet in the solar system of Earth were finally destroyed in 1,230 AD. In addition to operatives of the "Old Empire" who run the Earth prison operation, there were other beings from the "Old Empire" who came to Earth. Since Earth was no longer under the control of the "Old Empire" after their defeat by The Domain Forces, there was no police force to control military renegades, space pirates, miners, merchants and entrepreneurs who came to Earth to exploit the resources of the planet for personal gain, and many other nefarious reasons.

For example, the history of Earth, according to the Jewish people, describes the "Nephilim". [148 (Footnote)] Chapter 6 of The Book of Genesis, describes the origin of the "Nephilim" :

> "Now it came about, when men began to multiply on the face of the land, and daughters were born to them, that the "sons of God" saw that the daughters of men were beautiful; and they took wives for themselves, whomever they chose.

> The Nephilim were on the earth in those days, and also afterward, when the sons of God came in to the daughters of men, and they bore children to them. Those were the mighty men who were of old, men of renown."

The ancient Jewish people who wrote the history book called the Old Testament were slaves, herders and gatherers. Any modern technology, even a simple flashlight, would seem astounding and miraculous to them. They attributed any unexplainable phenomenon or technology to the workings of a "god". Unfortunately, this behavior is universal among all IS-BEs who have been given amnesia, and cannot remember their own experiences, training, technology, personality or identity.

Obviously, if these were men, and they mated with Earth
women, they were not "sons of god". They were IS-BEs
who inhabited biological bodies in order to take
advantage of the political situation in the "Old
Empire", or simply to indulge in physical sensation.
They set up small colonies of their own on Earth beyond
the reach of the police and tax authorities.

Coincidentally, one of the most serious crimes an IS-BE
could commit in the "Old Empire" was to violate income
tax regulations. Income taxes were used as a slavery
mechanism and as a punishment in the "Old Empire". The
slightest error in a tax report made an IS-BE
"untouchable", followed by imprisonment on Earth.

6,750 BCE --

Other Pyramid civilizations were set up by the "Old
Empire" on Earth. These were established in Babylon,
Egypt, China and Mesoamerica. The Mesopotamian area
provided service facilities, communication stations,
space ports, and stone quarry operations for these false
civilizations.

Ptah was the name given to the first in a succession of
administrators from the "Old Empire" who represented
themselves to the Earth population as "divine" rulers.

Ptah's importance may be understood when one learns that
the word "Egypt" is a Greek corruption of the phrase
"Het-Ka-Ptah," or "House of the Spirit of Ptah". Ptah,
was nick-named "The Developer". He was a construction
engineer. His high priest was given the title 'Great
Leader of Craftsmen'.

Ptah was also the god of reincarnation in Egypt. He
originated the "opening of the mouth ceremony" which was
performed by priests at funerals to "release souls" from
their corpses. Of course, when the "souls" were
released, they were captured, given amnesia, and
returned to Earth again.

The so-called "Devine" rulers who followed Ptah on Earth
were called "Ntr", meaning "Guardians or Watchers" by
the Egyptians. Their symbol was the Serpent, or Dragon
which represented a secret priesthood of the "Old
Empire" called the "Brothers of the Serpent".

"Old Empire" engineers used cutting tools of highly
concentrated light waves to quickly carve and excavate
stone blocks. [149] **(Footnote)** They also used force fields and
space craft to lift and transport blocks of stone
weighing hundred or thousands of tons each. The
placement on the ground of some of these structures will
be found to have geodetic or astronomical significance
relative to various stars in this galactic region.

The buildings are crude and impractical, compared to
building standards on most planets. As an engineer of
The Domain, I can attest that make-shift structures like
these would never pass inspection on a planet in The
Domain. Stone blocks such as those used in the pyramid
civilizations can still be seen, partially excavated, in
the stone quarries in the Middle East [150] **(Footnote)** and
elsewhere.

Most of the structures were hastily built "props", much
like the false facades of a western town on the set of a
motion picture. They appear to be real, and to have
some use or value, however, they have no value. They
have no useful purpose. The pyramids and all of the
other stone monuments erected by the "Old Empire" could
be called "mystery monuments". For what reason would
anyone waste so many resources to construct so many
useless buildings? To create a mysterious illusion.

The fact of the matter is that each one of the "divine
rulers" were IS-BEs who served as operatives of the "Old
Empire". They were certainly not "divine", although
they were IS-BEs.

6248 BCE --

The beginning of active warfare between The Domain Space
Command and the surviving remnants of the "Old Empire"
space fleet in this solar system that lasted nearly
7,500 years. It began when an installation was
established in the Himalaya mountains by a battalion of
the 3,000 officers and crew members of The Domain
Expeditionary Force. The installation was not fortified
as The Domain was not aware that the "Old Empire"
maintained Earth as a prison planet.

The Domain installation was attacked and destroyed by space forces of the "Old Empire" who continued to operate in the solar system of Earth. IS-BEs of The Domain battalion were captured, taken to Mars, given amnesia, and sent back to Earth to inhabit human biological bodies. They are still on Earth.

5,965 BCE --

Investigations into the disappearance of Domain forces in this solar system led to the discovery of "Old Empire" bases on Mars and elsewhere. The Domain took over the planet Venus [151] **(Footnote)** as a defensive position against the space forces of the "Old Empire". The Domain Expeditionary Force also monitors life forms on Venus which has a very dense, hot and heavy atmosphere of sulfuric acid clouds. There are a few life forms on Earth that can endure an atmospheric environment like Venus. [152] **(Footnote)**

The Domain also established secret installations or space stations in the Earth solar system. This solar system has a planet that is broken up -- the asteroid belt. [153] **(Footnote)** It provides a very useful low-gravity platform for take off and landing of space craft. It is used as a "galactic jump" between the Milky Way and adjoining galaxies. There aren't any planets at this end of the galaxy that can serve as a good galactic entering spot for incoming transport, and other ships. But this broken up planet makes a very ideal space station. As a result of our war against the "Old Empire", this area of the solar system is now a valuable possession of The Domain.

3,450 - 3,100 BCE --

The intervention into the affairs on Earth by the "Old Empire" operatives or "divine gods" was disrupted at this time by The Domain Forces. They were forced to replace themselves with human rulers. The First Dynasty of human Pharaohs who united Upper and Lower Egypt began with the rule of a Pharaoh who, coincidentally, was named "MEN". He established the capital city called Men-Nefer, "The Beauty of Men" in Egypt. This started the first succession of 10 human Pharaohs and a period of 350 years of chaos that followed in the administrative ranks of the "Old Empire".

3,200 BCE --

As I mentioned earlier, Earth was under attack between
The Domain and the "Old Empire" forces during this
period. Of course this does not make any sense to
archaeologists or historians on Earth, because the
Egyptian period is a space opera era period. Since
Earth historians have amnesia, they assume that this was
only a religious period.

Further, because the technology and civilizations
installed on Earth during this period were "pre-
packaged", they did not "evolve" on Earth. Of course,
there is no evidence anywhere on Earth of an
evolutionary transition which resulted in sophisticated
mathematics, language, writing, religion, architecture,
cultural traditions in Egypt or any of the pyramid
civilizations. These cultures, complete with all of the
details of racial body types, hair-styles, facial make-
up, rituals, moral codes and so forth, just "appeared"
as complete integrated packages.

The physical evidence suggests that all evidence of the
intervention of The Domain or "Old Empire" Forces, or
any other extraterrestrial activity, has been carefully
"cleaned up", so as not to create suspicion. The "Old
Empire" force does not want the IS-BEs of Earth to
suspect that they have been captured, transplanted to
Earth and brainwashed.

So, Earth historians continue to assume that Egyptian
priests were not supposed to have "ray guns" or other
technology of the "Old Empire". And, they suppose that
there was nothing going on, on Earth, except some
priests walking around saying 'Amen', which the
Christians still say.

3,172 BCE --

Layout of the astronomical grid that joins the key
mining sites and astronomical buildings of 'the gods' in
the Andes Mountains such as Tiahuanaco, [154] **(Footnote)** Cuzco,
Quito, the cities of Ollantaytambu, [155] **(Footnote)** Machupiccu [156]
**(Footnote)** and Pachacamac [157] **(Footnote)** for the mining of rare
metals, including tin for use in making bronze. Metals
were the property of "the gods", of course.

A great variety of entrepreneurial mining was done on
Earth at that time due to the war between the "Old
Empire" force and The Domain.  These miners did carve a
few sculptures of themselves.  They are seen wearing
mining helmets.  The Ponce Stela sculpture in the sunken
courtyard of the Kalasasaya temple is a crude rendering
of a stone worker using an electronic, light-wave
emitting stone cutter and carving tools, held in a
holster. [158] (Footnote)

The "Old Empire" has also maintained mining operations
on planets throughout the galaxy for a very long time.
The mineral resources of Earth are now a property of The
Domain.

2,450 BCE --

The "great" pyramid [159] (Footnote) and complex of pyramids
near Cairo were completed.  An inscription created by
the "Old Empire" administrators can be seen in the so-
called Pyramid texts. [160] (Footnote) The texts say that the
pyramid was built under the direction of Thoth, Son of
Ptah.  Of course there was never a King buried in the
chamber, since the pyramids were never intended to be
used as a burial chamber.

The great pyramid was located precisely at the exact
center of all of the land masses of Earth, [161] (Footnote) as
viewed from space. Obviously such precise measurements
require aerial perspective and a view of the land masses
of Earth from space.  Purely mathematical calculations
of the geodetic center of the continents of Earth could
not be made otherwise.

Shafts were constructed inside the pyramid to align with
the configuration of stars in the constellation of
Orion, Canus Majora, and specifically Sirius.  The
shafts are also aligned to the Big Dipper, where the
home planet of the "Old Empire" existed.  Also, Ainitak,
Alpha Draconis and Beta Ursa Minor. [162] (Footnote) These stars
are each one of the key systems in the "Old Empire" from
which IS-BEs were brought to Earth and dumped, as
unwanted merchandise.

The configuration of all the pyramids of the Giza
Plateau was intended to create a "mirror image", on

Earth of the solar system and certain constellations within the "Old Empire".

2,181 BCE --

MIN, became the God of Fertility of Egypt. The IS-BE, also known as Pan, was also a Greek god. Min or Pan, was an IS-BE who somehow managed to escape from the "Old Empire" amnesia system. [163] **(Footnote)**

2,160 - 2040 BCE --

One of the results of the intensifying battle between The Domain Forces and the "Old Empire" forces was that the control of the "divine rulers", was broken at this time. They finally left Egypt and returned to the "heavens", so to speak, in defeat. Human beings took over the ruling role as Pharaohs. The first human pharaoh moved the Capital city of Egypt from Memphis to Heracleopolis. [164] **(Footnote)**

1,500 BCE --

This is the date for the destruction of Atlantis given by the Egyptian high-priests, Psenophis of Heliopolis, and Sonchis of Sais, to the Greek sage Solon. [165] **(Footnote)** The Priests of Anu recorded that the Mediterranean area was invaded by "Atlantean" people about this time. Of course, these people were not from the ancient continent of Atlanta, in the Atlantic Ocean, which existed more than 70,000 years earlier.

These were refugees from the Minoan civilization on Crete escaping from the volcanic eruption and tidal waves of Mt. Thera that destroyed their civilization.

Plato's references to Atlantis were borrowed from the writings of the Greek philosopher Solon, who was given the information by the Egyptian priest who called Atlantis "Kepchu", which also happens to be the Egyptian name for the people of Crete. Some of the survivors of the Minoan volcanic disaster asked Egypt for help, since they were the only other civilization with high culture in the Mediterranean area at the time. [166] **(Footnote)**

1351 BCE - 1337 BCE --

The Domain Expeditionary Force actively waged a war of
religious conquest against the Egyptian mystery cult
called the Priest of Amun, also known as the "Old
Empire" Brothers of The Serpent.  During this time the
Pharaoh Akhenaten abolished the priesthood of Amun, and
moved the capital of Egypt from Thebes to the new
location at Amarna, at the exact geodetic center of
Egypt [167] **(Footnote).** However, this plot to overthrow the "Old
Empire" religious control was quickly spoiled.

1,193 BCE --

In the Near East and Achaea, the Greeks and Trojans
fought for supremacy, which ended in the destruction of
Troy as the finale of the Trojan War. [168] **(Footnote)** During
this same time, war was being fought out in the space of
the solar system between two forces for control of the
"space stations" surrounding Earth.  That period of 300
years was a very violent resistance to The Domain Forces
by the remnants of the "Old Empire" forces.  It did not
last long however, as it is futile to resist The Domain.

850 BCE --

Homer, the blind Greek poet, [169] **(Footnote)** wrote the stories
'the gods' as borrowed and modified from earlier sources
in Vedic texts, Sumerian texts, Babylonian and Egyptian
mythology.  His poems, as well as many other "myths" of
the ancient world are very accurate descriptions of the
exploits of IS-BE's on Earth who were able to avoid the
"Old Empire amnesia operation and operate without
biological bodies.

700 BCE --

The Vedic Hymns were first translated in the Greek
language.  This was the beginning of a cultural
revolution in Western civilization that transformed
crude and brutal tribal cultures into democratic
republics based on more reasonable conduct.

638 - 559 BCE --

Solon, a wise man from Greece, reported the existence of
Atlantis.  This was information he received from the
"Old Empire" high-priests, Psenophis of Heliopolis and
Sonchis of Sais, with whom he studied in Egypt. [170] **(Footnote)**

630 BCE --

Zoroaster [171] **(Footnote)** created religious practices in Persia around an IS-BE called Ahura Mazda. [172] **(Footnote)** This was yet another of the growing number of "monotheistic" gods put in place by operatives of The Domain to displace a panoply of "Old Empire" gods.

604 BCE --

Laozi, a philosopher who wrote a small book called "The Way", [173] **(Footnote)** was an IS-BE of great wisdom, who overcame the effects of the "Old Empire" amnesia / hypnosis machinery and escaped from Earth. His understanding of the nature of an IS-BE must have been very good to accomplish this.

According to the common legend, his last lifetime as a human was lived in a small village in China. He contemplated the essence of his own life. Like Guatama Siddhartha, he confronted his own thoughts, and past lives. In so doing, he recovered some of his own memory, ability and immortality.

As an old man, he decided to leave the village and go to the forest to depart the body. The village gatekeeper stopped him and begged him to write down his personal philosophy before leaving. Here is a small piece of advice he gave about "the way" he rediscovered his own spirit:

"He who looks will not see it;
He who listens will not hear it;
He who gropes will not grasp it.
The formless nonentity, the motionless source of motion.
The infinite essence of the spirit is the source of life.
Spirit is self.

Walls form and support a room,
yet the space between them is most important.
A pot is formed of clay,
yet the space formed therein is most useful.
Action is caused by the force of nothing on something,
just as the nothing of spirit is the source of all form.

One suffers great afflictions because one has a body.
Without a body what afflictions could one suffer?
When one cares more for the body than for his own spirit,
One becomes the body and looses the way of the spirit.

The self, the spirit, creates illusion.
The delusion of Man is that reality is not an illusion.
One who creates illusions and makes them more real than
reality, follows the path of the spirit and finds the
way of heaven".

593 BCE --

The Genesis story written by the Jewish people describe
"angels" or "sons of god" mating with women of Earth,
who bore them children.  These were probably renegades
from the "Old Empire".  They may also have been space
pirates or merchants from a system outside the galaxy
who came to steal mineral resources, or smuggle drugs.

The Domain has observed that there are many visitors to
Earth from neighboring planets and galaxies, but they
rarely stop and live here. What kind of beings would
live on a prison planet if they were not forced to do
so?

The same book also reports the story of a human named
Ezekiel who witnessed a spacecraft or aircraft landing
near Chebar River in Chaldea.  His description of the
craft uses very archaic language, technically, but is
nevertheless, quite an accurate description of an "Old
Empire" saucer or scout craft. It is similar to the
sighting of "vimanas" by the people in the foothills of
the Himalayas.

Their Genesis story also mentions that "Yahweh" designed
biological bodies to live for 120 years on Earth.
Biological bodies on most "Sun Type 12, Class 7" planets
are usually engineered to last for an average of about
150 years.  Human bodies on Earth last only about one
half as long.  We suspect this is because the prison
administrators have altered the biological material of
human bodies on Earth to die more frequently so that the
IS-BEs who inhabit them will recycle through the amnesia
mechanism more frequently. [174] **(Footnote)**

It should be noted that much of the "Old Testament" was written during the captivity of the Jews who were enslaved in Babylon, which was very heavily controlled by priests of the "Old Empire". The book introduces a false sense of time and a false concept of the origin of the creation.

The serpent is the symbol of the "Old Empire". It appears in the beginning of their creation story, or as the Greeks say, "Genesis", and causes the spiritual destruction of the first human beings, who are metaphorically represented by Adam and Eve.

The Old Testament, clearly influenced by the "Old Empire" Forces, gives a detailed description of the IS-BEs being induced into biological bodies on Earth. This book also describes many of the "Old Empire" brainwashing activities, including the installation of false memories, lies, superstitions, commands to "forget" and all manner of tricks and traps designed to keep IS-BEs on Earth. Most importantly, it destroys the awareness that humans are Immortal Spiritual Beings.

580 BCE --

The Oracle at Delphi was one temple in a network of many oracle temples. Each temple was a communication center. The "Old Empire" priests designated a local "god" for each temple. Each of the temples in this network were located at precisely 5 degrees of latitude intervals from the capital city of Thebes throughout the Mediterranean area as far north as the Baltic Sea.

The shrines served, among other things, as a grid, housing electronic beacons, later called "Omphalus Stones". [175] **(Footnote)** The grid arrangement of Oracle sites can only be seen from miles above the Earth. The original network of electronic communications beacons were disabled when the priesthood was dispersed, and were replaced by carved stones.

The symbol of the "Old Empire" priesthood is a Python, dragon or serpent. It was called the "earth-dragon" at Delphi, which is always represented in sculpture and vase-paintings as a serpent.

In Greek mythology the guardian of the Omphalus Stone at
the temple at Delphi was an oracle whose name was
Python, the serpent. [176] (Footnote) She was an IS-BE, who was
conquered by a "god" named Apollo.  He buried her under
the Omphalos stone.  This is a case of one "god" setting
up his temple on the grave of another.  This is a very
accurate euphemism for The Domain Force that detected
and disabled the "Old Empire" temple network on Earth.
It was one of the fatal blows to the "Old Empire" Force
in the solar system of Earth.

559 BCE --

The Commanding Officer of The Domain Battalion who was
lost in 5,965 BCE was detected and located by a search
party sent to Earth from The Domain Expeditionary Force.
He was incarnated as Cyrus II of Persia during this
time. [177] (Footnote)

A unique system of organization was used by Cyrus II [178]
(Footnote) and the members of that Battalion who followed
him from India through his progression of human lives on
Earth.  In part, it enabled them to build the largest
empire in the history of the Earth to that date.

The Domain Search Party who located him traveled around
the Earth searching for the lost Battalion for several
thousand years.  The party consisted of 900 officers of
The Domain, divided into teams of 300 each.  One team
searched the land, another team search the oceans and
the third team searched the space surrounding Earth.
There are many reports made in various human
civilizations concerning their activities, which humans
did not understand, of course.

The Domain Search Party devised a wide variety of
electronic detection devices needed to track the
electronic signature or wavelength of each of the
missing members of the Battalion.  Some were used in
space, others on land, and special devices were invented
to detect IS-BEs under water.

One of these electronic detection devices is referred to
as a "tree of life". [179] (Footnote) The device is literally a
tool designed to detect the presence of life, which is
an IS-BE.  This was a large electronic screen generator
designed to permeate wide areas.  To the ancient humans

on Earth it resembled a sort of tree, since is consists of an interwoven lattice of electronic field generators and receivers. The electronic field detects the presence of IS-BEs, whether the IS-BE is occupying a body, or if they are outside a body.

A portable version of this detection device was carried by each of the members of The Domain Search Party. Stone carvings in Sumeria show winged beings using pinecone-shaped instruments to scan the bodies of human beings. They are also shown carrying the power unit for the scanner which are depicted as stylized baskets or water buckets, being carried by eagle-headed, winged beings. [180] (Footnote)

Members of the aerial unit of The Domain Search Party, led by Ahura Mazda, were often called "winged gods" in human interpretations. Throughout the Persian civilization there are a great many stone relief carvings that depict winged space craft, that they called a "faravahar". [181] (Footnote)

Members of the Aquatic Unit of The Domain Search Party were called "Oannes" by local humans. [182] (Footnote) Stone carvings of the so-called Oannes are shown wearing silver diving suits. They lived in the sea and appeared to the human population to be men dressed to look like fish. Some members of the lost Battalion were found in the oceans inhabiting the bodies of dolphins or whales. [183] (Footnote)

On land, The Domain Search Party members were referred to as "Annunaki" [184] (Footnote) by the Sumerians, and "Nephilim", in the Bible. Of course, their true mission and activities were never disclosed to homo sapiens. Their activities have been purposefully disguised. Therefore, the human stories and legends about the Annunaki, and the other members of The Domain Search Party have not been understood and were badly misinterpreted.

In the absence of complete and accurate data, anyone observing a phenomenon will assume or hypothesize explanations in an attempt to make sense of the data. Therefore, although mythology and history may be based on factual events, they are likewise full of misunderstood and misinterpreted evaluations of the data, and embellished with assumptions, theories and hypotheses which are false.

The space unit of The Domain Expeditionary Force are shown flying in a "Winged-Disc". [185] (Footnote) This is an allusion to the spiritual power of the IS-BEs, as well as to the space craft used by The Domain Search Party.

The Commander of the lost Battalion, as Cyrus II, was an IS-BE who was regarded as a messiah on Earth by both the Jews, and the Muslims. In less than 50 years he established a highly ethical, and humanitarian philosophy which pervaded all of Western Civilization. [186] (Footnote)

His territorial conquests, organization of people and monumental building projects were unprecedented before or since. Such sweeping accomplishments in a short period of time could only have been achieved by a leader and a team of trained officers, pilots, engineers and crew members of a unit of The Domain, acting as a team, who had been trained and worked together for thousands of years.

Although we have discovered the location of many of the IS-BEs in the lost Battalion, The Domain has been unable to restore their memory and return them to active duty as yet.

Of course we cannot transport IS-BEs who are inhabiting biological bodies to the space stations of The Domain since there is no oxygen in our space craft. Also we do not maintain life support facilities for biological entities there. Our only hope has been to locate and rekindle the awareness, memory and identity of the IS-BEs of the Lost Battalion. One day they will be capable of rejoining us.

200 BCE --

The last remnant of the "Old Empire" pyramid civilization is at "Teotihuacán" [187] (Footnote). The Aztec name means "place of the gods" or "where men were transformed into gods". Like the astronomical configuration of the Giza pyramids in Egypt, the entire complex is a precise scale-model of the solar system that accurately reflects the orbital distances of the

inner planets, the asteroid belt, Jupiter, Saturn,
Uranus, Neptune, and Pluto.  Since the planet Uranus had
only been "discovered" with modern Earth telescopes in
1787, and Pluto not until 1930, it is apparent that the
builders had information from "other sources".

A common element of the Pyramid Civilizations around the
Earth is the constant use of the image of the snake,
dragon, or serpent.  This is because the beings who
planted these civilizations here want to create an
illusion that the "gods" are reptilian.  This is also a
part of an illusion designed to perpetuate amnesia.  The
beings who placed false civilizations on Earth are IS-
BEs, just like you.  Many of the biological bodies
inhabited by IS-BEs in the "Old Empire" are very similar
in appearance to the bodies on Earth.  The "gods" are
not reptiles, although they often behave like snakes.


1,034 - 1,124 AD --

The entire Arab world was enslaved by one man: Hasan
ibn-al-Sabbah [188] **(Footnote)**, the Old Man of the Mountain.  He
established the Hashshashin who operated a part of
Mohammedanism which controlled by terror and fear much
of India, Asia Minor and most of the Mediterranean
Basin.  They became a priesthood that used an extremely
effective mind-control mechanism and extortion tool that
enabled the "Assassins" to control the civilized world
for several hundred years.

Their method was simple.  Young men were kidnapped and
knocked unconscious with hashish. They were taken to a
garden filled with beautiful black-eyed houris in a
harem decorated with rivers of milk and honey.  The
young men were told that they were in paradise.  They
were promised they could return and live there forever
if they sacrificed themselves as an assassin of whomever
they were commanded to kill.  The men were knocked out
again, and shoved out into the world to carry out the
assassination mission.

Meanwhile, the Old Man of the Mountain sent a messenger
to the caliph or, whatever wealthy ruler from whom they
demanded payment, demanding camel-loads of gold, spices,
incense or other valuables.  If payment did not arrive
on time, the assassin would be sent to kill the
offending party.  There was virtually no defense against

the unknown assailant who wanted nothing more than to carry out his mission, be killed and return to "heaven".

This is a very crude example of how simple and effective a brainwashing and mind-control operation can be when it is used skillfully, and forcefully. It is a small scale demonstration of how the amnesia mind-control operation is used against the entire IS-BE population of Earth by the "Old Empire".

1119  AD --

The Knights Templar [189] **(Footnote)** was established as a Christian military unit after the First Crusade but quickly transformed into the basis for the international banking system to accumulate money to conduct the agenda of operatives for vestiges of the "Old Empire" on Earth.

1135 - 1230 AD --

The Domain Expeditionary Force completed the annihilation of the remaining remnants of the "Old Empire" space fleet operating in the solar system around Earth. Unfortunately, their long established thought control operation remains largely intact.

1307 AD --

The Knights Templar was disbanded by King Philip IV of France, who was deeply in debt to the Order. [190] **(Footnote)** He pressured Pope Clement V to condemn the Order's members, have them arrested, tortured them into giving false confessions, and burned them at the stake in an effort to erase his debt by seizing all of their wealth.

A majority of the Templars fled to Switzerland where they established an international banking system [191] **(Footnote)** which secretly controls the economy of Earth.

"Old Empire" operatives act as an unseen influence on international bankers. [192] **(Footnote)** The banks are operated covertly as a on-combatant provocateur to covertly promote and finance weapons and warfare between the nations of Earth. Warfare is an internal mechanism of control over the inmate population. [193] **(Footnote)**

The purpose of the senseless genocide and carnage of wars financed by these international banks is to prevent the IS-BEs of Earth from sharing open communication, cooperate together in activities that might enable IS-BEs to prosper, become enlightened, and escape their imprisonment."

# Chapter Ten

# A Lesson In Biology

(MATILDA O'DONNELL MACELROY PERSONAL NOTE)

"My debrief was also tape recorded as a back up and to add clarification to the stenographic notes. I debriefed immediately after my interview so that everything that was said was still fresh in my mind.

When I recounted these stories to the gallery stenographer I was still reeling a bit. The perspective on Earth history from the point of view of The Domain is very strange, to say the least. I wasn't sure if my uncomfortable feeling came from being dis-oriented, or if it came from being re-oriented. Either way, I felt unsteady and confused. Yet, at the same time, there was a ring of truth to it. I was elated and incredulous at the same time!

The stenographer looked askance at me more than a few times as she recorded the "history lesson" I passed on to her. I'm sure she thought I was losing my mind! Maybe she was right. However, if my mind had been filled with hypnotic suggestions and false memories by the "Old Empire", as Airl suggested, perhaps losing my mind would be a good idea!

I didn't have much time to ponder my own, personal thoughts about these things at the time. It was my duty to get all of the information I could from Airl and pass it on to the stenographer as soon as Airl was finished. My job was not to analyze the information, just report it as accurately as possible. The analysis would be left to the men in the gallery, or whomever else was receiving copies of the transcripts.

I also delivered a list of books and materials requested by Airl to the agent in the gallery room so these could be gathered and delivered to Airl. Each night after I left Airl, she spent the rest of the night reading or "scanning" the materials which had been delivered to her. The members of the gallery each received a transcript of the stenographic dictation to study, each looking for information that was of interest to them. In the morning after breakfast I reported back to the interview room to continue my interviews or "lessons" with Airl."

(OFFICIAL TRANSCRIPT OF INTERVIEW)

TOP SECRET

Official Transcript of the U.S. Army Air Force
Roswell Army Air Field, 509th Bomb Group
SUBJECT: ALIEN INTERVIEW, 28. 7. 1947, 1st Session

"The origins of this universe and life on Earth, as
discussed in the textbooks I have read, are very
inaccurate.  Since you serve your government as a
medical personnel, your duties require that you
understand biological entities.  So, I am sure that you
will appreciate the value of the material I will share
with you today.

The text of books I have been given on subjects related
to the function of life forms contain information that
is based on false memories, inaccurate observation,
missing data, unproven theories, and superstition.

For example, just a few hundred years ago your
physicians practiced bloodletting [194] **(Footnote)** as a means to
release supposed ill-humors from the body in an attempt
to relieve or heal a wide variety of physical and mental
afflictions.  Although this has been corrected somewhat,
many barbarisms are still being practiced in the name of
medical science.

In addition to the application of incorrect theories
concerning biological engineering, many primary errors
that Earth scientists make are the result of an
ignorance of the nature and relative importance of IS-
BEs as the source of energy and intelligence which
animate every life form.

Although it is not a priority of The Domain to intervene
in the affairs of Earth, The Domain Communications
Office has authorized me to provide you with some
information in an effort to provide a more accurate and
complete understanding of these things and thereby
enable you to discover more effective solutions to the
unique problems you face on Earth.

The correct information about the origins of biological
entities has been erased from your mind, as well as from
the minds of your mentors.  In order to help you regain
your own memory, I will share with you some factual
material concerning the origin of biological entities.

I asked Airl if she was referring to the subject of
evolution. Airl said, "No, not exactly".

You will find "evolution" mentioned in the ancient Vedic Hymns. [195] **(Footnote)** The Vedic texts are like folk tales or common wisdoms and superstitions gathered throughout the systems of The Domain. These were compiled into verses, like a book of rhymes. For every statement of truth, the verses contain as many half-truths, reversals of truth and fanciful imaginings, blended without qualification or distinction.

The theory of evolution assumes that the motivational source of energy that animates every life form does not exist. It assumes that an inanimate object or a chemical concoction can suddenly become "alive" or animate accidentally or spontaneously. Or, perhaps an electrical discharge into a pool of chemical ooze will magically spawn a self-animated entity.

There is no evidence whatsoever that this is true, simply because it is not true. Dr. Frankenstein did not really resurrect the dead into a marauding monster, except in the imagination of the IS-BE who wrote a fictitious story one dark and stormy night. [196] **(Footnote)**

No Western scientist ever stopped to consider who, what, where, when or how this animation happens. Complete ignorance, denial or unawareness of the spirit as the source of life force required to animate inanimate objects or cellular tissue is the sole cause of failures in Western medicine.

In addition, evolution does not occur accidentally. It requires a great deal of technology which must be manipulated under the careful supervision of IS-BEs. Very simple examples are seen in the modification of farm animals or in the breeding of dogs. However, the notion that human biological organisms evolved naturally from earlier ape-like forms is incorrect. No physical evidence will ever be uncovered to substantiate the notion that modern humanoid bodies evolved on this planet.

The reason is simple: the idea that human bodies evolved spontaneously from the primordial ooze of chemical interactivity in the dim mists of time is nothing more than a hypnotic lie instilled by the amnesia operation to prevent your recollection of the true origins of Mankind. Factually, humanoid bodies have existed in various forms throughout the universe for trillions of years.

This was compounded by the fact that The Vedic Hymns were brought to Earth 8,200 years ago by The Domain Expeditionary Force. While they were based in the Himalaya Mountains, the verses were taught to some of the local humans who memorized them. However, I should note that this was not an authorized activity for the crew of The Domain installation, although I am sure it seemed like an innocent diversion for them at the time.

The verses were passed along verbally from one generation to the next for thousands of years in the foothills and eventually spread throughout India. No one in The Domain credits any of the material in the Vedic Hymns as factual material, any more than you would use "Grimm's Fairy Tales" [197] **(Footnote)** as a guide for rearing children. However, on a planet where all of the IS-BEs have had their memory erased, one can understand how these tales and fantasies could be taken seriously.

Unfortunately, the humans who learned the Vedic verses passed them along to others saying that they came from "the gods". Eventually, the content of the verses were adopted verbatim as "truth". The euphemistic and metaphorical content of the Veda were accepted and practiced as dogmatic fact. The philosophy of the verses were ignored and the verses became the genesis of nearly every religious practice on the planet, especially Hinduism. [198] **(Footnote)**

As an officer, pilot and engineer of The Domain, I must always assume a very pragmatic point of view. I could not be effective or accomplish my missions if I were to use philosophical dogma or rhetoric as my operations manual. Therefore, our discussion of history is based on actual events that occurred long before any IS-BEs arrived on Earth, and long before the "Old Empire" came into power. I can relate part of this history from personal experience:

Many billions of years ago I was a member of a very large biological laboratory in a galaxy far from this one. It was called the "Arcadia Regeneration Company". [199] **(Footnote)** I was a biological engineer working with a large staff of technicians. It was our business to manufacture and supply new life forms to uninhabited planets. There were millions of star systems with millions of inhabitable planets in the region at that time.

There were many other biological laboratory companies at that time also. Each of them specialized in producing different kinds of life forms, depending on the "class" of the planet being populated. Over a long span of time these laboratories developed a vast catalogue of species throughout the galaxies. The majority of basic genetic material is common to all species of life. [200] **(Footnote)** Therefore, most of their work was concerned with manipulating alterations of the basic genetic pattern to produce variations of life forms that would be suitable inhabitants for various planetary classes.

The "Arcadia Regeneration Company" specialized in mammals for forested areas and birds for tropical regions. Our marketing staff negotiated contracts with various planetary governments and independent buyers from all over the universe. The technicians created animals that were compatible with the variations in climate, atmospheric and terrestrial density and chemical content. In addition we were paid to integrate our specimens with biological organisms engineered by other companies already living on a planet.

In order to do this our staff was in communication with other companies who created life forms. There were industry trade shows, publications and a variety of other information supplied through an association that coordinated related projects.

As you can imagine, our research required a great deal of interstellar travel to conduct planetary surveys. This is when I learned my skills as a pilot. The data gathered was accumulated in huge computer databases and evaluated by biological engineers. [201] **(Footnote)**

A computer is an electronic device that serves as an artificial "brain" or complex calculating machine. It is capable of storing information, making computations, solving problems and performing mechanical functions. In most of the galactic systems of the universe, very large computers are commonly used to run the routine administration, mechanical services and maintenance activities of an entire planet or planetary system.

Based on the survey data gathered, designs and artistic renderings were made for new creatures.  Some designs were sold to the highest bidder. Other life forms were created to meet the customized requests of our clients.

The design and technical specifications were passed along an assembly line through a series of cellular, chemical, and mechanical engineers to solve the various problems.  It was their job to integrate all of the component factors into a workable, functional and aesthetic finished product.

Prototypes of these creatures were then produced and tested in artificially created environments. Imperfections were worked out, modifications made and eventually the new life form was "endowed" or "animated" with a life force or spiritual energy before being introduced into the actual planetary environment for final testing.

After a new life form was introduced, we monitored the interaction of these biological organisms with the planetary environment and with other indigenous life-forms.  Conflicts resulting from the interaction between incompatible organisms were resolved through negotiation between ourselves and other companies.  The negotiations usually resulted in compromises requiring further modification to our creatures or to theirs or both.  This is part of a science or art you call "Eugenics". [202] (Footnote)

In some cases changes were made in the planetary environment, but not often, as planet building is much more complex than making changes to an individual life form.

Coincidentally, a friend and engineer with whom I used to work with at the Arcadia Regeneration Company -- a long time after I left the company -- told me that one of the projects they contracted to do, in more recent times, was to deliver life forms to Earth to replenish them after a war in this region of the galaxy devastated most of the life on the planets in this region of space. This would have been about seventy million years ago.

The skill required to modify the planet into an
ecologically interactive environment that will support
billions of diverse species was an immense undertaking.
Specialized consultants from nearly every biotechnology
company in the galaxy were brought in to help with the
project.

What you see now on Earth is the huge variety of life
forms left behind.  Your scientists believe that the
fallacious "theory of evolution" is an explanation for
the existence of all the life forms here.  The truth is
that all life forms on this and any other planet in this
universe were created by companies like ours.

How else can you explain the millions of completely
divergent and unrelated species of life on the land and
in the oceans of this planet?  How else can you explain
the source of spiritual animation which defines every
living creature?  To say it is the work of "god", is far
too broad.  Every IS-BE has many names and faces in many
times and places.  Every IS-BE is a god. When they
inhabit a physical object they are the source of Life.

For example, there are millions of species [203] **(Footnote)**  of
insects.  About 350,000 of these are species of beetles.
[204] **(Footnote)** There may be as many as 100 million species of
life forms on Earth at any given time.  In addition,
there are many times more extinct species of life on
Earth than there are living life forms.  Some of these
will be rediscovered in the fossil or geological records
of Earth.

The current "theory of evolution" of life forms on Earth
does not consider the phenomena of biological diversity.
Evolution by natural selection is science fiction.  One
species does not accidentally, or randomly evolve to
become another species, as the Earth textbooks indicate,
without manipulation of genetic material by an IS-BE.  [205]
**(Footnote)**

A simple example of IS-BE intervention is the selective
breeding of a species [206] **(Footnote)** on Earth.  Within the past
few hundred years several hundred dog breeds and
hundreds of varieties of pigeons and dozens of Koi fish
have been "evolved" in just a few years, beginning with

only one original breed.  Without active intervention by
IS-BEs, biological organisms rarely change.

The development of an animal like the 'duck-billed
platypus' required a lot of very clever engineering to
combine the body of a beaver with the bill of a duck and
make a mammal that lays eggs.  Undoubtedly, some wealthy
client placed a "special order" for it as a gift or
curious amusement.  I am sure the laboratory of some
biotechnical company worked on it for years to make it a
self-replicating life form!

The notion that the creation of any life form could have
resulted from a coincidental chemical interaction
moldering up from some primordial ooze is beyond
absurdity!  Factually, some organisms on Earth, such as
Proteobacteria, [207] (Footnote) are modifications of a Phylum [208]
(Footnote) designed primarily for "Star Type 3, Class C"
planets.  In other words, The Domain designation for a
planet with an anaerobic  atmosphere nearest a large,
intensely hot blue star, [209] (Footnote) such as those in the
constellation of Orion's Belt in this galaxy.

Creating life forms is very complex, highly technical
work for IS-BEs who specialize in this field.  Genetic
anomalies are very baffling to Earth biologists who have
had their memory erased.  Unfortunately, the false
memory implantations of the "Old Empire" prevent Earth
scientists from observing obvious anomalies.

The greatest technical challenge of biological organisms
was the invention of self-regeneration, or sexual
reproduction. It was invented as the solution to the
problem of having to continually manufacture replacement
creatures for those that had been destroyed and eaten by
other creatures.  Planetary governments did not want to
keep buying replacement animals.

The idea was contrived trillions of years ago as a
result of a conference held to resolve arguments between
the disputing vested interests within the biotechnology
industry.  The infamous "Council of Yuhmi-Krum" was
responsible for coordinating creature production.
[210] (Footnote)

A compromise was reached, after certain members of the
Council were strategically bribed or murdered, to author

an agreement which resulted in the biological phenomenon which we now call the "food chain".

The idea that a creature would need to consume the body of another life form as an energy source was offered as a solution by one of the biggest companies in the biological engineering business. They specialized in creating insects and flowering plants.

The connection between the two is obvious. Nearly every flowering plant requires a symbiotic relationship with an insect in order to propagate. The reason is obvious: both the bugs and the flowers were created by the same company. Unfortunately, this same company also had a division which created parasites and bacteria.

The name of the company roughly translated into English would be "Bugs & Blossoms" . They wanted to justify the fact that the only valid purpose of the parasitic creatures they manufactured was to aid the decomposition of organic material. There was a very limited market for such creatures at that time.

In order to expand their business they hired a big public relations firm and a powerful group of political lobbyists to glorify the idea that life forms should feed from other life forms. They invented a "scientific theory" to use as a promotion gimmick. The theory was that all creatures needed to have "food" as a source of energy. Before that, none of the life forms being manufactured required any external energy. Animals did not eat other animals for food, but consumed sunlight, minerals or vegetable matter only.

Of course, "Bugs & Blossoms" went into the business of designing and manufacturing carnivores. Before long, so many animals were being eaten as food that the problem of replenishing them became very difficult. As a 'solution', "Bugs & Blossoms" proposed, with the help of some strategically placed bribes in high places,  that other companies begin using 'sexual reproduction' as the basis for replenishing life-forms.  "Bugs & Blossoms" was the first company to  develop blueprints for sexual reproduction, of course.

As expected, the patent licenses for the biological engineering process [211] **(Footnote)** required to implant

stimulus-response mating, cellular division and pre-
programmed growth patterns for self-regenerating animals
were owned by "Bugs & Blossoms" too.

Through the next few million years laws were passed that
required that these programs be purchased by the other
biological technology companies.  These were required to
be imprinted into the cellular design of all existing
life-forms. It became a very expensive undertaking for
other biotechnology companies to make such an awkward,
and impractical idea work.

This led to the corruption and downfall of the entire
industry.  Ultimately, the 'food and sex' idea
completely ruined the bio-technology industry, including
"Bugs & Blossoms".  The entire industry faded away as
the market for manufactured life forms disappeared.
Consequently, when a species became extinct, there is no
way to replace them because the technology of creating
new life forms has been lost.  Obviously, none of this
technology was ever known on Earth, and probably never
will be.

There are still computer files on some planets far from
here which record the procedures for biological
engineering.  Possibly the laboratories and computers
still exist somewhere.  However, there is no one around
doing anything with them.  Therefore, you can understand
why it is so important for The Domain to protect the
dwindling number of creatures left on Earth.

The core concept behind 'sexual reproduction' technology
was the invention of a chemical/electronic interaction
called "cyclical stimulus-response generators".  [212] **(Footnote)**
This is an programmed genetic mechanism which causes a
seemingly spontaneous, recurring impulse to reproduce.
The same technique was later adapted and applied to
biological flesh bodies, including Homo Sapiens.

Another important mechanism used in the reproductive
process, especially with Homo Sapiens type bodies, is
the implantation of a "chemical-electrical trigger"
mechanism [213] **(Footnote)** in the body.  The "trigger" which
attracts IS-BEs to inhabit a human body, or any kind of
"flesh body", is the use of an artificially imprinted
electronic wave which uses "aesthetic pain" to attract
the IS-BE.

Every trap in the universe, including those used to capture IS-BEs who remain free, is "baited" with an aesthetic electronic wave. The sensations caused by the aesthetic wavelength are more attractive to an IS-BE than any other sensation. When the electronic waves of pain and beauty are combined together, this causes the IS-BE to get "stuck" in the body.

The "reproductive trigger" used for lesser life forms, such as cattle and other mammals, is triggered by chemicals emitted from the scent glands, combined with reproductive chemical-electrical impulses stimulated by testosterone, or estrogen. [214] **(Footnote)**

These are also interactive with nutrition levels which cause the life form to reproduce more when deprived of food sources. Starvation promotes reproductive activity as a means of perpetuating survival through future regenerations, when the current organism fails to survive. These fundamental principles have been applied throughout all species of life.

The debilitating impact and addiction to the "sexual aesthetic-pain" electronic wave [215] **(Footnote)** is the reason that the ruling class of The Domain do not inhabit flesh bodies. This is also why officers of The Domain Forces only use doll bodies. This wave has proven to be the most effective trapping device ever created in the history of the universe, as far as I know.

The civilizations of The Domain and the "Old Empire" both depend on this device to "recruit" and maintain a work force of IS-BEs who inhabit flesh bodies on planets and installations. These IS-BEs are the "working class" beings who do all of the slavish, manual, undesirable work on planets.

As I mentioned, there is a very highly regimented and fixed hierarchy or "class system" for all IS-BEs throughout the "Old Empire", and The Domain, as follows:

The highest class are "free" IS-BEs. That is, they are not restricted to the use of any type of body and may come and go at will, provided that they do not destroy or interfere with the social, economic or political structure.

Below this class are many strata of "limited" IS-BEs who
may or may not use a body from time to time.
Limitations are imposed on each IS-BE regarding range of
power, ability and mobility they can exercise.

Below these are the "doll body" classes, to which I
belong.   Nearly all space officers and crew members of
space craft are required to travel through intergalactic
space.   Therefore, they are each equipped with a body
manufactured from lightweight, durable materials.
Various body types have been designed to facilitate
specialized functions.   Some bodies have accessories,
such as interchangeable tools or apparatus for
activities such as maintenance, mining, chemical
management, navigation, and so forth. There are many
gradations of this body type which also serve as an
"insignia" of rank.

Below these are the soldier class.   The soldiers are
equipped with a myriad of weapons, and specialized
armaments designed to detect, combat and overwhelm any
imaginable foe.   Some   soldiers are issued mechanical
bodies.   Most soldiers are merely remote controlled
robots with no class designation.

The lower classes are limited to "flesh bodies".   Of
course, it is not possible for these to travel through
space for obvious reasons.   Fundamentally, flesh bodies
are far too fragile to endure the stresses of gravity,
temperature extremes, radiation exposure, atmospheric
chemicals and the vacuum of space.   There are also the
obvious logistical inconveniences of food, defecation,
sleep, atmospheric elements, and air pressure required
by flesh bodies, that doll bodies do not require.

Most flesh bodies will suffocate in only a few minutes
without a specific combination of atmospheric chemicals.
After 2 or 3 days the bacteria which live internally and
externally on the body cause severe odors to be emitted.
Odors of any kind are not acceptable in a space vessel.

Flesh can tolerate only a very limited spectrum of
temperatures, whereas in space the contrast of
temperatures may vary hundreds of degrees within
seconds.   Of course flesh bodies are utterly useless for
military duty.   A single shot from a hand-held,

electronic blast gun instantly turns a flesh body into a noxious vapor cloud.

IS-BEs who inhabit flesh bodies have lost much of their native ability and power.  Although it is theoretically possible to regain or rehabilitate these abilities, no practical means has been discovered or authorized by The Domain.

Even though space craft of The Domain travel trillions of "light years" in a single day, [216] **(Footnote)** the time required to traverse the space between galaxies is significant, not to mention the length of time to complete just one set of mission orders, which may require thousands of years.  Biological flesh bodies live for only a very short time -- only 60 to 150 years, at most -- whereas doll bodies can be re-used and repaired almost indefinitely.

The first development of biological bodies began in this universe about seventy-four trillion years ago.  It rapidly became a fad for IS-BEs to create and inhabit various types of bodies for an assortment of nefarious reasons:  especially for amusement, this is to experience various physical sensations vicariously through the body.

Since that time there has been a continuing "de-evolution" in the relationship of IS-BEs to bodies.  As IS-BEs continued to play around with these bodies, certain tricks were introduced to cause IS-BEs to get trapped inside a body so they were unable to leave again.

This was done primarily by making bodies that appeared sturdy, but were actually very fragile.  An IS-BE, using their natural power to create energy, accidentally injured a body when contacting it.  The IS-BE was remorseful about having injured this fragile body.  The next time they encountered a body they began to be "careful" with them.  In so doing, the IS-BE would withdraw or minimize their own power so as not to injure the body.  A very long and treacherous history of this kind of trickery, combined with similar misadventures eventually resulted in a large number of IS-BEs becoming permanently trapped in bodies.

Of course this became a profitable enterprise for some
IS-BEs who took advantage of this situation to make
slaves of others.  The resulting enslavement progressed
over trillions of years, and continues today.
Ultimately the dwindling ability of IS-BEs to maintain a
personal state of operational freedom and ability to
create energy resulted in the vast and carefully guarded
hierarchy or class system.  Using bodies as a symbol of
each class is used throughout the "Old Empire", as well
as The Domain.

The vast majority of IS-BEs throughout the galaxies of
this universe inhabit some form of flesh body.  The
structure, appearance, operation and habitat of these
bodies vary according to the gravity, atmosphere, and
climatic conditions of the planet they inhabit.  Body
types are predetermined largely by the type and size of
the star around which the planet revolves, the distance
from the star, the geological, as well as the
atmospheric components of the planet.

On the average, these stars and planets fall into
gradients of classification which are fairly standard
throughout the universe.  For example, Earth is
identified, roughly, as a "Sun Type 12, Class 7 planet".
That is a heavy gravity, nitrogen/oxygen atmosphere
planet, [217] **(Footnote)** with biological life-forms, in
proximity to a single, yellow, medium-size, low-
radiation sun or "Type 12 star".  The proper
designations are difficult to translate accurately due
to the extreme limitations of astronomical nomenclature
in the English language.

There are as many varieties of life forms as there are
grains of sands on the beach.  You can imagine how many
different creatures and types of bodies have been
manufactured by the millions of companies such as "Bugs
& Blossoms" for all of the myriad planetary systems
during the course of seventy-four trillion years!"

### (MATILDA O'DONNELL MACELROY PERSONAL NOTE)

"When Airl finished telling me this "story", there was a long, silent pause while I
muddled through all this in my mind.  Had Airl been reading science fiction books
and fantasy stories during the night?  Why would she tell me something so incredibly
far-fetched?  If there had not been a 40 inch tall alien, with gray "skin", and three

fingers on each hand and foot sitting directly across from me, I would not have believed a single word of it!

In retrospect, over the 60 years since Airl gave me this information, Earth doctors have begun to develop some of the biological engineering technology that Airl told me about right here on Earth. Heart bypasses, cloning, test tube babies, organ transplants, plastic surgery, genes, chromosomes, and so forth.

One thing is very sure: I have never looked at a bug or flower the same way since then, not to mention my religious belief in Genesis."

# Chapter Eleven

# A Lesson In Science

(MATILDA O'DONNELL MACELROY PERSONAL NOTE)

"The transcript of this interview is verbatim. There is nothing more I can add to it. It says everything".

(OFFICIAL TRANSCRIPT OF INTERVIEW)

TOP SECRET

Official Transcript of the U.S. Army Air Force
Roswell Army Air Field, 509th Bomb Group
SUBJECT: ALIEN INTERVIEW, 29. 7. 1947, 1st Session

"Today Airl told me about some very technical things. I took a few notes to remind myself, so I can repeat what she said as closely as possible. She began with an analogy about scientific knowledge:

Can you imagine how much progress could have been made on Earth if people like Johannes Gutenberg [218] (Footnote), Sir Isaac Newton, Benjamin Franklin, George Washington Carver, [219] (Footnote) Nicola Tesla, Jonas Salk, [220] (Footnote) and Richard Trevithick, [221] (Footnote) and many thousands of similar geniuses and inventors were living today?

Image what technical accomplishments might have been developed if men like these never died? What if they were never given amnesia and made to forget everything they knew? What if they continued to learn and work forever?

What level of technology and civilization could be attained if Immortal Spiritual Beings like these were allowed to continue to create -- in the same place and at the same time -- for billions or trillions of years?

Essentially, The Domain is one civilization that has existed for trillions of years with relatively

120

uninterrupted progress. Knowledge has been accumulated, refined, and improved upon in nearly every field of study imaginable -- and beyond imagining.

Originally, the interaction of IS-BE illusions or inventions created the very fabric of the physical universe -- the microcosm and the macrocosm. Every single particle of the universe has been imagined and brought into existence by an IS-BE. Everything created from an idea -- a thought with no weight or size or location in space.

Every speck of dust in space, from the size of the tiniest subatomic particle, to the size of a sun or a magelantic cloud the size of many galaxies, was created from the nothingness of a thought. Even the tiniest, individual cells were contrived and coordinated to enable a microbial entity to sense, and navigate through infinitesimally small spaces. These also came from an idea thought up by an IS-BE.

You, and every IS-BE on Earth, have participated in the creation of this universe. Even though you are now confined to a fragile body made of flesh; you live for only 65 short rotations of your planet around a star; you have been given overwhelming electric shock treatments to wipe out your memory; you must learn everything all over again each lifetime; in spite of all these circumstances, you are who you are and will always be. And, deep down, you still know that you are and what you know. You are still the essence of you.

How else can one understand the child prodigy? An IS-BE who plays concertos on a piano at three years of age, without formal training? Impossible, if they did not simply remember what they have already learned from thousands of lives spent in front of a keyboard in times untold, or on planets far away. They may not know how they know. They just know.

Humankind has developed more technology in the past 100 years than in the previous 2,000 years. Why? The answer is simple: the influence of the "Old Empire" over the mind and over the affairs of Mankind has been diminished by The Domain.

A renaissance [222] (Footnote) of invention on Earth began in 1,250 AD with the destruction of the "Old Empire" space fleet in the solar system. During the next 500 years, Earth may have the potential to regain autonomy and independence, but only to the degree that humankind can apply the concentrated genius of the IS-BEs on Earth to solve the amnesia problem.

However, on a cautionary note, the inventive potential of the IS-BEs who have been exiled to this planet is severely compromised by the criminal elements of the Earth population. Specifically, politicians, war-mongers and irresponsible physicists who create unlimited weapons such as nuclear bombs, chemicals, diseases and social chaos. These have the potential to extinguish all life forms on Earth, forever.

Even the relatively small explosions that were tested and used in the past two years on Earth have the potential to destroy all of life, if deployed in sufficient quantities. Larger weapons could consume all of the oxygen in the global atmosphere in a single explosion! [223] (Footnote)

Therefore, the most fundamental problems that must be solved in order to ensure that Earth will not be destroyed by technology, are social and humanitarian problems. The greatest scientific minds of Earth, in spite of mathematical or mechanical genius, have never addressed these problems.

Therefore, do not look to scientists to save Earth or the future of humanity. Any so-called "science" that is solely based on the paradigm [224] (Footnote) that existence is composed only of energy and objects moving through space is not a science. Such beings utterly ignore the creative spark originated by an individual IS-BE and collective work of the IS-BEs who continually create the physical universe and all universes. Every science will remain relatively ineffective or destructive to the degree that it omits or devaluates the relative importance of the spiritual spark that ignites all of creation and life.

Unfortunately this ignorance has been very carefully and forcefully instilled in human beings by the "Old Empire" to ensure that IS-BEs on this planet will not be able to recover their innate ability to create space, energy, matter and time, or any other component part of universes. As long as awareness of the immortal, powerful, spiritual "self" is ignored, humanity will remain imprisoned until the day of its own, self-destruction and oblivion.

Do not rely on the dogma of physical sciences to master the fundamental forces of creation any more than you would trust the chanted incantations of an incense-burning shaman. The net result of both of these is entrapment and oblivion. Scientists pretend to observe, but they only suppose that they see, and call it fact. Like the blind man, a scientist can not learn to see until he realizes that he is blind. The "facts" of Earth science do not include the source of creation. They include only the result, or byproducts of creation. The "facts" of science to not include any memory of the nearly infinite past experience of existence.

The essence of creation and existence cannot be found through the lens of a microscope or telescope or by any other measurement of the physical universe. One cannot comprehend the perfume of a flower or the pain felt by an abandoned lover with meters and calipers.

Everything you will ever know about the creative force and ability of a god can be found within you -- an Immortal Spiritual Being.

How can a blind man teach others to see the nearly infinite gradients that comprise the spectrum of light? The notion that one can understand the universe without understanding the nature of an IS-BE is as absurd as conceiving that an artist is a speck of paint on his own canvas. Or, that the lace on a ballet shoe is the choreographer's vision, or the grace of a dancer, or the electric excitement of opening night.

Study of the spirit has been booby-trapped by the thought control operation through religious superstitions they instill in the minds of men. Conversely, the study of the spirit and the mind have been prohibited by science which eliminates anything that is not measurable in the physical universe. Science is the religion of matter. It worships matter.

The paradigm of science is that creation is all, and the creator is nothing. Religion says the creator is all, and the creation is nothing. These two extremes are the bars of a prison cell. They prevent observation of all phenomenon as an interactive whole.

Study of creation without knowing the IS-BE, the source of creation, is futile. When you sail to the edge of a universe conceived by science, you fall off the end into an abyss of dark, dispassionate space and lifeless, unrelenting force. On Earth, you have been convinced that the oceans of the mind and spirit are filled with gruesome, ghoulish monsters that will eat you alive if you dare to venture beyond the breakwater of superstition.

The vested interest of the "Old Empire" prison system is to prevent you from looking at your own soul. They fear that you will see in your own memory the slave masters who keep you imprisoned. The prison is made of shadows in your mind. The shadows are made of lies, and pain, and loss, and fear.

The true geniuses of civilization are those IS-BEs who will enable other IS-BEs to recover their memory and regain self-realization and self-determination. This issue is not solved through enforcing moral regulation on behavior, or through the control of beings through mystery, faith, drugs, guns or any other dogma of a slave society. And certainly not through the use of electric shock and hypnotic commands!

The survival of Earth and every being on it depends on the ability to recover the memory of skills you have accrued through the trillenia; to recover the essence of yourself. Such an art, science, or technology has never been conceived in the "Old Empire". Otherwise, they would not have resorted to the "solution" that brought you to your current condition on Earth.

Neither has such technology ever been developed by The Domain. Until recently, the necessity of rehabilitating an IS-BE with amnesia has not been needed. Therefore, no one has ever worked on solving this problem. So far, unfortunately, The Domain has no solution to offer.

A few officers of The Domain Expeditionary Force have
taken it upon themselves to provide technology to Earth
during their off duty time.  These officers leave their
"doll" at the space station and, as an IS-BE, assume or
take over a biological body on Earth.  In some cases an
officer can remain on duty while they inhabit and
control other bodies at the same time.

This is a very dangerous and adventurous undertaking.
It requires a very able IS-BE to accomplish such a
mission, and return to base successfully.  One officer
who did this recently, while continuing to attend to his
official duties, was known on Earth as the electronics
inventor, Nicola Tesla. [225] **(Footnote)**

It is my intention, although is not a part of my mission
orders, to assist you in your efforts to advance
scientific and humanitarian progress on Earth.  My
intention is to help other IS-BEs to help themselves. In
order to solve the amnesia problem on Earth you will
need much more advanced technology, as well as social
stability to allow enough time for research and
development of techniques to free the IS-BE from the
body, and to free the mind of the IS-BE from amnesia.

Although The Domain has a long term interest in
maintaining Earth as a useful planet, it has no
particular interest in the human population of Earth,
other than its own personnel here.  We are interested in
preventing destruction, as well as accelerating the
development of technologies that will sustain the
infrastructures of the global biosphere, hydrosphere and
atmosphere.

To this end, you will discover, on very careful and
thorough examination, that my space craft contains a
wide assortment of technology that does not yet exist on
Earth.  If you distribute pieces of this craft to
various scientists for study, they will be able to
reverse engineer [226] **(Footnote)** some of the technology to the
extent that Earth has the raw materials required to
replicate these components.

Some features will be indecipherable.  Other features
cannot be duplicated as Earth does not have the natural
resources required to replicate them.  This is
especially true of the metals used to construct the

craft. Not only do these metals not exist on Earth, the refining process required to produce these metals took billions of years to develop.

It is also true of the navigation system which requires an IS-BE whose own personal wavelength has been specifically attuned to the "neural network" of the craft. [227] (Footnote) The pilot of the craft must possess a very high order of energy volition, discipline, training and intelligence to manipulate such a craft. IS-BEs on Earth are incapable of this expertise because it requires the use of an artificial body specifically created for this purpose.

Certain individual Earth scientists, some of whom are among the most brilliant minds in the history of the universe, will have their memory of this technology jogged when they examine the craft components. Just as some of the scientists and physicists on Earth have been able to "remember" how to recreate electric generators, internal combustion and steam locomotion, refrigeration, aircraft, antibiotics, and other tools of your civilization, they will also rediscover other vital technology in my craft.

The following are the specific systems embodied in my craft that contain useful components:

1) There is an assortment of microscopic wiring or fibers [228] (Footnote) within the walls of the craft that control such things as communications, information storage, computer function, and automatic navigation.

2) The same wiring is used for light, sub-light and ultra-light spectrum detection and vision. [229] (Footnote)

3) The fabrics of the interior of the craft [230] (Footnote) are far superior to any on Earth at this time and have hundreds or thousands of applications.

4) You will also find mechanisms for creating, amplifying and channeling light particles or waves as a form of energy. [231] (Footnote)

As an officer, pilot and engineer of The Domain Forces, I am not at liberty to discuss or convey the detailed operation or construction of the craft in any way, other

than what I have just disclosed. However, I am
confident that there are many competent engineers on
Earth who will develop useful technology with these
resources.

I am providing these details to you in the hope that the
greater good of The Domain will be served."

# Chapter Twelve

# A Lesson In Immortality

(MATILDA O'DONNELL MACELROY PERSONAL NOTE)

"I think the following transcript is pretty much self-explanatory."

(OFFICIAL TRANSCRIPT OF INTERVIEW)

TOP SECRET

Official Transcript of the U.S. Army Air Force
Roswell Army Air Field, 509th Bomb Group
SUBJECT: ALIEN INTERVIEW, 30. 7. 1947, 1st Session

Immortal Spiritual Beings, which I refer to as "IS-BEs",
for the sake of convenience, are the source and creators
of illusions. Each one, individually and collectively,
in their original, unfettered state of being, are an
eternal, all-powerful, all-knowing entity.

IS-BEs create space by imagining a location. The
intervening distance between themselves and the imagined
location is what we call space. An IS-BE can perceive
the space and objects created by other IS-BEs.

IS-BEs are not physical universe entities. They are a
source of energy and illusion. IS-BEs are not located
in space or time, but can create space, place particles
in space, create energy, and shape particles into
various forms, cause the motion of forms, and animate
forms. Any form that is animated by an IS-BE is called
life.

An IS-BE can decide to agree that they are located in
space or time, and that they, themselves, are an object,
or any other manner of illusion created by themselves or
another or other IS-BEs.

The disadvantage of creating an illusion is that an
illusion must be continually created. If not
continually created, it disappears. Continual creation
of an illusion requires incessant attention to every
detail of the illusion in order to sustain it.

A common denominator of IS-BEs seems to be the desire to
avoid boredom.  A spirit only, without interaction with
other IS-BEs, and the unpredictable motion, drama, and
unanticipated intentions and illusions being created by
other IS-BEs, is easily bored.

What if you could imagine anything, perceive everything,
and cause anything to happen, at will?  What if you
couldn't do anything else?  What if you always knew the
outcome of every game and the answer to every question?
Would you get bored?

The entire back time track of IS-BEs is immeasurable,
nearly infinite in terms of physical universe time.
There is no measurable "beginning" or "end" for an IS-
BE.  They simply exist in an everlasting now.

Another common denominator of IS-BEs is that admiration
of one's own illusions by others is very desirable.  If
the desired admiration is not forthcoming, the IS-BE
will keep creating the illusion in an attempt to get
admiration.  One could say that the entire physical
universe is made of unadmired illusions.

The origins of this universe began with the creation of
individual, illusionary spaces.  These were the "home"
of the IS-BE.  Sometimes a universe is a collaborative
creation of illusions by two or more IS-BEs.  A
proliferation of IS-BEs, and the universes they create,
sometimes collide or become commingled or merge to an
extent that many IS-BEs shared in the co-creation of a
universe.

IS-BEs diminish their ability in order to have a game to
play.  IS-BEs think that any game is better than no
game.  They will endure pain, suffering, stupidity,
privation, and all manner of unnecessary and undesirable
conditions, just to play a game.  Pretending that one
does not know all, see all and cause all, is a way to
create the conditions necessary for playing a game:
unknowns, freedoms, barriers and/or opponents and goals.
Ultimately, playing a game solves the problem of
boredom.

In this fashion, all of the space, galaxies, suns,
planets, and physical phenomena of this universe,

including life forms, places, and events have been
created by IS-BEs and sustained by mutual agreement that
these things exist.

There are as many universes as there are IS-BEs to
imagine, build and perceive them, each existing
concurrently within its own continuum. [232] **(Footnote)** Each
universe is created using its own unique set of rules,
as imagined, altered, preserved or destroyed by one or
more IS-BEs who created it. Time, energy, objects and
space, as defined in terms of the physical universe, may
or may not exist in other universes. The Domain exists
in such a universe, as well as in the physical universe.

One of the rules of the physical universe is that energy
can be created, but not destroyed.  So, the universe
will keep  expanding as long as IS-BEs keep adding more
new energy into it.  It is nearly infinite.  It is like
an automobile assembly line that never stops running and
none of the cars are ever destroyed.

Every IS-BE is basically good.  Therefore, an IS-BE does
not enjoy doing things to other IS-BEs which they
themselves do not want to experience.  For an IS-BE
there is no inherent standard for what is good or bad,
right or wrong, ugly or beautiful.  These ideas are all
based on the opinion of each individual IS-BE.

The closest concept that human beings have to describe
an IS-BE is as a god:  all-knowing, all-powerful,
infinite.  So, how does a god stop being a god?  They
pretend NOT to know.  How can you play a game of "hide
and seek" if you always know where the other person is
hiding?

You pretend NOT to know where the other players are
hiding, so you can go off to "seek" them.  This is how
games are created.  You have forgotten that you are just
"pretending".  In so doing, IS-BEs become entrapped and
enslaved inside a maze of their  own devising.

How does one create a cage, lock one's own self inside
the cage, throw away the key, and forget there is a key
or a cage, and forget there is an "inside" or "outside",
and even forget there is a self?  Create the illusion
that there is no illusion: the entire universe is real,
and that no other universe exists or can be created.

On Earth, the propaganda taught and agreed upon is that the gods are responsible, and that human beings are not responsible.  You are taught that  only a god can create universes.  So, the responsibility for every action is assigned to another IS-BE or god.  Never oneself.

No human being ever assumes personal responsibility for the fact that they, themselves -- individually and collectively -- are gods.  This fact alone is the source of entrapment for every IS-BE.

# Chapter Thirteen

# A Lesson In The Future

(MATILDA O'DONNELL MACELROY PERSONAL NOTE)

"I think this transcript speaks for itself also. I relayed Airl's exact communication as faithfully as possible. My superior officers became very alarmed about the possible military implications of what Airl said in this interview."

(OFFICIAL TRANSCRIPT OF INTERVIEW)

TOP SECRET

Official Transcript of the U.S. Army Air Force
Roswell Army Air Field, 509th Bomb Group
SUBJECT: ALIEN INTERVIEW, 31. 7. 1947, 1st Session

" 'It is my personal belief that the truth should not be sacrificed on the altar of political, religious or economic expediency. [233] **(Footnote)** As an officer, pilot and engineer of The Domain it is my duty to protect the greater good of The Domain and its possessions. However, we cannot defend ourselves against forces of which we are not aware.

The isolation of Earth from the rest of civilization prevents me from discussing many subjects with you at this time. Security and protocol prevent me from revealing any but the broadest, general statements about the plans and activities of The Domain. However, I can give you some information that you may find useful.

I must return to my assigned duties on the "space station" now. I have provided as much help as I feel ethically able to offer, given the requirements and constraints of my duties as an officer, pilot and engineer of The Domain Forces. Therefore, I will depart, as an IS-BE, from Earth within the next 24 hours.'

What this means is that Airl will leave her "doll" with us, as her craft is damaged beyond repair. We can examine, dissect and study the body at our leisure. She does not have any further use for it, nor does she have any personal feelings or attachments to it as others are readily available for her use.

Airl does not recommend that there is any technology in the body that Earth scientists will find useful, however. The technology of the body is simple, yet vastly beyond the reckoning of our current ability to analyze or reverse engineer any facet of it. The body is neither biological or mechanical, but a unique fabrication of materials and ancient technologies not found on any Earth-type planet.

As Airl mentioned previously, a very rigid and distinctive hierarchy of social, economic and cultural classes exists throughout The Domain which has remained unvaried and inviolate for many millennia. The body type and function assigned to an IS-BE officer varies specifically according to the rank, class, longevity, training level, command level, service record, and meritorious citations earned by each individual IS-BE, as with any other military insignia.

The body used by Airl is specifically designed for an officer, pilot and engineer of her rank and class. The bodies of her companions, which were destroyed in the crash, were not of the same rank or class, but of a junior rank. Therefore, the appearance, features, composition and functionality of those bodies were specialized, and limited to the requirements of their duties.

The junior officers whose bodies were damaged in the crash have left their bodies and returned to their duties on the space station. The damage suffered by their bodies was due primarily to the fact that they were officers of lower rank. They used bodies which were partially biological and therefore far less durable and resilient than hers.

Although The Domain will not hesitate to destroy any active vestiges of the "Old Empire" operations where ever they are discovered this is not our primary mission in this galaxy.  I am sure that the "Old Empire" mind-control mechanisms can be deactivated and destroyed eventually.  However, it is not possible to estimate how long this make take, as we do not understand the extent of this operation at this time.

We do know that the "Old Empire" force screen is vast enough to cover this end of the galaxy, at least.  We also know from experience that each force generator and trapping device is very difficult to detect, locate and destroy.  Also, it is not the current mission of The Domain Expeditionary Force to commit resources to this endeavor.

The eventual destruction of these devices may make it possible for your memory to be restored, simply by virtue of not having it erased after each lifetime. Fortunately, the memory of an IS-BE cannot be permanently erased.

There are many other active space civilizations who maintain various nefarious operations in this area, not the least of which is dumping unwanted IS-BEs on Earth. None of these craft are hostile or in violent opposition to The Domain Forces.  They know better than to challenge us!

For the most part The Domain ignores Earth and its inhabitants, except to ensure that the resources of the planet itself are not permanently spoiled.  This sector of the galaxy was annexed by The Domain and is the possession of The Domain, to do with or dispose of as it deems best.  The moon of Earth and the asteroid belt have become a permanent base of operations for The Domain Forces.

Needless to say, any attempt by humans or others to interfere in the activities of The Domain in this solar system -- even if it were possible, which it definitely is not -- will be terminated swiftly.  This is not a serious concern, as I mentioned earlier, since homo sapiens cannot operate in open space.

Of course we will continue with the next steps of The Domain Expansion Plan which has remained on schedule for billions of years. Over the next 5,000 years there will be increasing traffic and activity of The Domain Forces as we progress toward the center of this galaxy and beyond to spread our civilization through the universe.

If humanity is to survive, it must cooperate to find effective solutions to the difficult conditions of your existence on Earth. Humanity must rise above its human form and discover where they are, and that they are IS-BEs, and who they really are as IS-BEs in order to transcend the notion that they are merely biological bodies. Once these realizations have been made, it may be possible to escape your current imprisonment. Otherwise, there will be no future for the IS-BEs on Earth.

Although there are no active battles or war being waged between The Domain and the "Old Empire", there still exists the covert actions of the "Old Empire" taken against Earth through their thought control operation.

When one knows that these activities exist, the effects can be observed clearly. The most obvious examples of these actions against the human race can be seen as incidents of sudden, inexplicable behavior. A very recent instance of this occurred in the United States military just before the Japanese attack on Pearl Harbor. [234] (Footnote)

Just three days before the attack, someone in authority ordered all the ships in Pearl Harbor to go into port and secure for inspection. The ships were ordered to take all the ammunition out of their magazines, and store it below. On the afternoon before attack all of the admirals and generals were attending parties, even though two Japanese aircraft carriers were discovered standing right off Pearl Harbor.

The obvious action to take would have been to contact Pearl Harbor by telephone to warn them of the danger of a fight starting and to put the ammunition back and order the ships to get out of port into open sea.

About six hours before the Japanese attack began, a U.S.
navy ship sank a small Japanese submarine right outside
the harbor.  Instead of contacting Pearl Harbor by
telephone to report the incident,  a warning message was
put into top secret code, which took about two hours to
encode, and then it took another two hours to decode.
The word of warning to Pearl Harbor did not arrive until
10:00 AM Pearl Harbor time, Sunday -- 'two hours after
the Japanese attack destroyed the U.S. fleet.

How do things like this happen?

If the men who were responsible for these obviously
disastrous errors were stood up and asked bluntly to
justify their actions and intentions you would find out
that they were quite sincere in their jobs.  Ordinarily,
they do the very best they can do for people and
nations.  However, all of a sudden,  from some
completely unknown and undetectable source enters these
wild, unexplainable situations that just 'can't exist'.

The "Old Empire" thought control operation is run by a
small group of old "baboons" with very small minds.
They are playing insidious games with no purpose and no
goal other than to control and destroy IS-BEs who could
otherwise manage themselves perfectly well, if left
alone.

These types of artificially created incidents are being
forced upon the human race by the operators of the mind-
control prison system. The prison guards will always
promote and support oppressive or totalitarian
activities of IS-BEs on Earth.  Why not keep the inmates
fighting between themselves?  Why not empower madmen to
run the governments of Earth?  The men who run the
criminal governments of Earth mirror the commands given
them by covert thought-controllers of the "Old Empire".

The human race will continue to shadow box with this for
a long time -- as long as it remains the human race.
Until then, the IS-BEs on Earth will continue to live a
series of consecutive lives, over and over and over.
The same IS-BEs who lived during the rise and fall of
civilizations in India, China, Mesepotamia, Greece, and
Rome are inhabiting bodies in the present time in
America, France, Russia, Africa, and around the world.

In between each lifetime an IS-BE is sent back again, to begin all over, as though the new life was the only life they had ever lived.  They begin anew in pain, in misery, and mystery.

Some IS-BEs have been transported to Earth more recently than others.  Some IS-BEs have been on Earth only a few hundred years, so they have no personal experiences with the earlier civilizations of Earth.  They have no experiences of having lived on Earth, so could not remember a previous existence here, even if their memory was restored.  They might, however, remember lives they lived elsewhere on other planets and in other times.

Others have been here since the first days of Lemuria.  In any case, the IS-BEs of Earth are here forever, until they can break the amnesia cycle, conquer the electronic traps set up by their captors and free themselves.

Because The Domain has three thousand of their own IS-BEs in captivity on Earth also, they have an interest in solving this problem.  This problem has never been encountered or effectively solved before in the universe, as far as they know.  They will continue their efforts to free those IS-BEs from Earth, where and when it is possible, but it will require time to develop an unprecedented technology and the diligence to do so.'

**(EDITOR'S NOTE:** The following statement is a comment by Matilda.)

I think it is Airl's sincere desire, as one IS-BE to another, that the rest of our eternity will be as pleasant as possible."

# Chapter Fourteen

# Airl Reviews The Interview Transcripts

(MATILDA O'DONNELL MACELROY PERSONAL NOTE)

"Shortly after I finished recounting the previous interview with Airl to the stenographer, I was summoned urgently to the office of the Commanding Officer of the base. I was escorted by four heavily armed military policemen. When I arrived, I was asked to be seated in a very large, make-shift office that had been arranged with a conference table and chairs. In the office were several dignitaries I had seen at various times in "the gallery". I recognized a few of them because they were famous men.

I was introduced to these men, which included:

Army Air Force Secretary Symington, [235] (Footnote) General Nathan Twining, [236] (Footnote) General Jimmy Doolittle , [237] (Footnote) General Vandenberg, [238] (Footnote) and General Norstad. [239] (Footnote)

Much to my surprise Charles Lindbergh [240] (Footnote) was also in the office. Secretary Symington explained to me that Mr. Lindberg was there as a consultant to the chief of staff of the U.S. Air Force. There were several other men present in the room who were not introduced. I assume these men were personal aides to the officers or agents of some intelligence service.

All of this sudden attention, not only from the Secretary and generals, but from such world famous people as Mr. Lindbergh, and General Doolittle, made me realize how critically important my role as an "interpreter" for Airl was, as seen through the eyes of others. Until this time I was not really aware of this except in an peripheral sense. I suppose this was because I was so absorbed in details of the extraordinary situation. Suddenly, I began to grasp the magnitude of my role. I think that the presence of these men in that meeting was intended, in part, to impress me with this fact!

The Secretary instructed me not to be nervous. He said that I was not in any trouble. He asked me if I thought the alien would be willing to answer a list of questions they had prepared. He explained that they were very eager to discover many more details about Airl, the flying disc, The Domain, and many other subjects that Airl had disclosed in the interview transcripts. Of course, they were mainly interested in questions relating to the military security and the construction of the flying disc.

I told them that I was very sure that Airl had not changed her mind about answering questions, as nothing had changed that would cause her to trust the intentions of the

138

men in the gallery. I repeated that Airl had communicated everything that she was willing and at liberty to discuss already.

In spite of this, they insisted that I would ask Airl again if she would answer questions. And, if the answer was still "NO", I was to ask her if she would be willing to read the written copies of the transcripts of my interview "translations". They wanted to know if Airl would verify that my understanding and translation of our interviews was correct.

Since Airl could read English very fluently, the Secretary asked if they could be allowed to observe for themselves while Airl read the transcripts, and verify that they were correct in writing. They wanted her to write on a copy of the transcript whether the "translations" were correct, or not, and make a note of anything that was not accurate on the transcripts. Of course, I had no choice but to obey orders and I did exactly what the Secretary requested.

I was given a copy of the transcripts, with a signature page, which I was to show to Airl. After Airl completed her review, I was also directed to request that Airl sign the cover-page, attesting that all of the translations in the transcripts were correct, as amended by her.

About an hour later I entered the interview room, as instructed, with copies of the transcripts and signature page to deliver to Airl as the members of the gallery, including the Generals, (and Mr. Lindberg also, I presume) and others watched through the glass of the gallery room.

I went to my usual seat, sitting 4 or 5 feet across from Airl. I presented the envelope of transcripts to Airl, and passed on the instructions I had received from the Secretary, telepathically. Airl looked at me, and looked at the envelope, without accepting it.

Airl said: "If you have read them and they are accurate in your own estimation, there is no need for me to review them also. The translations are correct. You can tell your commander that you have faithfully conveyed a record of our communication."

I assured Airl that I had read them, and they were exact recordings of everything I told the transcription typist.

"Will you sign the cover page then?", I asked.

"No, I will not.", said Airl.

"May I ask why not?", I said. I was a little confused as to why she wasn't willing to do such a simple thing.

"If your commander does not trust his own staff to make an honest and accurate report to him, what confidence will my signature on the page give him? Why will he trust an ink mark on a page made by an officer of The Domain, if he does not trust his own, loyal staff?"

I didn't quite know what to say to that. I couldn't argue with Airl's logic, and I couldn't force her to sign the document either. I sat in my chair for a minute wondering what to do next. I thanked Airl and told her I needed to go ask my superiors for further instructions. I placed the envelope of the transcripts in the inside breast pocket of my uniform jacket and began to rise from my chair.

At that moment the door from the gallery room slammed open! Five heavily armed military police rushed into the room! A man in a white laboratory coat followed closely behind them. He pushed a small cart that carried a box-shaped machine with a lot of dials on the face of it.

Before I could react, two of the MPs grabbed Airl and held her firmly down in the overstuffed chair she had been sitting on since the first day of our interviews together. The two other MPs grabbed my shoulders and pushed me back down on my chair and held me there. The other MP stood directly in front of Airl, pointing a rifle directly at her, not more than six inches from her head.

The man in the lab coat quickly wheeled the cart behind Airl's chair. He deftly placed a circular head band over Airl's head and turned back to the machine on the cart. Suddenly, he shouted the word "clear!"

The soldiers who were holding Airl released her. At that instant I saw Airl's body stiffen and shudder. This lasted for about 15 or 20 seconds. The machine operator turned a knob on the machine and Airl's body slumped back into the chair. After a few seconds he turned the knob again and Airl's body stiffened as before. He repeated the same process several more times.

I sat in my chair, being held down all the while by the MPs. And I didn't understand what was going on. I was terrified and transfixed by what was happening! I couldn't believe it!

After a few minutes several other men wearing white lab coats entered the room. They briefly examined Airl who was now slumped listlessly in the chair. They mumbled a few words to each other. One of the men waved to the gallery window. A gurney was immediately rolled into the room by two attendants. These men lifted Airl's limp body onto the gurney, strapped her down across her chest and arms, and rolled it out of the room.

I was immediately escorted out of the interview room by the MPs and taken directly to my quarters, where I was locked in my room with the MPs remaining at guard outside the door.

After about half an hour there was a knock at the door to my quarters. When I opened it General Twining entered, together with the machine operator in the white lab coat. The General introduced the man to me as Dr. Wilcox. [241] **(Footnote)**. He asked me to accompany him and the doctor. We left the room, followed by the MPs. After several twists and turns through the complex we entered a small room where Airl had been wheeled on the gurney.

The General told me that Airl and The Domain were considered to be a very great military threat to the United States. Airl had been "immobilized" so that she could not depart and return to her base, as she said she would do in the interview. It would be a very grave risk to national security to allow Airl to report what she observed during her time at the base. So, it had been determined that decisive action was needed to prevent this.

The General asked me if I understood why this was necessary. I said that I did, although I most certainly did not agree that it was the least bit necessary and I certainly did not agree with the "surprise attack" on Airl and me in the interview room! However, I said nothing about this to the General because I was very afraid of what might happen to me and Airl if I protested.

Dr. Wilcox asked me to approach the gurney and stand next to Airl. Airl lay perfectly still and unmoving on the bed. I could not tell whether she was alive or dead. Several other men in white lab coats, who I assumed were also doctors, stood on the opposite side of the bed. They had connected two pieces of monitoring equipment to Airl's head, arms and chest. One of these devices I recognized from my training as a surgical nurse as an EEG machine [242] **(Footnote)** which is used to detect electrical activity in the brain. The other device was a normal hospital room vital signs monitor, which I knew would be useless since Airl did not have a biological body.

Dr. Wilcox explained to me that he had administered a series of "mild" electroshocks to Airl in an attempt to subdue her long enough to allow the military authorities time to evaluate the situation and determine what to do with Airl.

He asked me to attempt to communicate with Airl, telepathically.

I tried for several minutes but couldn't sense any communication from Airl. I couldn't even sense whether Airl was present in the body any longer!

"I think you must have killed her", I said to the doctor.

Dr. Wilcox told me that they would keep Airl under observation and that I would be asked to return later to try to establish communication with Airl again."

# Chapter Fifteen

# My Interrogation

(MATILDA O'DONNELL MACELROY PERSONAL NOTE)

"The next morning I was escorted from my quarters, under the guard of four MPs, to the interview room. Airl's overstuffed chair had been removed from the room and replaced by a small desk and several office chairs. I was asked to sit down and wait to be interviewed. After a few minutes Dr. Wilcox came into the office together with another man wearing a plain business suit. The man introduced himself as John Reid. [243] (Footnote)

Dr. Wilcox explained to me that Mr. Reid had been flown in from Chicago at the request of my superior officers to conduct a lie detector [244] (Footnote) test on me! My surprise at this statement was so obvious, that Dr. Wilcox noticed that I was obviously taken aback, and insulted, at the insinuation that I had ever lied about anything!

Nonetheless, Mr. Reid began to set up his polygraph device on the desk next to my chair, while Dr. Wilcox continued to explain, in a calm voice, that the test was being administered for my own protection. Since all of the interviews with the alien had been conducted telepathically, and Airl had declined to read and attest that the typed transcripts were accurate, the truth and accuracy of the statements contained in the transcripts depended entirely on my personal word alone. There was no other reliable way to test the accuracy of the transcripts without submitting me to a battery of tests and psychological examinations to determine, in the opinion of "experts", meaning himself, whether the transcripts should be taken seriously, or not.
The tone of his voice said very clearly, "or dismissed as the delusional ranting of a mere woman!"

Mr. Reid proceeded to strap a rubber tube around my chest, as well as an ordinary blood-pressure cuff around my upper arm. He then placed electrodes on the fingers and surfaces of my hands. He explained that he would be very objective during the interview because he had been thoroughly trained in scientific interrogation. This training was supposed to make his interrogation free from human error.

Mr. Reid explained to me that, in response to the questions he and Dr. Wilcox were going to ask me, that actual physiological changes would be transmitted through a small panel unit. The readings would then be tracked on moving graph paper, which he placed beside the machine on the desk. The parallel graphs on the paper would then be correlated and interpreted by Mr. Reid, with the "expert" assistance of Dr. Wilcox, to determine whether or not I was lying.

Both Mr. Reid and Dr. Wilcox asked me a series of innocuous questions to begin, which advanced into a more pointed interrogation about my interviews with Airl.

Here is what I remember about the questions:

"What is your name?"

"Matilda O'Donnell", I replied.

"What is your date of birth?"

"June 12th, 1924", I said.

"What is your age?"

"Twenty-three".

"Where were you born?"

"Los Angeles, California", I said.

(And so on, and so forth.)

"Are you able to communicate by telepathy?"

"No. I have never been able to do this with anyone except Airl." I said.

"Were any of the statements you made to the stenographer falsified?

"No", I answered.

"Have you intentionally or unintentionally imagined or fabricated any of the communication you claimed to have had with the alien?"

"No, of course not", I said.

"Are you intentionally attempting to deceive anyone?"

"No."

"Are you attempting to obstruct this test?"

"No."

"What color are your eyes?"

"Blue".

"Are you a Catholic?"

"Yes."

"Would you tell the same stories to your parish priest in a Catholic church confessional that you told to the stenographer here at the base?"

"Yes."

"Are you trying to hide anything from us?"

"No. Nothing."

"Do you believe everything the alien communicated to you?"

"Yes."

"Do you consider yourself to be a gullible person?"

"No."

The questions continued in this manner for more than an hour. Finally, I was unhooked from the polygraph machine and allowed to return to my quarters, still under guard by the MPs.

Later in the afternoon I returned to the interview room. This time the desk was replaced by a hospital gurney. Dr. Wilcox was accompanied by a staff nurse this time. He asked me to lie down on the gurney. He said that he had been requested to ask me the same series of questions that I answered for the lie detector test.

This time, however, I would respond to the questions under the influence of a "truth serum", [245] (Footnote) known as sodium pentothal. As a trained surgical nurse, I was familiar with this barbiturate drug as it was sometimes used as an anesthetic.

Dr. Wilcox asked me if I had any objection to submitting to such a test. I told him that I had nothing to hide. I cannot recall anything about this interview. I assumed that when I finished answering the questions I was escorted back to my room by the MPs, with their assistance this time, as I was too wobbly and woozy from the drug to navigate by myself. However, I had a very peaceful sleep that night.

Apparently neither of these interrogations yielded any suspicious results as I was not asked any more questions after that. Thankfully, I was left alone during the rest of my time at the base."

# Chapter Sixteen

# Airl Departs

(MATILDA O'DONNELL MACELROY PERSONAL NOTE)

"I remained at the base, mostly confined to my quarters, for another 3 weeks after Airl had been "incapacitated" by Dr. Wilcox. Once a day I was escorted to the room where Airl lay on the bed under continued surveillance by Dr. Wilcox, and others, I assume. Each time I went to the room, I was asked to try to communicate with Airl again. Each time there was no response. This saddened me a great deal. As the days continued I became increasing more certain and distressed that Airl was "dead", if that is the right word for it.

Every day, I re-read the transcripts of my interviews with Airl, searching for a clue that might remind me of something or help me in some way to re-establish communication with Airl. I still had the envelope in my possession with copies of the transcripts that Airl was asked to sign. To this day, I don't understand why no one ever asked me to return them. I suppose they forgot about the copy of the transcripts in all the excitement. I did not offer to return them. I kept them concealed under the mattress of my bed all the time I remained at the base, and have kept them with me ever since then. You will be the first person to see these transcripts.

Since Airl's body was not biological, the doctors could not detect whether the body was alive or dead unless it moved. Of course I knew that if Airl was not consciously animating the body as an IS-BE, the body would not move. I explained this to Dr. Wilcox. I explained this to him several times. Each time he just gave me a patronizing sort of smile, patted my arm, and thanked me for trying again.

At the end of the third week I was told by Dr. Wilcox that my services would no longer be needed because it had been decided by the military to move Airl to a larger, more secure military medical facility that was better equipped to deal with the situation. He didn't say anything about where the facility was located.

That was the last time I saw Airl's doll body.

The following day I received written orders, signed by General Twining. The orders said that I had completed my service to the U.S. military and was officially discharged from further duty and that I would receive an honorable discharge and a generous military pension. I would be also be relocated by the military, and given a new identity with the appropriate documents.

Along with the orders I received a document that I was instructed to read and sign. It was an oath of secrecy. The language of the document was full of "legalese", but the point was very clearly made that I was to never, ever discuss anything whatsoever with anyone whatsoever about anything whatsoever that I has seen, heard or experienced during my service in the military -- under pain of death as an Act of Treason against the United States of America!

As it turned out, I was placed into a Federal government witness protection program [248] **(Footnote)**, except that I would be protected from the government by the government. In other words, as long as I stayed quiet I could stay alive! The following morning I was placed aboard a small military transport plane and flown to a relocation destination. After being shuttled to several locations for short periods, I eventually I ended up in Glasgow, Montana near Fort Peck.

The night before I was scheduled to board the transport plane, as I lay in bed contemplating the whole affair and wondering what happened to Airl, and to me, I suddenly heard Airl's "voice". I sat bolt upright in my bed and turned on the light on the night stand! I looked around the room frantically for a few seconds. Then I realized that it was Airl, the IS-BE. Her body was not in the room with me, of course, and it didn't need to be.

She said "Hello!". The tone of her thought was plain and friendly. It was unmistakably Airl. I did not have the least doubt about that!

I thought, "Airl? Are you still here?" She answered that she was "here", but not in a body on Earth. She had returned to her post at The Domain base when the doctor and MPs attacked us in the interview room. She was pleased to perceive that I was well, and that I was going to be released unharmed.

I wondered how she escaped from them. I was worried that they might have injured Airl by the shock machine. Airl said that she was able to leave the body before the shock was administered and avoided the electric current running through the body. She wanted to let me know that she was safe and not to worry about her. I was very relieved, to say the least!

I asked Airl if I would every see her again. Airl reassured me that we are both IS-BEs. We are not a physical bodies. Now that she had located me in space and time we would always stay in communication. Airl wished me well and my communication with her ended for the moment."

# Post Script from Mrs. MacElroy

**EDITOR' NOTE**: The following message was enclosed in a separate envelope marked "READ ME LAST", together with the original letter, the transcripts and the other notes of explanation I received in the envelope from Mrs. MacElroy. This is what the message said:

"The other documents in this envelope are the end of the story, as far as what happened back in 1947. However, several months after the government got me settled at my final relocation destination, I continued my communication with Airl on a regular basis.

It has been almost exactly 40 years since the crash at Roswell. Since then it has become obvious to me that I have been able to communicate telepathically with Airl for one reason: I am one of the 3,000 members of the Lost Battalion. At this time, all of the members of the Lost Battalion have been located on Earth as a result of The Domain Annunaki Mission and their use of the "Tree of Life" detection device.

Through my communication with Airl, I have recovered some of my memory of lives I've spent on Earth over the past 8,000 years. Most of these memories are not especially important compared to the long backtrack of events, but it has been a necessary stepping stone to regaining my awareness and ability as an IS-BE.

I can also remember some dim patches of my life in The Domain Expeditionary Force. I was a nurse there too. For the most part I've been a nurse over and over and over again down through the ages. I stick with being a nurse because it is familiar to me. And, I enjoy the work of helping people, as well as members of the race of biological beings in The Domain whose bodies look more like insects than mammals, especially their hands. Even doll bodies need some repair once in awhile, too.

As I remember more about my past, I realize that the rest of my life is in the future. Eternity is not just in the past. Eternity is in the future. At this point I am still not able to fully return to The Domain. I am sentenced to eternal imprisonment, like all other IS-BEs in the living Hell called Earth, until we can disable the "Old Empire" force screens.

Because I won't keep my biological body much longer now, I am intensely aware that very soon I will be recycled through the amnesia process of the "Old Empire", and stuck back into another baby body to start all over again -- without any memory of what went before.

As you know, members of The Domain Expeditionary Force have been working to solve this problem for thousands of years. Airl says that even though The Domain has located all of the Lost Battalion officers and crew, the success of freeing them depends on the IS-BEs who are already on Earth. The Domain Central Command cannot authorize any personnel or resources, at this time, to conduct a "rescue mission" as this in not the primary mission of The Domain Expeditionary Force in this galaxy.

So, if IS-BEs on Earth are going to escape from this prison, it will have to be an "inside job", so to speak. The inmates will have to figure out how to get themselves out. Various methods of recovering the memory and ability of IS-BEs have been developed over the past 10,000 years on Earth, but none have proven to be consistently effective so far.

Airl mentioned that the most significant breakthrough was made by Gautama Siddhartha about 2,500 years ago. However, the original teachings and techniques taught by The Buddha have been altered or lost over the millennia since then. The practical techniques of his philosophy were perverted into robotic religious rituals by priests as a self-serving instrument of control or slavery.

However, another major advance occurred recently. An acquaintance of The Commanding Officer of The Domain Expeditionary Force Space Station is an IS-BE who had once been an important engineer and officer in the "Old Empire" Space Fleet. He become an "untouchable" himself about 10,000 years ago and was sentenced to Earth for leading a mutiny against the oppressive

regime of the "Old Empire". The engineer was trained
in Advanced Scientific Improvisation Theory thousands
of years ago. This man has applied his expertise to
helping The Domain solve the apparently unsolvable
problem of rescuing the members of the Lost
Battalion, as well as the IS-BEs on Earth.

Careful observation and experimental analysis of the
mechanics of memory in IS-BEs by he and his wife, who
assisted him, led to the realization that IS-BEs can
recover from amnesia and also regain lost abilities.
Together they discovered and developed effective
methods that they used to rehabilitate their own
memories. They eventually codified their methods so
that others can safely be trained to apply them to
themselves and others, without detection by the "Old
Empire" thought control operators.

Their research also revealed that IS-BEs can occupy
and operate more than one body at the same time --
a fact that previously was thought to be uniquely
limited to officers of The Domain.

One example of this fact is that the engineer, in a
previous lifetime on Earth, was Suleiman The
Magnificent [247] **(Footnote)** . His assistant was a harem girl
who rose up from slavery to become his wife and rule
the Ottoman empire with him. [248] **(Footnote)** Simultaneously,
she inhabited another body and ruled her own empire
as Queen Elizabeth. [249] (Footnote) As the Queen of England,
she never married, because she was already married to
the Sultan of the Ottoman Empire!

In a later life he was incarnated as Cecil Rhodes.
[250] **(Footnote)**. During his life as Rhodes she was, again,
a princess, this time from Poland. [251] **(Footnote)** As such,
she pursued Rhodes unsuccessfully toward the end of
his life. However, in their next incarnation they met
again, were married, had a family, and again, worked
together successfully all of their lives.

Several other notable examples of this phenomena were
observed. For example, the process of refining steel
was invented by the same IS-BE who inhabited two
bodies simultaneously. One was named Kelly [252] **(Footnote)**
who lived in Kentucky, and the other was a man named

Bessemer [253] **(Footnote)** who lived in England. They both conceived the same process at the same time.

Another example is Alexander Graham Bell [254] **(Footnote)** the inventor of the telephone, which was invented by several others at the same time, including Elisha Gray. [255] **(Footnote)** The telephone was conceived concurrently in several locations around the world all at once. This was a single IS-BE of such tremendous energy and ability that he was able to operate several bodies in several different locations while conducting complex research work!

Thanks to these revelations, The Domain has been able to return some IS-BEs of the Lost Battalion to active duty on a limited, part-time basis. For example, two young girls who occupy biological bodies on Earth are now, at the same time, working as active members of The Domain Expeditionary Force on the asteroid space station as operators of a communication switchboard. These operators relay messages between The Domain Expeditionary Force and The Domain Command Headquarters.

Recently, I, myself have been able to resume some of my own duties for The Domain Expeditionary Force while continuing to live on Earth. This is not an easy task however, and can only be done while my biological body is sleeping.

It makes me very, very happy to know that we may not have to stay on Earth forever! There is hope of escape, not just for the Lost Battalion, but for many other IS-BEs on Earth.

However, all IS-BEs could be helped to become more aware of the actual situation on Earth through the information in this envelope. This is why I sent these letters and transcripts to you. I want you to get these documents published. I want IS-BEs on Earth to have a chance to find out what is really happening on Earth.

Most people will not believe any of it, I'm sure. It seems too incredible. No "reasonable" person would ever believe a word of it. However, it only seems "incredible" to an IS-BE whose memory has been erased and replaced with false information inside the electronically controlled illusion of a prison planet. We must not allow the apparent incredibility of our situation to prevent us from confronting the reality of it.

Frankly, "reasons" have nothing to do with reality. There are no reasons. Things are what they are. If we don't face the facts of our situation, we're going to stay under the thumb of the "Old Empire" forever! The biggest weapon the "Old Empire" has left now is our ignorance of what they are doing to all the IS-BEs on Earth. Disbelief and secrecy are the most effective weapons they have!

The government agencies that classified the enclosed transcripts as "TOP SECRET" are run by IS-BEs who are nothing more than mindless automatons covertly ordered about through hypnotic commands given by the "Old Empire" prison operators. They are the unknowing slaves of unseen slave masters -- and all the more enslaved by their willingness to be slaves.

Most of the IS-BEs on Earth are good, honest, able beings: artists, managers, geniuses, free thinkers and revolutionaries who have harmed no one, really. They are no threat to anyone except the criminals who have imprisoned them.

They must find out about the "Old Empire" amnesia and hypnosis operation. They must remember their own past lives. The only way this will ever happen is to communicate, coordinate and fight back. We have to tell other people and they have to discuss it openly with each other. Communication is the only effective weapon against secrecy and oppression.

This is why I am asking you to tell this story. Please share these transcripts with as many people as you can. If the people of Earth are told what is really going on here, perhaps they will begin to remember who they are, and where they came from.

For now, we can begin our own release and rescue with words. We can be free again. We can be ourselves again. Perhaps I will meet you in person, with or without a body, somewhere in our Eternal Future.

Good Luck To All Of Us,

Matilda O'Donnell MacElroy

**-- END OF MRS. MACELROY DOCUMENTS --**

# Appendix: Editor's Footnotes

---

[1] "..."War of the Worlds, and The Invasion from Mars"..."

"... the day before Halloween, on Oct. 30, 1938, when millions of Americans tuned in to a popular radio program that featured plays directed by, and often starring, Orson Welles. The performance that evening was an adaptation of the science fiction novel The War of the Worlds, about a Martian invasion of the Earth. But in adapting the book for a radio play, Welles made an important change: under his direction the play was written and performed so it would sound like a news broadcast about an invasion from Mars, a technique that, presumably, was intended to heighten the dramatic effect.

As the play unfolded, dance music was interrupted a number of times by fake news bulletins reporting that a "huge flaming object" had dropped on a farm near Grovers Mill, New Jersey. As members of the audience sat on the edge of their collective seat, actors playing news announcers, officials and other roles one would expect to hear in a news report, described the landing of an invasion force from Mars and the destruction of the United States. The broadcast also contained a number of explanations that it was all a radio play, but if members of the audience missed a brief explanation at the beginning, the next one didn't arrive until 40 minutes into the program.

At one point in the broadcast, an actor in a studio, playing a newscaster in the field, described the emergence of one of the aliens from its spacecraft. "Good heavens, something's wriggling out of the shadow like a gray snake," he said, in an appropriately dramatic tone of voice. "Now it's another one, and another. They look like tentacles to me. There, I can see the thing's body. It's large as a bear and it glistens like wet leather. But that face. It...it's indescribable. I can hardly force myself to keep looking at it. The eyes are black and gleam like a serpent. The mouth is V-shaped with saliva dripping from its rimless lips that seem to quiver and pulsate....The thing is raising up. The crowd falls back. They've seen enough. This is the most extraordinary experience. I can't find words. I'm pulling this microphone with me as I talk. I'll have to stop the description until I've taken a new position. Hold on, will you please, I'll be back in a minute."

As it listened to this simulation of a news broadcast the audience concluded that it was hearing an actual news account of an invasion from Mars. People packed the roads, hid in cellars, loaded guns, even wrapped their heads in wet towels as protection from Martian poison gas, in an attempt to defend themselves against aliens, oblivious to the fact that they were acting out the role of the panic-stricken public that actually belonged in a radio play.

News of the panic (which was conveyed via genuine news reports) quickly generated a national scandal. There were calls, which never went anywhere, for government regulations of broadcasting to ensure that a similar incident wouldn't happen again.

In a prescient column, in the New York Tribune, Dorothy Thompson foresaw that the broadcast revealed the way politicians could use the power of mass communications to create theatrical illusions, to manipulate the public."

-- Reference: http://www.transparencynow.com/welles.htm

[2] "...Majestic-12 documents."

**"Majestic 12" or "MJ-12".** (NOTE: All of the following information and/or assertions concerning the MJ-12 documents are those of the authors of the following website: http://www.majesticdocuments.com)

*"Operation Majestic-12 was established by special classified presidential order on September 24, 1947 at the recommendation of Secretary of Defense James Forrestal and Dr. Vannevar Bush, Chairman of the Joint Research and Development Board. The goal of the group was to exploit everything they could from recovered alien technology.*

*Buried in a super-secret "MAJIC EYES ONLY" classification that was above TOP SECRET — long before the modern top secret codeword special access programs of today — Major General Leslie R. Groves (who commanded the Manhattan Project to deliver the atomic bomb) kept just one copy of the details of crashed alien technology in his safe in Washington, D.C.*

*Ambitious, elite scientists such as Vannevar Bush, Albert Einstein, and Robert Oppenheimer, and career military people such as Hoyt Vandenberg, Roscoe Hillenkoetter, Leslie Groves, and George Marshall, along with a select cast of other experts, feverishly and secretively labored to understand the alien agenda, technology, and their implications.*

*Einstein and Oppenheimer were called in to give their opinion, drafting a six-page paper titled "Relationships With Inhabitants Of Celestial Bodies." They provided prophetic insight into our modern nuclear strategies and satellites, and expressed agitated urgency that an agreement be reached with the President so that scientists could proceed to study the alien technology.*

*The extraordinary recovery of fallen airborne objects in the state of New Mexico, between July 4 – July 6, 1947, caused the Chief of Staff of the Army Air Force's Interplanetary Phenomena Unit, Scientific and Technical Branch, Counterintelligence Directorate to initiate a thorough investigation. The special unit was formed in 1942 in response to two crashes in the Los Angeles area in late February 1942. The draft summary report begins "At 2332 MST, 3 July 47, radar stations in east Texas and White Sands Proving Ground, N.M. tracked two unidentified aircraft until they both dropped off radar. Two crash sites have been located close to the WSPG. Site LZ-1 was located at a ranch near Corona, Approx. 75 miles northwest of the town of Roswell. Site LZ-2 was located approx. 20 miles southeast of the town of Socorro, at latitude 33-40-31 and longitude 106-28-29".*

*The first-ever-known UFO crash retrieval case occurred in 1941 in Cape Girardeau, Missouri. This crash kicked off early reverse-engineering work, but it did not create a unified intelligence effort to exploit possible technological gains apart from the Manhattan Project uses.*

*The debris from the primary field of the 1947 crash 20 miles southeast of Socorro, New Mexico was called ULAT-1 (Unidentified Lenticular Aerodyne Technology), and it excited metallurgists with its unheard-of tensile and shear strengths. The fusion nuclear (called neutronic at that time) engine used heavy water and deuterium with an oddly arranged series of coils, magnets, and electrodes — descriptions that resemble the "cold fusion" studies of today.*

*Harry Truman kept the technical briefing documents of September 24, 1947 for further study, pondering the challenges of creating and funding a secret organization before the CIA* existed (although the Central Intelligence Group or CIG did exist) and before there was a legal procedure of funding non-war operations.

In April 1954, a group of senior officers of the U.S. intelligence community and the Armed Forces gathered for one of the most secret and sensational briefings in history. The subject was Unidentified Flying Objects — not just a discussion of sightings, but how to recover crashed UFOs, where to ship the parts, and how to deal with the occupants. For example, in the "Special Operations Manual (SOM1-01) Extraterrestrial Entities Technology Recovery and Disposal," MAJESTIC–12 "red teams" mapped out UFO crash retrieval scenarios with special attention given to press blackouts, body packaging, and live alien transport, isolation, and custody.

Majestic Documents.com is not another rehash of the famous Roswell story — it contains over 500 pages (and growing) of newly surfaced documents, many of which date years before the Roswell crash. Unlike other websites, a central theme of validating authenticity is woven throughout the site while telling the exciting story of the U.S. government's work on retrieval and analysis of extraterrestrial hardware and alien life forms from 1941 to present."

-- Reference: http://www.majesticdocuments.com/

[3] **"Like Ripley said..."**

**Robert LeRoy Ripley** *(December 25, 1893 - May 27, 1949) was a cartoonist, entrepreneur, and amateur anthropologist who created the world famous Ripley's Believe It or Not! newspaper panel series, featuring odd but true facts from around the world. Subjects covered in Ripley's cartoons and text ranged from sports feats to little known facts about unusual and exotic sites, but what ensured the concept's popularity may have been that Ripley also included items submitted by readers, who supplied photographs of a wide variety of small town American trivia, ranging from unusually shaped vegetables to oddly marked domestic animals, all documented by photographs and then engagingly depicted by Ripley's prolific pen."*

-- Reference: Wikipedia.org

[4] **"...Voltaire..."**

**"François-Marie Arouet** (21 November 1694 – 30 May 1778), better known by the pen name **Voltaire**, was a French Enlightenment writer, essayist, deist and philosopher known for his wit, philosophical sport, and defense of civil liberties, including freedom of religion and the right to a fair trial. He was an outspoken supporter of social reform despite strict censorship laws and harsh penalties for those who broke them. A satirical polemicist, he frequently made use of his works to criticize Christian Church dogma and the French institutions of his day. Many of Voltaire's works and ideas would influence important thinkers of both the American and French Revolutions."

-- Reference: Wikipedia.org

[5] **"... old Underwood typewriter..."**

*The **Underwood Typewriter Company** was a manufacturer of typewriters headquartered in New York City, New York. Underwood produced what is considered the first widely* *successful, modern typewriter.* **By 1939, Underwood had produced five million machines.**

*From 1874 the Underwood family made typewriter ribbons and carbon paper, and were among a number of firms who produced these goods for Remington. When Remington decided to start producing ribbons themselves, the Underwoods apparently decided to get into the business of manufacturing typewriters.*

*The original Underwood typewriter was invented by German-American Franz X. Wagner, who showed it to entrepreneur John T. Underwood. Underwood supported Wagner and bought the company, recognizing the importance of the machine. Underwood No. 1 and No. 2s, made between 1896 and 1900, had "Wagner Typewriter Co." printed on the back.*

*Underwood started adding addition and subtraction devices to their typewriters in about 1910. During World War II Underwood produced M1 carbines for the war effort. Olivetti bought a controlling interest in Underwood in 1959, and completed the merger in October 1963, becoming known in the US as Olivetti-Underwood with headquarters in New York City, and entering the electromechanical calculator business. The Underwood name last appeared on Olivetti portable typewriters produced in Spain in the 1980s.*

-- Reference: Wikipedia.org

### [6] "...personal Hell..."

*"The modern English word Hell is derived from Old English hel, helle (about 725 AD) and ultimately from Proto-Germanic halja, meaning "one who covers up or hides something".*

-- Reference: Wikipedia.org

### [7] "...Top Secret"...

*"**Top Secret** is the highest acknowledged level of classified information in many countries, where it is defined as material that would cause "exceptionally grave damage" to national security if disclosed. The term **top secret** can be applied to information, actions, organizations, projects, etc. of which any knowledge is highly restricted."*

-- Reference: Wikipedia.org

### [8] "... self-administered euthanasia...."

*"The term euthanasia comes from the greek words "eu" and "thanatos" which combined means "well-death" or "dying well". Hippocrates mentions euthanasia in the Hippocratic Oath, which was written between 400 and 300 B.C. The ancient Greeks and Romans generally did not believe that life needed to be preserved at any cost and were, in consequence, tolerant of suicide in cases where no relief could be offered to the dying or, in the case of the Stoics and Epicureans, where a person no longer cared for his life."*

-- Reference: Wikipedia.org

### [9] "...County Meath, Ireland..."

*"Meath (the "middle") was formed from the eastern part of the province of Midhe - see Kings of Mide - but now forms part of Leinster. Historically this province of Meath included all of the*

*current county as well as all of Westmeath and parts of Cavan, Longford, Louth, Offaly, Dublin and Kildare. The High King of Ireland sat at Tara in Meath. The archaeological complex of Brú na Bóinne is 5,000 years old and includes the burial sites of Newgrange, Knowth and Dowth, in the northeast of the county."*

-- Reference: Wikipedia.org

[10] **"...The Great Mound" at Knowth, and Dowth, the "Fairy Mound of Darkness". These are sacred "cairns" or massive stone structures that were erected about 3,700 BCE and engraved with indecipherable hieroglyphs..."**

*"The astronomical significance of Kerbstone 51, the "Stone of the Seven Suns", at Dowth: If moonlight were to shine on the back stone of the eastern passage at Knowth, it would illuminate a map of the moon itself, the world's oldest known depiction of the lunar maria\*. The carvings are about 4800 years old. The next oldest depiction of the maria known to science is that by Leonardo da Vinci in about 1505 AD.*

*\* **Lunar maria** (singular: mare, two syllables) are large, dark, basaltic plains on Earth's Moon, formed by ancient volcanic eruptions. They were dubbed maria, Latin for "seas", by early astronomers who mistook them for actual seas. They are less reflective than the "highlands" as a result of their iron-rich compositions, and hence appear dark to the naked eye. The maria cover about 16% of the lunar surface, mostly on the near-side visible from Earth. The few maria on the far-side are much smaller, residing mostly in very large craters where only a small amount of flooding occurred. -- Reference: Wikipedia*

*The mythology about Dowth speaks of a bull and seven cows, it seems likely that the site has some connection with the constellation of Taurus, the Bull, which contains the open cluster the Pleiades, otherwise known as "The Seven Sisters". This constellation was very important around the year 3000BC, when the Boyne Valley mounds were being constructed, as it contained the Sun on the Spring Equinox, that very important moment of the year when the Sun's path along the ecliptic crossed the celestial equator heading northwards. It is the Sun's position among the zodiac stars at this time which determines the current 'age' – i.e. the "Age of Taurus".*

*Another interesting phenomenon which occurs at this time is what is known to astronomers as a 'heliacal rising' of the Pleiades. This happens when the stars in question rise at the eastern horizon but are quickly lost in the glare of the rising sun. It is interesting to note that the Egyptians, and the Dogon tribe in Africa, (See: **The Oz Factors**) among others, used the same Dowth-like 'sun-wheel' symbols to signify a heliacal rising.*

*If these 'sun-wheel' symbols do represent the heliacal rising of the Pleiades, it tells us something very significant about the Neolithic people – they were aware of the great cycle of precession, the slow wobble of the Earth's axis which causes the celestial pole to shift over time, resulting in the Vernal Equinox point, that place where the Sun crosses the celestial equator, moving backwards, or westwards, through the Zodiac over a huge 25,800-year period. This Vernal point moves just one degree (about two widths of the full moon) every 72 years, and spends on average 2,150 years in each of the twelve constellations of the Zodiac."*

-- Reference: http://www.mythicalireland.com/ancientsites/dowth/candlelight.html

[11] **"...In ancient Irish religion and mythology this (Tara) was the sacred place of dwelling for the "gods"..."**

" Sitting on top of the King's Seat (Forradh) of Temair is the most famous of Tara's monuments - Ireland's ancient coronation stone - the Lia Fail or "Stone of Destiny", which was brought here according to mythology by the godlike people, the Tuatha Dé Danann, as one of their sacred objects. It was said to roar when touched by the rightful king of Tara.

A new theory suggests Tara was the ancient capital of the lost kingdom of Atlantis. The mythical land of Atlantis was Ireland, according to a new book.  There are a large number of monuments and earthen structures on the Hill of Tara. The earliest settlement at the site was in the Neolithic, and the Mound of the Hostages was constructed in or around 2500BC."

-- Reference:  http://www.mythicalireland.com/ancientsites/tara/

[12]  "...the Military - Industrial Complex that President Eisenhower warned us about in his farewell address..."

"A **military-industrial complex** (MIC) is composed of a nation's armed forces, its suppliers of weapons systems, supplies and services, and its civil government.

The term "MIC" is most often used in reference to the United States, where it gained popularity after its use in the farewell address of President Dwight D. Eisenhower. In the penultimate draft of the address, **Eisenhower initially used the term *military-industrial-congressional complex*,** and thus indicated the essential role that the United States Congress plays in the propagation of the military industry.  But, it is said, that the president chose to strike the word *congressional* in order to placate members of the legislative branch of the federal government.

It is sometimes used more broadly to include the entire network of contracts and flows of money and resources among individuals as well as institutions of the defense contractors, The Pentagon, and the Congress and Executive branch. This sector is intrinsically prone to Principal-agent problem, moral hazard, and rent seeking. Cases of political corruption have also surfaced with regularity.

**President of the United States** (and former General of the Army) **Dwight D. Eisenhower** later used the term in his **Farewell Address to the Nation on January 17, 1961**:

"A vital element in keeping the peace is our military establishment. Our arms must be mighty, ready for instant action, so that no potential aggressor may be tempted to risk his own destruction...

This conjunction of an immense military establishment and a large arms industry is new in the American experience. The total influence — economic, political, even spiritual — is felt in every city, every statehouse, every office of the federal government. We recognize the imperative need for this development. Yet we must not fail to comprehend its grave implications. Our toil, resources and livelihood are all involved; so is the very structure of our society.

In the councils of government, we must guard against the acquisition of unwarranted influence, whether sought or unsought, by the **military-industrial complex**. The potential for the disastrous rise of misplaced power exists and will persist.

We must never let the weight of this combination endanger our liberties or democratic processes. We should take nothing for granted. Only an alert and knowledgeable citizenry can compel the proper meshing of the huge industrial and military machinery of defense with our peaceful methods and goals so that security and liberty may prosper together."

-- Reference: Wikipedia.org

[13] "... Roswell Army Air Field (RAAF)..."

"In May 1946, the Army Air Forces (AAF) gave SAC the responsibility of delivering the atomic bomb. Only one of the command's bombardment units, the 509th at Walker Air Force Base (then Roswell Field) in New Mexico, was trained and ready for the atomic bomb mission. The 509th Wing, training on the B-29 aircraft, dropped the first atomic bomb on Japan."

-- Reference: http://www.strategic-air-command.com/bases/Walker_AFB.htm

[14] "...July 8, 1947, the Roswell Army Air Field (RAAF) issued a press release stating that personnel from the field's 509th Bomb Group had recovered a crashed "flying disc" from a ranch near Roswell, New Mexico..."

THE FOLLOWING LIST OF WITNESSES AND TESTIMONY REGARDING THE "CRASHED FLYING DISC" INCIDENT THAT MRS. MACELROY DESCRIBES IN HER LETTER:

NOTE: Testimonial, Signed Affidavits, Photos And Other Resource Materials About The Incident Can Be Viewed At The Following Website:

-- http://roswellproof.homestead.com/index.html

(Copyright ©2001 by David Rudiak. E-Mail: drudiak@lmi.net )

"When we look at the contents of the message in conjunction with witness testimony, the evidence clearly points to an actual flying saucer crash, as astonishing as this conclusion may seem to many.

This testimony is gone into in much greater detail elsewhere in this Website. It consists primarily of numerous and consistent descriptions of highly anomalous debris and to a lesser extent of alien bodies. Here are a few key witnesses:

Major Jesse Marcel: Then the intelligence chief at Roswell and the first to investigate sheep rancher Mack Brazel's find, Marcel confirmed in a number of interviews 30 years later that the crash debris had highly anomalous properties and was "not of this Earth." Marcel also spoke of Ramey's weather balloon cover-up at Fort Worth. Note particularly highly laudatory post-Roswell evaluations by base commander Col. William Blanchard, Gen. Ramey, and future USAF Chief of Staff Col. John Ryan.

Lt. Walter Haut: Former Roswell base public information officer who issued the base press release. Haut's "deathbed" sealed affidavit has just been published. In it he confesses to seeing the spacecraft and bodies in base Hangar 84/P-3 and tells us the mysterious press release was General Ramey's idea to divert press and public attention away from the closer and more important craft/body site.

**Sgt Frederick Benthal:** *Army photographer flown in from Washington D.C., said he photographed alien bodies in a tent at crash site and saw large quantities of crash debris being hauled away in trucks.*

**PFC Elias Benjamin:** *Roswell MP, said he escorted the alien bodies from the heavily guarded base Hangar P-3 to the base hospital, and saw a live one being worked on by doctors; was threatened afterwards if he didn't keep quiet.*

**1st Lt. Chester P. Barton:** *A crypto specialist and assigned to an MP unit, Barton said he was ordered to the crash site 45 minutes north of town to check on the cleanup, saw a football-field-size burn impact area heavily guarded by MPs, scattered metal debris, was told radiation was at the site, heard archeologists had first discovered it, and also heard bodies were taken to base hospital and then to Fort Worth. Because of what he saw, he knew that the balloon explanation was ridiculous and there had been a cover-up. However, Barton was unusual in being a flying saucer crash skeptic, instead thinking that it was maybe a B-29 crash and nuclear accident.*

**Bill Brazel Jr.:** *Rancher Mack Brazel's son, Bill Brazel independently corroborated many details of Marcel's testimony, including the strange debris, the large, elongated debris field, and his father's story of an explosion in the middle of a violent electrical storm.*

**Louis Rickett:** *One of the regular Army CIC agents in Marcel's office, Rickett confirmed the anomalous quality of the debris, a major cleanup operation at Brazel's ranch, high secrecy, and being involved in a subsequent investigation to determine the trajectory of the craft. He was also told by others about the shape of the main craft. Like Chester Barton, he placed the main impact site a 45 minute drive north of Roswell.*

**Brig. Gen. Arthur Exon:** *Though not a direct participant, Exon was stationed at Wright Field at the time, over flew the area soon afterwards, and was later commanding officer of Wright-Patterson AFB. Exon when first interviewed flatly stated, "Roswell was the recovery of a craft from space." Among other things, he confirmed the existence of two main crash sites. Exon also said he heard that bodies were recovered and confirmed the debris was highly anomalous based on testing done by labs at Wright-Patterson. Exon added that he was aware of other crash-recoveries that occurred while he was C/O at Wright-Patterson.*

**Steven Lovekin** *(served in the White House Army Signal Corp during Eisenhower and Kennedy administrations, 1959-1961) Although like Exon not a direct participant, Lovekin said he received 1959 Pentagon briefings and being shown a metallic beam with symbols from a 1947 N.M. crash (presumably Roswell) plus being told of **either 3 or 5 aliens being recovered, one initially alive.** He also said he was shown very compelling photographic and radar evidence of UFOs. He also testified of the threats against military personnel given this information if they were to publicly reveal it. Finally, he told of Eisenhower's concern over losing control of the situation with power falling into the hands of private corporations given access to the materials.*

**Brig. Gen. Thomas Dubose:** *Gen. Ramey's Chief of Staff in 1947, Dubose handled the high-level phone communications between Roswell, Fort Worth, and Washington. Dubose went on record many times about the high secrecy involved (including the matter going directly to the White House), receiving direct orders from Washington to instigate a cover-up, Gen. Ramey's weather balloon cover story, and a highly secret shipment of debris from Roswell to Fort Worth, Washington, and Wright Field. Dubose's damning testimony made him a complete nonentity in the Air Force's 1995 Roswell report, which didn't even bother to* identify him in the photos taken of Gen. Ramey with his weather balloon. (Visit the website to view Dubose's Air Force biography, his sworn affidavit, and a more detailed discussion of his testimony which the Air Force was so eager to avoid.)

**Sgt. Robert Slusher and PFC Lloyd Thompson:** Crew members on a mysterious B-29 flight from Roswell to Fort Worth on July 9, 1947, transporting a large wooden crate in the bomb bay surrounded by an armed guard. Upon arrival, the plane was met by high brass and a mortician. This is probably the flight referred to in the Ramey memo that would ship whatever was "in the 'disc'" to Fort Worth by a B-29 Special Transport plane. New witnesses to the flight, including daughter of the head security guard, saying that alien bodies were inside the crate.

**Frank Kaufmann:** A highly controversial witness claiming to be one of the exclusive members of a special CIC-team (Army Counter-Intelligence Corp) in charge of the Roswell recovery operation. Nonetheless, some of Kaufmann's claims seem to be corroborated by the Ramey message, including the existence of such a team, the recovery of an intact "disk" with bodies inside about 35 miles north of Roswell base, and the special team being responsible for the initial Roswell base press release. Kaufmann also testified to knowing of a wooden crate guarded in a hangar with the bodies packed inside awaiting shipment, perhaps the same crate independently described by Slusher and Thompson.

**Glenn Dennis:** A Roswell mortician and another highly controversial witness, Dennis spoke of receiving strange calls from the base about preservation techniques and child-sized coffins. Dennis also claimed to be at the Roswell base hospital, seeing unusual debris in the back of an ambulance including a pod-like object perhaps alluded to in the Ramey message, and being threatened. He also claimed to know a Roswell nurse who assisted in a preliminary autopsy at the base hospital and who described the aliens to him.

The nurse subsequently disappeared. However, attempts to identify the mystery nurse have proven to be a complete failure after Dennis provided a false name. However, also see some corroborative evidence immediately following Dennis' affidavit, such as David Wagnon, a medical technician, who remembered the nurse fitting Dennis' description, as did Pete Anaya, who said the pretty nurse he knew and encountered at the base hangar telling him of the bodies there subsequently disappeared.

Roswell police chief L. M. Hall stated that Dennis was telling him of calls from the base about small coffins for the aliens only a few days after the crashed saucer story broke in the Roswell papers. Similarly, **S/Sgt. Milton Sprouse** also said he heard of the coffin call from Dennis and a medic friend told him of the alien bodies and autopsy at the hospital.

The medic and doctors and **nurses involved in the autopsy all immediately were transferred and their fate remained unknown.** In addition, other independent witnesses have provided first and second-hand testimony about small bodies being found with details very similar to those provided by Dennis, including **Walter Haut, Frederick Benthal, Eli Benjamin,** and relatives of "Pappy" Henderson.

**Family and friends of Oliver "Pappy" Henderson:** Henderson was one of the senior pilots at Roswell. When the first public stories of a Roswell saucer crash began circulating in 1981, Henderson confided to family and friends of being the pilot who flew bodies of the aliens and crash wreckage to Wright Field. He also claimed to have seen the craft and bodies, and provided a description of the aliens.

**Sgt. Robert E. Smith:** *A member of an air transport unit at Roswell, Smith said he helped load crates filled with debris for transport by C-54's, including one flown by Henderson and his crew. Smith was also among the witnesses to describe the mysterious "memory foil" which he said was in the crates. He further described strangers to the base dressed in plainclothes and flashing ID cards for some unknown project, perhaps part of the special CIC-team mentioned in the Ramey memo and by Frank Kaufmann. Finally he claimed that distant cousin of his was with the Secret Service and was there at the base representing President Truman. (The same name was also provided by Kaufmann.)*

**S/Sgt. Earl V. Fulford:** *In the engineering squadron, Fulford said he participated in the large debris field cleanup guarded by MPs, handled the mysterious "memory foil," saw what may have been the tarped crash object on a flatbed truck being towed to Hangar 84, and in the middle of the night was made to load a large wooden crate into an idling C-54.*

**Earl Zimmerman:** *Formerly with AFOSI (AF counterintelligence). While in officers' club heard many rumors about flying saucer crash and of it being investigated under the guise of an airplane crash. Several times observed Gen. Ramey and Charles Lindbergh being at base unannounced in connection with this. Like Robert Smith, spoke of seeing an unknown CIC man being at base. Col. Blanchard told him it was OK. Later worked with astronomer Dr. Lincoln LaPaz and corroborated story of Roswell CIC man Lewis Rickett that LaPaz investigated Roswell afterwards with the help of the CIC to try to determine objects trajectory. Again an airplane crash was the cover story.*

**Lt. Robert Shirkey:** *Then the assistant operations officer, Shirkey witnessed the loading of the*
*B-29 that took Major Marcel to Fort Worth to see Gen. Ramey. He said he saw boxes of debris being carried on board, including an I-beam with raised markings and a large piece of metal, brushed stainless steel in color, obviously not part of a tinfoil radar target. He was told it was from a flying saucer. Along with witness Robert Porter, he also stated that the plane's pilot was Deputy Commanding Officer Lt. Col. Payne Jennings, who was now the Acting C/O with Col. Blanchard officially on leave. Nine days later, Shirkey was abruptly transferred to the Philippines to a post that didn't exist. Jennings personally flew him to his next assignment.*

**Sgt. Robert Porter:** *Was on Marcel's flight to Fort Worth and was handed wrapped packages of debris samples. Said that flight was piloted by Deputy base commander Jennings. He was told on board that the crash material was from a flying saucer. Later, they told him it was a weather balloon. Said debris was loaded onto another plane.*

**Art McQuiddy:** *Former editor of the Roswell Morning Dispatch. Said base commander Col. Blanchard admitted to authorizing base press release and of strange material being found by his men.*

**Judd Roberts:** *Co-owner of Roswell radio station KGFL owner. Spoke of how they wire-recorded an interview with rancher Mack Brazel for later airing, then withdrew it about receiving warnings from Washington about losing their license. Testified to seeing a military cordon around Brazel crash site.*

**William Woody:** *Another witness to a military cordon thrown up up north of town along the main highway, blocking access to the west.*

**Lydia Sleppy:** *Albuquerque teletype operator and one of earliest witnesses. Stated that the story phoned in from field by Roswell radio reporter Johnny McBoyle about seeing the*

163

crashed saucer and hearing of bodies was intercepted and cut-off on the teletype wire by the FBI.

**Loretta Proctor:** Neighbor of rancher Mack Brazel. Brazel told her and her husband of finding strange material before going to Roswell, and showing them a wood-like piece that couldn't be cut or burned. They advised him to go to Roswell and report it. Brazel was detained at the base and complained bitterly of his treatment when he returned.

**Sally Strickland Tadolini:** Another neighbor of Brazel's. Although only 9 years old at the time, remembered Mack Brazel's grown son Bill Brazel bringing over a piece of metallic-looking debris with memory properties to show to her family (incident corroborated by her mother). Described it as tough, resembled a smooth "fabric" like silk or satin, and, of course, unfolded itself to its original shape after being crumpled up. Independently corroborated Bill Brazel's story of finding material and also Marcel's of a metallic fabric material with memory properties which he could blow through (therefore not balloon material). Also remembered the adults talking about Mack Brazel's bad treatment at hands of military.

**Dr. Jesse Marcel Jr.:** 11-year old son of Major Marcel in 1947, recounts how his father woke up his mother and himself in the middle of the night when he returned from the debris field, showing them the pieces of a "flying saucer." Among other material, he distinctly remembers a small metallic "I-beam" with purplish "hieroglyphics."

---

[15] **"... the Commanding General of the Eighth Air Force..."**

"General Roger M. Ramey was a major player in the Roswell Incident, but information on him is hard to come by. Even though he became a fairly important Air Force general in the early 1950s, for some reason the Air Force biographical Web page on their generals doesn't list him.

Ramey was born in 1903 in Sulphur Springs, Texas, but grew up in Denton, Texas, about 40 miles north of Fort Worth. He graduated from North Texas State Teachers College in Denton and wanted to study medicine. But he won a rodeo competition and "preferred working on a ranch to books."

He was the mess sergeant in a local National Guard unit, and the captain insisted young "Cowboy" Ramey take the competitive examination for entrance to the U.S. Military Academy, winning the West Point appointment. He entered West Point in 1924.

**July 26, 1946:** Ramey wrote Roswell intelligence chief Major Jesse Marcel a commendation for his work during Crossroads, citing his important contributions to security, his handling of complex intelligence matters, and the perfection of his staff briefings. A year later, Marcel was to handle the initial investigation into the strange crash debris found by rancher Mac Brazel near Roswell and fly the debris to Fort Worth for examination by Gen. Ramey.

**June 30, 1947:** Ramey and his intelligence chief were giving press interviews and debunking the new flying saucer phenomenon.

**July 6, 1947:** Ramey spent all day attending an air show in his home town of Denton, TX (and probably visiting relatives). Meanwhile, back in Fort Worth with Ramey away from the base, his chief of staff, Brig. Gen. Thomas Dubose, said he first learned of the find at Roswell by phone from SAC acting chief of staff Gen. McMullen. According to Dubose,

McMullen ordered debris samples flown immediately to Washington by "colonel courier," first stopping in Fort Worth. The whole operation was carried out under the strictest secrecy, said Dubose. McMullen ordered him not to tell anyone, not even Ramey.

*July 8, 1947:* The infamous Roswell base flying disk press release and Ramey's subsequent debunking of it as a weather balloon. According to Dubose, McMullen ordered the cover-up in another phone call to Dubose from Washington. Both Dubose and Roswell intelligence chief Jesse Marcel said the weather balloon was not what Marcel brought from Roswell, being nothing but a cover story to get rid of the press.

-- Reference: Wikipedia.org

### [16] "... U.S. Women's Army Air Force..."

"The Women's Army Corps (WAC) was the women's branch of the US Army. It was created as an auxiliary unit, the Women's Army Auxiliary Corps in 1942, and converted to full status as the WAC in 1943. About 150,000 American women served in the WAAC and WAC during World War II. They were the first women other than nurses to serve with the Army."

-- Reference: Wikipedia.org

### [17] "...Flight Nurse"...

"The Flight Nurse Badge is issued in two different versions, one for the Navy and the other for the Air Force. To be awarded the Flight Nurse Badge, a service member must be a commissioned officer and a Registered Nurse and must also complete training normally befitting the award of the Aircrew Badge. The Flight Nurse Badge is then presented after a probationary period of in-flight instruction and observation."

-- Reference: Wikipedia.org

### [18] ..."Sheridan Cavitt of the Counter Intelligence Officer"...
(Please see the following Footnote)

### [19] "... I was asked to accompany Mr. Cavitt, the Counter Intelligence officer, to the crash site as the driver of his vehicle ...

"Most of the testimony in this (the following) document is from the 1992 book "Crash at Corona" by Stanton Friedman and Don Berliner, published in the United States by Paragon House. That book contains lots of other interesting material, including material regarding another crash site in New Mexico.

*Sequence of Events:*

On July 2, 1947, during the evening, a flying saucer crashed on the Foster Ranch near Corona, New Mexico. The crash occurred during a severe thunderstorm. (The military base nearest the crash site is in Roswell, New Mexico; hence, Roswell is more closely associated with this event than Corona, even though Corona is closer to the crash site.)

On July 3, 1947, William "Mac" Brazel (rhymes with "frazzle") and his 7-year-old neighbor Dee Proctor found the remains of the crashed flying saucer. Brazel was foreman of the Foster Ranch. The pieces were spread out over a large area, perhaps more than half a mile long. When Brazel drove Dee back home, he showed a piece of the wreckage to Dee's parents, Floyd and Loretta Proctor. They all agreed the piece was unlike anything they had ever seen.

On July 6, 1947, Brazel showed pieces of the wreckage to Chaves County Sheriff George Wilcox. Wilcox called Roswell Army Air Field (AAF) and talked to Major Jesse Marcel, the intelligence officer. Marcel drove to the sheriff's office and inspected the wreckage. Marcel reported to his commanding officer, Colonel William "Butch" Blanchard. Blanchard ordered Marcel to get someone from the Counter Intelligence Corps, and to proceed to the ranch with Brazel, and to collect as much of the wreckage as they could load into their two vehicles.

Soon after this, military police arrived at the sheriff's office, collected the wreckage Brazel had left there, and delivered the wreckage to Blanchard's office. The wreckage was then flown to Eighth Air Force headquarters in Fort Worth, and from there to Washington.

Meanwhile, Marcel and Sheridan Cavitt of the Counter Intelligence Corps drove to the ranch with Mac Brazel. They arrived late in the evening. They spent the night in sleeping bags in a small out-building on the ranch, and in the morning proceeded to the crash site.

On July 7, 1947, Marcel and Cavitt collected wreckage from the crash site. After filling Cavitt's vehicle with wreckage, Marcel told Cavitt to go on ahead, that Marcel would collect more wreckage, and they would meet later back at Roswell AAF. Marcel filled his vehicle with wreckage. On the way back to the air field, Marcel stopped at home to show his wife and son the strange material he had found.

On July 7, 1947, around 4:00 pm, Lydia Sleppy at Roswell radio station KSWS began transmitting a story on the teletype machine regarding a crashed flying saucer out on the Foster Ranch. Transmission was interrupted, seemingly by the FBI.

On July 8, 1947, in the morning, Marcel and Cavitt arrived back at Roswell AAF with two carloads of wreckage. Marcel accompanied this wreckage, or most it, on a flight to Fort Worth AAF.

On July 8, 1947, around noon, Colonel Blanchard at Roswell AAF ordered Second Lieutenant Walter Haut to issue a press release telling the country that the Army had found the remains of a crashed a flying saucer. Haut was the public information officer for the 509th Bomb Group at Roswell AAF. Haut delivered the press release to Frank Joyce at radio station KGFL. Joyce waited long enough for Haut to return to the base, then called Haut there to confirm the story. Joyce then sent the story on the Western Union wire to the United Press bureau.

On July 8, 1947, in the afternoon, General Clemence McMullen in Washington spoke by telephone with Colonel (later Brigadier General) Thomas DuBose in Fort Worth, chief of staff to Eighth Air Force Commander General Roger Ramey. McMullen ordered DuBose to tell Ramey to quash the flying saucer story by creating a cover story, and to send some of the crash material immediately to Washington.

On July 8, 1947, in the afternoon, General Roger Ramey held a press conference at Eighth Air Force headquarters in Fort Worth in which he announced that what had crashed at

*Corona was a weather balloon, not a flying saucer. To make this story convincing, he showed the press the remains of a damaged weather balloon that he claimed was the actual wreckage from the crash site. (Apparently, the obliging press did not ask why the Army hurriedly transported weather balloon wreckage to Fort Worth, Texas, site of the press conference, from the crash site in a remote area of New Mexico.)*

*The only newspapers that carried the initial flying saucer version of the story were evening papers from the Midwest to the West, including the Chicago Daily News, the Los Angeles Herald Express, the San Francisco Examiner, and the Roswell Daily Record. The New York Times, the Washington Post, and the Chicago Tribune were morning papers and so carried only the cover-up story the next morning.*

*At some point, a large group of soldiers were sent to the debris field on the Foster Ranch, including a lot of MPs whose job was to limit access to the field. A wide search was launched well beyond the limits of the debris field. Within a day or two, a few miles from the debris field, the main body of the flying saucer was found, and a mile or two from that several bodies of small humanoids were found.*

*The military took Mac Brazel into custody for about a week, during which time he was seen on the streets of Roswell with a military escort. His behavior aroused the curiosity of friends when he passed them without any sign of recognition. Following this period of detention, Brazel repudiated his initial story."*

--- Reference: http://ufo.jack.sk/unidentified-flying-objects/roswell/

[20] **"...I discovered that one of the personnel on board the craft had survived the crash... "**

**The following is a verbatim copy** of the signed Affidavit submitted on 8-7-1991 by Glenn Dennis, a mortician, in Roswell, N.M. at the time of the incident described in the letter from Mrs. MacElroy: (**PLEASE NOTE**: Mrs. MacElroy is **NOT** the same nurse that Mr. Dennis mentions in his Affidavit. Although no official identification has been made, several witnesses have identified "Nurse X" as 1st Lt. Adeline "Eileen" Fanton.)

### *"AFFIDAVIT OF GLENN DENNIS*

*(1) My name is Glenn Dennis*

*(2) My address is: XXXXXXXXXX*

*(3) I am ( ) employed as: _____ ( ) retired,*

*(4) In July 1947, I was a mortician, working for the Ballard Funeral Home in Roswell, which had a contract to provide mortuary services for the Roswell Army Air Field. One afternoon, around 1:15 or 1:30, I received a call from the base mortuary officer who asked what was the smallest size hermetically sealed casket that we had in stock. He said, "We need to know this in case something comes up in the future." He asked how long it would take to get one, and I assured him I could get one for him the following day. He said he would call back if they needed one.*

*(5) About 45 minutes to an hour later, he called back and asked me to describe the preparation for bodies that had been lying out on the desert for a period of time. Before I*

could answer, he said he specifically wanted to know what effect the preparation procedures would have on the body's chemical compounds, blood and tissues. I explained that our chemicals were mainly strong solutions of formaldehyde and water, and that the procedure would probably alter the body's chemical composition. I offered to come out to the base to assist with any problem he might have, but he reiterated that the information was for future use. I suggested that if he had such a situation that I would try to freeze the body in dry ice for storage and transportation.

(6) Approximately a hour or an hour and 15 minutes later, I got a call to transport a serviceman who had a laceration on his head and perhaps a fractured nose. I gave him first aid and drove him out to the base. I got there around 5:00 PM.

(7) Although I was a civilian, I usually had free access on the base because they knew me. I drove the ambulance around to the back of the base infirmary and parked it next to another ambulance. The door was open and inside I saw some wreckage. There were several pieces which looked like the bottom of a canoe, about three feet in length. It resembled stainless steel with a purple hue, as if it had been exposed to high temperature. There was some strange-looking writing on the material resembling Egyptian hieroglyphics. Also there were two MPs present.

(8) I checked the airman in and went to the staff lounge to have a Coke. I intended to look for a nurse, a 2nd Lieutenant, who had been commissioned about three months earlier right out of college. She was 23 years of age at the time (I was 22). I saw her coming out of one of the examining rooms with a cloth over her mouth. She said, "My gosh, get out of here or you're going to be in a lot of trouble." She went into another door where a Captain stood. He asked me who I was and what I was doing here. I told him, and he instructed me to stay there. I said, "It looks like you've got a crash; would you like me to get ready?" He told me to stay right there. Then two MPs came up and began to escort me out of the infirmary. They said they had orders to follow me out to the funeral home.

(9) We got about 10 or 15 feet when I heard a voice say, "We're not through with that SOB. Bring him back." There was another Captain, a redhead with the meanest-looking eyes I had ever seen, who said, "You did not see anything, there was no crash here, and if you say anything you could get into a lot of trouble." I said, "Hey look mister, I'm a civilian and you can't do a damn thing to me." He said, "Yes we can; somebody will be picking your bones out of the sand." There was a black Sergeant with a pad in his hand who said, "He would make good dog food for our dogs." The Captain said, "Get the SOB out." The MPs followed me back to the funeral home.

(10) The next day, I tried to call the nurse to see what was going on. About 11:00 AM, she called the funeral home and said, "I need to talk to you." We agreed to meet at the officers club. She was very upset. She said, "Before I talk to you, you have to give me a sacred oath that you will never mention my name, because I could get into a lot of trouble." I agreed.

(11) She said she had gone to get supplies in a room where two doctors were performing a prelimary autopsy. The doctors said they needed her to take notes during the procedure. She said she had never smelled anything so horrible in her life, and the sight was the most gruesome she had ever seen. She said, "This was something no one has ever seen." As she spoke, I was concerned that she might go into shock.

(12) She drew me a diagram of the bodies, including an arm with a hand that had only four fingers; the doctors noted that on the end of the fingers were little pads resembling suction

cups. She said the head was disproportionately large for the body; the eyes were deeply set; the skulls were flexible; the nose was concave with only two orifices; the mouth was a fine slit, and the doctors said there was heavy cartilage instead of teeth. The ears were only small orifices with flaps. They had no hair, and the skin was black--perhaps due to exposure in the sun. She gave me the drawings.

(13) There were three bodies; two were very mangled and dismembered, as if destroyed by predators; one was fairly intact. They were three-and-a-half to four feet tall. She told me the doctors said: "This isn't anything we've ever see before; there's nothing in the medical textbooks like this." She said she and the doctors became ill. They had to turn off the air conditioning and were afraid the smell would go through the hospital. They had to move the operation to an airplane hangar.

(14) I drove her back to the officers' barracks. The next day I called the hospital to see how she was, and they said she wasn't available. I tried to get her for several days, and finally got one of the nurses who said the Lieutenant had been transferred out with some other personnel. About 10 days to two weeks later, I got a letter from her with an APO number. She indicated we could discuss the incident by letter in the future. I wrote back to her and about two weeks later the letter came back marked "Return to Sender--DECEASED." Later, one of the nurses at the base said the rumor was that she and five other nurses had been on a training mission and had been killed in a plane crash.

(15) Sheriff George Wilcox and my father were very close friends. The Sheriff went to my folks' house the morning after the events at the base and said to my father, "I don't know what kind of trouble Glenn's in, but you tell your son that he doesn't know anything and hasn't seen anything at the base." He added, "They want you and your wife's name, and they want your and your children's addresses." My father immediately drove to the funeral home and asked me what kind of trouble I was in. He related the conversation with Sheriff Wilcox, and so I told him about the events of the previous day. He is the only person to whom I have told this story until recently.

(16) I had filed away the sketches the nurse gave me that day. Recently, at the request of a researcher, I tried to locate my personal files at the funeral home, but they had all been destroyed.

(17) I have not been paid or given anything of value to make this statement, which is the truth to the best of my recollection.

Signed: Glenn Dennis
Date: 8-7-91"

-- Reference: http://roswellproof.homestead.com/Dennis.html
(Copyright ©2001 by David Rudiak. E-Mail: drudiak@lmi.net )

---

[21] "...telepathic thought..."

"Telepathy, from the Greek τελε, tele meaning "remote" and πάθεια, patheia meaning "to be affected by", describes the purported transfer of information on thoughts or feelings between individuals by means other than the five classical senses. The term was coined in 1882 by the classical scholar Fredric W. H. Myers, a founder of the Society for Psychical Research, specifically to replace the earlier expression thought-transference. A person who is able to make use of telepathy is said to be able to read the minds of others. Telepathy, along with psychokinesis forms the main branches of parapsychological research, and many studies seeking to detect and understand telepathy have been done within the field.

Telepathy is a common theme in fiction and science fiction, with many superheroes and supervillains having telepathic abilities. Such abilities include both sensing the thoughts of others, and controlling the minds of other people. Transhumanists believe that technologically enabled telepathy, called "techlepathy", will be the inevitable future of humanity, and seek to develop practical, safe devices for directly connecting human nervous systems."

-- Reference: Wikipedia.org

[22] **"...I was the only women at the site..."**

*"Another story about the alien bodies and a vanishing nurse came from Pete and Ruben Anaya, who said they picked up N.M. Lt. Governor Joseph Montoya outside the large base hangar. Besides the hangar being heavily guarded by MPs, they said there was a base nurse (or maybe two different nurses) who came outside the hangar and spoke briefly with them. Ruben said she told him that the bodies were "not from this world" and then noticed one of them moving. Ruben said he then went to take a look and also glimpsed two small bodies from a distance under sheets inside the hangar and one of them moving. He described the nurse he spoke to as blondish and heavyset. [Note: Of the five nurses that are pictured in the base yearbook from around June/July 1947, none of them appear blondish or heavyset, though.*

*In contrast, Pete Anaya said he knew the nurse he spoke to from the Officer's Club (his brother Ruben worked there as a cook), had danced with her once the previous Halloween at a party, said she resembled his wife Mary, and was a beautiful women with beautiful hair. He wanted to go inside the hangar to see what was going on, and she told him he didn't want to see anything. After that, he said he never saw her again. (Source: Tim Shawcross, The Roswell File, 1997)*

*Former Roswell police chief **L.M. Hall** remembered Dennis telling him only a few days after the newspaper stories of the crashed flying saucer, about strange calls from the base for child-size caskets "to ship or bury those aliens."*

*Another witness that recently came forth to corroborate parts of Dennis' story was **S/Sgt. Milton Sprouse**, then a B-29 crew chief with the 830th Bomb Squadron. Sprouse said he spoke to Dennis several years later while Dennis handled a funeral for a friend. Dennis told him he had received a call from the base for five children's caskets for a crash that had happened 2 or 3 days before. Thus it seems that Dennis' story of the child casket call is not of recent origin but dates back to the original event itself.*

*Sprouse said the bodies were taken to a hangar heavily guarded by MPs with machine guns. He also said he knew something about the autopsy initially described by Dennis. A fellow staff sergeant in his barracks, who worked as an emergency room medic at the base hospital, was called out there. When he came back he related that an autopsy on one or two of the "humanoid bodies" had been carried out by two doctors and two nurses. His friend said he had seen the bodies. Similar to Dennis' nurse, the sergeant was transferred the following day and nobody ever found out what became of him.*

*Sprouse also heard that the doctors and nurses involved with the autopsy were also transferred and nobody found out what became of them either. Five members of his ground crew were also sent to the ranch to help clean up the debris field. They told him the material was "out of this world," including foil that when crumpled returned to its original shape."*

-- Reference: (San Diego Union-Tribune story, 10/26/2007; North County Times story, 9/30/2007 --San Diego, Riverside)

### [23] "...prehensile..."

*"The word is derived from the Latin term prehendere, meaning "to grasp." It is the quality of an organ that has adapted for grasping or holding. Examples of prehensile body parts include the tails of New World monkeys and opossums, the trunks of elephants, the tongues of giraffes, the lips of horses and the proboscides of tapir. The hands of primates are all prehensile to varying degrees, and many species (even a few humans) have prehensile feet as well. The claws of cats are also prehensile. Many extant lizards have prehensile tails (geckos, chameleons, and a species of skink). The fossil record shows prehensile tails in lizards (Simiosauria) going back many million years to the Triassic period .*

*Prehensility is an evolutionary adaptation that has afforded species a great natural advantage in manipulating their environment for feeding, digging, and defense. It enables many animals, such as primates, to use tools in order to complete tasks that would otherwise be impossible without highly specialized anatomy. For example, chimpanzees have the ability to use sticks to fish for termites and grubs. However, not all prehensile organs are applied to tool use- the giraffe tongue, for instance, is instead used in feeding and self-cleaning behaviors."*

-- Reference: Wikipedia.org

### [24] "... able to detect waves or particles beyond the visual spectrum of light."

*The **visible spectrum** (or sometimes called the **optical spectrum**) is the portion of the electromagnetic spectrum that is visible to (can be detected by) the human eye. Electromagnetic radiation in this range of wavelengths is called **visible light** or simply light. A typical human eye will respond to wavelengths in air from about 380 to 750 nm. The corresponding wavelengths in water and other media are reduced by a factor equal to the refractive index. In terms of frequency, this corresponds to a band in the vicinity of 400-790 terahertz. A light-adapted eye generally has its maximum sensitivity at around 555 nm (540 THz), in the green region of the optical spectrum. The spectrum does not, however, contain all the corlors that the human eyes and brain can distinguish. Brown, pink, and magenta are absent, for example, because they need a mix of multiple wavelengths, preferably shades of red.*

*Wavelengths visible to the eye also pass through the "optical window", the region of the electromagnetic spectrum which passes largely unattenuated through the Earth's atmosphere (although blue light is scattered more than red light, which is the reason the sky is blue). The response of the human eye is defined by subjective testing, but the atmospheric windows are defined by physical measurement. The "visible window" is so called because it overlaps the human visible response spectrum; the near infrared windows lie just out of human response window, and the Medium Wavelength and Long Wavelength or Far Infrared are far beyond the human response region.*

*The eyes of many species perceive wavelengths different from the spectrum visible to the human eye. For example, many insects, such as bees, can see light in the ultraviolet, which* is useful for finding nectar in flowers. For this reason, plant species whose life cycles are linked to insect pollination may owe their reproductive success to their appearance in ultraviolet light, rather than how colorful they appear to our eyes."

-- Reference: Wikipedia.org

[25] "... this may have included the full range of the electromagnetic spectrum..."

"The **electromagnetic spectrum** is the range of all possible electromagnetic radiation. The "electromagnetic spectrum" (usually just spectrum) of an object is the characteristic distribution of electromagnetic radiation from that object.

The electromagnetic spectrum extends from below the frequencies used for modern radio (at the long-wavelength end) through gamma radiation (at the short-wavelength end), covering wavelengths from thousands of kilometres down to a fraction the size of an atom. It's thought that the short wavelength limit is the vicinity of the Planck length, and the long wavelength limit is the size of the universe itself, although in principle the spectrum is infinite and continuous."

-- Reference: Wikipedia.org

[26] "... her gaze seemed to penetrate right through me, as though she had "x-ray vision".

"In fictional stories, **X-ray vision** has generally been portrayed as the ability to see through layers of objects at the discretion of the holder of this superpower. People often pretend to have this ability through the use of X-ray glasses, which are a special type of "joke-around" or prank-gag toys with the secret of its "x-ray properties" being unknown. The goal is usually to see through clothing, usually to determine if someone is carrying a concealed weapon, but sometimes for purpose of seeing a person's private parts. In the non-fictional realm, X-rays have many practical uses in the fields of science and medicine. While there are devices currently extant which can "see" through clothing (using terahertz waves), most are quite bulky. However, there are night vision equipped video cameras that can be modified to see through clothing at a frequency just below visible light."

-- Source Reference: Wikipedia.org

[27] ..."Technically, from a medical standpoint, I would say that Airl's body could not even be called "alive"."

"The word "**organism**" may broadly be defined as an assembly of molecules that function as a more or less stable whole and has the properties of life. However, many sources, lexical and scientific, add conditions that are problematic to defining the word.

The Oxford English Dictionary defines an organism as "[an] individual animal, plant, or single-celled life form" This definition problematically excludes non-animal and plant multi-cellular life forms such as some fungi and protista. Less controversially, perhaps, it excludes viruses and theoretically-possible man-made non-organic life forms.

Chambers Online Reference provides a much broader definition: "any living structure, such as a plant, animal, fungus or bacterium, capable of growth and reproduction". The definition "any life form capable of independent reproduction, organic or otherwise" would encompass all cellular life, as well as the possibility of synthetic life capable of independent reproduction, but would exclude viruses, which are dependent on the biochemical machinery of a host cell for reproduction. Some may use a definition that would also include viruses."

-- Source Reference: Wikipedia.org

[28] "...in space there is not gravity..."

"The terms **gravitation** and **gravity** are mostly interchangeable in everyday use, but in scientific usage a distinction may be made. "Gravitation" is a general term describing the attractive influence that all objects with mass exert on each other, while "gravity" specifically refers to a force that is supposed in some theories (such as Newton's) to be the cause of this attraction. By contrast, in general relativity gravitation is due to space-time curvatures that cause inertially moving objects to accelerate towards each other.

**Isaac Newton's theory of universal gravitation** is a physical law describing the gravitational attraction between bodies with mass. It is a part of classical mechanics and was first formulated in Newton's work Philosophiae Naturalis Principia Mathematica, published in 1687. In modern language it states the following:

Every point mass attracts every other point mass by a force pointing along the line intersecting both points. The force is proportional to the product of the two masses and inversely proportional to the square of the distance between the point masses:

where:

- $F$ is the magnitude of the gravitational force between the two point masses,
- $G$ is the gravitational constant,
- $m_1$ is the mass of the first point mass,
- $m_2$ is the mass of the second point mass,
- $r$ is the distance between the two point masses."

-- Reference: Wikipedia.org

[29] "...stenographer..."

"Shorthand is an abbreviated and/or symbolic writing method that increases speed or brevity of writing as compared to a normal method of writing a language. The process of writing in shorthand is called stenography, from the Greek stenos (narrow) and graphē (writing). It has also been called brachygraphy, from Greek brachys (short) and tachygraphy, from Greek tachys (swift, speedy), depending on whether compression or speed of writing is the goal. Many forms of shorthand exist. A typical shorthand system provides symbols or abbreviations for words and common phrases, which allow someone well trained in the system to write as quickly as people speak. Shorthand was used more widely in the past, before the invention of recording and dictation machines."

-- Reference: Wikipedia.org

[30] "... INVESTIGATION OF "BURNING CLOUDS" / RADIATION / EXPLOSIONS..."

"July 16, 1945..." -- The **first test of a nuclear device** was made in the desert north of Alamogordo, New Mexico. **Roswell, New Mexico is only 117 miles from Alamogordo.**

**NOTE**: In 1932 that British explorers in Model-A Fords first visited this area of western Egypt, where they discovered a mysterious yellow-green glass scattered across the surface. Ever since, Libyan Desert Glass has fascinated scientists, who have dreamed up all sorts of ideas about how it could have formed. It's too silica rich to be volcanic. In some ways it resembles the tektites generated by the high pressures associated with asteroid impacts. Vincenzo de Michele visited the Egyptian Museum in Cairo, and noticed that one of King Tutankhamun's jeweled breastplates contained a carved scarab that looked suspiciously like a piece of the glass. A simple optical measurement confirmed the match in 1998. **Nuclear explosions are hot enough to fuse surface materials into glass, much like the first atomic explosion generated yellow - green glass at the Trinity, New Mexico site in 1945.** Many similar sites around the world that are associated with unexplainable "cataclysmic" events reveal the same yellow - green glass. **This "yellow-green glass" has been discovered in strata of rock which contain dinosaur fossils all over the world.**

June 30, 1947 -- "The Evaluation of the Atomic Bomb as a Military Weapon", made by the Atomic Energy Commission was received by President Truman. With a brilliant flourish of suicidal logic, that only the military, politicians other lunatics are capable of fathoming, the recommendation of the Commission, based on explosions of bombs in Alamogordo, New Mexico, on innocent civilians in two Japanese cities, and on the Marshall Islands, was as follows: (Seriously, you can't make this shit up, folks!)

"PART III -- Conclusions and Recommendations

Section One - CONCLUSIONS

1. The Board has reached the following major conclusions:
(1) If used in numbers, atomic bombs not only can nullify any nation's military effort, but can demolish its social and economic structures and prevent their reestablishment for long periods of time. With such weapons, especially if employed in conjunction with other weapons of mass destruction as, for example, pathogenic bacteria, it is quite possible to depopulate vast areas of the earth's surface, leaving only vestigial remnants of man's material works.
(2) The threat of the uncontrolled use of the atomic bomb and of other weapons of mass destruction is a threat to mankind and to civilization. Only the outlawing of all war and the setting up on an adequate international control of weapons of mass destruction can lift this threat from the peoples of the world.
(3) In the absence of absolute guarantees of abiding peace, the United States has not alternative but to continue the manufacture and stockpiling of weapons of nuclear fission and to carry on continuous research and development for their improvement in the means of their delivery."
(REFERENCE: President's Secretary's File, Truman Papers.
( http://www.trumanlibrary.org/whistlestop/study_collections/bomb/large/index.php )

July 8, 1947 -- Alien space craft crashes at Roswell, NM while investigation nuclear testing in the area.-- The Editor

[31] "...trillions..."

One thousand thousand = one million.  ( 1,000,000 )
One thousand million = one billion.  ( 1,000,000,000 )
One thousand billion = one **trillion**.  ( 1,000,000,000,000 )

*"The English names for large numbers are coined from the Latin names for small numbers n by adding the ending -illion suggested by the name "million." Thus billion and trillion are coined from the Latin prefixes bi- (n = 2) and tri- (n = 3), respectively.*

*In recent years, American usage has eroded the European number definitions, particularly in Britain and to a lesser extent in other countries. This is primarily due to American finance, because Americans insist that $1,000,000,000 be called a billion dollars. In 1974, the government of Prime Minister Harold Wilson announced that henceforth "billion" would mean $10^9$ and not $10^{12}$ in official British reports and statistics.  Anyone who uses the words "billion" and "trillion" internationally should make clear which meaning of those words is intended."*

-- Reference:  Russ Rowlett and the University of North Carolina at Chapel Hill.

[32] **"...her name was Gertrude something or other..."**

This was probably Gertrude R. Schmeidler, who was a notable experimental psychologist and parapsychologist at the time.  She published journal articles and books about how various factors and traits affect a person's extrasensory perception (ESP) abilities.

Studied the role of women in parapsychology, and formed groups and institutes interested in the study of ESP, such as the American Society for Psychical Research, the Duke University Parapsychology Laboratory, and the Parapsychology Foundation, Inc.

Reflected in much of her research is the work for which Schmeidler is most notable, the development of the metaphor of the sheep and goats. She determined through several cycles of ESP card-guessing experiments that "sheep" (persons who believed that success was possible in ESP tasks) scored higher than "goats" (those who rejected the possibility of success).

-- Reference:  http://library.duke.edu/

[33] **"...Krishnamurti..."**

*"**Jiddu Krishnamurti** (May 12, 1895 – February 17, 1986) was born into a Telugu Brahmin family in Madanapalle, India, and in 1909 met C.W. Leadbeater on the private beach at the Theosophical Society headquarters at Adyar in Madras (now Chennai), India. He was subsequently raised under the tutelage of Annie Besant and C.W. Leadbeater, leaders of the Society at the time, who believed him to be a "vehicle" for an expected "World Teacher". As a young man, he disavowed this idea and dissolved a world-wide organization (the Order of the Star) established to support it. He spent the rest of his life traveling the world as an individual speaker, speaking to large and small groups, as well as with interested individuals. He was a well-known writer and speaker on fundamental philosophical and spiritual subjects. His subject matter included (but was not limited to): the purpose of meditation, human relationships, and how to enact positive change in global society. At the age of 34, he publicly renounced the fame and messiah status he had gained from being proclaimed the new incarnation of the Maitreya Buddha by the Theosophical Society, and spent the rest of his life publishing regularly and holding public talks, mostly in South Asia, Europe and the*

United States. At age 90 he addressed the United Nations on the subject of peace and awareness, and was awarded the 1984 UN Peace Medal."

-- Reference: Wikipedia.org

[34] **"...The powers that be..."**

*"Meaning -- The established government of authority.*

*Origin -- From the Bible, Romans 13:1 (King James Version): "Let every soul be subject unto the higher powers. For there is no power but of God: **The powers that be** are ordained of God."*

-- Reference: Wikipedia.org

[35] **"...Columbus..."**

*"The name Christopher Columbus is the Anglicization of the Latin **Christophorus Columbus**. Also well known are his name's rendering in modern Italian as **Cristoforo Colombo**, in Portuguese as **Cristóvão Colombo** (formerly Christovam Colom), and in Spanish as **Cristóbal Colón**."*

-- Reference: Wikipedia.org

**"Pre-Columbian trans-oceanic contacts** *involve the interactions between the indigenous peoples of the Americas and peoples of other continents – Europe, Africa, Asia, or Oceania – before the arrival of Christopher Columbus in 1492. Many such events have been proposed at various times, based on historical reports, archaeological finds, and cultural comparisons."*

**(Please refer to the following website address for details of many other contacts with the "new world" before Columbus):**
*http://en.wikipedia.org/wiki/Pre-Columbian_trans-oceanic_contact*

[36] **"...unexplored universe..."**

That is, **"unexplored"** by homo sapiens. Much like Columbus, who "discovered" the Western Hemisphere, which had not yet been explored by Europeans, it had obviously been explored by the millions of indigenous inhabitants long before Europe existed.

If any of the information in the "Alien Interview" transcripts is factual, it appears that the universe has been very, very thoroughly explored indeed -- but not be humans.
**-- The Editor**

[37] **"...show us on a map of the stars which is the star of your home planet..."**

*"There are probably more than 100 billion ($10^{11}$) galaxies in the observable universe. Most galaxies are 1,000 to 100,000 parsecs (approximately $3.086 \times 1016$ m, 3.262 light-years or 19,176,075,967,324.937 miles) in diameter and are usually separated by distances on the order of millions of parsecs (or megaparsecs). Intergalactic space (the space between galaxies) is filled with a tenuous gas of an average density less than one atom per cubic meter.*

*Beginning in the 1990s, the Hubble Space Telescope yielded improved observations. Among other things, it established that the missing dark matter in our galaxy cannot solely consist of inherently faint and small stars. The Hubble Deep Field, an extremely long exposure of a relatively empty part of the sky, provided evidence that **there are (at least) 125 billion galaxies in the universe**."*

-- Reference: Wikipedia.org

[38] **"... a Japanese language specialist from the Navy ..."**

*"John A. Kneubuhl, was of mixed Samoan/American ancestry, John was an acclaimed Pacific Island playwright who died in 1992. Born of Samoan, English and German ancestry, Kneubuhl grew up in his Samoan grandmother's thatched hut until he was 13 years old. He was educated at Punahou and Yale and wrote plays for the Honolulu Community Theater. He joined the US Navy in 1942, entering the US Navy Japanese Language School at the University of Colorado in July 1942 and graduated in August 1943. He served as a Navy Japanese Language Officer. After the War, he spent 20 years as a TV writer in Hollywood, writing scripts for the Wild, Wild West, Waterfront, Markham, West Point Story, and other shows. **John wrote the story for the Star Trek: The Original Series episode "Bread and Circuses"**, although he did not receive screen credit in the finished episode.*
***Overview****: Captain Kirk and his companions are forced to fight in gladiatorial games on a planet modeled after the Roman Empire."*

-- References: Wikipedia.org and
http://209.85.173.104/search?q=cache:zIAm_bPdRQEJ:ucblibraries.colorado.edu/archives/collections/jlsp/interpreter131.doc+language+expert,+1947&hl=en&ct=clnk&cd=3&gl=us.

[39] **"... the Japanese people have a great number of homonyms..."**

*"In linguistics, a **homonym** is one of a group of words that share the same spelling and the same pronunciation but have different meanings. Some sources only require that homonyms share the same spelling or pronunciation (in addition to having different meanings). Examples of homonyms are stalk (which can mean either part of a plant or to follow someone around), bear (animal) and bear (carry), left (opposite of right) and left (past tense of leave). Some sources also consider the following trio of words to be homonyms, but others designate them as "only" homophones: to, too and two (actually, to, to, too, too and two, being "for the purpose of" as in "to make it easier", the opposite of "from", also, excessively, and "2", respectively). The word **"homonym"** comes from the conjunction of the Greek prefix homo- (meaning same) and suffix -onym (meaning name). Thus, it refers to two or more distinct words sharing the "same name"."*

-- Reference: Wikipedia.org

[40] **"...standard Chinese characters..."**

*"A **Chinese character** or **Han character** (simplified Chinese: 汉字; traditional Chinese: 漢字; pinyin: Hànzi) is a logogram used in writing Chinese, Japanese, sometimes Korean, and formerly Vietnamese. The number of **Chinese characters contained in the Kangxi dictionary is approximately 47,035**, although a large number of these are rarely used variants accumulated throughout history. Studies carried out in China have shown **that full literacy requires a knowledge of between three and four thousand characters.***

*In the Chinese writing system, each character corresponds to a single spoken syllable. A majority of words in all modern varieties of Chinese are poly-syllabic and thus require two or more characters to write. Cognates in the various Chinese languages/dialects which have the same or similar meaning but different pronunciations can be written with the same character. In addition, **many Chinese characters were adopted according to their meaning by the Japanese and Korean languages to represent native words, disregarding pronunciation altogether.**"*

-- Reference: Wikipedia.org

[41] **"...McGuffey's Eclectic Readers..."**

*"**McGuffey's Eclectic Readers** were written by William Holmes McGuffey who began teaching school at the age of 14. He was a professor of ancient languages at Miami University from 1826 until his resignation in 1836. He then served as president of Cincinnati College (1836-1839) and Ohio University (1839-1843). Returning to Cincinnati, McGuffey taught at Woodward College from 1843 until 1845, when he became a professor of moral philosophy at the University of Virginia. He was ordained as a Presbyterian minister in 1829. It was during his years at Miami when McGuffey was approached to write a series of readers for school children. In addition to the work done on these by William Holmes McGuffey, he was assisted by his brother, Alexander Hamilton McGuffey, who also compiled a speller and had sole responsibility for the Fifth Reader. Alexander taught school while working on his law degree and opened a law office in Cincinnati in 1839. The McGuffey Readers sold over 125,000,000 copies.*

*McGuffey became a "roving" teacher at the age of 14, beginning with 48 students in a one room school in Calcutta, Ohio. The size of the class was just one of several challenges faced by the young McGuffey. In many one-teacher schools, children's ages varied from six to twenty-one. McGuffey often worked 11 hours a day, 6 days a week in a succession of frontier schools. He had a remarkable ability to memorize, and could commit to mind entire books of the Bible.*

*The first Reader taught reading by using the phonics method, the identification of letters and their arrangement into words, and aided with slate work. The second Reader came into play once the student could read, and helped them to understand the meaning of sentences while providing vivid stories which children could remember. The third Reader taught the definitions of words, and was written at a level equivalent to the modern 5th or 6th grade. The fourth Reader was written for the highest levels of ability on the grammar school level, which students completed with this book.*

*McGuffey's Readers were among the first textbooks in America that were designed to become progressively more challenging with each volume. They used word repetition in the text as a learning tool, which built strong reading skills through challenging reading. Sounding-out, enunciation and accents were emphasized. Colonial-era texts had offered dull lists of 20 to 100 new words per page for memorization. In contrast, McGuffey used new vocabulary words in the context of real literature, gradually introducing new words and carefully repeating the old.*

*McGuffey believed that teachers should study the lessons as well as their students and suggested they read aloud to their classes. He also listed questions after each story for he believed in order for a teacher to give instruction, one must ask questions. The Readers emphasized spelling, vocabulary, and formal public speaking, which, in 19th century America, was a more common requirement than today.*

**Henry Ford cited McGuffey's Readers as one of his most important childhood influences.** *He was an avid fan of McGuffey's Readers first editions, and claimed as an adult to be able to quote from McGuffey's by memory at great length. Ford republished all six Readers from the 1857 edition, and distributed complete sets of them, at his own expense, to schools across the United States.*

*McGuffey's Readers contain many derogatory references to ethnic and religious minorities. For example, Native Americans are referred to as "savages". There are those who regard the references in the book to the Jews and Judaism as anti-Semitic. For instance, in Neil Baldwin's Henry Ford and the Jews, the author makes the case that Henry Ford's self-avowed anti-Semitism originated with his study of McGuffey's as a schoolboy. Baldwin cites numerous anti-semitic references to Shylock and to Jews attacking Jesus and Paul. He also quotes the Fourth Reader to the effect that "Jewish authors were incapable of the diction and strangers to the morality contained in the gospel." The readers further characterize Jews as "Christ killers" and labels their reverence of the Old Testament as "superstitious," and teach that Jews have been rejected by God for being "unfaithful"."*

You may download text versions of the McGuffy's Reader from the following website: http://www.gutenberg.org/etext/14640

[42] "... the phonics method ..."

**"Phonics** *refers to an instructional method for teaching children to read English. Phonics involves teaching children to connect sounds with letters or groups of letters (e.g., that the sound /k/ can be represented by c, k, or ck spellings) and teaching them to blend the sounds of letters together to produce approximate pronunciations of unknown words."*

-- Reference: Wikipedia.org

[43] "... brought in a set of the *Encyclopedia Britannica...*"

*"The **Encyclopædia Britannica** is a general English-language encyclopaedia published by Encyclopædia Britannica, Inc., a privately held company. The Britannica has a popular reputation for summarizing all of human knowledge. To further their education, many have devoted themselves to reading the entire Britannica, taking anywhere from three to 22 years to do so. When Fat'h Ali became the Shah of Persia in 1797, he was given a complete set of the Britannica's 3rd edition, which he read completely; after this feat, he extended his royal title to include "Most Formidable Lord and Master of the Encyclopædia Britannica." Writer George Bernard Shaw claimed to have read the complete 9th edition—except for the science articles—and Richard Evelyn Byrd took the Britannica as reading material for his five-month stay at the South Pole in 1934.*

*The articles in the Britannica are aimed at educated adult readers, and written by a staff of 19 full-time editors and over 4,000 expert contributors. It is widely perceived as the most scholarly of encyclopaedias. Since the 3rd edition, the Britannica has enjoyed a popular and critical reputation for general excellence. On the release of the 14th edition, Time magazine dubbed the Britannica the "Patriarch of the Library". In a related advertisement, naturalist William Beebe was quoted as saying that the Britannica was "beyond comparison because there is no competitor." References to the Britannica can be found throughout English literature, most notably in one of Arthur Conan Doyle's favorite Sherlock Holmes stories, "The Red-Headed League"."*

-- Reference: Wikipedia.org

[44]  "...her favorite books were *Alice's Adventures in Wonderland* ...'"

*"Alice's Adventures in Wonderland* (1865) is a work of literary nonsense written by English author Charles Lutwidge Dodgson under the pseudonym Lewis Carroll, considered a classic example of the genre and of English literature in general. It tells the story of a girl named Alice who falls down a rabbit-hole into a fantastic realm populated by peculiar and anthropomorphic creatures. The tale is filled with allusions to Dodgson's friends (and enemies), and to the lessons that British schoolchildren were expected to memorize. The tale plays with logic in ways that have made the story of lasting popularity with adults as well as children. It is considered to be one of the most characteristic examples of the genre of literary nonsense, and its narrative course and structure has been enormously influential, mainly in the fantasy genre."

-- Reference: Wikipedia.org

[45]  "...Don Quixote de la Mancha..."

"An early novel written by Spanish author Miguel de Cervantes Saavedra. Cervantes created a fictional origin for the story based upon a manuscript by the invented Moorish historian, Cide Hamete Benengeli. The work was published in two volumes: the first in 1605, and the second in 1614.

The protagonist, Alonso Quixano, is a country gentleman who has read so many stories of chivalry that he descends into fantasy and becomes convinced he is a knight errant. Together with his earthy squire Sancho Panza, the self-styled "Don Quixote de la Mancha" sets out in search of adventure. The "lady" for whom Quixote seeks to toil is Dulcinea del Toboso, an imaginary object crafted from a neighboring farm girl (her real name is Aldonza Lorenzo) by the illusion-struck "knight" to be the object of his courtly love. "Dulcinea" is totally unaware of Quixote's feelings for her, nor does she actually appear in the novel.

Published in two volumes a decade apart, Don Quixote is the most influential work of literature to emerge from the Spanish Golden Age and perhaps the entire Spanish literary canon. As a founding work of modern Western literature, it regularly appears at or near the top of lists of the greatest works of fiction ever published and is the best-selling non-religious, non-political work of fiction of all time."

-- Reference: Wikipedia.org

[46]  "...One Thousand and One Nights..."

"One Thousand and One Nights (Arabic: كتاب ألف ليلة وليلة - kitāb 'alf laylah wa-laylah; Persian: هزار و یک شب - *Dezār-o yak šab*) is a collection of stories collected over thousands of years by various authors, translators and scholars in various countries. These collections of tales trace their roots back to ancient Arabia and Yemen, ancient India, ancient Persia (especially the Sassanid Hazār Afsān Persian: هزار افسان, lit. Thousand Tales), ancient Egypt, ancient Mesopotamian Mythology, ancient Syria, and medieval Arabic folk stories from the Caliphate era. Though an original manuscript has never been found several versions date the collection's genesis to somewhere between AD 800-900.

The main frame story concerns a Persian king and his new bride. The king, Shahryar, upon discovering his former wife's infidelity has her executed and then declares all women to be unfaithful. He begins to marry a succession of virgins only to execute each one the next morning. Eventually the vizier cannot find any more virgins. Scheherazade, the vizier's daughter, offers herself as the next bride and her father reluctantly agrees. On the night of their marriage, Scheherazade tells the king a tale, but does not end it. The king is thus forced to keep her alive in order to hear the conclusion. The next night, as soon as she finishes the tale, she begins (and only begins) another. So it goes for 1,001 nights.

The tales vary widely: they include historical tales, love stories, tragedies, comedies, poems, burlesques, various forms of erotica, and Muslim religious legends. Numerous stories depict djinn, magicians, and legendary places, which are often intermingled with real people and geography; the historical caliph Harun al-Rashid is a common protagonist, as are his alleged court poet Abu Nuwas and his vizier, Ja'far al-Barmaki. Sometimes a character in Scheherazade's tale will begin telling other characters a story of his own, and that story may have another one told within it, resulting in a richly-layered narrative texture.

The different versions have different individually detailed endings (in some Scheherazade asks for a pardon, in some the king sees their children and decides not to execute his wife, in some other things happen that make the king distracted) but they all end with the king giving his wife a pardon and sparing her life.

The narrator's standards for what constitutes a cliffhanger seem broader than in modern literature. While in many cases a story is cut off with the hero in danger of losing his life or another kind of deep trouble, in some parts of the full text Scheherazade stops her narration in the middle of an exposition of abstract philosophical principles or complex points of Islamic philosophy, and in one case during a detailed description of human anatomy according to Galen—and in all these cases turns out to be justified in her belief that the king's curiosity about the sequel would buy her another day of life.

The Indian folklore is represented by certain animal stories, which reflect influence from ancient Sanskrit fables. The Jataka is a collection of 547 stories, which are for the most part moral stories with an ethical purpose. The Tale of the Bull and the Ass and the linked Tale of the Merchant and his Wife are found in the frame stories of both the Jataka and the Arabian Nights."

-- Reference: Wikipedia.org

[47] "... Adventures of Huckleberry Finn..."

"Adventures of Huckleberry Finn (1884) (often shortened to Huck Finn) by Mark Twain. The book is noted for its innocent young protagonist, its colorful description of people and places along the Mississippi River, and its sober and often scathing look at entrenched attitudes, particularly racism. The drifting journey of Huckleberry Finn and his friend, runaway slave Jim, down the Mississippi River on their raft may be one of the most enduring images of escape and freedom in all of American literature."

-- Reference: Wikipedia.org

[48] "... Gulliver's Travels ..."

"Gulliver's Travels (1726, amended 1735), officially Travels into Several Remote Nations of the World, in Four Parts. By Lemuel Gulliver, First a Surgeon, and then a Captain of several Ships, is a novel by Jonathan Swift that is both a satire on human nature and a parody of the *"travellers' tales" literary sub-genre. It is Swift's best known full-length work, and a classic of English literature. The book became tremendously popular as soon as it was published (John Gay said in a 1726 letter to Swift that "it is universally read, from the cabinet council to the nursery"), and it is likely that it has never been out of print since then. The book presents itself as a simple traveller's narrative with the disingenuous title Travels into Several Remote Nations of the World, its authorship assigned only to "Lemuel Gulliver, first a surgeon, then a captain of several ships"."*

-- Reference: Wikipedia.org

### [49] "...Peter Pan..."

*Peter Pan is a character created by Scottish novelist and playwright J. M. Barrie (1860–1937). A mischievous boy who flies and magically refuses to grow up, Peter Pan spends his never-ending childhood adventuring on the small island of Neverland as the leader of his gang the Lost Boys, interacting with fairies and pirates, and from time to time meeting ordinary children from the world outside.*

*Barrie never described Peter's appearance in detail, leaving much of it to the imagination of the reader and the interpretation of anyone adapting the character. He describes him as a beautiful boy with a beautiful smile, "clad in skeleton leaves and the juices that flow from trees".*

*Peter is mainly an exaggerated stereotype of a boastful and careless boy. He is quick to point out how great he is. Peter has a nonchalant, devil-may-care attitude, and is fearlessly cocky when it comes to putting himself in danger. Barrie writes that when Peter thought he was going to die on Marooner's Rock, he felt scared, yet he felt only one shudder run through him when any other person would've felt scared up until death. With his blissful unawareness of the tragedy of death, he says, "To die will be an awfully big adventure".*

*Peter's archetypal ability is his refusal to grow up. Barrie did not explain how he was able to do this, leaving the implication that it was by an act of will.*

*Peter is a skilled swordsman, with the skill to rival even Captain Hook, whose hand he cut off in a duel. He has remarkably keen vision and hearing. Peter Pan is said to be able to do almost anything. Peter has an effect on the whole of Neverland and its inhabitants when he is there. Barrie states that the island wakes up when he returns from his trip to London. Peter is the leader of the Lost Boys, a band of boys who were lost by their parents, and came to live in Neverland. He is friends with Tinker Bell, a common fairy who is often jealously protective of him."*

-- Reference: Wikipedia.org

### [50] "...The Legend of Sleepy Hollow... "

*"A short story by Washington Irving contained in his collection The Sketch Book of Geoffrey Crayon, Gent., written while he was living in Birmingham, England, and first published in 1820. With Irving's companion piece "Rip Van Winkle", "The Legend of Sleepy Hollow" is among the earliest American fiction still read today.*

The story is set circa 1790 in the Dutch settlement of Tarry Town, New York, in a secluded glen called Sleepy Hollow. It tells the story of Ichabod Crane, a lanky schoolmaster from Connecticut, who competes with Abraham "Brom Bones" Van Brunt, the town rowdy, for the hand of 18-year-old Katrina Van Tassel, only daughter of a wealthy farmer. As Crane leaves a party at the Van Tassel home on an autumn night, he is pursued by the Headless Horseman, supposedly the ghost of a Hessian trooper who lost his head to a cannonball during "some nameless battle" of the American Revolutionary War and who "rides forth to the scene of battle in nightly quest of his head." Crane disappears from town, leaving Katrina to marry Brom Bones, who was "to look exceedingly knowing whenever the story of Ichabod was related."

-- Reference: Wikipedia.org

[51] ...one-way glass..."

"A **two-way mirror**, also called a **one-way mirror**, is a mirror which is partially reflective and partially transparent. It is used with a darkened room on one side and a well-lit room on the other, allowing those in the darkened room to see into the lighted room but not vice versa.

The glass is coated with (or in some cases encases a layer of) a very thin almost transparent layer of metal (generally aluminum). The result is what appears to be a mirror from one side, and tinted glass from the other. A viewer in the brightly lit area has difficulty seeing into the darkened room, through what appears to be a mirror.

To take full advantage of the partially mirrored surface, the target side should be brightly lit, to obscure any hint of light coming through the glass from the viewer's side. The darkened room is only completely obscured when it is in complete darkness. Sometimes a darkened curtain or a double door type vestibule is used to keep the viewer's side darkened.

A flashlight held against the glass can be used to illuminate the darkened viewer's side, allowing someone on the lit side to see through.  Two-way mirrors are used for:

- providing security, through covert viewing of public spaces
- for the protection of covert cameras
- for some police interrogation rooms"

-- Reference: Wikipedia.org

[52] "...Sanskrit of the Vedic Hymns..."

"**Sanskrit** (संस्कृता वाक् sa□sk□tā vāk, for short संस्कृतम् sa□sk□tam) is a classical language of South Asia, a liturgical language of Hinduism, Buddhism, Sikhism, Jainism, and one of the 23 official languages of India.

Its position in the cultures of South and Southeast Asia is akin to that of Latin and Greek in Europe and it has evolved into, as well as influenced, many modern-day languages of the world. It appears in pre-Classical form as Vedic Sanskrit, with the language of the Rigveda being the oldest and most archaic stage preserved. Dating back to as early as 1500 BCE, Vedic Sanskrit is the earliest attested Indo-Aryan language, and one of the earliest attested members of the Indo-European language family.

The corpus of Sanskrit literature encompasses a rich tradition of poetry and drama as well as scientific, technical, philosophical and religious texts. Today, Sanskrit continues to be widely used as a ceremonial language in Hindu religious rituals in the forms of hymns and mantras. Spoken Sanskrit is still in use in a few traditional institutions in India, and there are some attempts at revival.

The scope of this article is the Classical Sanskrit language as laid out in the grammar of Panini, around the 4th century BCE."

-- Reference: Wikipedia.org

[53] **"Part of the search required interaction with the human population that inhabited the adjoining at that time."**

-- **Editor's Note:** (The western borders of Pakistan include the **Khyber Pass** and **Bolan Pass**, traditional invasion routes between Central Asia. The closest civilization using Sanskrit at the date and nearest the location of "The Domain Base" would have been in the foothills of the Himalayas. This was the in the area of "**Mehrgarh**", an early beginning of the Indus Valley civilization which has been recently excavated.)

"(**Bolan Pass** (Urdu: □□□ □□□□□) is a mountain pass through the Toba Kakar Range of mountains in western Pakistan, 120 kilometres from the Afghanistan border. Strategically located, traders, invaders, and nomadic tribes have also used it as a gateway to and from the South Asia.)

The **Khyber Pass**, (also spelled Khaiber or Khaybar) (Urdu: □□□ □□□□) (altitude: 1,070 m , 3,510 ft) is the mountain pass that links Pakistan and Afghanistan. Throughout history it has been an important trade route between Central Asia and South Asia and a strategic military location.

"**Mehrgarh** is now seen as a precursor to the Indus Valley Civilization. "Discoveries at Mehrgarh changed the entire concept of the Indus civilization," according to Ahmad Hasan Dani, professor emeritus of archaeology at Quaid-e-Azam University, Islamabad, "There we have the whole sequence, right from the beginning of settled village life.

The Kachi plain and in the Bolan basin (are) situated at the Bolan peak pass, one of the main routes connecting southern Afghanistan, eastern Iran, the Balochistan hills and the Indus valley. This area of rolling hills is thus located on the western edge of the Indus valley, where, around 2500 BC, a large urban civilization emerged at the same time as those of Mesorpotamia and the ancient Egyptian empire. For the first time in the Indian subcontinent, a continuous sequence of dwelling-sites has been established from 7000 BC to 500 BC. The chalcolithic people of Mehrgarh also had contacts with contemporaneous cultures in northern Afghanistan, northeastern Iran and southern central Asia.
in April 2006, it was announced in the scientific journal Nature that the oldest (and first early Neolithic) evidence for the drilling of human teeth in vivo (i.e. in a living person) was found in Mehrgarh. According to the authors, their discoveries point to a tradition of proto-dentistry in the early farming cultures of that region. "Here we describe eleven drilled molar crowns from nine adults discovered in a Neolithic graveyard in Pakistan that dates from 7,500 to 9,000 years ago."

-- Reference: Wikipedia.org

184

[54] "... they reported sighting *"vimanas"* or space craft in the area.."

*"A **vimāna** (Sanskrit: विमान) is a mythical flying machine, described in the Sanskrit epics. The predecessors of the flying vimanas of the Sanskrit epics are the flying chariots employed by various gods in the Vedas.*

*The first flying vimana mentioned in Hindu mythology:*

> *"The Pushpaka chariot that resembles the Sun and belongs to my brother was brought by the powerful Ravana; that aerial and excellent car going everywhere at will .... that car resembling a bright cloud in the sky ... and the King [Rama] got in, and the excellent car at the command of the Raghira, rose up into the higher atmosphere.'*

*The Rigveda does not mention Vimanas, but verses RV 1.164.47-48 have been taken as evidence for the idea of "mechanical birds":*

> *"Dark the descent: the birds are golden-coloured; up to the heaven they fly robed in the waters.*
> *Again descend they from the seat of Order, and all the earth is moistened with their fatness."*
> *"Twelve are the fellies, and the wheel is single; three are the naves. What man hath understood it?*
> *Therein are set together spokes three hundred and sixty, which in nowise can be loosened." (trans. Griffith)*

*In Dayananda Saraswati's "translation", these verses become:*

> *"jumping into space speedily with a craft using fire and water ... containing twelve stamghas (pillars), one wheel, three machines, 300 pivots, and 60 instruments."*

*But likelier in the original Indian symbolism when that hymn was composed, the wheel is a year, the 12 "fellies" are months (lunations), and the 360 spokes are days.*

*In the Ramayana, the pushpaka ("flowery") vimana of Ravana is described as follows:*

> *"The Pushpaka chariot that resembles the Sun and belongs to my brother was brought by the powerful Ravana; that aerial and excellent car going everywhere at will .... that car resembling a bright cloud in the sky ... and the King [Rama] got in, and the excellent car at the command of the Raghira, rose up into the higher atmosphere.'*

*It is the first flying vimana mentioned in Hindu mythology (as distinct from the gods' flying horse-drawn chariots).*

*Pushpaka was originally made by Maya for Kubera, the God of wealth, but was later stolen, along with Lanka, by his half-brother, the demon king Ravana.*

*One example is that the Asura Maya had a Vimana measuring twelve cubits in circumference, with four strong wheels. Apart from 'blazing missiles', the poem records the use of other deadly weapons. 'Indra's Dart' (Indravajrā) operated via a circular 'reflector'.*

185

When switched on, it produced a 'shaft of light' which, when focused on any target, immediately 'consumed it with its power'.

In one exchange, the hero, Krishna, is pursuing his enemy, Salva, in the sky, when Salva's Vimana, the Saubha, is made invisible in some way. Undeterred, Krishna immediately fires off a special weapon: "I quickly laid on an arrow, which killed by seeking out sound".

Many other terrible weapons are described in the Mahabharata, but the most fearsome of all is the one used against the Vrishis. The narrative records:

> "Gurkha flying in his swift and powerful Vimana hurled against the three cities of the Vrishnis and Andhakas a single projectile charged with all the power of the Universe. An incandescent column of smoke and fire, as brilliant as ten thousands suns, rose in all its splendour. It was the unknown weapon, the Iron Thunderbolt, a gigantic messenger of death which reduced to ashes the entire race of the Vrishnis and Andhakas."

-- Reference: Wikipedia.org

[55] " I have now scanned all of the books and material you provided me. This has been processed through the computers of the space station in this region, translated into my own language and relayed back to me. "

**Editors Note** -- Apparently Airl is able to "scan" something she sees through the lenses of her "doll body" eyes, upload the data to a computer on the "space station", have it processed and downloaded to her? Or, maybe she does it telepathically? This is not clarified anywhere in the transcripts or notes.

[56] "... I was "outside" of my body, looking down from the ceiling..."

"An **out-of-body experience (OBE)**, is an experience that typically involves a sensation of floating outside of one's body and, in some cases, perceiving one's physical body from a place outside one's body (autoscopy). About one in ten people has reported having an out-of-body experience at some time in their lives. It is claimed that those experiencing an OBE sometimes observe details which were unknown to them beforehand.

The first extensive scientific study of OBEs was made by Celia Green (1968). She collected written, first-hand accounts from a total of 400 subjects, recruited by means of appeals in the mainstream media, and followed up by questionnaire. some 80% reported feeling they were a 'disembodied consciousness', with no external body at all.

Another form of a spontaneous OBE occurs during a near death experience (NDE). The phenomenology of an NDE usually includes physiological, psychological and transcendental factors (Parnia, Waller, Yeates & Fenwick, 2001) such as impressions of being outside the physical body (an out-of-body experience), Typically the experience follows a distinct progression, starting with the sensation of floating above one's body and seeing the surrounding area."

-- Reference: Wikipedia.org

[57] "...509th Bomber Squadron..."

"The **509th Composite Group** was an air combat unit of the United States Army Air Forces during the Second World War and as the **509th Operations Group**, is a current unit of the United States Air Force. It was tasked with developing and employing a combat delivery system for the Atomic bomb and conducted the attacks on Hiroshima and Nagasaki, Japan, in August 1945.

The group later became a medium bombardment group of the Strategic Air Command, as the combat component of the 509th Bomb Wing, before being inactivated in 1952. Its lineage, honors, and history were also bestowed on the like-numbered wing in 1947.

The 509th Composite Group was constituted on December 9, 1944, and activated on December 17, 1944, at Wendover Army Air Field, Utah, commanded by Colonel Paul W. Tibbets. Colonel Tibbets had been assigned to organize and command a combat group to develop the means of delivering an atomic weapon by airplane against targets in Germany and Japan. Because the flying squadrons of the group consisted of both bomber and transport aircraft, the group was designated as a "composite" rather than a "bombardment" unit.

The mission profile for both atomic missions called for weather scouts to precede the strike force by an hour, reporting weather conditions in code over each proposed target. The strike force consisted of a bombing aircraft, with the aircraft commander responsible for all decisions in reaching the target and the bomb commander (weaponeer) responsible for all decisions regarding dropping of the bomb; a blast instrumentation aircraft which would fly the wing of the strike aircraft and drop instruments by parachute into the target area; and a camera ship, which would also carry scientific observers. Each mission would have one "spare" aircraft accompanying it as far as Iwo Jima to take over carrying the bomb if the strike aircraft encountered mechanical problems.

The Hiroshima mission was flown as planned and executed without significant problems or diversion from plan. The Nagasaki mission, however, originally targeted Kokura and encountered numerous problems which resulted in the bombing of the secondary target, a delay in bombing of almost two hours, detonation of the bomb some distance from the designated aiming point, and a diversion of the strike force to emergency landings on Okinawa because of a lack of fuel. However the basic objectives of the mission were met despite the problems.

Lieutenant Jacob Beser flew on both attack aircraft (the only man to do so), although Maj. Charles W. Sweeney and crew observed Hiroshima from The Great Artiste and dropped the bomb on Nagasaki from Bockscar. Lawrence H. Johnston of Project Alberta observed all three nuclear explosions, including the Trinity test.

While the Nagasaki mission was in progress, two B-29's of the 509th took off from Tinian to return to Wendover. Lt.Col. Classen, the deputy group commander, in the unnamed victor 94 and crew B-6 in Jabit III, together with their ground crews, were sent back to stage for the possibility of transporting further bomb assemblies to Tinian. However the plutonium cores were still at Site Y, and on August 13 Gen. Groves ordered that all shipments of material be stopped. His order reached Los Alamos in time to keep the third bomb from being shipped. The first Atomic War lasted 9 days, August 6 through August 15, 1945.

After the Nagasaki mission the group continued combat operations, making another series of pumpkin bomb attacks (12 dropped) on August 14. With the announcement of the Japanese *surrender, however, the 509th CG flew three further training missions involving 31 sorties on August 18, 20, and 22, then stood down from operations."*

**See Article at Wikipedia.org**: *Atomic bombings of Hiroshima and Nagasaki*

-- Reference: Wikipedia.org

[58] **"... nuclear weapons which have been tested in New Mexico."**

*"The first nuclear weapons test was conducted in Alamogordo, New Mexico, on July 16, 1945, during the Manhattan Project, and given the codename "Trinity". The test was originally to confirm that the implosion-type nuclear weapon design was feasible, and to give an idea of what the actual size and effects of a nuclear explosion would be before they were used in combat against Japan. While the test gave a good approximation of many of the explosion's effects, it did not give an appreciable understanding of nuclear fallout, which was not well understood by the project scientists until well after the atomic bombings of Hiroshima and Nagasaki."*

-- Reference: Wikipedia.org

[59] "...radiation..."

*"The dangers of radioactivity and of radiation were not immediately recognized.* **Acute effects of radiation were first observed** *in the use of X-rays when the Serbo-Croatian-American electric engineer* **Nikola Tesla intentionally subjected his fingers to X-rays in 1896**. *He published his observations concerning the burns that developed, though he attributed them to ozone rather than to X-rays.* **His injuries healed later**.*

*The genetic effects of radiation, including the effects on cancer risk, were recognized much later. In 1927 Hermann Joseph Muller published research showing genetic effects, and in 1946 was awarded the Nobel prize for his findings.*

*Before the biological effects of radiation were known, many physicians and corporations had begun marketing radioactive substances as patent medicine and radioactive quackery. Examples were radium enema treatments, and radium-containing waters to be drunk as tonics. Marie Curie spoke out against this sort of treatment, warning that the effects of radiation on the human body were not well understood (Curie later died from aplastic anemia assumed due to her work with radium, but later examination of her bones showed that she had been a careful laboratory worker and had a low burden of radium. A more likely cause was her exposure to unshielded X-ray tubes while a volunteer medical worker in WWI). By the 1930s, after a number of cases of bone necrosis and death in enthusiasts, radium-containing medical products had nearly vanished from the market."*

-- Reference: Wikipedia.org

[60] ..."the space craft was struck by a bolt of lighting"...

*"**Lightning** is an atmospheric discharge of electricity, which typically occurs during thunderstorms, and sometimes during volcanic eruptions or dust storms. The leader of a bolt of lightning can travel at speeds of 60,000 m/s, and can reach temperatures approaching*

*30,000 °C (54,000 °F), hot enough to fuse soil or sand into glass channels. There are over 16 million lightning storms every year."*

-- Reference: Wikipedia.org

[61] ..."**electronic wavelength**"...

*"In physics, **wavelength** is the distance between repeating units of a propagating wave of a given frequency. It is commonly designated by the Greek letter lambda (λ). Examples of wave-like phenomena are light, water waves, and sound waves. In a wave, a property varies with the position. For example, this property can be the air pressure for a sound wave, or the magnitude of the electric or the magnetic field for light. The wavelengths of frequencies audible to the human ear (20 Hz–20 kHz) are between approximately 17 m and 17 mm, respectively. Visible light ranges from deep red, roughly 700 nm to violet, roughly 400 nm (430–750 THz). For other examples, see **electromagnetic spectrum**."*

-- Reference: Wikipedia.org

[62] ..."**space opera**" civilization"...

*"It was not until the 1920s that the **space opera** proper appeared in the pulp magazines Weird Tales and Amazing Stories. Unlike earlier stories of space adventure, which either related the invasion of Earth by extraterrestrials, or concentrated on the invention of a space vehicle by a genius inventor, pure space opera simply took space travel for granted (usually by setting the story in the far future), skipped the preliminaries, and launched straight into tales of derring-do among the stars.*

*The first stories of this type were J. Schlossel's The Second Swarm (Spring 1928) in Amazing Stories Quarterly and Edmond Hamilton's Crashing Suns (August-September 1928) and The Star Stealers (February 1929) in Weird Tales . Similar stories by other writers followed through 1929 and 1930; by 1931 the space opera was well-established as a dominant sub-genre of science fiction.*

*The transition from the older space-voyage story to the space opera can be seen in the works of **E. E. "Doc" Smith**. His first published work, The Skylark of Space (August-October 1928, Amazing Stories), merges the traditional tale of a scientist inventing a space-drive with planetary romance in the style of **Edgar Rice Burroughs**; but by the time of the sequel, Skylark Three (August-October 1930, **Amazing Stories**) which introduces the space faring race of the Fenachrone, Smith had moved closer to a space opera mode.*

*Space opera in its most familiar form was a product of 1930s-40s pulp magazines. Like early science fiction in general, space opera borrowed much of its style from established adventure, crime, and thriller genres. Notable influences included stories that described adventures on exotic or uncivilized frontiers, e.g. the American West, Africa, or the Orient. The imagined future of space opera included immense space liners, intrepid explorers of unknown worlds, pirates of the space ways, and tough but incorruptible space police.*

***E. E. "Doc" Smith's later* Lensman Series** *and the works of Edmond Hamilton, John W. Campbell, and Jack Williamson in the 1930s and 1940s were popular with readers and much imitated by other writers. By the early 1940s, the repetitiousness and extravagance of some of these stories led to objections from some fans."*

-- Reference: Wikipedia.org

**63** "... European explorers who "discovered" and "claimed" the New World for The Holy Father, The Pope..."

"...On the death of Pope Innocent VIII (1484–1492), the three likely candidates for the Holy See were cardinals Borgia, Ascanio Sforza and Giuliano della Rovere. While there was never substantive proof of simony, the rumor was that Borgia, by his great wealth, succeeded in buying the largest number of votes, including that of Sforza, whom, popular rumor had it, he bribed with four mule-loads of silver.

**Pope Alexander VI** (1 January 1431 – 18 August 1503), born **Roderic Llançol**, later **Roderic de Borja y Borja** (Italian: **Borgia**) was Pope from 1492 to 1503. He is the most controversial of the secular popes of the Renaissance, and **his surname (Italianized as Borgia) became a byword for the debased standards of the papacy of that era.**

Della Rovere was bankrolled to the cost of 200,000 gold ducats by the King of France, with another 100,000 supplied by the Republic of Genoa. Borgia was elected on 11 August 1492, assuming the name of Alexander VI. Giovanni di Lorenzo de' Medici, later to become Pope Leo X, sharply criticized the election and warned of dire things to come:

**"Now we are in the power of a wolf, the most rapacious perhaps that this world has ever seen. And if we do not flee, he will inevitably devour us all."**

-- Reference: Wikipedia.org

**64** "...1493 AD -- "The Requirement"...

"The Requirement was published as a papal "bull", issued by the infamous Pope Alexander VI, (Rodrigo Borgia), Roman Catholic Pope from 1492 until his death, is the most memorable of the Popes of the Renaissance.

Because of the pre-existence of millions of people living in the Americas in 1493, the King of Spain, had a small twinge of fear at the prospect that God might become angry at him for all the murder, theft and mayhem he endorsed in the New World. So, he persuaded Pope Alexander VI to sanction an official proclamation intended to dissolve the stain of bloody culpability from the King's own immortal soul. This document, called "The Requirement", was supposed to be read, whether translated into the native language of the inhabitants or not, to the citizens of every foreign nation just prior to their conquest. The gist of the proclamation was to inform the soon to be vanquished that their lands were being "donated" to Spain.

The Requirement read, in part:

"I, (name of the Conquistador), servant of the high and mighty Kings of Castile and Leon, conquerors of barbarian peoples, and being their messenger and Captain, hereby notify and inform you ... that God Our Lord, One and Eternal, created Heaven and Earth and a man and a woman from whom you and I and all the multitude begotten from these over the past five thousand and some years since the world was made ... And so I request and require you ... to recognize the Church as your Mistress and as Governess of the World and Universe, and the High Priest, called the Pope, in Her name, and His Majesty (the King of Spain) in Her place, as Ruler and Lord King ... And if you do not do this ... with the help of

God I shall come mightily against you, and I shall make war on you everywhere and in every way that I can, and I shall subject you to the yoke and obedience of the Church and His Majesty, and I shall seize your women and children, and I shall make them slaves, to sell and dispose of as His Majesty commands, and I shall do all the evil and damage to you that I am able. And I insist that the deaths and destruction that result from this will be your fault."

One of the first to hear The Requirement were the chiefs of the Maya, whose scale of time for the creation of life on Earth did not begin a mere 5,000 years earlier, as suggested by the Pope, rather the Mayan measured original creation in millions of years by the astronomical calendars they kept, which tracked the solar year accurately to within a few seconds a year. Their comment upon hearing The Requirement was, "The Holy Father has indeed been generous with others' property".

The Requirement was originally intended as a response to complaints by Spanish clerics that the wars against the Native American peoples were unjust. Comparing them to Spain's wars against the Moors, the clerics claimed that Muslims had knowledge of Christ and rejected Him, so that waging a Crusade against them was legitimate. In contrast, wars against the Native Americans, who had never come into contact with Christianity were unacceptable. The Requirement was intended as a legal loophole to place the native population in the position of having rejected Christianity. It stated: "We protest that any deaths that result from this [rejection of Christianity] are your fault…"

Many critics of the conquistadors' policies were appalled by the flippant nature of the Requirement, and the priest, Bartolomeo de Las Casas, said in response to it that he did not know whether to laugh or to cry. While the conquistadors were encouraged to use an interpreter to read the Requirement, this was not absolutely necessary, and in many cases, it was read out to an uncomprehending populace. In some instances, it was read to barren beaches and empty villages, long after the natives had fled, to prisoners after they were captured, or even from the decks of ships once they had just spotted the coast. Nevertheless, for the conquistadors, it provided a religious justification for attacking and enslaving the native population, and because of its potential to enrich the coffers of Spain, the Requirement was not generally questioned."

-- Reference: Wikipedia.org

The net result of the "discovery" of the "New World" which wasn't really "new" as it had been around as long as any other continent, and had a larger population than Europe, was as follows:

1) hundreds of indigenous cultures were eradicated  2) approximately 100 million people were killed by disease and war brought upon them by "aliens" 3) 100 million people from the Gold Coast of Africa were enslaved, and/ or murdered by Europeans in an effort to replace the "labor force" of slaughtered indigenous population of the Western Hemisphere 4) nearly all of the priceless literature, history, cultural and artistic artifacts of the Western hemisphere were destroyed 5) most of the gold and gems mined over a period of thousands of years by indigenous people were stolen and shipped off the a handful of greedy, idiotic, uneducated, filthy, disease-ridden, superstitious, murderous, thieves in Europe who squandered it on mindless self-indulgences. -- **The Editor**

[65] *"... They are interested primarily in the "low gravity" satellites in this space station which consists mainly of the dark side of the moon...".*

"According to the NASA Astronaut Neil Armstrong the aliens have a base on the Moon and (the aliens) *told us in no uncertain terms to get off and stay off the Moon!*

*Sound far fetched? Milton Cooper, a Naval Intelligence Officer tells us that not only does the Alien Moon Base exist but the U.S. Naval Intelligence Community refers to the Alien Moon Base as "Luna," that there is a huge mining operation going on there, and that is where the aliens keep their huge mother ships while the trips to Earth are made in smaller "flying saucers".*

*LUNA: The Alien base on the far side of the Moon. It was seen and filmed by the Apollo astronauts. A base, a mining operation using very large machines, and the very large alien craft described in sighting reports as mother ships exist there. -Milton Cooper*

*Did Apollo 11 Encounter UFOs on the Moon? from the Book "Above Top Secret" by Timothy Good.*

*According to hitherto unconfirmed reports, both Neil Armstrong and Edwin "Buzz" Aldrin saw UFOs shortly after their historic landing on the Moon in Apollo 11 on 21 July 1969. I remember hearing one of the astronauts refer to a "light" in or on a carter during the television transmission, followed by a request from mission control for further information. Nothing more was heard.*

*According to a former NASA employee Otto Binder, unnamed radio hams with their own VHF receiving facilities that bypassed NASA's broadcasting outlets picked up the following exchange:*

*NASA: What's there? Mission Control calling Apollo 11...*

*Apollo: These "Babies" are huge, Sir! Enormous! OH MY GOD! You wouldn't believe it! I'm telling you there are other spacecraft out there, lined up on the far side of the crater edge! They're on the Moon watching us!*

*In 1979, Maurice Chatelain, former chief of NASA Communications Systems confirmed that Armstrong had indeed reported seeing two UFOs on the rim of a crater. "The encounter was common knowledge in NASA," he revealed, "but nobody has talked about it until now."*

*Soviet scientists were allegedly the first to confirm the incident. "According to our information, the encounter was reported immediately after the landing of the module," said Dr. Vladimir Azhazha, a physicist and Professor of Mathematics at Moscow University. "Neil Armstrong relayed the message to Mission Control that two large, mysterious objects were watching them after having landed near the moon module. But his message was never heard by the public-because NASA censored it. "*

*According to another Soviet scientist, Dr. Aleksandr Kazantsev, Buzz Aldrin took color movie film of the UFOs from inside the module, and continued filming them after he and Armstrong went outside. Dr. Azhazha claims that the UFOs departed minutes after the astronauts came out on to the lunar surface.*

*Maurice Chatelain also confirmed that Apollo 11's radio transmissions were interrupted on several occasions in order to hide the news from the public. Before dismissing Chatelain's* sensational claims, it is worth noting his impressive background in the aerospace industry and space program. His first job after moving from France was as an electronics engineer with Convair, specializing in telecommunications, telemetry, and radar. In 1959 he was in charge of an electromagnetic research group, developing new radar and telecommunications systems for Ryan. One of his eleven patents was an automatic flights to the Moon. Later, at North American Aviation, Chatelain was offered the job of designing and building the Apollo communications and data-processing systems.

Chatelain claims that "all Apollo and Gemini flights were followed, both at a distance and sometimes also quite closely, by space vehicles of extraterrestrial origin-flying saucers, or UFOs, if you want to call them by that name. Every time it occurred, the astronauts informed Mission Control, who then ordered absolute silence." He goes on to say:

"I think that Walter Schirra aboard Mercury 8 was the first of the astronauts to use the code name 'Santa Claus' to indicate the presence of flying saucers next to space capsules. However, his announcements were barely noticed by the general public.

It was a little different when James Lovell on board the Apollo 8 command module came out from behind the moon and said for everybody to hear:

'PLEASE BE INFORMED THAT THERE IS A SANTA CLAUS.'

Even though this happened on Christmas Day 1968, many people sensed a hidden meaning in those words."

Rumors persist. NASA may well be a civilian agency, but many of its programs are funded by the defense budget and most of the astronauts are subject to military security regulations. Apart from the fact that the National Security Agency screens all films and probably radio communications as well. We have the statements by Otto Binder, Dr. Garry Henderson and Maurice Chatelain that the astronauts were under strict orders not to discuss their sightings. And Gordon Cooper has testified to a United Nations committee that one of the astronauts actually witnessed a UFO on the ground. If there is no secrecy, why has this sighting not been made public?

A certain professor, who wished to remain anonymous, was engaged in a discussion with Neil Armstrong during a NASA symposium.

Professor: What REALLY happened out there with Apollo 11?

Armstrong: It was incredible, of course we had always known there was a possibility, the fact is, we were warned off! (by the Aliens). There was never any question then of a space station or a moon city.

Professor: How do you mean "warned off"?

Armstrong: I can't go into details, except to say that their ships were far superior to ours both in size and technology - Boy, were they big!... and menacing! No, there is no question of a space station.

Professor: But NASA had other missions after Apollo 11?

*Armstrong: Naturally-NASA was committed at that time, and couldn't risk panic on Earth. But it really was a quick scoop and back again.*

*Armstrong confirmed that the story was true but refused to go into further detail, beyond admitting that the CIA was behind the cover-up.*

*Reasonable activity of an alien civilization showed up unexpectedly close to us. We were not ready for it psychologically*

*We still can come across publications trying to find an answer to the question: Are we alone in the universe? At the same time, presence of reasonable creatures has been detected just close to our home, in the Moon. However, the discovery was immediately classified as secret, as it was so much incredible that even could shake the already existing social principles, reports Russia's newspaper "Vecherny Volgograd."*

*Here is an extract from the official press-release:*

*"NASA scientists and engineers participating in exploration of Mars and Moon reported results of their discoveries at a briefing at the Washington national press club on March 21, 1996. It was announced for the first time that man-caused structures and objects had been discovered on the Moon." The scientists spoke rather cautiously and evasively about the functioning objects, with the exception of UFO. They always mentioned the man-caused objects as possible, and pointed out the information was still under study, and official results would be published later.*

*It was mentioned at the briefing as well that the Soviet Union used to own some photo materials proving presence of reasonable activity on the Moon. And although it wasn't identified what kind of reasonable activity it was, thousands of photo-and video materials photographed from the Apollo and the Clementine space station demonstrated many parts on the lunar surface where the activity and its traces were perfectly evident. The video films and photos made by U.S. astronauts during the Apollo program were demonstrated at the briefing. And people were extremely surprised why the materials hadn't been presented to the public earlier. And NASA specialists answered: "It was difficult to forecast the reaction of people to the information that some creatures had been or still were on the Moon. Besides, there were some other reasons to it, which were beyond NASA."*

*Specialist for lunar artifacts Richard Hoagland says that NASA is still trying to veil photo materials before they are published in public catalogues and files, they do retouching or partially refocus them while copying. Some investigators, Hoagland is among them, suppose that an extraterrestrial race had used the Moon as a terminal station during their activity on the Earth. The suggestions are confirmed by the legends and myths invented by different nations of our planet.*

*Ruins of lunar cities stretched along many kilometers, huge transparent domes on massive basements, numerous tunnels and other constructions make scientists reconsider their opinions concerning the lunar problems. How the Moon appeared and principles of its revolving around the Earth still pose a great problem for scientists.*

*Some partially destroyed objects on the lunar surface can't be placed among natural geological formations, as they are of complex organization and geometrical structure. In the upper part of Rima hadley, not far from the place where the Apollo-15 had landed, a* construction surrounded with a tall D-shaped wall was discovered. As of now, different artifacts have been discovered in 44 regions.

The NASA Goddard Space Flight Center, the Houston Planetary Institute and specialists from the bank of space information are investigating the regions. Mysterious terrace-shaped excavations of the rock have been discovered near the Tiho crater. The concentric hexahedral excavations and the tunnel entry at the terrace side cant be results of natural geological processes; instead, they look very much like open cast mines.

A transparent dome raised above the crater edge was discovered near the crater Copernicus. The dome is unusual as it is glowing white and blue from inside. A rather unusual object, which is unusual indeed even for the Moon, was discovered in the upper part of the Factory area. A disk of about 50 meters in diameter stands on a square basement surrounded with rhombi walls. In the picture, close to the rhombi, we can also see a dark round embrasure in the ground, which resembles an entry in an underground caponier. There is a regular rectangular area between Factory and the crater Copernicus which is 300 meters wide 400 meters long.

Apollo 10 astronauts made a unique picture (AS10-32-4822) of a one-mile long object called Castle, which is hanging at the height of 14 kilometers and casts a distinct shadow on the lunar surface. The object seems to be consisting of several cylindrical units and a large conjunctive unit. Internal porous structure of the Castle is clearly seen in one of the pictures, which makes an impression that some parts of the object are transparent.

As it turned out at the briefing where many NASA scientists were present, when Richard Hoagland had requested originals of the Castle pictures for the second time, no pictures were found there at all. They disappeared even from the list of pictures made by the Apollo 10 crew. Only intermediate pictures of the object were found in the archives, which unfortunately don't depict the internal structure of the object.

When Apollo-12 crew landed on the lunar surface, they saw that the landing was observed by a half-transparent pyramidal object. It was hanging just several meters above the lunar surface and shimmered with all rainbow colors against the black sky.

In 1969, when the film about astronauts traveling to the Sea of Storms was demonstrated (the astronauts saw the strange objects once again, which were later called "striped glasses"), NASA finally understood what consequences such kind of control could bring. Astronaut Mitchell answered the question about his feelings after a successful return the following: "My neck still aches as I had to constantly turn my head around because we felt we were not alone there. We had no choice but pray." Johnston, who worked at the Houston Space Center and studied photos and video materials done during the Apollo program, discussed the artifacts with Richard Hoagland and said, the NASA leadership was awfully annoyed with the great number of anomalous, to put it mildly, objects on the Moon. It was even said that piloted flights to the Moon could be banned in the programs network.

Investigators are especially interested in ancient structures resembling partially destroyed cities. The orbital shooting reveals an astonishingly regular geometry of square and rectangular constructions. They resemble our terrestrial cities seen from the height of 5-8 kilometers. A mission control specialist commented on the pictures: "Our guys observed ruins of the Lunar cities, transparent pyramids, domes and God knows what else, which are currently hidden deep inside the NASA safes, and felt like Robinson Crusoe when he suddenly came across prints of human bare feet on the sand of the desert island." What do geologists and scientists say after studying the pictures of lunar cities and other anomalous objects? They say, such objects can't be natural formations. "We should admit they are artificial, especially the domes and pyramids." Reasonable activity of an alien civilization showed up unexpectedly close to us. We were not ready for it psychologically, and some people hardly believe they are true even now."

Translated by Maria Gousseva (original source = http://english.pravda.ru/main/2002/10/05/37771.html)

-- Source: http://www.ufocasebook.com/moon.html

[66] "... synthesized from gypsum..."

"**Gypsum** is a common mineral, with thick and extensive evaporite beds in association with sedimentary rocks. Deposits are known to occur in strata from as early as the Permian age. Gypsum is deposited in lake and sea water, as well as in hot springs, from volcanic vapors, and sulfate solutions in veins. Hydrothermal anhydrite in veins is commonly hydrated to gypsum by groundwater in near surface exposures. It is often associated with the minerals halite and sulfur.

The word gypsum is derived from the aorist form of the Greek verb μαγειρεύω, "to cook", referring to the burnt or calcined mineral. Because the gypsum from the quarries of the Montmartre district of Paris has long furnished burnt gypsum used for various purposes, this material has been called plaster of Paris. It is also used in foot creams, shampoos and many other hair products.

Because gypsum dissolves over time in water, gypsum is rarely found in the form of sand. However, the unique conditions of the White Sands National Monument in the US state of New Mexico have created a 710 km² (275 sq mile) expanse of white gypsum sand, enough to supply the construction industry with drywall for 1,000 years."

-- Reference: Wikipedia.org

[67] "... electromagnetic force..."

"In physics, the **Lorentz force** is the force on a point charge due to electromagnetic fields. Lorentz introduced this force in 1892. However, the discovery of the Lorentz force was before Lorentz's time. In particular, it can be seen at equation (77) in Maxwell's 1861 paper On Physical Lines of Force. Later, Maxwell listed it as equation "D" of his 1864 paper, A Dynamical Theory of the Electromagnetic Field, as one of the eight original Maxwell's equations. In this paper the equation was written as follows:

$$E = v \times (\mu H) - \frac{\partial A}{\partial t} - \nabla \phi$$

where

> **A** is the magnetic vector potential,
> φ is the electrostatic potential,
> **H** is the magnetic field **H**,

*μ is magnetic permeability.*

*Although this equation is obviously a direct precursor of the modern Lorentz force equation, it actually differs in two respects:*

- *It does not contain a factor of q, the charge. Maxwell didn't use the concept of charge. The definition of **E** used here by Maxwell is unclear. He uses the term electromotive force. He operated from Faraday's electro-tonic state **A**, which he considered to be a momentum in his vortex sea. The closest term that we can trace to electric charge in Maxwell's papers is the density of free electricity, which appears to refer to the density of the aethereal medium of his molecular vortices and that gives rise to the momentum **A**. Maxwell believed that **A** was a fundamental quantity from which electromotive force can be derived.*
- *The equation here contains the information that what we nowadays call **E**, which today can be expressed in terms of scalar and vector potentials according to*

$$\mathbf{E} = -\nabla\phi - \frac{\partial \mathbf{A}}{\partial t}$$

*The fact that **E** can be expressed this way is equivalent to one of the four modern Maxwell's equations, the Maxwell-Faraday equation.*

*Despite its historical origins in the original set of eight Maxwell's equations, the Lorentz force is no longer considered to be one of "Maxwell's equations" as the term is currently used (that is, as reformulated by Heaviside). It now sits adjacent to Maxwell's equations as a separate and essential law.*

### Significance of the Lorentz force

*While the modern Maxwell's equations describe how electrically charged particles and objects give rise to electric and magnetic fields, the Lorentz force law completes that picture by describing the force acting on a moving point charge q in the presence of electromagnetic fields. The Lorentz force law describes the effect of **E** and **B** upon a point charge, but such electromagnetic forces are not the entire picture. Charged particles are possibly coupled to other forces, notably gravity and nuclear forces. Thus, Maxwell's equations do not stand separate from other physical laws, but are coupled to them via the charge and current densities. The response of a point charge to the Lorentz law is one aspect; the generation of **E** and **B** by currents and charges is another.*

*In real materials the Lorentz force is inadequate to describe the behavior of charged particles, both in principle and as a matter of computation. The charged particles in a material medium both respond to the **E** and **B** fields and generate these fields. Complex transport equations must be solved to determine the time and spatial response of charges, for example, the Boltzmann equation or the Fokker–Planck equation or the Navier-Stokes equations. For example, see magnetohydrodynamics, fluid dynamics, electrohydrodynamics, superconductivity, stellar evolution. An entire physical apparatus for dealing with these matters has developed. See for example, Green–Kubo relations and Green's function (many-body theory).*

*Although one might suggest that these theories are only approximations intended to deal with large ensembles of "point particles", perhaps a deeper perspective is that the charge-*

bearing particles may respond to forces like gravity, or nuclear forces, or boundary conditions."

-- Reference: Wikipedia.org

[68] "... quadrillion..."

"**Quadrillion** may mean either of the two numbers:

1,000,000,000,000,000 (one thousand million million; $10^{15}$; SI prefix peta) - increasingly common meaning in English language usage.

1,000,000,000,000,000,000,000,000 ($10^{24}$; SI prefix yotta) - increasingly rare meaning in English language usage."

-- Reference: Wikipedia.org

[69] "...points of origin to establish age and duration."

"So far scientists have not found a way to determine the exact age of the Earth directly from Earth rocks because Earth's oldest rocks have been recycled and destroyed by the process of plate tectonics. If there are any of Earth's primordial rocks left in their original state, they have not yet been found. Nevertheless, scientists have been able to determine the probable age of the Solar System and to calculate an age for the Earth by assuming that the Earth and the rest of the solid bodies in the Solar System formed at the same time and are, therefore, of the same age.

The ages of Earth and Moon rocks and of meteorites are measured by the decay of long-lived radioactive isotopes of elements that occur naturally in rocks and minerals and that decay with half lives of 700 million to more than 100 billion years to stable isotopes of other elements. These dating techniques, which are firmly grounded in physics and are known collectively as radiometric dating, are used to measure the last time that the rock being dated was either melted or disturbed sufficiently to rehomogenize its radioactive elements."

-- Reference: http://pubs.usgs.gov/gip/geotime/age.html

[70] "... The physical universe itself is formed from the convergence and amalgamation of many other individual universes..."

"A **creation myth** is a supernatural mytho-religious story or explanation that describes the beginnings of humanity, earth, life, and the universe (cosmogony), usually as a deliberate act of "creation" by a supreme being. Many accounts of creation share broadly similar themes. Common motifs include the fractionation of the things of the world from a primordial chaos; the separation of the mother and father gods; land emerging from an infinite and timeless ocean; or creation ex nihilo (Latin: out of nothing)."

-- Reference: Wikipedia.org

[71] "... energy and forms can be created, but not destroyed..."

"In physics, the **law of conservation of energy** states that the total amount of energy in any isolated system remains constant but cannot be recreated, although it may change forms, e.g. friction turns kinetic energy into thermal energy. In thermodynamics, the first law of thermodynamics is a statement of the conservation of energy for thermodynamic systems, and is the more encompassing version of the conservation of energy. In short, the law of conservation of energy states that energy can not be created or destroyed, it can only be changed from one form to another."

-- Reference: Wikipedia.org

[72] "... **Tales of magic, sorcery and enchantment, fairy tales and mythology** speak of such things..."

**Magic**, sometimes known as **sorcery**, is a conceptual system that asserts human ability to control the natural world (including events, objects, people, and physical phenomena) through mystical, paranormal or supernatural means. The term can also refer to the practices employed by a person asserting this influence, and to beliefs that explain various events and phenomena in such terms. In many cultures, magic is under pressure from, and in competition with, scientific and religious conceptual systems.

Adherents to magic believe that it may work by one or more of the following basic principles:

- *Natural forces that cannot be detected by science at present, and in fact may not be detectable at all. These magical forces are said to exist in addition to and alongside the four fundamental forces of nature: gravity, electromagnetism, the strong force and the weak force.*

- *Intervention of spirits similar to these hypothetical natural forces, but with their own consciousness and intelligence. Believers in spirits will often describe a whole cosmos of beings of many different kinds, sometimes organized into a hierarchy.*

*Aleister Crowley preferred the spelling magick, defining it as "the science and art of causing change to occur in conformity with the will." By this, he included "mundane" acts of will as well as ritual magic. In Magick in Theory and Practice, Chapter XIV, Crowley says:*

> *"What is a Magical Operation? It may be defined as any event in nature which is brought to pass by Will. We must not exclude potato-growing or banking from our definition. Let us take a very simple example of a Magical Act: that of a man blowing his nose." "*

-- Reference: Wikipedia.org

[73] "...they will capture other **IS-BEs as slaves**..."

"The word slave in the English language originates from the Middle English sclave, from the Old French esclave, the Medieval Latin sclavus, the early Greek sklabos, from sklabenoi, Slavs, of Slavic origin; akin to Old Russian Slovene, an East Slavic tribe. The term sclavus originally referred to the Slavs of Eastern and Central Europe, as many of these people had been captured and then sold as slaves by Otto the Great and his successors. The former Latin word for "slave" was servus (cf. English serf)."

The evidence for slavery predates written records. It can be found in almost all cultures and continents. Slavery can be traced to the earliest records, such as the Code of Hammurabi in Mesopotamia (~1800 BC), which refers to slavery as an already established institution. In important exception occurred under the reign of the Achaemenid Empire in Persia in 500 BC. The forced labor of women in some ancient and modern cultures may also be identified as slavery. Slavery, in this case, includes sexual services.

Historically, most slaves were captured in wars or kidnapped in isolated raids, but some persons were sold into slavery by their parents, or by themselves, as a means of surviving extreme conditions. Most slaves were born into that status, to parents who were enslaved. Ancient Warfare often resulted in slavery for prisoners and their families, who were either killed, ransomed or sold as slaves. Captives were often considered the property of those who captured them and were looked upon as a prize of war. Slavery may originally have been more humane than simply executing those who would return to fight if they were freed, but the effect led to widespread enslavement of particular groups of people. Those captured sometimes differed in ethnicity, nationality, religion, or race from their enslavers, but often were the same as the captors. The dominant group in an area might take captives and turn them into slaves with little fear of suffering the like fate. The possibility always existed of reversals of fortune, as when Seneca warned, at the height of the Roman Empire, when powerful nations fought among themselves, anyone might find himself enslaved."

-- Reference: Wikipedia.org

[74] "...asteroid belt..."

"The **asteroid belt** is the region of the Solar System located roughly between the orbits of the planets Mars and Jupiter. It is occupied by numerous irregularly shaped bodies called asteroids or minor planets. More than half the mass within the main belt is contained in the four largest objects: Ceres, 4 Vesta, 2 Pallas, and 10 Hygiea. All of these have mean diameters of more than 400 km, while Ceres, the main belt's only dwarf planet, is about 950 km in diameter. The remaining bodies range down to the size of a dust particle. The asteroid material is so thinly distributed that multiple unmanned spacecraft have traversed it without incident."

-- Reference: Wikipedia.org

[75] "... the Big Dipper constellation..."

"Within Ursa Major the stars of the Big Dipper have Bayer designations in consecutive Greek alphabetical order from the bowl to the handle.

| Proper Name | Bayer Designation | Apparent Magnitude | Distance (L Yrs) |
|---|---|---|---|

Dubhe α        124
    UMa1.8

M    β
era UM 2.4  79
k    a

| Phecda | γ UMa | 2.4 | 84 |

Megrez   δ       81
      UMa3.3

Ali   ε
oth  UM 1.8  81
  a

Mi   ζ
zar  UM 2.1  78
  a

Al   η
kai  UM 1.9  101
d  a

*Near Mizar is a star called Alcorr and together they are informally known as the Horse and Rider. At magnitude 4.1, Alcor would normally be relatively easy to see with the unaided eye, but its proximity to Mizar renders it more difficult to resolve, and it has served as a traditional test of sight. In the 17th century, Mizar itself was discovered to be a binary star system — the first telescopic binary found. The component stars are known as Mizar A and Mizar B. In 1889, Mizar A was discovered to in fact be a binary as well, the first spectroscopic binary discovered, and with the subsequent discovery that Mizar B itself is also a binary, in total Mizar currently is known to be at least a quadruple star system."*

-- Reference: Wikipedia.org

[76] **"... the body of the Archduke of Austria..."**

*"**Franz Ferdinand** (December 18, 1863 – June 28, 1914) was an Archduke of Austria-Este, Prince Imperial of Austria and Prince Royal of Hungary and Bohemia, and from 1896 until his death, heir presumptive to the Austro-Hungarian throne. His assassination in Sarajevo precipitated the Austrian declaration of war. **This caused countries allied with Austria-Hungary** (the Central Powers) and countries allied with Serbia (the Entente Powers) **to declare war on each other, starting World War I.***

*In 1889, Franz Ferdinand's life changed dramatically. His cousin Crown Prince Rudolf committed suicide at his hunting lodge in Mayerling, leaving Franz Ferdinand's father, Archduke Karl Ludwig, as first in line to the throne. However his father renounced his succession rights a few days after the Crown Prince's death. Henceforth, Franz Ferdinand was groomed to succeed.*

*On June 28, 1914, at approximately 11:15 am, Franz Ferdinand and his wife were killed in Sarajevo, the capital of the Austro-Hungarian province of Bosnia and Herzegovina, by Gavrilo Princip, a member of Young Bosnia and one of several (a few) assassins organized by The Black Hand (Црна рука/Tsrna Ruka). The event, known as the Assassination in Sarajevo, triggered World War I.*

*Franz and Sophie had previously been attacked when a bomb was thrown at their car. It missed them, but many civilians were injured. Franz and Sophie both insisted on going to see all those injured at the hospital. As a result of this, Princip saw them and shot Sophie in* the abdomen. Franz was shot in the jugular and was still alive when witnesses arrived to his aid, but it was too late; he died within minutes.

The assassinations, along with the arms race, nationalism, imperialism,, militarism, and the alliance system all contributed to the beginning of World War I, which began less than two months after Franz Ferdinand's death, with Austria-Hungary's declaration of war against Serbia."

-- Reference: Wikipedia.org

[77] ..."force field"...

"Originally a term coined by Michael Faraday to provide an intuitive paradigm, but theoretical construct, for **the behavior of electromagnetic fields, the term force field refers to the lines of force one object (the "source object") exerts on another object or a collection of other objects. An object might be a mass particle or an electric or magnetic charge, for example**. The lines do not have to be straight, in the Euclidean geometry case, but may be curved. Faraday called these theoretical connections between objects lines of force because the objects are most directly connected to the source object along this line.

**Examples of force fields:**

- A local Newtonian gravitational field near Earth ground typically consists of a uniform array of vectors pointing in one direction---downwards, towards the ground; its force field is represented by the Cartesian vector , where points in a direction away from the ground, and m refers to the mass, and g refers to the acceleration due to gravity.
- A global Gravitational field consists of a spherical array of vectors pointing towards the center of gravity. Its classical force field, in spherical coordinates, is represented by the vector, , which is just Newton's Law of Gravity, with the radial unit vector pointing towards the origin of the sphere (center of the Earth).
- A conservative Electric field has an electric charge (or a smeared plum pudding of electric charges) as its source object. In the case of the point charges, the force field is represented by , where is the position vector that represents the straightest line between the source charge and the other charge.
- A static Magnetic field has a magnetic charge (a magnetic monopole or a charge distribution).
- The electromagnetic force is given by the Lorentz force formula, which in SI units is, "

-- Reference: Wikipedia.org

[78] "Electroshock..."

"The story of electric shock began in 1938, when Italian psychiatrist Ugo Cerletti visited a Rome slaughterhouse to see what could be learned from the method that was employed to butcher hogs. In Cerletti's own words, "As soon as the hogs were clamped by the [electric] tongs, they fell unconscious, stiffened, then after a few seconds they were shaken by convulsions.... During this period of unconsciousness (epileptic coma), the butcher stabbed and bled the animals without difficulty....

"At this point I felt we could venture to experiment on man, and I instructed my assistants to be on the alert for the selection of a suitable subject."

202

Cerletti's first victim was provided by the local police - a man described by Cerletti as "lucid and well-oriented." After surviving the first blast without losing consciousness, the victim overheard Cerletti discussing a second application with a higher voltage. He begged Cerletti, "Non una seconda! Mortifiere!" ("Not another one! It will kill me!")

Ignoring the objections of his assistants, Cerletti increased the voltage and duration and fired again. With the "successful" electrically induced convulsion of his victim, Ugo Cerletti brought about the application of hog-slaughtering skills to humans, creating one of the most brutal techniques of psychiatry.

*Electric shock is also called electro-convulsive "therapy" or treatment (ECT), electroshock therapy or electric shock treatment (EST), electrostimulation, and electrolytic therapy (ELT). All are euphemistic terms for the same process: sending a searing blast of electricity through the brain in order to alter behavior." (Reference: http://www.sntp.net/ect/ect3.htm)

Today Electroshock therapy (ECT) is most often used as a treatment for severe major depression which has not responded to other treatment, and is also used in the treatment of mania, catatonia, schizophrenia and other disorders. It first gained widespread use as a form of treatment in the 1940s and 50s. Today, an estimated 1 million people worldwide receive ECT every year, usually in a course of 6-12 treatments administered 2 or 3 times a week.

Electroconvulsive therapy has "side-effects" which include confusion and memory loss for events around the time period of treatment. ECT have been shown to cause persistent memory loss. It is the effects of ECT on long-term memory that give rise to much of the concern surrounding its use. The acute effects of ECT include **amnesia**.

Registered nurse Barbara C. Cody reports in a letter to the *Washington Post* that her life "was forever changed by 13 outpatient ECTs I received in 1983. Shock 'therapy' totally and permanently disabled me. "EEGs [electroencephalograms] verify the extensive damage shock did to my brain. **Fifteen to 20 years of my life were simply erased**; only small bits and pieces have returned. I was also left with short-term memory impairment and serious cognitive deficits. **"Shock 'therapy' took my past, my college education, my musical abilities, even the knowledge that my children were, in fact, my children."**

**Ernest Hemingway**, American author, committed suicide shortly after Electric Shock treatment at the Menninger Clinic in 1961. He is reported to have said to his biographer, *"Well, what is the sense of ruining my head and erasing my memory, which is my capital, and putting me out of business? It was a brilliant cure but we lost the patient...."*

-- Reference: Wikipedia.org

[79] "...electric voltage..."

"The general public may consider household mains circuits (100–250 V AC), which carry the highest voltages they normally encounter, to be high voltage. For example, an installer of heating, ventilation and air conditioning equipment may be licensed to install 24 Volt control circuits, but may not be permitted to connect the 240 volt power circuits of the equipment.

**Voltages over approximately 50 volts can usually cause dangerous amounts of current to flow through a human being** touching two points of a circuit.

*Voltages of greater than 50 V are capable of producing heart fibrillation if they produce electric currents in body tissues which happen to pass through the chest area. The electrocution danger is mostly determined by the low conductivity of dry human skin. If skin is wet, or if there are wounds, or if the voltage is applied to electrodes which penetrate the skin, then even voltage sources below 40 V can be lethal if contacted."*

-- Reference: Wikipedia.org

[80] **"...Post hypnotic suggestions..."**

*"The ability of a human to be induced into a form of behavior or thinking pattern after coming out of the hypnotic state.* **Post hypnotic suggestions are administered by the hypnotist and may optionally include a time scope. An altered sense of perception or behavioral pattern may be "programmed" into the person under hypnosis.** *Certain sequences of events may be set as triggers to enter or exit the post-hypnotic pattern. The behavior patterns resemble conditioned reflexes, though administered without classical behavior alteration techniques.*

*Examples:*

**Any number, color, object, etc. may be induced to be ignored by the patient after full consciousness.** *A certain keyword starts the suggestion and a different word ends it.* **The patient will not know nor use the item to be ignored. He/she may state that the sea is colored red, if suggested to ignore the color blue.** *A count of eleven may be achieved if asked to count ones fingers if a number -say 5- is suggested to be ignored. Thus the patient counts 1-2-3-4-6-7-8-9-10-11*

**Different type of behavior patterns may be induced** *such as forcing the patient to recite a certain sentence* **whenever anyone says out loud the special keyword.** *The patient is fully aware of the conditioned action but it is very difficult, if not impossible, to restrain from doing it.* **Sweating, loss of coordination and full lack of concentration plagues the patient until he/she performs the programmed action.**

**An object may be set to be perceived as invisible** *and it will be fully ignored and evaded during the period of suggestion. Experiments may be performed with a coffee mug, induced to be invisible. If the mug is put on top of a page with writing, the patient will only read the parts not covered by the mug. Even though the sentences may make no sense, nothing is seemingly wrong to the suspected. It is difficult to suggest an object be invisible, yet stay tactile. Usually* **the object is completely ignored by all senses.** *Thus, the mug in the example* **will reportedly not exist, even when the patient is touching it.**

*Stage hypnotists will sometimes perform shows in which they hypnotize participants to think they are some celebrity and behave exactly like them. John Mohl, stage hypnotist and member of The National Guild of Hypnotists, says that* **he has often hypnotized people to become someone else***! Mohl noticed that adults often became a celebrity while Middle or High School students usually become something much more creative or imaginative."*

-- Reference: Wikipedia.org

[81] **"... Untouchables..."**

"In the Indian caste system, a Dalit, often called an **untouchable**, or an **outcaste**, is a person who according to traditional Hindu belief does not have any "varnas". Varna refers to the Hindu belief that most humans were supposedly created from different parts of the body of the divinity Purusha. The part from which a varna was supposedly created defines a person's social status with regard to issues such as whom they may marry and which professions they may hold. Dalits fall outside the varnas system and have historically been prevented from doing any but the most menial jobs. (However, a distinction must be made between lower-caste people and Pariahs.) Included are leather-workers (called chamar), carcass handlers (called mahar),poor farmers and landless labourers, night soil scavengers (called bhangi or chura), street handicrafters, folk artists, street cleaners, dhobi, etc.

Traditionally, they were treated as pariahs in South Asian society and **isolated in their own communities**, to the point that **even their shadows were avoided by the upper castes**. Discrimination against Dalits still exists in rural areas in the private sphere, in ritual matters such as access to eating places and water sources. It has largely disappeared, however, in urban areas and in the public sphere, in rights of movement and access to schools. The earliest rejection of discrimination, at least in spiritual matters, was made as far back as the Bhagavada Gita, which says that no person, no matter what, is barred from enlightenment There are an estimated 160 million Dalits in India."

Reference: Wikipedia.org

"Human rights abuses against these people, known as Dalits, are legion. A random sampling of headlines in mainstream Indian newspapers tells their story: "Dalit boy beaten to death for plucking flowers"; "Dalit tortured by cops for three days"; "Dalit 'witch' paraded naked in Bihar"; "Dalit killed in lock-up at Kurnool"; "7 Dalits burnt alive in caste clash"; "5 Dalits lynched in Haryana"; "Dalit woman gang-raped, paraded naked"; "Police egged on mob to lynch Dalits".

"Dalits are not allowed to drink from the same wells, attend the same temples, wear shoes in the presence of an upper caste, or drink from the same cups in tea stalls," said Smita Narula, a senior researcher with Human Rights Watch, and author of Broken People: Caste Violence Against India's "Untouchables." Human Rights Watch is a worldwide activist organization based in New York. India's Untouchables are relegated to the lowest jobs, and live in constant fear of being publicly humiliated, paraded naked, beaten, and raped with impunity by upper-caste Hindus seeking to keep them in their place. Merely walking through an upper-caste neighborhood is a life-threatening offense. Nearly 90 percent of all the poor Indians and 95 percent of all the illiterate Indians are Dalits."

Reference:
http://news.nationalgeographic.com/news/2003/06/0602_030602_untouchables.html

[82] "...political prisoners..."

"A **political prisoner** is someone held in prison or otherwise detained, perhaps under house arrest, for his/her involvement in political activity.

political prisoners are arrested and tried with a veneer of legality, where false criminal charges, manufactured evidence, and unfair trials are used to disguise the fact that an individual is a political prisoner. This is common in situations which may otherwise be decried nationally and internationally as a human rights violation and suppression of a political dissident. A political prisoner can also be someone that has been denied bail *unfairly, denied parole when it would reasonably have been given to a prisoner charged with a comparable crime, or special powers may be invoked by the judiciary.*

*Particularly in this latter situation, whether an individual is regarded as a political prisoner may depend upon subjective political perspective or interpretation of the evidence. Governments typically reject assertions that they hold political prisoners.*

***Examples****:*

*In the **Soviet Union**, **dubious psychiatric diagnoses** were sometimes used to confine political prisoners. In **Nazi Germany**, "Night and Fog" prisoners were among the first victims of fascist repression. In **North Korea**, entire families are jailed if one family member is suspected of anti-government sentiments."*

-- Reference: Wikipedia.org

[83] "... His commanding officer ordered that a battle cruiser be dispatched..."

**Editor's Note: The only Wikipedia.org reference to the term "battle cruiser" is a US or British Navy ships. Another interesting and entertaining reference is as follows:**

*"The **Honorverse** is the semi-official name for the setting of a **military science fiction series** of stories **by David Weber** featuring Honor Harrington, the Nelsonesque heroine in a series reminiscent of C. S. Forester's Horatio Hornblower book series. The books are popular in the United States and new releases regularly make The New York Times Best Seller list.*

*The following list refers to starship classes within different areas of Honorverse:*

*These starship classes are in the People's Republic of Haven:*

- ***Cimeterres-class****: LAC*
- ***Program 13-class****: LAC*
- ***Bastogne-class****: destroyer*
- ***City-class****: destroyer*
- ***Desforge-class****: destroyer*
- ***Frigate-class I****: light cruiser*
- ***Conqueror-class****: light cruiser*
- ***Charles Wade Pope-class****: light cruiser*
- ***Brillance-class****: light cruiser*
- ***Mars-A-class****: heavy cruiser*
- ***Mars-B-class****: heavy cruiser*
- ***Scimitar-class****: heavy cruiser*
- ***Sword-class****: heavy cruiser*
- ***Tiger-class****: battlecruiser*
- ***Warlord-class****: battlecruiser*
- ***Sultan-class****: battlecruiser*
- ***Triumphant-class****: battleship*
- ***Nouveau Paris-class****: dreadnought - Formally thought to be the New Boston-class*
- ***Rousseau-class****: dreadnought*
- ***DuQuesne-class****: superdreadnought*

- **Sovereign of Space-class**: *pod-superdreadnaught*
- **Temeraire-class**: *pod-superdreadnaught*
- **Astra-class**: *LAC Carrier*
- **Aviary-class**: *LAC Carrier"*

-- Reference: Wikipedia.org

[84] **"...a few hundred miles north of the equator on Mars in the Cydonia region."**

This statement was made by Airl in 1947. The following photographs of this area were not taken by NASA satellites in the 1970s!

( The following internet links shows maps of a complex of artificial looking structures which some people have referred to a the "Pyramid Complex, The Face on Mars, and other geological features that are strikingly similar to symbols and architecture found in Mesoamerican and Egyptian pyramid civilizations. Notice how the "pyramids and face structures look as though they have been partially destroyed! Had there been an "Old Empire" base at this location, which was destroyed by a cruiser attack from The Domain Force, it base would have been significantly damaged. )

http://www.greatdreams.com/cydonia.htm

http://www.qtm.net/~geibdan/cydonia.html

*"In addition, a team of scientists from the United States Geological Survey reported at the recent annual Lunar and Planetary Science Conference in Houston, Texas, that images taken by NASA's Mars-orbiting spacecraft Mars Odyssey show what appear to be cave entrances where primitive life forms – "past or present microbial life" – could have been sheltered, and where water could exist in liquid form.*

*A more detailed perusal of the report reveals that the spacecraft actually photographed, in both visual and infrared, puzzling dark circular structures associated with these caves - structures ranging in size from 100 to 250 meters (330 to 825 feet). Picking up the hardly-noticed story in its June 2007 issue, the prestigious journal Scientific American has now provided additional information: Seven such "football size" caverns were identified; they are 425 feet deep. "*

-- Reference: Wikipedia.org

[85] **"... mind control..."**

**"Mind control** (or "brainwashing") refers to a broad range of psychological tactics able to subvert an individual's control of his own thinking, behavior, emotions, or decisions. The concept is **closely related to hypnosis**, but differs in practical approach.

*William Sargant connected Pavlov's findings (the Russian researcher who experimented on stimulus-response mechanism with dogs) to the ways people learned and internalized belief systems. Conditioned behavior patterns could be changed by stimulated stresses beyond a dog's capacity for response, in essence causing a breakdown. This could also be caused by intense signals, longer than normal waiting periods, rotating positive and negative signals and changing a dog's physical condition, as through illness. Depending on the dog's initial* personality, this could possibly cause a new belief system to be held tenaciously. Sargant also connected Pavlov's findings to the **mechanisms of brain-washing**....

**"Though men are not dogs, they should humbly try to remember how much they resemble dogs in their brain functions, and not boast themselves as demigods. They are gifted with religious and social apprehensions, and they are gifted with the power of reason; but all these faculties are physiologically entailed to the brain. Therefore the brain should not be abused by having forced upon it any religious or political mystique that stunts the reason, or any form of crude rationalism that stunts the religious sense."** (p. 274)

Psychologist Margaret Singer describes **six conditions which would create an atmosphere in which thought reform is possible**. Singer states that these conditions involve no need for physical coercion or violence.

- Keep the victim unaware of what is going on and how he is being changed a step at a time.
- Control the victim's social and/or physical environment; especially control the victim's time.
- Systematically create a sense of powerlessness in the victim. This is accomplished by getting victims away from their normal social support group for a period of time and into an environment where the majority of people are already group members.
    - The victims serve as models of the attitudes and behaviors of the group and speak an in-group language.
    - Strip victims of their main occupation (quit jobs, drop out of school) or source of income or have them turn over their income (or the majority of) to the group.
    - Once stripped of your usual support network, your confidence in your own perception erodes.
    - As your sense of powerlessness increases, your good judgment and understanding of the world are diminished. (ordinary view of reality is destabilized)
    - As group attacks your previous worldview, it causes you distress and inner confusion; yet you are not allowed to speak about this confusion or object to it -- leadership suppresses questions and counters resistance.
    - This process is sped up if you are kept tired.
- Manipulate a system of rewards, punishments and experiences in such a way as to inhibit behavior that reflects the victim's former social identity.
    - Manipulation of experiences can be accomplished through various methods of trance induction, including leaders using such techniques as paced speaking patterns, guided imagery, chanting, long prayer sessions or lectures, and lengthy meditation sessions.
    - Your old beliefs and patterns of behavior are defined as irrelevant or evil. Leadership wants these old patterns eliminated, so the victims must suppress them.
    - Victims get positive feedback for conforming to the group's beliefs and behaviors and negative feedback for old beliefs and behavior.
- Manipulate a system of rewards, punishments, and experiences in order to promote learning the group's ideology or belief system and group-approved behaviors.
    - Good behavior, demonstrating an understanding and acceptance of the group's beliefs, and compliance are rewarded while questioning, expressing doubts or criticizing are met with disapproval, redress and possible rejection.

If one expresses a question, he or she is made to feel that there is
something inherently wrong with them to be questioning.

- The only feedback victims get is from the group, they become totally
  dependent upon the rewards given by those who control the environment.
- Victims must learn varying amounts of new information about the beliefs of
  the group and the behaviors expected by the group.
- The more complicated and filled with contradictions the new system is and
  the more difficult it is to learn, the more effective the conversion process will
  be.
- Esteem and affection from peers is very important to new recruits. Approval
  comes from having the new victim's behaviors and thought patterns conform
  to the models (victims). Victims' relationship with peers is threatened
  whenever they fail to learn or display new behaviors. Over time, the easy
  solution to the insecurity generated by the difficulties of learning the new
  system is to inhibit any display of doubts -- new recruits simply acquiesce,
  affirm and act as if they do understand and accept the new ideology.

- Put forth a closed system of logic and an authoritarian structure that permits no
  feedback and refuses to be modified except by leadership approval or executive
  order.
  - The group has a top-down, pyramid structure. The leaders must have verbal
    ways of never losing.
  - Victims are not allowed to question, criticize or complain -- if they do, the
    leaders allege that the victim is defective -- not the organization or the
    beliefs.
  - The individual is always wrong -- the system, its leaders and its belief are
    always right.
  - Remolding of the individual victim happens in a closed system. As victims
    learn to modify their behavior in order to be accepted in this closed system,
    they change -- begin to speak the language -- which serves to further isolate
    them from their prior beliefs and behaviors."

### Social psychology tactics

A contemporary view of mind control sees it as an intensified and persistent use of well
researched social psychology principles like compliance, conformity, persuasion,
dissonance, reactance, framing or emotional manipulation.

One of the most notable proponents of such theories is social psychologist Philip Zimbardo,
former president of the American Psychological Association:

> "I conceive of mind control as a phenomena encompassing all the ways in
> which personal, social and institutional forces are exerted to induce
> compliance, conformity, belief, attitude, and value change in others.
>
> "Mind control is the process by which individual or collective freedom of
> choice and action is compromised by agents or agencies that modify or
> distort perception, motivation, affect, cognition and/or behavioral outcomes. It
> is neither magical nor mystical, but a process that involves a set of basic
> social psychological principles."

In Influence, Science and Practice, social psychologist Robert Cialdini argues that mind
control is possible through the covert exploitation of the unconscious rules that

underlie and facilitate healthy human social interactions. He states that common social rules *can be used to prey upon the unwary*, and he titles them as follows:

- *"Reciprocation: The Old Give and Take...and Take"*
- *"Commitment and Consistency: Hobgoblins of the Mind"*
- *"Social Proof: Truths Are Us"*
- *"Liking: The Friendly Thief"*
- *"Authority: Directed Deference"*
- *"Scarcity: The Rule of the Few"*

*Using these six broad categories, he offers specific examples of both mild and extreme mind control (both one on one and in groups), notes the conditions under which each social rule is most easily exploited for false ends, and offers suggestions on how to resist such methods."*

Reference: Wikipedia.org

[86] **"... remote thought control..."**

**EDITOR'S NOTE:** If "hypersonic sound" (see reference below) can already be used on Earth, which has been using electricity for only 150 years, imagine a technology that has been refined over millions of years, that could transmit <u>thoughts</u> that are precisely targeted to an individual person across millions of miles of space.

*"The lunatic is in my head,"* sang Pink Floyd on their landmark "Dark Side of the Moon" album released 35 years ago. "There's someone in my head but it's not me."

**In 2008, there is a chance that the voice inside your head may be trying to sell you something.** Advertisers are using a new acoustic technology to project advertising slogans directly into your head. And not everyone is happy about the aural intrusion.

In fact, **the space between your ears may be the newest battleground in the conflict between privacy and technology.** The technique is called hypersonic sound and it was created by inventor Woody Norris. **Hypersonic sound (HSS)** projection enables sound to be directed precisely to one individual without any spillover.

In tandem with an ultrasonic emitter and a signal processor/amplifier, HSS projects a column of modulated ultrasonic frequencies into the air. The ultrasonic frequencies are inaudible by themselves, but the interaction of the frequencies with the air create sounds that can be heard by anyone inside the column. Hypersonic sound can direct sound as precisely as a laser beam can direct light.

One only needs to be standing in the path of an HSS beam in order to hear the sound. However, the sensation to those hearing is that the sound is being projected from inside their skull.

Pretty cool, thinks inventor Norris. Or pretty creepy if you don't know what's going on. It is already being done from a billboard on Prince Street in New York City.

Advertising for a television show called "Paranormal State," which airs on the Arts and Entertainment Network (A&E), has been sent through HSS to unsuspecting pedestrians who trigger a sensor as they stroll by. The sound that is emitted can be heard only by them.

Science and technology writer Clive Thompson, has written about the Prince Street billboard for Wired magazine. He experienced HSS himself, writing that it felt "creepy" to hear a woman's voice whisper, "Who's there? Who's there?"

It used to be that we could at least be guaranteed privacy in the space between our ears. That is no longer true, thanks to the invention of "in-head advertising."

**The freedom to think our own thoughts without artificial manipulation from outside sources may be our latest civil rights battle."**
By RUTH N. GELLER
HumanistNetworkNews.org
April 2, 2008

-- Reference: http://humaniststudies.org/enews/?id=342&showAll=true

[87] "... the remote mind-control operation..."

"One of the earliest examples of **remote control was developed in 1893 by Nikola Tesla**, and described in his patent, U.S. Patent 613,809, named "Method of an Apparatus for Controlling Mechanism of Moving Vehicle or Vehicles".

"In 1903, Leonardo Torres Quevedo presented the Telekino at the Paris Academy of Science, accompanied by a brief, and making an experimental demonstration. In the same year, he obtained a patent in France, Spain, Great Britain, and the United States. The Telekino consisted of a robot that executed commands transmitted by electromagnetic waves. It constituted the world's first apparatus for radio control and was a pioneer in the field of remote control. In 1906, in the presence of the king and before a great crowd, Torres successfully demonstrated the invention in the port of Bilbao, guiding a boat from the shore. Later, he would try to apply the Telekino to projectiles and torpedoes, but had to abandon the project for lack of financing.

The first remote-controlled model airplane flew in 1932, and **the use of remote control technology for military purposes** was worked intensively during the Second World War, one result of this being the German Wasserfall missile."

**Remote control technology is also used in space travel,** for instance the Russian Lunokhod vehicles were remote-controlled from the ground. **Direct remote control of space vehicles** at greater distances from the earth is not practical due to increasing signal delay times."

Reference: Wikipedia.org

[88] "... mind control..."

Editor's Note: The most famously publicized evidence of the use of mind-control operations is the CIA project, "MK-ULTRA":

"Project **MK-ULTRA**, or **MKULTRA**, was the code name for a covert CIA mind-control and chemical interrogation research program, run by the Office of Scientific Intelligence, that began in the early 1950s and continued at least through the late 1960s. There is much published evidence that the project involved the surreptitious use of many types of drugs, as well as other methodology, to manipulate individual mental states and to alter brain function.

Project MK-ULTRA was first brought to wide public attention in 1975 by the U.S. Congress, through investigations by the Church Committee, and by a presidential commission known as the Rockefeller Commission. Investigative efforts were hampered by the fact that CIA Director Richard Helms ordered all MK-ULTRA files destroyed in 1973.

Although the CIA insists that MK-ULTRA-type experiments have been abandoned, 14-year CIA veteran Victor Marchetti has stated in various interviews that the CIA routinely conducts disinformation campaigns and that CIA mind control research continued. In a 1977 interview, Marchetti specifically called the CIA claim that MK-ULTRA was abandoned a 'cover story.'.

On the Senate floor in 1977, Senator Ted Kennedy said:

The Deputy Director of the CIA revealed that over thirty universities and institutions were involved in an 'extensive testing and experimentation' program which included covert drug tests on unwitting citizens 'at all social levels, high and low, native Americans and foreign.' Several of these tests involved the administration of LSD to 'unwitting subjects in social situations.' At least one death, that of Dr. [Frank] Olson, resulted from these activities. The Agency itself acknowledged that these tests made little scientific sense. The agents doing the monitoring were not qualified scientific observers.

A precursor of the MK-ULTRA program began in 1945 when the Joint Intelligence Objectives Agency was established and given direct responsibility for Operation Paperclip. **Operation Paperclip was a program to recruit former Nazi spies, scientists and experts in torture and brain washing,** some of whom had just been identified and prosecuted as war criminals during the Nuremberg Trials.

Several secret U.S. government projects grew out of Operation Paperclip. These projects included Project CHATTER (established 1947), and Project BLUEBIRD (established 1950), which was later renamed to Project ARTICHOKE in 1951. Their purpose was to study mind-control, interrogation, behavior modification and related topics.

Headed by Dr. Sidney Gottlieb, **the MK-ULTRA project was started on the order of CIA director Allen Dulles on April 13, 1953,** largely in response to Soviet, Chinese, and North Korean use of mind-control techniques on U.S. prisoners of war in Korea. The CIA wanted to use similar methods on their own captives. The CIA was also interested in being able to manipulate foreign leaders with such techniques, and would later invent several schemes to drug Fidel Castro.

Experiments were often conducted without the subjects' knowledge or consent. In some cases, academic researchers being funded through grants from CIA front organizations were unaware that their work was being used for these purposes.

In 1964, the project was renamed MK-SEARCH. The project attempted to produce a perfect truth drug for use in interrogating suspected Soviet spies during the Cold War, and **generally to explore any other possibilities of mind control.**

An MK-ULTRA program tagged "Operation Teapot" involved the testing of pregnant women with radiation, among other things. Also under this program, U.S. army soldiers were dosed with LSD to study the effects of panic.

212

Another MK-ULTRA effort, Subproject 54, was the Navy's top secret "Perfect Concussion" program, which *used sub aural frequency blasts to erase memory*. During this program LSD's corollary effect on controlled and channeled mass panic was discovered.

MK-ULTRA head Sidney Gottlieb was involved with both Operation Teapot and Subproject 54. The U.S. government officially denied involvement until 1995 when an official apology was issued to the pregnant women and to the affected U.S. army soldiers. However no apologies were offered to the affected U.S. Navy soldiers or to a group of Oregon prison inmates, whose testicles were irradiated without their knowledge. Compensation for medical treatment resulting from these experiments has been disputed and remains tied up in arbitration more than 40 years after the fact. Since 1995, most of the associated files have been reclassified as Top Secret.

Because most MK-ULTRA records were deliberately destroyed in 1973 by order of then CIA Director Richard Helms, it has been difficult, if not impossible, for investigators to gain a complete understanding of the more than 150 individually funded research sub-projects sponsored by MK Ultra and related CIA programs.

### Aims

**The Agency poured millions of dollars into studies probing dozens of methods of influencing and controlling the mind.** One 1955 MK-ULTRA document gives an indication of the size and range of the effort; this document refers to the study of an assortment of mind-altering substances described as follows:

1. Substances which will promote illogical thinking and impulsiveness to the point where the recipient would be discredited in public.
2. Substances which increase the efficiency of mentation and perception.
3. Materials which will prevent or counteract the intoxicating effect of alcohol.
4. Materials which will promote the intoxicating effect of alcohol.
5. Materials which will produce the signs and symptoms of recognized diseases in a reversible way so that they may be used for malingering, etc.
6. **Materials which will render the induction of hypnosis easier** or otherwise enhance its usefulness.
7. Substances which will enhance the ability of individuals to withstand privation, torture and coercion during interrogation and so-called "brain-washing".
8. Materials and physical **methods which will produce amnesia** for events preceding and during their use.
9. Physical methods of producing shock and confusion over extended periods of time and capable of surreptitious use.
10. Substances which produce physical disablement such as paralysis of the legs, acute anemia, etc.
11. Substances which will produce "pure" euphoria with no subsequent let-down.
12. Substances which alter personality structure in such a way that the tendency of the recipient to become dependent upon another person is enhanced.
13. A material which will cause mental confusion of such a type that the individual under its influence will find it difficult to maintain a fabrication under questioning.
14. Substances which will lower the ambition and general working efficiency of men when administered in undetectable amounts.
15. Substances which promote weakness or distortion of the eyesight or hearing faculties, preferably without permanent effects.

16. A knockout pill which can surreptitiously be administered in drinks, food, cigarettes, as an aerosol, etc., which will be safe to use, provide a maximum of amnesia, and be suitable for use by agent types on an ad hoc basis.
17. A material which can be surreptitiously administered by the above routes and which in very small amounts will make it impossible for a man to perform any physical activity whatsoever.

Historians have learned that **creating a "Manchurian Candidate" subject through "mind control" techniques was undoubtedly a goal of MK-ULTRA and** related CIA projects.

## Budget

**A secretive arrangement granted a percentage of the CIA budget.** The MK-ULTRA director was granted six percent of the CIA operating budget in 1953, without oversight or accounting.

## Experiments

CIA documents suggest that "chemical, biological and radiological" means were investigated for the purpose of mind control as part of MK-ULTRA.

## Drugs

### LSD

Early efforts focused on LSD, which later came to dominate many of MK-ULTRA's programs.

Experiments included administering LSD to CIA employees, military personnel, doctors, other government agents, prostitutes, mentally ill patients, and members of the general public in order to study their reactions. LSD and other drugs were usually administered without the subject's knowledge and informed consent, a violation of the Nuremberg Code that the U.S. agreed to follow after WWII.

Efforts to "recruit" subjects were often illegal, even discounting the fact that drugs were being administered (though actual use of LSD, for example, was legal in the United States until October 6, 1966). In Operation Midnight Climax, the CIA set up several brothels to obtain a selection of men who would be too embarrassed to talk about the events. The men were dosed with LSD, and the brothels were equipped with one-way mirrors and the "sessions" were filmed for later viewing and study.

Some subjects' participation was consensual, and in many of these cases, the subjects appeared to be singled out for even more extreme experiments. In one case, volunteers were given LSD for 77 consecutive days.

LSD was eventually dismissed by MK-ULTRA's researchers as too unpredictable in its effects. Although useful information was sometimes obtained through questioning subjects on LSD, not uncommonly the most marked effect would be the subject's absolute and utter certainty that they were able to withstand any form of interrogation attempt, even physical torture.

### Other drugs

Another technique investigated was connecting a barbiturate IV into one arm and an amphetamine IV into the other. The barbiturates were released into the subject first, and as soon as the subject began to fall asleep, the amphetamines were released. The subject would begin babbling incoherently at this point, and it was sometimes possible to ask questions and get useful answers.

Other experiments involved heroin, morphine, temazepam (used under code name MK-SEARCH), mescaline, psilocybin, scopolamine, marijuana, alcohol, and sodium pentothal.

### Hypnosis

Declassified MK-ULTRA documents indicate hypnosis was studied in the early 1950s. Experimental goals included: the creation of "hypnotically induced anxieties," "hypnotically increasing ability to learn and recall complex written matter," studying hypnosis and polygraph examinations, "hypnotically increasing ability to observe and recall complex arrangements of physical objects," and studying "relationship of personality to susceptibility to hypnosis."

### Canadian experiments

The experiments were exported to Canada when the CIA recruited Scottish **psychiatrist Donald Ewen Cameron**, creator of the "psychic driving" concept, which the CIA found particularly interesting. **Cameron had been hoping to correct schizophrenia by erasing existing memories** and completely rebuilding the psyche. He commuted from Albany, New York to Montreal every week to work at the Allan Memorial Institute of McGill University and was paid $69,000 from 1957 to 1964 to carry out MKULTRA experiments there.

In addition to LSD, **Cameron also experimented with various paralytic drugs as well as electroconvulsive therapy at thirty to forty times the normal power.** His "driving" experiments consisted of putting subjects into drug-induced coma for weeks at a time (up to three months in one case) while playing tape loops of noise or simple repetitive statements. His experiments were typically carried out on patients who had entered the institute for minor problems such as anxiety disorders and postpartum depression, many of whom suffered permanently from his actions. His treatments resulted in victims' incontinence, **amnesia**, forgetting how to talk, forgetting their parents, and thinking their interrogators were their parents. His work was inspired and paralleled by the British **psychiatrist** Dr William Sargant at St Thomas' Hospital, London, and Belmont Hospital, Surrey, who also experimented extensively and very damagingly on his patients without their consent and was equally involved with the Intelligence Services.

It was during this **era that Cameron became known worldwide as <u>the first chairman of the World Psychiatric Association</u>** as well as president of the American and Canadian psychiatric associations. Cameron had also been a member of the Nuremberg medical tribunal only a decade earlier.

### Revelation

In 1973, **CIA Director Richard Helms ordered all MK-ULTRA files destroyed.** *Pursuant to this order, most CIA documents regarding the project were destroyed, making a full investigation of MK-ULTRA all but impossible.*

*In December 1974, The New York Times reported that the CIA had conducted illegal domestic activities, including experiments on U.S. citizens, during the 1960s. That report prompted investigations by the U.S. Congress, in the form of the Church Committee, and by a presidential commission known as the Rockefeller Commission that looked into **domestic activities of the CIA, the FBI, and intelligence-related agencies of the military**.*

**In the summer of 1975, congressional Church Committee reports and the presidential Rockefeller Commission report revealed to the public for the first time that the CIA and the Department of Defense had conducted experiments on both unwitting and cognizant human subjects as part of an extensive program to influence and control human behavior through the use of psychoactive drugs such as LSD and mescaline and other chemical, biological, and psychological means.** *They also revealed that at least one subject had died after administration of LSD.*

*The congressional committee investigating the CIA research, chaired by Senator Frank Church, concluded that "[p]rior consent was obviously not obtained from any of the subjects". The committee noted that the "experiments sponsored by these researchers ... call into question the decision by the agencies not to fix guidelines for experiments."*

*In Canada, the issue took much longer to surface, becoming widely known in 1984 on a CBC news show, The Fifth Estate. **It was learned that not only had the CIA funded Dr. Cameron's efforts, but perhaps even more shockingly, the Canadian government was fully aware of this, and had later provided another $500,000 in funding to continue the experiments.** This revelation largely derailed efforts by the victims to sue the CIA as their U.S. counterparts had, and the Canadian government eventually settled out of court for $100,000 to each of the 127 victims.*

### U.S. General Accounting Office Report

*The U.S. General Accounting Office issued a report on September 28, 1994, which stated that between 1940 and 1974, DOD and other national security agencies studied thousands of human subjects in tests and experiments involving hazardous substances.*

*The quote from the study:*

*... Working with the CIA, the Department of Defense gave hallucinogenic drugs to thousands of "volunteer" soldiers in the 1950's and 1960's. In addition to LSD, the Army also tested quinuclidinyl benzilate, a hallucinogen code-named BZ. Many of these tests were conducted under the so-called MKULTRA program, established to counter perceived Soviet and Chinese advances in brainwashing techniques. Between 1953 and 1964, the program consisted of 149 projects involving drug testing and other studies on unwitting human subjects...*

### Extent of participation

*44 American colleges or universities, 15 research foundations or chemical or pharmaceutical companies and the like, 12 hospitals or clinics (in addition to those associated with universities), and 3 prisons are known to have participated in MKULTRA.*

### Famous subjects

*Considerable evidence supports the contention that Unabomber Theodore Kaczynski participated in CIA-sponsored MK-ULTRA experiments conducted at Harvard University by Henry A. Murray, a professor in Social Relations, from the fall of 1959 through the spring of 1962. Kaczynski was a precocious, though impressionable, sixteen-year-old when he began his participation; his assigned code name was "Lawful." He emerged, years later, as a terrorist and has been sentenced to life in prison without the possibility of parole.*

*"Merry Prankster" Ken Kesey, author of One Flew Over the Cuckoo's Nest, volunteered for* **MK-ULTRA experiments** *while a student at Stanford University.* **Kesey's ingestion of LSD during these experiments led directly to his widespread promotion of the drug and the subsequent development of hippie culture."**

Reference: Wikipedia.org

### [89] ..."Dark Ages"...

*"It is generally accepted that the concept* **(Dark Ages)** *was created by Petrarch in the 1330s. Writing of those who had come before him, he said, "Amidst the errors there shone forth men of genius, no less keen were their eyes, although they were surrounded by darkness and dense gloom." Christian writers had traditional metaphors of "light versus darkness" to describe "good versus evil". Petrarch was the first to co-opt the metaphor and give it secular meaning by reversing its application. Classical Antiquity, so long considered the "dark" age for its lack of Christianity, was now seen by Petrarch as the age of "light" because of its cultural achievements, while Petrarch's time, lacking such cultural achievements, was seen as the age of darkness.*

*As an Italian, Petrarch saw the Roman Empire and the classical period as expressions of Italian greatness. He spent much of his time traveling through Europe rediscovering and republishing the classic Latin and Greek texts. He wanted to restore the classical Latin language to its former purity. Humanists saw the preceding 900-year period as a time of stagnation. They saw history unfolding, not along the religious outline of St. Augustine's Six Ages of the World, but in cultural (or secular) terms through the progressive developments of classical ideals, literature, and art.*

*Petrarch wrote that history had had two periods: the classic period of the Greeks and Romans, followed by a time of darkness, in which he saw himself as still living. Humanists believed one day the Roman Empire would rise again and restore classic cultural purity, and so by the late 14th and early 15th century, humanists such as Leonardo Bruni believed they had attained this new age, and that a third, Modern Age had begun. The age before their own, which Petrarch had labeled dark, thus became a "middle" age between the classic and the modern."*

Reference: Wikipedia.org

*"The early modern period is seen as a flowering of the Renaissance, in what is often known as the "Scientific Revolution", viewed as a foundation of modern science. Historians like Howard Margolis hold that the Scientific Revolution began in 1543, when Nicolaus Copernicus received the first copy of his De Revolutionibus, printed in Nuremberg (Nürnberg) by Johannes Petreius. Most of its contents had been written years prior, but the publication had been delayed. Copernicus died soon after receiving the copy.*
*Further significant advances were made over the following century by Galileo Galilei, Christiaan Huygens, Johannes Kepler, and Blaise Pascal. During the early seventeenth century, Galileo made extensive use of experimentation to validate physical theories, which is the key idea in the modern scientific method. Galileo formulated and successfully tested several results in dynamics, in particular the Law of Inertia. In Galileo's Two New Sciences, a dialogue between the characters Simplicio and Salviati discuss the motion of a ship (as a moving frame) and how that ship's cargo is indifferent to its motion. Huygens used the motion of a boat along a Dutch canal to illustrate an early form of the conservation of momentum.*
*The scientific revolution is considered to have culminated with the publication of the Philosophiae Naturalis Principia Mathematica in 1687 by the mathematician, physicist, alchemist and inventor Sir Isaac Newton (1643-1727). In 1687, Newton published the Principia, detailing two comprehensive and successful physical theories: Newton's laws of motion, from which arise classical mechanics; and Newton's Law of Gravitation, which describes the fundamental force of gravity. Both theories agreed well with experiment. The Principia also included several theories in fluid dynamics.*

*After Newton defined classical mechanics, the next great field of inquiry within physics was the nature of electricity."*

Reference: Wikipedia.org

*"Electricity would remain little more than an intellectual curiosity for over two millennia until 1600, when the English physician William Gilbert made a careful study of electricity and magnetism, distinguishing the lodestone effect from static electricity produced by rubbing amber. He coined the New Latin word electricus ("of amber" or "like amber", from ηλεκτρον [elektron], the Greek word for "amber") to refer to the property of attracting small objects after being rubbed. This association gave rise to the English words "electric" and "electricity", which made their first appearance in print in Thomas Browne's Pseudodoxia Epidemica of 1646.*

*Further work was conducted by Otto von Guericke, Robert Boyle, Stephen Gray and C. F. du Fay. In the 18th century, Benjamin Franklin conducted extensive research in electricity, selling his possessions to fund his work. In June 1752 he is reputed to have attached a metal key to the bottom of a dampened kite string and flown the kite in a storm-threatened sky. He observed a succession of sparks jumping from the key to the back of his hand, showing that lightning was indeed electrical in nature.*

*In 1791 Luigi Galvani published his discovery of bioelectricity, demonstrating that electricity was the medium by which nerve cells passed signals to the muscles. Alessandro Volta's battery, or voltaic pile, of 1800, made from alternating layers of zinc and copper, provided scientists with a more reliable source of electrical energy than the electrostatic machines* previously used. André-Marie Ampère discovered the relationship between electricity and magnetism in 1820; Michael Faraday invented the electric motor in 1821, and Georg Ohm mathematically analyzed the electrical circuit in 1827.

While it had been the early nineteenth century that had seen rapid progress in electrical science, the late nineteenth century would see the greatest progress in electrical engineering. Through such people as Nikola Tesla, Thomas Edison, George Westinghouse, Ernst Werner von Siemens, Alexander Graham Bell and Lord Kelvin, electricity was turned from a scientific curiosity into an essential tool for modern life, becoming a driving force for the Second Industrial Revolution."

Reference: Wikipedia.org

<sup>92</sup> "... Sir Isaac Newton..."

"**Sir Isaac Newton** (4 January 1643 – 31 March 1727) was an English physicist, mathematician, astronomer, theologian, natural philosopher, and alchemist. His treatise **Philosophiæ Naturalis Principia Mathematica** was published in 1687, and said to be the **greatest single work in the history of science**, described universal gravitation and the **three laws of motion**, laying the groundwork for **classical mechanics**, which **dominated the scientific view of the physical universe for the next three** centuries and is **the basis for modern engineering**. He showed that the motions of objects on Earth and of celestial bodies are governed by the same set of natural laws by demonstrating the consistency between Kepler's **laws of planetary motion** and his **theory of gravitation**, thus removing the last doubts about heliocentrism and advancing the scientific revolution.

In mechanics, Newton enunciated the **principles of conservation of momentum** and angular momentum. In optics, **he invented the reflecting telescope** and developed a **theory of colour** based on the observation that a prism decomposes white light into a visible spectrum. He also formulated an **empirical law of cooling** and studied the **speed of sound**.

In mathematics, Newton shares the credit with Gottfried Leibniz for the **development of the calculus**. He also demonstrated the generalized **binomial theorem**, developed the so-called **"Newton's method" for approximating the zeroes of a function**, and contributed to the study of power series.

In a 2005 poll of the Royal Society of who **had the greatest effect on the history of science**, Newton was deemed much more influential than Albert Einstein."

Reference: Wikipedia.org

<sup>93</sup> "...between lifetimes."

"**Dr. Carl Sagan** was a noted scientist, teacher and skeptic. Sagan was a founding member of a group that set out to debunk unscientific claims, and wrote the book The Demon-Haunted World in which he said that there were several areas in parapsychology which deserved serious study:

"**At the time of writing there are three claims in the ESP field which, in my opinion, deserve serious study:** (1) that by thought alone humans can (barely) affect random number generators in computers; **(2)** that people under mild sensory deprivation can receive thoughts or images "projected" at them; and **(3)** that young children sometimes report the details of a previous life, which upon checking turn out to be accurate and which they could not have known about in any way other than reincarnation. I pick these claims not because I think they're likely to be valid (I don't), but as examples of contentions that might be true."

"**University of Virginia psychiatrists Dr. Jim Tucker and Professor Ian Stevenson** have published books and peer-reviewed research papers about their work in examining cases of early childhood past life memories and birthmarks. The most detailed collections of personal reports in favor of reincarnation have been published by Professor Ian Stevenson, in books such as **Twenty Cases Suggestive of Reincarnation**.

Stevenson has spent over 40 years devoted to the study of children who have spoken about past lives. In each case, Stevenson methodically documents the child's statements. Then, he identifies the deceased person the child allegedly identifies with, and verifies the facts of the deceased person's life that match the child's memory. **Stevenson believes that his meticulous methods rule out all possible "normal" explanations for the child's memories.** However, it should be noted that a significant proportion of the University of Virginia's reported cases of reincarnation originate in Eastern societies, where dominant religions often permit the concept of reincarnation. In India — where this phenomenon is quite common — if a child from a poor family claims to be the reincarnated person from a rich family, this can lead to the child to be adopted by that family, a motive that has led to children making fraudulent reincarnation claims.

Stevenson has said about the 2500 cases of children who appeared to remember past lives, which he and his associates investigated:

"**My conclusion so far is that reincarnation** is not the only explanation for these cases, but that it **is the best explanation we have** for the stronger cases, by which I mean those in which a child makes a considerable number (say 20 or 30) of correct statements about another person who lives in a family that lives quite remote from his own and with which his family has had no prior contacts. When we talk about remoteness, we don't necessarily just mean physical distance. We know that two families can live only 10 kilometers apart and yet they can be very remote because they belong to different economic and social classes."

Professor Stevenson has also matched **birthmarks** and **birth defects** to **wounds** and **scars** on the deceased, **verified by medical records such as autopsy photographs**. Stevenson's research into birthmarks and congenital defects has particular importance for the demonstration of reincarnation, since it furnishes objective and graphic evidence of reincarnation, superior to the (often fragmentary) memories and reports of the children and adults questioned, which even if verified afterwards probably cannot be assigned the same."

Reference: Wikipedia.org

[94] "... **lost civilizations of Atlantis...**"

The following website has most of the popular information about Atlantis:

http://www.lost-civilizations.net/atlantis.html

[95] "... **and Lemuria...**"

"The rise and fall of the Lemurian civilization cannot be accurately documented, though many have gone in quest of this mythological continent. Lost civilizations have been known to rise and fall - or just appear and disappear without explanation. As with Atlantis one can only speculate as to what happened, based on archaeological evidence, legends, theories pieced together by researchers, and for some, metaphysical channelings.

The exact location of Lemuria varies with different researchers and authors, though it is part of the mysteries of the Pacific region flowing into the American continent, just as Atlantis is linked to the Atlantic land areas that stretch to the Mediterranean Sea. Wherever you believe the location of Lemuria to be, it is linked with the Ring of Fire. This area has become active with a Tsunami in December 26, 2004, powerful earthquakes and volcanoes that continue, after being dormant for many years. It would seem that the legends of ancient Lemuria speak to us once again with warning signs - as they supposedly did to the Lemurians - before the continent - or group of islands - fell into the sea.

The fate of Lemuria, also known as Pacifica, Mu, and what Cayce called Zu or Oz, is not unlike that proposed for Atlantis. It is much like the destiny of humanity foreseen in our timeline by prophets of old and modern-day clairvoyants. The legends are all the same ... a thriving, advanced culture that suddenly manifested out of nowhere. Their origins and downfall are linked to destruction when their continent sank beneath the 'sea' due to natural cataclysms and human imbalance."

-- Reference: http://www.crystalinks.com/lemuria.html

[96] "...polar shift"...

"In 1852, mathematician Joseph Adhemar suggested that the accumulation of thick ice at the poles periodically caused the earth to flip and the equator to move to where the poles were. An early mention of a shifting of the Earth's axis can be found in an 1872 article entitled "Chronologie historique des Mexicains" which interpreted ancient Mexican myths as evidence for four periods of global cataclysms that had begun around 10,500 B.C.

The novel Geyserland: Empiricisms in Social Reform. Being Data and Observations Recorded by the Late Mark Stubble, M.D., Ph.D. (1908) by Richard Hatfield used the device of a fictional study to locate a blissful nation of pure Communism at the North Pole on the island of Atlantis. This fictional Utopia was destroyed by a pole shift set in 9262 B.C.

Hugh Auchincloss Brown, an electrical engineer, advanced a theory of catastrophic pole shift influenced by Adhemar's earlier model. Brown also argued that accumulation of ice at the poles caused recurring tipping of the axis. identifying cycles of approximately 7 millennia.

**Charles Hapgood** is now perhaps the best remembered early proponent, from in his books **The Earth's Shifting Crust** (1958) **(which includes a foreword by Albert Einstein)** and **Path of the Pole** (1970). Hapgood, building on Adhemar's much earlier model, speculated that the ice mass at one or both poles over-accumulates and destabilizes the earth's rotational balance, causing slippage of all or much of earth's outer crust around the earth's core, which retains its axial orientation. Based on his own research, he argued that each shift took approximately five thousand years, followed by 20 to 30 thousand year periods with no polar movements. Also, in his calculations, the area of movement never covered

221

more than 40 degrees. His examples of recent locations for the North Pole include the Yukon Territory, Hudson Bay, and in the Atlantic Ocean between Iceland and Norway.

This is an example of slow pole shift motion, which displays the most minor alterations and no destruction. A more dramatic view assumes more rapid changes, with dramatic alterations of geography and localized areas of destruction due to earthquakes and tsunamis. Several recent books propose changes that take place in weeks, days, or even hours, resulting in a variety of doomsday scenarios.

Regardless of speed, the results of a shift occurring results in major climate changes for most of the earth's surface, as areas that were formerly equatorial become temperate, and areas that were temperate become either more equatorial or more arctic.

Hapgood wrote to Canadian librarian, Rand Flem-Ath, encouraging him in his pursuit of scientific evidence to back Hapgood's claim and in his expansion of the theory. Flem-Ath published the results of this work in 1995 in When the Sky Fell co-written with his wife, Rose.

Other theories which are not dependent upon polar ice masses include those involving:

- a high-velocity asteroid or comet which hits Earth at such an angle that the lithosphere moves independent of the mantle
- a high-velocity asteroid or comet which hits Earth at such an angle that the entire planet shifts axis.
- an unusually magnetic celestial object which passes close enough to Earth to temporarily reorient the magnetic field, which then "drags" the lithosphere about a new axis of rotation. Eventually, the sun's magnetic field again determines the Earth's, after the intruding celestial object "returns" to a location from which it cannot influence Earth.
- perturbations of the topography of the core-mantle boundary, perhaps induced by differential core rotation and shift of its axial rotation vector, leading to CMB mass redistributions. See, e.g., Bowin.
- mass redistributions in the mantle from mantle avalanches or other deformations. See, e.g., Ladbury, and Steinberger and O'Connell."

-- Reference: Wikipedia.org

[97] "... Totalitarian..."

"Totalitarianism is a concept used in political science that describes a state that regulates nearly every aspect of public and private behavior. Totalitarian regimes or movements maintain themselves in political power by means of secret police, propaganda disseminated through the state-controlled mass media, personality cults, regulation and restriction of free discussion and criticism, single-party states, the use of mass surveillance, and widespread use of terror tactics.

Many consider the first totalitarian regimes to have begun in the 20th century, which include the communist regimes of the Soviet Union and Cuba, as well as totalitarianism of Nazi Germany, Fascist Italy, Spain under Franco, Portugal under Salazar, as well as others. However some argue that totalitarianism has existed centuries prior, such as in ancient China under the political leadership of Prime Minister Li Si who helped the Qin dynasty unify China. Li Si adopted the political philosophy of Legalism as the ruling philosophical thought of China and restricted political activities and destroyed all literature and killed scholars who did not support Legalism. Totalitarianism was also used by the Spartan state in Ancient Greece. Its "educational system" was part of the totalitarian military society. The oligarchy running the state machine dictated every aspect of life, including the rearing of children."

-- Reference: Wikipedia.org

[98] "...planetary governments, regulated by a brutal social, economic, and political hierarchy..."

"A hierarchy (in Greek: hieros, 'sacred', and arkho, 'rule') is a system of ranking and organizing things or people, where each element of the system (except for the top element) is a subordinate to a single other element.

A hierarchy can link entities either directly or indirectly, and either vertically or horizontally. The only direct links in a hierarchy, insofar as they are hierarchical, are to one's immediate superior or to one of one's subordinates, although a system that is largely hierarchical can also incorporate other organizational patterns. Indirect hierarchical links can extend "vertically" upwards or downwards via multiple links in the same direction. All parts of the hierarchy which are not vertically linked to one another can nevertheless be "horizontally" linked by traveling up the hierarchy to find a common direct or indirect superior, and then down again. This is akin to two co-workers, neither of whom is the other's boss, but both of whose chains of command will eventually meet."

Many human organizations, such as governments, educational institutions, businesses, churches, armies and political movements are hierarchical organizations, at least officially; commonly seniors, called "bosses", have more power than their subordinates. Thus the relationship defining this hierarchy is "commands" or "has power over". Some analysts question whether power "actually" works in the way the traditional organizational chart indicates, however. This view tends to emphasize the significance of the informal organization."

-- Reference: Wikipedia.org

[99] "...royal monarch as its figurehead."

"In politics, a **figurehead**, by metaphor with the carved figurehead at the prow of a sailing ship, is a person who holds an important title or office yet executes little actual power. Common figureheads include constitutional monarchs, such as the Emperor of Japan, or presidents in parliamentary democracies, such as the President of Israel.

While the authority of a figurehead is generally symbolic, respect and access to high levels of government can give them significant influence on some events. An example would be Emperor Hirohito's involvement in World War II. In parliamentary systems, presidents are figureheads at times of peace (delegated such powers as convening or dismissing the national legislature), but at wartime they are often commanders in chief.

Sometimes a figurehead can be exploited in times of emergency. For example, Indian Prime Minister Indira Gandhi used the figurehead President of India to issue unilateral decrees that allowed her to bypass parliament when it no longer supported her.

The word can also have more sinister overtones, and refer to a powerless leader who should be exercising full authority, yet is actually being controlled by a more powerful figure behind the throne.

The tendency of this word to drift, like many words that are in a strong process of changed meanings, into the pejorative is beginning to make it unsuitable to apply to a head of state with limited constitutional authority, such that its use may become increasingly inappropriate in referring to monarchs and presidents in parliamentary systems."

-- Reference: Wikipedia.org

[100] "... united by a egalitarian esprit de corps..."

*"Esprit de corps, when discussing the morale of a group, is an intangible term used for the capacity of people to maintain belief in an institution or a goal, or even in oneself and others. According to Alexander H. Leighton, "morale is the capacity of a group of people to pull together persistently and consistently in pursuit of a common purpose".*

*Egalitarian, (derived from the French word égal, meaning equal) is a political doctrine that holds that all people should be treated as equals from birth. Generally it applies to being held equal under the law, the church, and society at large. In actual practice, one may be considered an egalitarian in most areas listed above, even if not subscribing to equality in every possible area of individual difference. For example, one might support equal rights in race matters but not in gender issues, or vice versa."*

-- Reference: Wikipedia.org

[101] "... Many of the IS-BEs on Earth are here because they are violently opposed to totalitarian governments..."

-- **Editor's Note:** Coincidentally, or perhaps NOT coincidentally, almost one year after this interview, the novel "1984" by **George Orwell**, which was published in June of 1948. The state of the U.S. government has grown to mirror many of the features described by Orwell in the book, "Nineteen Eighty-Four". It is easy to speculate that Orwell may have been "influenced" by an IS-BE of The Domain while writing this book. Or, at the very least, he was one of the IS-BEs sentenced to Earth because he is one of "**... the IS-BEs on Earth are here because they are violently opposed to totalitarian governments...**".

**The following description of the basis for Orwell's "1984" are taken verbatim from Wikipedia.org. It is a very close description of the "Old Empire" government:**

*"Much of Oceanic society is based upon Stalin's Soviet Union. The "Two Minutes' Hate" was the ritual demonization of State enemies and rivals; Big Brother resembles Joseph Stalin; the Party's archenemy, Emmanuel Goldstein, resembles Leon Trotsky (both are Jewish, both have the same physiognomy, and Trotsky's real surname was 'Bronstein'). Another suggested inspiration for Goldstein is Emma Goldman, the famous Anarchist figure. Doctored photography is a propaganda technique and the creation of unpersons in the story, analogous to Stalin's enemies being made nonpersons and being erased from official photographic records; the police treatment of several characters recalls the Moscow Trials of the Great Purge."*

There a <u>very</u> many interesting parallels between the concepts discussed by Orwell in "1984", and the description of the "Old Empire" government and the Earth prison planet activities in the transcripts of the "Alien Interviews" with Airl.

For example, a few of these are parallels cited in the following excerpt from the internet encyclopedia, Wikipedia.org:

"The **Thought Police** capture Winston and Julia in their sanctuary bedroom and they are separately <u>interrogated</u> at the Ministry of Love, where <u>**the regime's opponents are tortured and killed**</u>, but sometimes released (to be executed at a later date); Charrington, the shop keeper who rented them the room reveals himself an officer of the Thought Police. **In the Ministry of Love torture chamber**, O'Brien tells **Smith that he will be <u>cured</u> of his hatred for the Party**. During a session, he explains to Winston **that torture's purpose is to alter his way of thinking**, not to extract a fake confession, adding that **once <u>cured</u> — <u>accepting reality</u> as the Party describes — he then will be <u>executed</u>; <u>electroshock torture</u> will achieve that,** continuing until O'Brien decides Winston is cured."

For complete comparative analysis, read the book, "1984" or read the entire reference to the book on the internet at **Wikipedia.org**, excerpted below:

"**Nineteen Eighty-Four** (also titled **1984**), by George Orwell (the pen name of Eric Arthur Blair), is an English dystopian novel about life in a dictatorship as lived by Winston Smith, an intellectual worker at the Ministry of Truth, and his degradation when he runs afoul of the totalitarian government of Oceania, the state in which he lives in the year 1984.

Orwell's influences
In the essay Why I Write, Orwell explains that all the serious work he wrote since the Spanish Civil War in 1936 was "written, directly or indirectly, against totalitarianism and for democratic socialism." Therefore, Nineteen Eighty-Four is an anti-totalitarian cautionary tale about the betrayal of a revolution by its defenders. He already had stated distrust of totalitarianism and betrayed revolutions in Homage to Catalonia and Animal Farm. Coming Up For Air, at points, celebrates the personal and political freedoms lost in Nineteen Eighty-Four.

The novel's title, its terms and its language (Newspeak), and its author's surname are bywords for personal privacy lost to national state security. The adjective "Orwellian" denotes totalitarian action and organization; the phrase: Big Brother is Watching You connotes pervasive, invasive surveillance. The following quotation has become famous:

War is Peace
Freedom is Slavery
Ignorance is Strength

Although the novel has been banned or challenged in some countries, it, along with Brave New World, by Aldous Huxley, and Fahrenheit 451, by Ray Bradbury, is among literature's most famous dystopias. In 2005, Time magazine listed it among the best one hundred English-language novels published since 1923.

Nineteen Eighty-Four introduces Oceania, one of the world's three intercontinental totalitarian super-states. The story occurs in London, the "chief city of Airstrip One", itself a province of Oceania that "had been called England or Britain". Posters of "Big Brother", the Party leader, with the caption BIG BROTHER IS WATCHING YOU, dominate the city landscapes; two-way television (the telescreen) dominates the private and public spaces of the populace.

Oceania's people are in three classes — (i) the Inner Party, (ii) the Outer Party, and (iii) the "Proles". This government, the Party, controls them via the Ministry of Truth (MiniTru), where Winston Smith, the protagonist, works; he is a member of the Outer Party. His job in MiniTru is the continual rewriting and altering of history so that the government is always right and correct: destroying evidence, amending newspaper articles, deleting the existence of people identified as "unpersons".

The story begins on April 4, 1984: "It was a bright cold day in April, and the clocks were striking thirteen." The date is questionable, because it is what Winston Smith perceives. In the story's course, he concludes it as irrelevant, because the State can arbitrarily alter it; the year 1984 and its world are transmutable.

The novel does not render the world's full history to 1984. Indeed, because the book Winston reads is given to him by a Party member, it is possible that the book itself is meant to be a deception, and the history of the world of 1984 is somewhat different. Winston's recollections, and what he reads in The Theory and Practice of Oligarchical Collectivism, by Emmanuel Goldstein, reveal that after the Second World War, the United Kingdom fell to civil war, becoming part of Oceania. Simultaneously, the Soviet Union encompassed mainland Europe, forming Eurasia; the third super state, Eastasia, comprises the east Asian countries around China and Japan.

There was an atomic war, fought mainly in Europe, western Russia, and North America. It is unclear what occurred first: the civil war wherein the Party assumed power or the United States' annexation of the British Empire or the war during which Colchester was bombed.

During the Second World War, George Orwell repeatedly said that British democracy, as it existed before 1939, would not survive the war; the question being: Would it end via Fascist coup d'état (from above) or via Socialist revolution (from below)? During the war, Orwell admitted events proved him wrong: "What really matters is that I fell into the trap of assuming that 'the war and the revolution are inseparable' "

-- Reference: Wikipedia.org

[102] "... Wars are fought with electronic cannon."...

"I have not thought it hazardous to predict, that wars in the future will be waged by electrical means." -- Nikola Tesla, 1915

Tesla made some remarkable claims concerning a "teleforce" weapon. The press called it a "peace ray" or death ray. In total, the components and methods included:

1. An apparatus for producing manifestations of energy in free air instead of in a high vacuum as in the past. This, according to Tesla in 1934, was accomplished.
2. A mechanism for generating tremendous electrical force. This, according to Tesla, was also accomplished.
3. A means of intensifying and amplifying the force developed by the second mechanism.

4. A new method for producing a tremendous electrical repelling force. This would be the projector, or gun, of the invention.

Tesla worked on plans for a directed-energy weapon between the early 1900s till the time of his death. In 1937, Tesla composed a treatise entitled "The Art of Projecting Concentrated Non-dispersive Energy through the Natural Media" concerning charged particle beams. Tesla published the document in an attempt to expound on the technical description of a "superweapon that would put an end to all war". This treatise of the particle beam is currently in the Nikola Tesla Museum archive in Belgrade. It described an open ended vacuum tube with a gas jet seal that allowed particles to exit, a method of charging particles to millions of volts, and a method of creating and directing nondispersive particle streams (through electrostatic repulsion).

Records of his indicate that it was based on a narrow stream of atomic clusters of liquid mercury or tungsten accelerated via high voltage (by means akin to his magnifying transformer). Tesla gave the following description concerning the particle gun's operation: [The nozzle would] send concentrated beams of particles through the free air, of such tremendous energy that they will bring down a fleet of 10,000 enemy airplanes at a distance of 200 miles from a defending nation's border and will cause armies to drop dead in their tracks."

-- Reference: Wikipedia.org

[103] "... like the Axis powers..."

"The **Axis powers**, also interpreted as **Axis alliance, Axis nations, Axis countries** or sometimes just the **Axis** were those countries opposed to the Allies during World War II. The three major Axis powers, Nazi Germany, Fascist Italy, and Imperial Japan were part of a military alliance on the signing of the Tripartite Pact in September 1940, which officially founded the Axis powers. At their zenith, the Axis powers ruled empires that dominated large parts of Europe, Africa, East and Southeast Asia and the Pacific Ocean, but World War II ended with their total defeat. Like the Allies, membership of the Axis was fluid, and some nations entered and later left the Axis during the course of the war.

The term was first used by Benito Mussolini, in November 1936, when he spoke of a Rome-Berlin axis arising out of the treaty of friendship signed between Italy and Germany on October 25, 1936. Mussolini declared that the two countries would form an "axis" around which the other states of Europe would revolve. This treaty was forged when Italy, originally opposed to Germany, was faced with opposition to its war in Abyssinia from the League of Nations and received support from Germany. Later, in May 1939, this relationship transformed into an alliance, called by Mussolini the "Pact of Steel"."

-- Reference: Wikipedia.org

[104] "...Vedic Hymns..."

The Vedas are very exhaustive scriptures. Each veda contains several sections and thousands of hymns. Some of the Vedic hymns, especially the hymns of the Rig veda, are considered to be at least 6000-8000 years old. The Vedas are believed to be revealed scriptures, because they are considered to be divine in origin. Since they were not written by any human beings but were only heard in deep meditative states, they are commonly referred a "those that were heard".

Here is one of the most famous hymns from the Rig Vega: :The Hymn of Creation"

*"A time is envisioned when the world was not, only a watery chaos (the dark, "indistinguishable sea") and a warm cosmic breath, which could give an impetus of life. Notice how thought gives rise to desire (when something is thought of it can then be desired) and desire links non-being to being (we desire what is not but then try to bring it about that it is). Yet the whole process is shrouded in mystery.*

*Where do the gods fit in this creation scheme?*

*The non-existent was not; the existent was not at that time. The atmosphere was not nor the heavens which are beyond. What was concealed? Where? In whose protection? Was it water? An unfathomable abyss?*

*There was neither death nor immortality then. There was not distinction of day or night. That alone breathed windless by its own power. Other than that there was not anything else.*

*Darkness was hidden by darkness in the beginning. All this was an indistinguishable sea. That which becomes, that which was enveloped by the void, that alone was born through the power of heat.*

*Upon that desire arose in the beginning. This was the first discharge of thought. Sages discovered this link of the existent to the nonexistent, having searched in the heart with wisdom.*

*Their line [of vision] was extended across; what was below, what was above? There were impregnators, there were powers: inherent power below, impulses above.*

*Who knows truly? Who here will declare whence it arose, whence this creation? The gods are subsequent to the creation of this. Who, then, knows whence it has come into being?*

*Whence this creation has come into being; whether it was made or not; he in the highest heaven is its surveyor. Surely he knows, or perhaps he knows not."*

-- Reference: Wikipedia.org

[105] "... the Aryan people..."

*"The Vedic term **arya-** in its earliest attestations has a **meaning of "stranger"**, but "stranger" in the sense of **"potential guest"**. The Sanskrit lexicon defines **Arya** as mahākula kulīnārya **"being of a noble family"**, sabhya **"having gentle or refined behavior and demeanor"**, sajjana **"being well-born and respectable"**, and sādhava **"being virtuous, honourable, or righteous"**. Arya, is a title of honor and respect given to certain people for noble behavior.*

*The **Aryan race** was a term used in the early 20th century by European racial theorists who believed strongly in the division of humanity into biologically distinct races with differing characteristics. Such writers believed that the Proto-Indo-Europeans constituted a specific race that had expanded across parts of Europe, Iran and small parts of northern India. This*

228

usage tends to merge the Sanskrit meaning of "noble" or "elevated" with the idea of distinctive behavioral and ancestral ethnicity marked by language distribution.

Nazism portrayed their interpretation of an "Aryan race" as the only race capable of, or with an interest in, creating and maintaining culture and civilizations, while other races are merely capable of conversion, or destruction of culture. These arguments derived from late nineteenth century racial hierarchies. Some Nazis were also influenced by Madame Blavatsky's The Secret Doctrine (1888) where she postulates "Aryans" as the fifth of her "Root Races", dating them to about a million years ago, tracing them to Atlantis,

Because of historical racist use of Aryan, and especially use of Aryan race in connection with the propaganda of Nazism, the word is sometimes avoided in the West as being tainted, in the same manner as the **swastika symbol**. Currently, India and Iran are the only countries to use the word Aryan in a demographic denomination."

-- Reference: Wikipedia.org

### [106] "... the Vedic Hymns..."

"The term **veda** means **"knowledge, (sacred) lore"** embraces a body of writings the origin of which is **ascribed to divine revelation** (shruti, literally "hearing"), and which forms the foundation of the Brahmanical system of religious belief. This **sacred canon** is divided into three or (according to a later scheme) four co-ordinate collections, likewise called **Veda**:

(I) the Rig-veda, or lore of praise (or **hymns**); (2) the Samaveda, or lore of tunes (or chants); (3) the Yajurveda, or lore of prayer (or sacrificial formulas); and (4) the Atharvaveda, or lore of the Atharvans. Each of these four Vedas consists primarily of a collection (samihita) of sacred, mostly poetical, texts of a devotional nature, called mantra. This entire body of texts (and particularly the first three collections) is also frequently referred to as the trayi vidya, or threefold wisdom, of hymns (rik), tune or chant (saman), and prayer (yajus), the fourth Veda, if at all included, being in that case classed together with the Rik."

-- Reference: Wikipedia.org

### [107] "...Vishnu..."

"Vishnu is **the All-Pervading essence of all beings**, the master of and beyond the past, present and future, the creator and destroyer of all existences, one who supports, sustains and governs the Universe and originates and develops all elements within. **In the Rigveda, Vishnu is mentioned 93 times.**

The traditional Sanskrit explanation of the name Vi□□u involves the root viś, meaning "to settle, to enter", or "to pervade", and a suffix nu, translating to approximately "the All-Pervading One".

He has nine avatars, or 'incarnations' (which) are described as having occurred in the past, with one still to happen at the end of Kali Yuga. The Bhagavad Gita mentions their purpose as being to vanquish negative forces."

-- Reference: Wikipedia.org

### [108] "...past lives."

A "past lives" scenario automatically infers a "future life" in the context of an amnesia and prison planet operation. This implies the phenomenon of reincarnation:

*"Reincarnation literally "to be made flesh again", is a doctrine or metaphysical belief that some essential part of a living being (in some variations only human beings) survives death to be reborn in a new body. This essential part is often referred to as the spirit or soul, the "higher" or "true" self, "divine spark", or "I". According to such beliefs, a new personality is developed during each life in the physical world, but some part of the self remains constant throughout the successive lives.*

*Belief in reincarnation is an ancient phenomenon. This doctrine is a central tenet within the majority of Indian religious traditions, such as Hinduism (including Yoga, Vaishnavism, and Shaivism), Jainism, and Sikhism. The idea was also entertained by some Ancient Greek philosophers. Many modern Pagans also believe in reincarnation as do some New Age movements, along with followers of Spiritism, practitioners of certain African traditions, and students of esoteric philosophies such as Kabbalah, Sufism and Gnostic and Esoteric Christianity. The Buddhist concept of Rebirth although often referred to as reincarnation differs significantly from the Hindu-based traditions and New Age movements in that there is no "self" (or eternal soul) to reincarnate.*

*During recent decades, a significant minority of people in the West have developed a belief in reincarnation. Notable exceptions include Henry Ford and General George Patton.*

*Henry Ford was convinced he had lived before, most recently as a soldier killed at the battle of Gettysburg. A quote from the San Francisco Examiner from August 26, 1928 described Ford's beliefs:*

> *"I adopted the theory of Reincarnation when I was twenty-six. Religion offered nothing to the point. Even work could not give me complete satisfaction. Work is futile if we cannot utilize the experience we collect in one life in the next. When I discovered Reincarnation it was as if I had found a universal plan I realized that there was a chance to work out my ideas. Time was no longer limited. I was no longer a slave to the hands of the clock. Genius is experience. Some seem to think that it is a gift or talent, but it is the fruit of long experience in many lives. Some are older souls than others, and so they know more. The discovery of Reincarnation put my mind at ease. If you preserve a record of this conversation, write it so that it puts men's minds at ease. I would like to communicate to others the calmness that the long view of life gives to us."*

*General George S. Patton was a staunch believer in reincarnation and, along with many other members of his family, often claimed to have seen vivid, lifelike visions of his ancestors. In particular, Patton believed he was a reincarnation of Carthaginian General Hannibal.*

*The most detailed collections of personal reports in favor of reincarnation have been published by Professor Ian Stevenson, from the University of Virginia, in books such as Twenty Cases Suggestive of Reincarnation.*

*Stevenson spent over 40 years devoted to the study of children who have apparently spoken about a past life. In each case, Professor Stevenson methodically documented the child's* statements. Then he identified the deceased person the child allegedly identified with, and verified the facts of the deceased person's life that matched the child's memory. He also matched birthmarks and birth defects to wounds and scars on the deceased, verified by medical records such as autopsy photographs.

In a fairly typical case, a boy in Beirut spoke of being a 25-year-old mechanic, thrown to his death from a speeding car on a beach road. According to multiple witnesses, the boy provided the name of the driver, the exact location of the crash, the names of the mechanic's sisters and parents and cousins, and the people he went hunting with -- all of which turned out to match the life of a man who had died several years before the boy was born, and who had no apparent connection to the boy's family.

Stevenson believed that his strict methods ruled out all possible "normal" explanations for the child's memories. However, it should be noted that a significant majority of Professor Stevenson's reported cases of reincarnation originate in Eastern societies, where dominant religions often permit the concept of reincarnation. Following this type of criticism, Stevenson published a book on European cases suggestive of reincarnation."

-- Reference: Wikipedia.org

[109] "...Moses..."

"The cartouche of Akhenaten's god and heavenly father, the Aten, bore the name Imram. In the Bible, Moses is referred to as the son of Amram, the Hebrew equivalent.

**The name of the Egyptian deity Aten transliterates into the Hebrew word Adon**. Adon, which is translated by English Bibles as "the Lord" (and Adonai, translated as "my Lord") is used along with Jehovah (Yhwh) in the Bible as the exclusive personal names of God. Moreover, in ancient times, the name Jehovah (Yhwh) was written, but never spoken. Whenever the written name Jehovah (Yhwh) was to be read out loud, Adon (Aten) was voiced instead. The written form of Adon is infrequent, however, its limited usage is significant, especially in the first six books of the Bible (See under "LORD" in Strong's Exhaustive Concordance), where it is reserved for the following applications alone: **Moses addresses God using the title Adon/Aten (Exodus 4:10,13; 5:22; 34:9; Numbers 14:17; Deuteronomy 3:23; 7:26; 10:17); Moses, himself, is addressed both by Aaron (Ex.32:22; Num.12:11) and by Joshua (Numbers 11:28) using the title Adon/Aten; and Joshua also addresses God using the title Adon/Aten (Joshua 5:14 b; 7:7).** As mentioned above, there is an established relationship between the literature of the Egyptian 18th Dynasty and the Bible. Psalm 104 is an embellishment of the Hymn to the Aten which was found by archaeologists at the city of Akhetaten."

http://www.domainofman.com/ankhemmaat/moses.html

"Recent and non-Biblical view places Moses as a noble in the court of the Pharaoh Akhenaten. A significant number of scholars, from Sigmund Freud to Joseph Campbell, suggest that Moses may have fled Egypt after Akhenaten's death (ca. 1334 BC) when many of the pharaoh's monotheistic reforms were being violently reversed. The principal ideas behind this theory are: **the monotheistic religion of Akhenaten being a possible predecessor to Moses' monotheism**, and the "Amarna Letters", written by nobles to Akhenaten, which describe raiding bands of "Habiru" attacking the Egyptian territories in Mesopotamia."

-- Reference: Wikipedia.org

[110] **"...Amenhotep III..."**

*"**Amenhotep III,** meaning Amun is Satisfied was the ninth pharaoh of the Eighteenth dynasty. According to different authors, he ruled Egypt from June 1391 BC-December 1353 BCE or June 1388 BCE to December 1351 BC/1350 BCE after his father Thutmose IV died. Amenhotep III was the son of Thutmose IV by Mutemwia, a minor wife of Amenhotep's father. Amenhotep III fathered two sons with his Great Royal Wife Tiye, a great queen known as the progenitor of monotheism via the Crown Prince Tuthmose who predeceased his father, and his second son, Akhenaten, who ultimately succeeded him to the throne."*

-- Reference: Wikipedia.org

[111] **"...Akhenaten..."**

*"**Akhenaten,** meaning Effective spirit of Aten, first known as Amenhotep IV (sometimes read as Amenophis IV and meaning Amun is Satisfied) before his first year, was a Pharaoh of the Eighteenth dynasty of Egypt. He is especially noted for attempting to compel the Egyptian population in the monotheistic worship of Aten, although there are doubts as to how successful he was at this.*

*Amenhotep IV succeeded his father after Amenhotep III's death at the end of his 38-year reign, possibly after a coregency lasting between either 1 to 2 or 12 years. Suggested dates for Akhenaten's reign (subject to the debates surrounding Egyptian chronology) are from 1353 BCE - 1336 BCE or 1351 BCE – 1334 BCE Akhenaten's chief wife was Nefertiti.*

*His religious reformation appears to have begun with his decision to celebrate a Sed festival in his third regnal year – a highly unusual step, since a Sed-festival, a sort of royal jubilee intended to reinforce the Pharaoh's divine powers of kingship, was traditionally held in the thirtieth year of a Pharaoh's reign.*

*Year eight marked the beginning of construction on his new capital, Akhetaten ('Horizon of Aten'), at the site known today as Amarna. In the same year, Amenhotep IV officially changed his name to Akhenaten ('Effective Spirit of Aten') as evidence of his shifting religious perspective. Very soon afterward he centralized Egyptian religious practices in Akhenaten, though construction of the city seems to have continued for several more years. In honor of Aten, Akhenaten also oversaw the construction of some of the most massive temple complexes in ancient Egypt, including one at Karnak, close to the old temple of Amun. In these new temples, Aten was worshipped in the open sunlight, rather than in dark temple enclosures, as had been the previous custom. Akhenaten is also believed to have composed the Great Hymn to the Aten.*

*Initially, Akhenaten presented Aten as a variant of the familiar supreme deity Amun-Ra (itself the result of an earlier rise to prominence of the cult of Amun, resulting in Amun becoming merged with the sun god Ra), in an attempt to put his ideas in a familiar Egyptian religious context. However, by Year 9 of his reign Akhenaten declared that Aten was not merely the supreme god, but the only god, and that he, Akhenaten, was the only intermediary between Aten and his people. He ordered the defacing of Amun's temples throughout Egypt, and in a number of instances inscriptions of the plural 'gods' were also removed.*

Aten's name is also written differently after Year 9, to emphasize the radicalism of the new regime, which included a ban on idols, with the exception of a rayed solar disc, in which the rays (commonly depicted ending in hands) appear to represent the unseen spirit of Aten, who by then was evidently considered not merely a sun god, but rather a universal deity. It is important to note, however, that representations of the Aten were always accompanied with a sort of "hieroglyphic footnote", stating that the representation of the sun as All-encompassing Creator was to be taken as just that: a representation of something that, by its very nature as something transcending creation, cannot be fully or adequately represented by any one part of that creation."

This Amarna period is also associated with a serious outbreak of a pandemic, possibly the plague, or polio, or perhaps the world's first recorded outbreak of influenza, which came from Egypt and spread throughout the Middle East, killing Suppiluliuma I, the Hittite King. Influenza is a disease associated with the close proximity of water fowl, pigs and humans, and its origin as a pandemic disease may be due to the development of agricultural systems that allow the mixing of these animals and their wastes.

Some of the first archaeological evidence for this agricultural system is during the Amarna period of Ancient Egypt, and the pandemic that followed this period throughout the Ancient Near East may have been the earliest recorded outbreak of influenza. However, **the precise nature of this Egyptian plague remains unknown and Asia has also been suggested as a possible site of origin of pandemic influenza in humans**. The prevalence of disease may help explain the rapidity with which the site of Akhetaten was subsequently abandoned. **It may also explain why later generations considered the gods to have turned against the Amarna monarchs**. The black plague has also been suggested due to the fact that at Amarna the traces of the plague have been found."

-- Reference: Wikipedia.org

[112] **"... Nefertiti...**

**"Nefertiti** (pronounced at the time something like *nafrati.ta) (c. 1370 BCE - c. 1330 BCE) was the Great Royal Wife (or chief consort/wife) of the Egyptian Pharaoh Akhenaten. She was the mother-in-law and probable stepmother of the Pharaoh Tutankhamun. Nefertiti may have also ruled as pharaoh in her own right under the name Neferneferuaten briefly after her husband's death and before the accession of Tutankhamun, although this identification is doubted by the latest research. Her name roughly translates to "the beautiful (or perfect) one has arrived". She also shares her name with a type of elongated gold bead, called "nefer", that she was often portrayed as wearing. She was made famous by her bust, now in Berlin's Altes Museum.

Nefertiti's parentage is not known with certainty, but it is now generally believed that she was the daughter of AY later to be pharaoh. Another theory that gained some support identified Nefertiti with the Mitanni princess Tadukhipa. The name Nimerithin has been mentioned in older scrolls, as an alternative name, but this has not yet been officially confirmed. It has also been suggested that Nefertiti was a daughter or relative of Amenhotep III, or of the high Theban nobility. Another theory places Nefertiti as the daughter of Sitamun, half-sister of Amenhotep III. Queen Iaret was Sitamun's mother. Iaret held important hereditary titles that ceased to exist after the ascension of Amenhotep III. Sitamun is elevated to Great Royal Wife beside Tiye but there is no indication that she ever had children and if so with whom. There is some evidence based upon the titles of each of these women that suggests that they were somehow related to one another in her family... Her name means "beautiful one".

Nefertiti only worshiped one god by the name of Aten. Depending on which reconstruction of the genealogy of the ancient Egyptian pharaohs is followed, her husband Akhenaten may have been the father or half-brother of the Pharaoh Tutankhaten (later called Tutankhamen).

She had six known daughters with the Pharaoh Akhenaten. This is a list with suggested years of birth:

- Meritaten: Before year one or the very beginning of year one.(1356 BC).
- Meketaten: Year 1 or three (1349 BC).
- **Ankhesenpaaten, later queen of Tutankhamun**
- Neferneferuaten Tasherit: Year 6 (1344 BC)
- Neferneferure: Year 9 (1341 BC).
- Setepenre: Year 11 (1339 BC)."

-- Reference: Wikipedia.org

[113] "... **Tutankhamun**..."

"He was the son of Akhenaten, also known as Amenhotep IV, and his minor wife Queen Kiya. Queen Kiya's title was "Greatly Beloved Wife of Akhenaten" so it is possible that she could have borne him an heir. Supporting this theory, images on the tomb wall in the tomb of Akhenaten show a royal fan bearer standing next to Kiya's death bed, fanning what is either a princess or more likely a wet nurse holding a baby, which would indicate that the wet nurse was holding the boy-king-to-be.

Tutankhamun was only nine or ten years old when he became pharaoh, and reigned for approximately ten years, making him nineteen years old at death. In historical terms Tutankhamun significance stems from his rejection of the radical religious innovations introduced by his predecessor Akenhaten and that his tomb, uniquely, in the Valley of the Kings was discovered almost completely intact -- the most complete ancient Egyptian tomb ever found. As Tutankhamun began his reign at such an early age, his vizier and eventual successor Ay was probably making most of the important political decisions during Tutankhamun's reign."

-- Reference: Wikipedia.org

[114] ..."**Brothers of the Snake**"...

"It cannot be overemphasized that the **serpent** or **snake** plays no role in the teachings or ritual of regular Freemasonry. Its introduction as a fastener for masonic aprons is easily seen as the work of regalia manufacturers. That said, the symbolic usages of the snake are of interest to students of religion, esoterica, and of history.

On the other hand, George Oliver writes that the **serpent** is a "significant symbol in Freemasonry : Moses' rod changed into a **serpent**, "The serpentine emblem of Masonry... is a bright symbol of Hope; for the promised Deliverer will open the gates of Heaven to his faithful followers by bruising its head, and they shall enter triumphantly, trampling on its prostrate body." "A striking emblem of Christianity triumphant; and bearing an undoubted reference to the promise made to Adam after his unhappy fall." In mainstream Christian beliefs, the **snake** represents temptation and evil: the snake is the servant of Satan. But it has also had its more positive significance.

In ancient Egyptian mythology the world was created by four powers, one of which was the sun god **Amun-Ra** who took the form of a **snake** and emerged from the water to inseminated the cosmic egg, the kneph, which was created by the other gods. In another story, a god named Hathor transformed himself into a poisonous snake called Agep and killed Seth. He also guarded the wheat fields where the spirit of Horus was said to live, bringing the sheaf of wheat to be regarded as the symbol of rebirth. W. Bro. H. Meij suggests that this is the root of the masonic usage of an ear of corn in the Fellowcraft degree.

In Greek mythology Zeus freed two eagles which met at the centre of the world, sometimes called the navel of the earth, which is guarded by a snake called Pytho. The symbol Serpens Candivorens, a snake biting its tail, represents the unending cycle of nature between destruction, and new creation, life and death. The Greeks called this figure Ouroboros. Chinese mythology maintained that the world was surrounded by two entwined snakes, which symbolized the power and wisdom of the creator. In another legend the Buddha was attacked by a snake which bound itself seven times around his waist. Due to the inner strength of the Buddha, the snake could not kill him but instead became his follower.

Astrologers, or those interested in the historical development of astrology, will point out that some systems include a thirteenth sign of the zodiac known as Ophiuchus Serpentarius, the Serpent Holder. This constellation lies between Sagittarius and Libra, somewhat over Scorpio. In the sixteenth and seventeenth centuries this constellation was called Alpheichius. Known as the "God of Invocation", this house was named after the legendary healer, Ophiuchus (Asclepius). The two serpents in his hands later replaced the twin ribbons around the caduceus which became a symbol for physicians."

-- Reference: freemasonry.bcy.ca/symbolism/serpent.html

[115] **"...assassinated by the Priests of Amen..."**

"The High Priest of Amun or First Prophet of Amun was the highest ranking priest in the priesthood of the ancient Egyptian god Amun.

"Maya" was the High Priest of Amen until year 4 of Akhenaten. Redford speculates that Maya is short for Ptahmose and that Ptahmose served from the end of the reign of Amenhotep III until the beginning of the time of Akhenaten.

"Parennefer" was the High Priest of Amen during the reigns of Tutankhamen and Horemheb."

-- Reference: Wikipedia.org

[116] **"...Moses..."**

"(The Exodus of Hebrew slave from Egypt, led by Moses) may have occurred around 1400s BC, since the Amarna letters, written ca. forty years later to Pharaohs Amenhotep III and Amenhotep IV (Akhenaten) indicate that Canaan was being invaded by the "Habiru" — whom some scholars in the 1950s to 1970s interpret to mean "Hebrews".

Exodus 34:29-35 tells that after meeting with God the skin of Moses' face became radiant, frightening the Israelites and leading Moses to wear a veil. Jonathan Kirsch, in his book

235

*Moses: A Life*, thought that, since he subsequently had to wear a veil to hide it, Moses' face was disfigured by a sort of "divine radiation burn".

-- Reference: Wikipedia.org

[117] .. Yahweh..."

*"The cartouche of Akhenaten's god and heavenly father, the Aten, bore the name Imram. In the Bible, Moses is referred to as the son of Amram, the Hebrew equivalent.* **The name of the Egyptian deity Aten transliterates into the Hebrew word Adon**. *Adon, which is translated by English Bibles as "the Lord" (and Adonai, translated as "my Lord") is used along with Jehovah (Yhwh) in the Bible as the exclusive personal names of God. Moreover, in ancient times, the name Jehovah (Yhwh) was written, but never spoken. Whenever the written name Jehovah (Yhwh) was to be read out loud, Adon (Aten) was voiced instead. The written form of Adon is infrequent, however, its limited usage is significant, especially in the first six books of the Bible (See under "LORD" in Strong's Exhaustive Concordance), where it is reserved for the following applications alone:* **Moses addresses God using the title Adon/Aten (Exodus 4:10,13; 5:22; 34:9; Numbers 14:17; Deuteronomy 3:23; 7:26; 10:17); Moses, himself, is addressed both by Aaron (Ex.32:22; Num.12:11) and by Joshua (Numbers 11:28) using the title Adon/Aten; and Joshua also addresses God using the title Adon/Aten (Joshua 5:14 b; 7:7).** *As mentioned above, there is an established relationship between the literature of the Egyptian 18th Dynasty and the Bible. Psalm 104 is an embellishment of the Hymn to the Aten which was found by archaeologists at the city of Akhetaten."*

-- Reference: http://www.domainofman.com/ankhemmaat/moses.html

**"Yahweh** *is an English rendition of* יהוה, *the name of the God of Israel. During the Babylonian captivity, the Hebrew language spoken by the Jews was replaced by the Aramaic language of their Babylonian captors, which was closely related to Hebrew and, while sharing many vocabulary words in common, contained some words that sounded the same or similar but had other meanings. In Aramaic, the Hebrew word for "blaspheme" used in Leviticus 24:16, "Anyone who blasphemes the name of YHWH must be put to death" carried the meaning of "pronounce" rather than "blaspheme".*

-- Reference: Wikipedia.org

[118] "...Torah...decoded..."

**"The Bible Code** *is a best-selling controversial book by Michael Drosnin, first published in 1997. A sequel, The Bible Code II, was published in 2002 and also reached best-seller status.*

*Drosnin describes an alleged "Bible code", in which messages are encoded in the Hebrew bible. The messages are purported to be hidden in the Torah, and can be deciphered by placing the letters of various Torah passages at equal intervals in a text that has been formatted to fit inside a graph.*

*Drosnin suggests that the Code was written by extraterrestrial life (which he claims also brought the DNA of the human genetic code to Earth). Drosnin elaborates on this theory in The Bible Code II, suggesting that the alien who brought the code left the key to the code in a steel obelisk. Drosnin attempted to find this obelisk, which he believes is buried near the*

*Dead Sea. Drosnin's book is based on the technique described in the paper "Equidistant Letter Sequences in the Book of Genesis" by Professor Eliyahu Rips of the Hebrew University in Israel with Doron Witztum and Yoav Rosenberg."*

-- Reference: Wikipedia.org

[119] **"... Buddha ..."**

*"The following points are the the few of the fundamentals of the teachings attributed to Gautama Buddha:*

*The Four Noble Truths: that suffering is an inherent part of existence; that the origin of suffering is ignorance and the main symptoms of that ignorance are attachment and craving; that attachment and craving can be ceased; and that following the Noble Eightfold Path will lead to the cessation of attachment and craving and therefore suffering.*

*The Noble Eightfold Path: right understanding, right thought, right speech, right action, right livelihood, right effort, right mindfulness, and right concentration.*

*Dependent origination: that any phenomenon 'exists' only because of the 'existence' of other phenomena in a complex web of cause and effect covering time past, present and future.*

*Because all things are thus conditioned and transient (anicca), they have no real independent identity (anatta).*

*Anicca (Sanskrit: anitya): That all things are impermanent.*

*Anatta (Sanskrit: anātman): That the perception of a constant "self" is an illusion.*

*Dukkha (Sanskrit: duḢkha): That all beings suffer from all situations due to unclear mind.*

*According to tradition, the Buddha emphasized ethics and correct understanding. He questioned the average person's notions of divinity and salvation. He stated that gods are subjected to karma themselves; and the Buddha is solely a guide and teacher for the sentient beings who must tread the path of Nirvā Ḣa themselves to attain the spiritual awakening called bodhi and see truth and reality as it is. The Buddhist system of insight and meditation practice is not believed to have been revealed divinely, but by the understanding of the true nature of the mind, which must be discovered by personally treading a spiritual path guided by the Buddha's teachings."*

-- Reference: Wikipedia.org

[120] **"... Laozi..."**

*"The Daodejing, often called simply the Laozi after its reputed author, describes the Dao (or Tao) as the mystical source and ideal of all existence: it is unseen, but not transcendent, immensely powerful yet supremely humble, being the root of all things. According to the Daodejing, humans have no special place within the Dao, being just one of its many ("ten thousand") manifestations. People have desires and free will (and thus are able to alter their own nature). Many act "unnaturally", upsetting the natural balance of the Dao. The Daodejing intends to lead students to a "return" to their natural state, in harmony with Dao. Language and conventional wisdom are critically assessed. Taoism views them as inherently biased and artificial, widely using paradoxes to sharpen the point.*

*Wu wei, literally "non-action" or "not acting", is a central concept of the Daodejing. The concept of wu wei is very complex and reflected in the words' multiple meanings, even in English translation; it can mean "not doing anything", "not forcing", "not acting" in the* theatrical sense, "creating nothingness", "acting spontaneously", and "flowing with the moment."

Laozi used the term broadly with simplicity and humility as key virtues, often in contrast to selfish action. On a political level, it means avoiding such circumstances as war, harsh laws and heavy taxes. Some Taoists see a connection between wu wei and esoteric practices, such as the "sitting in oblivion" (emptying the mind of bodily awareness and thought) found in the Zhuangzi.

Taoism is a religion addressing the quest of immortality."

-- Reference: Wikipedia.org

[121] "...Zoroaster..."

"The best known (**Zoroastrians** were the) Magi, the "Wise Men from the East" in the Bible, (who brought gifts to Bethlehem) and whose graves Marco Polo claimed to have seen in what is today the district of Saveh, near Tehran, Iran. In English, the **term is the origin of the words magic and magician.**

"Many traits of Zoroastrianism can be traced back to the culture and beliefs of the proto-Indo-Iranian period, and Zoroastrianism consequently **shares** some **elements with the historical Vedic religion that also has its origins in that era**.

Central to Zoroastrianism is the **emphasis on moral choice, to choose between the responsibility and duty for which one is in the mortal world**, or to give up this duty and so facilitate the work of druj. Similarly, **predestination is rejected** in Zoroastrian teaching. Humans bear responsibility for all situations they are in, and in the way they act to one another. **Reward, punishment, happiness and grief all depend on how individuals live their life.**

In Zoroastrianism, good transpires for those who do righteous deeds. Those who do evil have themselves to blame for their ruin. Zoroastrian morality is then to be summed up in the simple phrase, **"good thoughts, good words, good deeds"**.

There is one universal and transcendental God, Ahura Mazda, the one uncreated creator and to whom all worship is ultimately directed.

Ahura Mazda's creation — evident as truth and order — is the antithesis of chaos, falsehood and disorder. The resulting conflict involves the entire universe, including humanity, which has an active role to play in the conflict.

Active participation in life through good thoughts, good words and good deeds is necessary to ensure happiness and to keep the chaos at bay. This active participation is a central element in Zoroaster's concept of free will."

-- Reference: Wikipedia.org

[122] "The land masses continually crack, crumble and drift."

"**Plate tectonics** (from Greek τέκτων, tektōn "builder" or "mason") is a theory of geology that has been developed to explain the observed evidence for large scale motions of the Earth's lithosphere. The theory encompassed and superseded the older theory of continental drift *from the first half of the 20th century and the concept of seafloor spreading developed during the 1960s.*

*The outermost part of the Earth's interior is made up of two layers: above is the lithosphere, comprising the crust and the rigid uppermost part of the mantle. Below the lithosphere lies the asthenosphere. Although solid, the asthenosphere has relatively low viscosity and shear strength and can flow like a liquid on geological time scales. The deeper mantle below the asthenosphere is more rigid again. This is, however, not because of cooler temperatures but due to high pressure.*

*The lithosphere is broken up into what are called tectonic plates — in the case of Earth, there are seven major and many minor plates. The lithospheric plates ride on the asthenosphere. These plates move in relation to one another at one of three types of plate boundaries: convergent or collision boundaries, divergent or spreading boundaries, and transform boundaries. Earthquakes, volcanic activity, mountain-building, and oceanic trench formation occur along plate boundaries. The lateral movement of the plates is typically at speeds of 5 - 10 centimeters / yr."*

-- Reference: Wikipedia.org

[123] " **The magnetic poles of the planet shift radically about once every 20,000 years".**

*"The **pole shift theory** is a hypothesis that the axis of rotation of a planet has not always been at its present-day locations or that the axis will not persist there; in other words, that its physical poles had been or will be shifted. Pole shift theory is almost always discussed in the context of Earth, but other solar system bodies may have experienced axial reorientation during their existences.*

*Pole shift theories are not to be confused with plate tectonics, the well-accepted geological theory that the Earth's surface consists of solid plates which shift over a fluid asthenosphere; nor with continental drift, the corollary to plate tectonics which maintains that locations of the continents have moved slowly over the face of the earth, resulting in the gradual emerging and breakup of continents and oceans over hundreds of millions of years.*

*Pole shift theories are also not to be confused with Geomagnetic reversal, the periodic reversal of the earth's magnetic field (effectively switching the north and south magnetic poles). Geomagnetic reversal has more acceptance in the scientific community than pole shift theories."*

-- Reference: Wikipedia.org

[124] " **This operation is managed by the secret police...**"

*"**Secret police** (sometimes **political police**) are a police organization which operates in secrecy to maintain national security against internal threats to the state. **Secret police forces are typically associated with totalitarian regimes**, as they are often used to maintain the political power of the state rather than uphold the rule of law. Secret police are law enforcement organizations officially endowed with authority superior to civil police forces, **operating outside the normal boundaries of the law**, and they are often accountable only to the executive branch of the government. **They operate entirely or partially in secrecy**; i.e., most or all of their operations are obscure and hidden from the general public and from*

all government officials, except for the topmost executive officials. **Secret police organizations have often been used as an instrument of political repression**. *States where the secret police wield significant power are sometimes referred to as police states. Secret police differ from the domestic security agencies in modern liberal democracies, because domestic security agencies are generally subject to government regulation, reporting requirements, and other accountability measures. Despite such oversight, there still exists the possibility of domestic-security agencies acting unlawfully and taking on some characteristics of secret police.*

*Secret police not only have the traditional police authority to arrest and detain, but in some cases they are given unsupervised control of the length of detention, assigned to implement punishments independent of the public judiciary, and allowed to administer those punishments without external review. The tactics of investigation and intimidation used by secret police enable them to accrue so much power that they usually operate with little or no practical restraint.* **Secret-police organizations employ internal spies and civilian informants to find protest leaders or dissidents,** *and they may also employ agents provocateurs to incite political opponents to perform illegal acts against the government, whereupon such opponents may be arrested.* **Secret police may open mail, tap telephone lines, use various techniques to trick, blackmail, or coerce relatives or friends of a suspect into providing information. The secret police are renowned for raiding homes between midnight and dawn, to apprehend people suspected of dissent.**

**People apprehended by the secret police are often arbitrarily arrested and detained without due process.** *While in detention,* **arrestees may be tortured or subjected to inhumane treatment**. *Suspects may not receive a public trial, and instead may be convicted in a kangaroo court-style show trial, or by a secret tribunal.*

*Secret police have been used by many types of governments.* **Secret police forces in dictatorships and totalitarian states usually use violence and acts of terror to suppress political opposition and dissent, and may use death squads to carry out assassinations and "disappearances".** *Although secret police normally do not exist in democratic states there are different varieties of democracy and, in times of emergency or war, a democracy may lawfully grant its policing and security services additional or sweeping powers, which may be seen or construed as a secret police."*

-- Reference: Wikipedia.org

[125] "...using false provocation operations to disguise their activities..."

*"False flag operations are covert operations conducted by governments, corporations, or other organizations, which are designed to appear as if they are being carried out by other entities. The name is derived from the military concept of flying false colors; that is, flying the flag of a country other than one's own.* **False flag operations are not limited to war** *and counter-insurgency operations, and* **have been used in peacetime**; *for example, during Italy's strategy of tension.*

*During the Italian strategy of tension in which several bombings in the 1970s, attributed to far-left organizations, were in fact carried out by far-right organizations cooperating with the Italian secret services (see Operation Gladio, 1969 Piazza Fontana bombing, 1972 Peteano attack by Vincenzo Vinciguerra, 1973 assassination attempt of former Interior Minister Mariano Rumor, 1980 Bologna massacre, etc. and various investigations, for example by Guido Salvini). In France, the Masada Action and Defense Movement, supposedly a Zionist* group, was really a neo-fascist terrorist group which hoped to increase tension between Arabs and Jews in France.

False flag tactics were also employed during the Algerian civil war, starting in the mid-1994. Death squads composed of DRS(Département du Renseignement et de la Sécurité) security forces disguised themselves as Islamist terrorists and committed false flag terror attacks. Such groups included the OJAL (Organisation of Young Free Algerians) or the OSSRA (Secret Organisation for the safeguard of the Algerian Republic) According to Roger Faligot and Pascal Kropp (1999), the OJAL reminded of "the Organization of the French Algerian Resistance (ORAF), a group of counter-terrorists created in December 1956 by the DST (Direction de la Surveillance du Territoire / Territorial Surveillance Directorate) whose mission was to carry out terrorist attacks with the aim of quashing any hopes of political compromise."

**On the night of Feb. 27, 1933 the Reichstag building was set on fire. At the urging of Hitler, Hindenburg responded the next day by issuing an emergency decree "for the Protection of the people and the State," which stated: "Restrictions on personal liberty, on the right of free expression of opinion, including freedom of the press; on the rights of assembly and association; and violations of the privacy of postal, telegraphic and telephonic communications and warrants for house searches, orders for confiscations as well as restrictions on property, are also permissible beyond the legal limits otherwise prescribed."** After 74 years, the question of who actually started the Reichstag fire is still unknown and occasionally debated.

**There are various 9/11 conspiracy theories (and a very large body of hard evidence - Editor) which say the September 11, 2001 attacks on the US were a false flag operation."**

-- Reference: Wikipedia.org

[126] **"... mind-control methods developed by government psychiatrists..."**

"William Sargant was a consultant to the British Secret Intelligence Service (MI5/MI6). In 1953 he associated with Frank Olson, Deputy Acting Head of Special Operations for the CIA, investigating the use of mind-bending drugs at the Biological Warfare Centre at Porton Down.

In 1944 he collaborated with Slater in writing An Introduction to Physical Methods of Treatment in Psychiatry, **a textbook on biological psychiatry that included lobotomy and shock therapy and remained in print for three decades.**

**William Sargant was a pioneer in methods of placing false memories into patients.** He attested at the 1977 U.S. Senate hearing, **"that the therapist should deliberately distort the facts of the patient's life-experience to achieve heightened emotional response and abreaction. In the drunken state of narcoanalysis patients are prone to accept the therapist's false constructions."**

In 1957 William Sargant published one of the first books on the psychology of brainwashing, Battle for the Mind. William Sargant connected Pavlov's findings to the ways people learned and internalized belief systems. Conditioned behavior patterns could be changed by stimulated stresses beyond a dog's capacity for response, in essence causing a breakdown.

This could also be caused by intense signals, longer than normal waiting periods, rotating positive and negative signals and changing a dog's physical condition, as through illness. Depending on the dog's initial personality, this could possibly cause a new belief system to be held tenaciously. Sargant also connected Pavlov's findings to the mechanisms of brainwashing in religion and politics.

Sargant and Dr Ewen Cameron of **Project MKULTRA** notoriety, were friends and colleagues who shared and exchanged views and information on brainwashing and de-patterning techniques and their mutual researches in this area. Both men had extensive CIA and British Secret Intelligence Service connections.

**The aim** of Cameron, Sargant and the CIA's **researches was to find a way to obliterate the memories** of an allied spy ('de-patterning') **and implant false memories at a deep level** so that if that spy was captured in his adoptive country, he would be incapable under duress or even torture of revealing his true American/British allegiance. **He would only be able to reveal the falsely implanted memories that supported his assumed persona.** This concept became termed 'The Manchurian Candidate' after the novel. **The extensive use of 'heroic' doses of** <u>**Electron Convulsive Shock Treatment**</u> combined with Deep Sleep Treatment (narcosis), anti-depressants, tape-loops, insulin coma therapy, and other drugs in this context, **was designed to** <u>**induce catastrophic memory loss**</u> **which would then supposedly** <u>**be replaced with false memories and ideas**</u> (via tape loops, hypnosis, LSD or conversations while the person was drugged).

**In addition to LSD, Cameron also experimented with various paralytic drugs, as well as electroconvulsive therapy at 30 to 40 times the normal power.** His "driving" **experiments consisted of putting subjects into drug-induced coma for months on end** (up to three in one case) while playing tape loops of noise or simple repetitive statements. His experiments were typically carried out on patients who had entered the institute for minor problems such as anxiety disorders and post-partum depression, many of whom suffered permanently from his actions."

-- Reference: Wikipedia.org

[127] ..."**Earth is a "ghetto" planet...**"

"**Ghetto**" is also used figuratively to indicate geographic areas with a concentration of any type of person.

**Ghetto is formed in three ways:**

- As ports of entry for racial minorities, and immigrant racial minorities.
- When the majority uses compulsion (typically violence, hostility, or legal barriers) to force minorities into particular areas.
- When the majority is willing and able to pay more than the minority to live with its own kind.

During World War II ghettos in occupied Europe 1939-1944 were established by the Nazis to confine Jews and sometimes Gypsies into tightly packed areas of the cities of Eastern Europe turning them into **de-facto concentration camps and death camps in the Holocaust.**"

-- Reference: Wikipedia.org

"... Holocaust..."

*"**The Holocaust** (from the Greek □λόκαυστον (holókauston): holos, "completely" and kaustos, "burnt"), is the term generally used to describe the killing of approximately six million European Jews during World War II, as part of a program of deliberate extermination planned and executed by the National Socialist (Nazi) regime in Germany led by Adolf Hitler.*

***Other groups were persecuted and killed by the regime, including the Roma; Soviets, particularly prisoners of war; ethnic Poles; other Slavic people; the disabled; gay men; and political and religious dissidents.***

***The persecution and genocide were accomplished in stages.*** *Legislation to remove the Jews from civil society was enacted years before the outbreak of World War II. Concentration camps were established in which inmates were used as **slave labour** until they died of exhaustion or disease. Where the Third Reich conquered new territory in eastern Europe, specialized units called Einsatzgruppen murdered Jews and **political opponents** in mass shootings. Jews and Roma were **crammed into ghettos** before being transported hundreds of miles by freight train to extermination camps where, if they survived the journey, the majority of them were killed in gas chambers. Every arm of Germany's bureaucracy was involved in the logistics of the mass murder, turning the country into what one Holocaust scholar has called "a genocidal state."*

-- Reference: Wikipedia.org

129 "..."final solution"..."

"Holocaust documenters argue that the medicalization of social problems and systematic euthanasia of people in German mental institutions in the 1930s provided the institutional, procedural, and doctrinal origins of the mass murder of the 1940s. **The Nuremberg Trials convicted a number of psychiatrists who held key positions in Nazi regimes.**"

-- Reference: Lapon, Lenny (1986). *Mass Murderers in White Coats : Psychiatric Genocide in Nazi Germany and the United States.*

<u>**The tie between Hitler and the eugenic psychiatrists**</u> *was so close that much of Mein Kampf is literally indistinguishable in language and in tone from the major international journals and psychiatric textbooks of the time. To **quote from** a few of many such passages in **Mein Kampf**:*

"To demand that defective people be prevented from propagating equally defective offspring is a demand for the clearest reason and, if systematically executed, represents the most humane act of mankind ..."

"Those who are physically and mentally unhealthy and unworthy must not perpetuate their ;suffering in the bodies of their children ..."

"A prevention of the faculty and opportunity to procreate on the part of the physically degenerate and the mentally sick ... would not only free humanity from an immeasurable misfortune but would lead to a recovery which today seems scarcely conceivable."

_Hitler received support from psychiatrists and social scientists around the world after he took power_. Many articles in the world's leading medical journals monitored _and heaped praise on Hitler's eugenic legislation and policies_.

Records uncovered by Abrams at the hospital confirm that the _extermination had begun as a part of a national psychiatric program before Hitler took on the systematic murder of the Jews_. Hundreds of patients had been shipped off to psychiatric extermination centers prior to the end of 1941, when the national program was largely abandoned and local state mental hospitals took over "the action" on their own.

_The psychiatric extermination program_ was not a hidden, secret shame of psychiatry - at least, not at the start. _It was organized by leading professors of psychiatry_ and directors of mental hospitals through a series of national meetings and workshops. So-called euthanasia forms were circulated to individual hospitals, and _final approval of each death was then given in Berlin by a committee of the nation's outstanding psychiatrists_. By January 1940 patients were being shipped to six special extermination centers staffed by psychiatrists.

In late 1941, public outrage and lack of enthusiasm from Hitler pushed the program underground, but _between 100,000 and 200,000 German mental patients had been killed_. From then on, individual institutions, such as that at Kaufbeuren, continued to act on their own, even admitting new patients for the purpose of murdering them. At the end of the war, many large institutions were entirely empty, and estimates from various war-crime tribunals, including Nuremberg, estimate _the number of dead to be between 250,000 and 300,000, mostly inmates of psychiatric hospitals_ and homes for the retarded...

_Psychiatrist Frederic Wertham_, by no means a radical critic of his profession, **deserves the credit for being the first to describe the role of psychiatry in Nazi Germany**: ...

**"The tragedy is that the PSYCHIATRISTS did not have to have an order. They _acted on their own. They were not carrying out a death sentence pronounced by somebody else. They were the legislators who laid down the rules for deciding who was to die_; they were the administrators who worked out the procedures, provided the patients and the places, _and decided the methods of killing_; they _pronounced a sentence of life or death in each individual case; they were the executioners_ who carried the sentences out or -- without being coerced to do so -- surrendered their patients to be killed in other institutions; _they supervised and often watched the slow deaths_..."**

By November 1, 1941, the first extermination camps were being built: first Belzec, then Sobibor, Treblinka, Chelmno and Majdanek, and finally Auschwitz-Birkenau.

At first, vague plans were made in Nazi Germany to deport all European Jews to Madagascar. **Adolf Eichmann**, in particular, supported this option before **the Wannsee Conference of 1942**, where he was made privy to the exact details of the **"Final Solution"**.

**SS chief Heinrich Himmler** stated:

"However cruel and tragic each individual case may be, this method is still the mildest and best, if one rejects the Bolshevik method of physical extermination of a people out of inner conviction as un-German and impossible."

The original plan was to use the Royal Navy after Britain's defeat to exile all of Europe's Jews to Madagascar. However, since the British were not defeated as anticipated by the Nazis, the Madagascar Plan had to be abandoned.

The extermination process in Belzec, Sobibor and Treblinka was similar to the method used in the six extermination camps in Germany and Austria, but hugely scaled up for killing whole transports of people at a time.

**Victims would hand over their valuables, which became property of the German Reichsbank. They then undressed, and their clothes were searched for jewelry and other valuables. Victims were then marched into the gas chamber and packed tightly to minimize the available fresh air. An engine created carbon monoxide gas which was then discharged through gas pipes, killing the occupants. Their corpses were cremated after any gold dental fillings were removed. The mass murder was carefully tracked and documented.**

For example, the intercepted Höfle Telegram sent by SS-Sturmbannführer Hermann Höfle on January 11, 1943 to SS-Obersturmbannführer **Adolf Eichmann in Berlin listed 1,274,166 total arrivals to the four camps of Aktion Reinhard through the end of 1942**, as well as the total arrivals by camp for the last two weeks of 1942.

The structure of all camps was nearly identical. From the reception area with ramp and undressing barracks, the Jews entered a narrow, camouflaged path (called sluice or tube) to the extermination area with gas chambers, pits and cremation grids. The SS and Trawnikis stayed in a separate area. Barbed wire fences, partially camouflaged with pine branches, surrounded the camp and separated the different parts. Unlike Auschwitz, no electric fences were used. Wooden watchtowers guarded the camp.

Approximately 2 million Jews lost their lives in Belzec, Sobibor, Treblinka and Majdanek in the course of Operation Reinhard. Approximately 178,045,960 German Reichsmark worth of Jewish property (today's value: around 700,000,000 $US or 550,000,000 Euros) was stolen. This money went not only to German authorities, but also to single individuals (SS and police men, camp guards, non-Jewish inhabitants of towns and villages with ghettos or adjacent camps)."

-- Reference: Wikipedia.org

[130] "... the "Old Empire", whose headquarters located near one of the "tail stars" in the Ursa Major (Big Dipper)..."

The "Tail Stars" of Ursa Major are **Alcor, Alioth**, and **Alkaid**."

-- Reference: Wikipedia.org

[131] "... radioactivity..."

"Nuclear weapons emit large amounts of electromagnetic radiation as visible, infrared, and ultraviolet light. The chief hazards are burns and eye injuries. On clear days, these injuries can occur well beyond blast ranges. The light is so powerful that it can start fires that spread rapidly in the debris left by a blast. The range of thermal effects increases markedly with weapon yield. Thermal radiation accounts for between 35-45% of the energy released in the explosion, depending on the yield of the device.

*The first atomic bomb actually used in war time was dropped on Hiroshima on August 6th, 1945 killing between 130,000 and 150,000 people by the end of that year. Those who survived the bombing are rapidly aging now after struggling for many years.*

*In Hiroshima, a tremendous fire storm developed within 20 minutes after detonation and destroyed many more buildings and homes. A fire storm has gale force winds blowing in towards the center of the fire from all points of the compass.*

*Mr. Hiroshi Sawachika was 28 years old when the bomb was dropped. He was an army doctor stationed at the army headquarters in Ujina. When he was exposed, he was inside the building at the headquarters, 4.1 km from the hypocenter. Being rather far from the hypocenter, he was not seriously injured. Afterwards, he was very busy getting medical treatment to the survivors.*

*INTERVIEWER: How many patients did you treat on August 6?*

*ANSWER: Well, at least 2 or 3 thousand on that very day if you include those patients whom I gave directions to. I felt that as if once that day started, it never ended. I had to keep on and on treating the patients forever. It was the longest day of my life. Later on, when I had time to reflect on that day, I came to realize that we, doctors learned a lot through the experience, through the suffering of all those people. It's true that the lack of medical knowledge, medical facilities, integrated organization and so on prevented us from giving sufficient medical treatment. Still there was a lot for us, medical doctors to learn on that day. I learned that the nuclear weapons which gnaw the minds and bodies of human beings should never be used. Even the slightest idea using nuclear arms should be completely exterminated the minds of human beings. Otherwise, we will repeat the same tragedy. And we will never stop being ashamed of ourselves."*

-- Reference: Wikipedia.org

[132] **"...Atlanta..."**

*"Atlantis was a continent. Its capital was called by the same name or by that of Poseidonis, and was located on an island next to its coast. After this continent sunk under the seas, only the peaks of its loftiest mountains remained above the water, forming what the ancients later knew as the Islands of the Blest, and which we know as those of Indonesia.*

*Atlantis created a worldwide empire, and had colonies the world over. These colonies, as usual, attempted to duplicate the motherland, as colonists are wont to do. Atlantis and Lemuria have been grossly distorted and misplaced by all sorts of investigators in what concerns both their epochs and their sizes and locations. Indeed, Atlantis and Lemuria coexisted side by side, at more or less the same date.*

*More exactly, Lemuria was the archetypal Atlantis, the same as Eden or Paradise, the site of origin of both Mankind and Civilization. From there, the Lemurian Atlanteans colonized the nearby region of India, which became its "twin" and partner. In mythical terms, we can say that Lemuria-Indonesia was the Mother, and that Atlantis-India was the Father of all the other civilizations.*

*Our Atlantean heritage also encompasses the arts and techniques such as Agriculture and Animal Domestication, the greatest inventions ever. Without the domesticated plants and animals — most or all of which originated in Atlantis, and often embody an advanced use of*

246

*genetic engineering — Civilization could never have developed at all. Besides these, a series of inventions of mysterious origins, who came to us from the dawn of time, are also owed to Atlantis and Lemuria: metallurgy, stone masonry and sculpture, paper, the alphabet, medicinal drugs, gunpowder, weaving, and so on."*

Reference: http://www.atlan.org/

[133] "...Lemur..."

*"Lemuria is the name of a hypothetical "lost land" variously located in the Indian and Pacific Oceans. Its 19th century origins lie in attempts to account for discontinuities in biogeography. Though Lemuria has passed out of the realm of conventional science, it has been adopted by occult writers, as well as some Tamil writers of India. Accounts of Lemuria differ according to the requirements of their contexts, but all share a common belief that a continent existed in ancient times and sank beneath the ocean as a result of geological change, often cataclysmic.*

*Lemuria entered the lexicon of the Occult through the works of Madame Blavatsky, who claimed in the 1880s to have been shown an ancient, pre-Atlantean Book of Dzyan by the Mahatmas. Kumari Kandam is a sunken kingdom sometimes compared with Lemuria. According to these modernist interpretations of motifs in classical Tamil literature — the epics Cilappatikaram and Manimekalai that describe the submerged city of Puhar — the Dravidians originally came from land south of the present day coast of South India that became submerged by successive floods. There are various claims from Tamil authors that there was a large land mass connecting Australia and the present day Tamil Nadu coast.*

*It is interesting to note that Madame Blavatsky described the Lemurians (her third root race) as being colored black and described the Negroid race, the Dravidians and* **the Australoids, Papuans and Melanesians as being descended from them.**

*prior to the acceptance of continental drift, biologists frequently postulated submerged land masses in order to account for populations of land-based species now separated by barriers of water. Similarly, geologists tried to account for striking resemblances of rock formations on different continents. The first systematic attempt was made by Melchior Neumayr in his book Erdgeschichte in 1887. Many hypothetical submerged land bridges and continents were proposed during the 19th century, in order to account for the present distribution of species.*

*As Lemuria gained some acceptance within the scientific community, it began to appear in the works of other scholars. Ernst Haeckel, a German Darwinian taxonomist, proposed Lemuria as an explanation for the absence of "missing link" fossil records. According to another source, Haeckel put forward this thesis prior to Sclater (but without using the name 'Lemuria'). Locating the origins of the human species on this lost continent, he claimed the fossil record could not be found because it had sunk beneath the sea.*

*Other scientists hypothesized that Lemuria had extended across parts of the Pacific oceans, explaining distributions of species across Asia and the Americas.*

*The Lemuria theory disappeared completely from conventional scientific consideration after the theories of plate tectonics and continental drift were accepted by the larger scientific community. According to the theory of plate tectonics (which is nowadays the only accepted paradigm in geology), Madagascar and India were indeed once part of the same landmass (thus accounting for geological resemblances), but plate movement caused India to break away millions of years ago, and move to its present location. The original landmass broke apart - it did not sink beneath the sea level."*

-- Reference: Wikipedia.org

[134] ..."Lake Toba in Sumatra"...

*The **Toba eruption** (the **Toba event**) occurred at what is now Lake Toba about 67,500 to 75,500 years ago. It had an estimated Volcanic Explosivity Index of 8 (described as "mega-colossal"), making it possibly the largest explosive volcanic eruption within the last twenty-five million years. The total amount of erupted material was about 2800 cubic km (670 cubic miles) — around 2,000 km³ of ignimbrite that flowed over the ground and around 800 km³ that fell as ash, with the wind blowing most of it to the west.*

*By contrast, the 1980 eruption of Mount St. Helens ejected around 1.2 cubic km of material, whilst the largest volcanic eruption in historic times, at Mount Tambora in 1815, emitted the equivalent of around 100 cubic kilometers of dense rock and created the "Year Without a Summer" as far away as North America."*

*The Toba eruption was the latest of a series of at least three caldera-forming eruptions which have occurred at the volcano. Earlier calderas were formed around 700,000 and 840,000 years ago.*

*To give an idea of its magnitude, consider that although the eruption took place in Indonesia, it deposited an ash layer approximately 15 cm (6 in) thick over __the entire Indian subcontinent__; at one site in __central India__, the **Toba ash layer today is up to 6 m (20 feet) thick and parts of Malaysia were covered with 9 m of ashfall**. In addition it has been calculated that $10^{10}$ metric tons of sulphuric acid was ejected into the atmosphere by the event, causing acid rain fallout."*

-- Reference: Wikipedia.org

[135] "...Mt. Krakatoa..."

*"Mt. Krakatoa is a volcanic island in the Sunda Strait between Java and Sumatra in Indonesia. The name is used for the island group, the main island (also called Rakata), and the volcano as a whole. It has erupted repeatedly, massively, and with disastrous consequences throughout recorded history. The best known eruption culminated in a series of massive explosions on August 26-27 1883, which was among the most violent volcanic events in modern times. With a Volcanic Explosivity Index of 6, it was equivalent to 200 megatonnes of TNT — about 13,000 times the yield of the Little Boy bomb (13 to 16 KT), which devastated Hiroshima, Japan.*

*The 1883 eruption ejected more than 25 cubic kilometres of rock, ash, and pumice, and generated the loudest sound historically reported: the cataclysmic explosion was distinctly heard as far away as Perth in Australia approx. 1,930 miles (3,110 km), and the island of Rodrigues near Mauritius approx. 3,000 miles (5,000 km). Near Krakatoa, according to official records, 165 villages and towns were destroyed and 132 seriously damaged, at least 36,417 (official toll) people died, and many thousands were injured by the eruption, mostly from the tsunamis which followed the explosion.*

The eruption destroyed two thirds of the island of Krakatoa. Eruptions at the volcano since 1927 have built a new island in the same location, called Anak Krakatau (child of Krakatoa)."

-- Reference: Wikipedia.org

[136] "... colossal volcanic explosion..."

"A **supervolcano** is a volcano that produces the largest and most voluminous kinds of eruption on Earth. The explosivity of such eruptions varies, but the volume of ejected tephra is enough to radically alter the landscape and **severely affect global climate for years**, with cataclysmic consequences for life VEI-8 volcanic events have included eruptions at the following locations. Estimates of the volume of erupted material are given in parentheses.

- _Lake Taupo_, _North Island_, _New Zealand_ - _Oruanui eruption_ 26,500 years ago (1,170 km³)
- **Lake Toba, Sumatra, Indonesia - 75,000 years ago (2,800 km³)**
- Yellowstone Caldera, Wyoming, United States - 2.2 million years ago (2,500 km³) and 640,000 years ago (1,000 km³)
- La Garita Caldera, Colorado, United States - Source of the truly enormous eruption of the Fish Canyon Tuff 27.8 million years ago (~5,000 km³)

**The Lake Toba eruption** plunged the Earth into a volcanic winter, eradicating an estimated 60% of the human population (although humans managed to survive, even in the vicinity of the volcano), and was responsible for the formation of sulfuric acid in the atmosphere.

Many other supermassive eruptions have also occurred in the geological past."

-- Reference: Wikipedia.org

[137] "... due to atmospheric pollution as well as an extensive period during which radiation from the sun is deflected back into space, and cause global cooling..."

"**Nuclear winter** is a hypothetical global climate condition that is predicted to be a possible outcome of a large-scale nuclear war. It is thought that severely cold weather can be caused by detonating large numbers of nuclear weapons, especially over flammable targets such as cities, where large amounts of smoke and soot would be injected into the Earth's stratosphere. **The term has also been applied to one of the after-effects of an supervolcano eruption**.

A global average surface cooling of –7°C to –8°C persists for years, and after a decade the cooling is still –4°C (Fig. 2). Considering that the global average cooling at the depth of the last ice age 18,000 yr ago was about –5°C, this would be a climate change unprecedented in speed and amplitude in the history of the human race. The temperature changes are largest over land ... Cooling of more than –20°C occurs over large areas of North America and of more than –30°C over much of Eurasia, including all agricultural regions."

-- Reference: Wikipedia.org

[138] "...The global cataclysm that destroyed the dinosaurs..."

*"In the past 600 million years there have been five major mass extinctions that on average extinguished half of all species. The largest mass extinction to have affected life on Earth was in the Permian-Triassic, which ended the Permian period 250 million years ago and killed off 90% of all species. The last such mass extinction led to the demise of the dinosaurs and has been found to have coincided with a large asteroid impact; this is the Cretaceous–Tertiary extinction event. There is no solid evidence of impacts leading to the four other major mass extinctions, though a recent report from Ohio State scientists stated that they have located a 483-km diameter impact crater beneath the East Antarctic Ice Sheet which may date back about 250 million years, based on gravity measurements, which might associate it with the Permian-Triassic extinction event.*

*In 1980, physicist Luis Alvarez, his son, geologist Walter Alvarez, and nuclear chemists Frank Asaro and Helen V. Michael from the University of California, Berkeley discovered **unusually high concentrations of <u>iridium</u>**, an element that is rare in the Earth's crust but relatively abundant in many meteorites. From the amount and distribution of iridium present in the 65 million year old "iridium layer", the Alvarez team later estimated that an asteroid of 10–14 kilometers must have collided with the earth. This iridium layer at the K–T boundary has been found worldwide at 100 different sites. **Multidirectionally shocked quartz** (coesite), which is only known to form as the result of large impacts or <u>**atomic bomb explosions**</u>, has also been found in the same layer at more than 30 sites. **Soot and ash at levels tens of <u>thousands times normal levels</u>** were found with the above."*

-- Reference: Wikipedia.org

*"The geologic record of terminal Cretaceous environmental events indicates that **iridium** and other associated elements **were not deposited instantaneously** but during a time interval spanning some 10,000 to 100,000 years. The available geologic evidence favors a mantle rather than meteoritic origin for these elements. These results are in accord with the scenario of a series of intense eruptive volcanic events occurring during a relatively short geologic time interval and **not with the scenario of a single large asteroid impact event**."*

-- Reference: *Article: Terminal Cretaceous Environmental Events*
Charles B. Officer [1] and Charles L. Drake [2]

[1] Research professor in the Earth Sciences Department, Dartmouth College, Hanover, New Hampshire 03755.
[2] Professor in the Earth Sciences Department, Dartmouth College, Hanover, New Hampshire 03755.

[139] **"Atomic explosions cause atmospheric fallout much like that of volcanic eruptions."**

*"Oct. 26, 2007 -- New evidence dug from the shores of the Bay of Bengal supports the radical idea that it was a series of monumental volcanic eruptions that wiped out the dinosaurs, not a meteor impact in the Gulf of Mexico. The discovery confirms two important things, said Keller: First, that the most massive Deccan eruption and the K-T mass extinction happened at the same time. Second, that the later, final eruption is timed right to have slowed the recovery of many living things. This latter matter of the slow recovery has long been a mystery to paleontologists, she said."*

-- Reference: http://dsc.discovery.com/news/2007/10/26/dinosaur-volcano.html

*"A new statistical study of mass extinctions throughout the history of life on Earth is backing up the idea that no single meteor, volcanic eruption or other lone gunman is ever to blame, even in the case of the Cretaceous-Tertiary event that brought the end of dinosaurs 65 million years ago.*

*Instead, the worst die-offs happen when some sort of interminable, multi-generational pressure on life is combined with a few powerful blows. It's what is now being called the press/pulse theory of mass extinctions.*

*The theory "is essentially a more eloquent way of saying what I and many other paleontologists have been saying for many years," said Gerta Keller of Princeton University. "Namely that the impact-kill hypothesis is all wrong. Impacts alone could not have been the killing mechanism for the K-T or any of the other major mass extinctions."*

*In the late Cretaceous case massive volcanism — the Deccan Traps eruption in India — and attendant climate change, coincided with an impact that pushed highly stressed biota over the brink."*

-- Reference: http://dsc.discovery.com/news/2006/10/20/extinction_pla.html

### [140] "... Rwenzori Mountains..."

*"The highest Rwenzoris are permanently snow-capped, and they, along with Mount Kilimanjaro and Mount Kenya are the only such in Africa. The Ruwenzoris are often identified with the "Mountains of the Moon" mentioned by Ptolemy. The Ruwenzori are known for their vegetation, ranging from tropical rainforest through alpine meadows to snow; and for their animal population, including forest elephants, several primate species and many endemic birds."*

-- Reference: Wikipedia.org

### [141] ..." Pyrenees Mountains"...

*"The Pyrenees are named after Pyrene (fire in Greek) who was the daughter of Bebryx and was raped by Herakles. Terrified at **giving birth to a <u>serpent</u>, she fled to the mountains and was either buried or eaten by wild animals**. Herodotus located this legend in his map of the Oikumene as early as 450 BC."*

-- Reference: Wikipedia.org

### [142] "... steppes of Mongolia..."

*"In the chaos of the late twelfth century, a chieftain named Temüjin finally succeeded in uniting the Mongol tribes between Manchuria and **the Altai Mountains**. In 1206, he took the title **Genghis Khan**, and he and his successors began **expanding the Mongol Empire into the largest contiguous land empire in world history**, going as far northwest as the Kievan Rus, and as far south as northern Vietnam, Tibet, Iran."*

-- Reference: Wikipedia.org

**...** **"plunder their possessions."**

*"Looting, sacking, plundering, despoiling, or pillaging is the indiscriminate taking of goods by force as part of a military or political victory, or during a catastrophe or riot, such as during war, natural disaster, or rioting. The term is also used in a broader (some would argue metaphorical) sense, to describe egregious instances of theft and embezzlement, such as the "plundering" of private or public assets by corrupt or overly greedy corporate executives or government authorities. The proceeds of all these activities can be described as loot, plunder, or pillage.*

*Looting originally referred primarily to the plundering of villages and cities not only by victorious troops during warfare, but also by civilian members of the community. For example, see War and Peace, which describes widespread looting by Moscow's citizens before Napoleon's troops enter the town, and looting by French troops elsewhere; also note the looting of art treasures by the Nazis during WWII."*

-- Reference: Wikipedia.org

144 **"...Tiahuanaco..."**

For more detailed information about the archaeology of this site, visit the following websites:

http://www.sacredsites.com/americas/bolivia/tiahuanaco.html
http://www.viewzone.com/tia.html
http://www.world-mysteries.com/mpl_6.htm

145 **"...the shift of the poles of the planet...".**

*"Charles Hapgood first came to public attention in the mid-1950s with his theory of earth crust displacement, a radical geological idea which attracted the curiosity and support of Albert Einstein. The Einstein-Hapgood correspondence is a forgotten page in the history of science. Rose and I obtained these letters (ten from Einstein to Hapgood) from Albert Einstein's Archives in the Fall of 1995. They show, for the first time, just how extensively Albert Einstein was involved in assisting Charles Hapgood in the development of the theory. This correspondence is detailed in The Atlantis Blueprint. Here is a brief summary:*

*In his second reply (24 November 1952) to Hapgood, Einstein wrote that the idea of earth crust displacement should not be ruled out "apriori" just because it didn't fit with what we wanted to believe about the earth's past. What was needed, Einstein claimed, was solid "geological and paleontological facts."*

*For six months, Hapgood gathered geological evidence to support the idea of an earth crust displacement. On the 3rd of May 1953 he forwarded thirty-eight pages of this evidence to Einstein. Central to his argument was Hapgood's evidence that Lesser Antarctica was ice-free at the same time that North America lay smothered in ice. Einstein responded (8 May 1953):*

*"I find your arguments very impressive and have the impression that your hypothesis is correct. One can hardly doubt that significant shifts of the crust have taken place repeatedly and within a short time."*

He urged Hapgood to follow up on evidence of "earth fractures". A month later (11 June 1953) Hapgood sent Einstein forty-two pages of evidence on earth fractures and the evolution of the ice sheets.

Einstein wrote (17 December 1953) Hapgood urging him to address the "centrifugal momentum" problem. Hapgood responded with four pages on this problem and thirty-seven pages of "paleontological evidence" including the frozen mammoths of Arctic Siberia. Einstein was now convinced. On the 18th of May 1954, Einstein wrote a very favorable foreword for Hapgood's book EARTH'S SHIFTING CRUST: A KEY TO SOME BASIC PROBLEMS OF EARTH SCIENCE (published in 1958 by Pantheon Books, New York). The Foreword begins:

"I frequently receive communications from people who wish to consult me concerning their unpublished ideas. It goes without saying that these ideas are very seldom possessed of scientific validity. The very first communication, however, that I received from Mr. Hapgood electrified me. His idea is original, of great simplicity, and - if it continues to prove itself of great importance to everything that is related to the history of the earth's surface. ... I think that this rather astonishing, even fascinating, idea deserves the serious attention of anyone who concerns himself with the theory of the earth's development."

-- Reference:  When the Sky Fell, Rand and Rose Flemth-Ath

[146]  **"The alignment of the Pyramids of Giza on the ground matches perfectly the alignment of the constellation of Orion as seen in the sky from Giza...".**

"(Robert) Bauval is specifically known for the Orion Correlation Theory (OCT). This proposes a relationship between the fourth dynasty Egyptian pyramids of the Giza Plateau and the alignment of certain stars in the constellation of Orion.

One night, while working in Saudi Arabia, he took his family and a friend's family up into the sand dunes of the Arabian desert for a camping expedition. His friend pointed out Orion, and mentioned that Mintaka, the smaller more easterly of the stars making up Orion's belt was offset slightly from the others. Bauval then made a connection between the layout of the three main stars in Orion's belt and the layout of the three main pyramids in the Giza necropolis."

-- Reference:  Wikipedia.org

[147]  **"... Heliopolis..."**

"Heliopolis has been occupied since the Predynastic Period, with extensive building campaigns during the Old and Middle Kingdoms. Today, unfortunately, it is mostly destroyed, its temples and other buildings having been used for the construction of medieval Cairo; most information about it comes from textual sources.

According to Diodorus Siculus Heliopolis was built by Actis, one of the sons of Helios and Rhode, who named the city after his father. While all Greek cities were destroyed during the flood, the Egyptian cities including Heliopolis survived. The chief deity of Heliopolis was the god Atum, who was worshipped in the primary temple.

*The city was also the original source of the worship of the Ennead pantheon, although in later times, as Horus gained in prominence, worship focused on the synchrentistic solar deity Ra-harakhty (literally Ra, (who is) Horus of the Two Horizons).*

*During the Amarna Period, Pharoah Akhenaten introduced monotheistic worship of Aten, the deified solar disc. As the capital of Egypt for a period of time, grain was stored in Heliopolis for the winter months, when many people would descend on the town to be fed, leading to it gaining the title place of bread. The Book of the Dead goes further and describes how Heliopolis was the place of multiplying bread, <u>recounting a myth in which Horus feeds the masses there with only 7 loaves, which is the basis of the Bible New Testament parable.</u>"*

-- Reference: Wikipedia.org

[148] **"...Nephilim..."**

*"The Nephilim were an antediluvian race (pre-flood) race which are referred to in the Bible as giants.". -- Reference: http://www.nwcreation.net/nephilim.html*

*"Genesis 6:4 states "The Nephilim were on the earth in those days --and also afterwards-- when the sons of God went to the daughters of men and had children by them. They were the heroes of old, men of renown." The Nephilim were a race of giants that were produced by the sexual union of the sons of God (presumably fallen angels) and the daughters of men. Translated from the Hebrew texts, "Nephilim" means "fallen ones." They were renowned for their strength, prowess, and a great capacity for sinfulness.*

*The origination of the Nephilim begins with a story of the fallen angels. Shemhazai, an angel of high rank, led a sect of angels in a descent to earth to instruct humans in righteousness. The tutelage went on for a few centuries, but soon the angels pined for the human females. After lusting, the fallen angels instructed the women in magic and conjuring, mated with them, and produced hybrid offspring: the Nephilim.*

*The Nephilim were gigantic in stature. Their strength was prodigious and their appetites immense. Upon devouring all of humankind's resources, they began to consume humans themselves. The Nephilim attacked and oppressed humans and were the cause of massive destruction on the earth.*

*Two texts of central import to the story of the Nephilim, the Bible and the Dead Sea Scrolls, mention several names for the Nephilim. The diverse kinds of these giants are cited in several passages. They are variously referred to as Emim, or "Terrors" (Gen. 14:5; Deut. 2:10), Rephaim, or "Weakeners" or "Dead Ones" (2 Sam. 23:13; 1 Chron. 11:15), Gibborim, or "Giant Heroes" (Job 16:4), Zamzummim, or "Achievers" (Deut. 2:10), Anakim, or "Long-necked" (Deut. 2:10; Josh. 11:22, 14:15), and Awwim or "Devastators" and "Serpents." Other giants are mentioned in these texts as well, such as Goliath (2 Sam. 21:19), a giant with twelve fingers and twelve toes who is mentioned as one of the Rephaim (2 Sam. 21:20), and a tall Egyptian (1 Chron. 11:23). The passage of Numbers 13:26-33 recounts the Nephilim of Canaan that Joshua and the other Hebrew spies saw. Furthermore, according to Judaic lore, a certain one of the Nephilim, Arba, built a city, Kiriath Arba, which was named for its builder and is now known as Hebron.*

*The wickedness of the Nephilim carried with it a heavy toll. Genesis 6:5 alludes to the corruption that the Nephilim had caused amongst humans and themselves: "The Lord saw how great man's wickedness on the earth had become..." Their evil rebellion had incurred*

254

both the wrath and grief of God. God instructed the angel Gabriel to ignite a civil war among the Nephilim. He also chose Enoch, a righteous man, to inform the fallen angels of the judgment pronounced on them and their children. God did not allow the fallen angels any peace, for they could not lift their eyes to heaven and were later to be chained. The end of the Nephilim came about in the war incited by Gabriel, in which the giants eventually annihilated each other."

-- Reference: http://www.pantheon.org/articles/n/nephilim.html

[149] "...used cutting tools of highly concentrated light waves and electronic energy..."

"A *laser* is an electronic-optical device that emits coherent light radiation. The term "laser" is an acronym for Light Amplification by Stimulated Emission of Radiation. A typical laser emits light in a narrow, low-divergence monochromatic (single-coloured, if the laser is operating in the visible spectrum), beam with a well-defined wavelength. In this way, laser light is in contrast to a light source such as the incandescent light bulb, which emits light over a wide area and over a wide spectrum of wavelengths.

The first working laser was demonstrated in May 1960 by Theodore Maiman at Hughes Research Laboratories. Recently, lasers have become a multi-billion dollar industry. The most widespread use of lasers is in optical storage devices such as compact disc and DVD players, in which the laser (a few millimeters in size) scans the surface of the disc. Other common applications of lasers are bar code readers, laser printers and laser pointers.

In industry, lasers are used for cutting steel and other metals and for inscribing patterns (such as the letters on computer keyboards). Lasers are also commonly used in various fields in science, especially spectroscopy, typically because of their well-defined wavelength or short pulse duration in the case of pulsed lasers. Lasers are used by the military for range finding, target identification and illumination for weapons delivery. Lasers used in medicine are used for internal surgery and cosmetic applications.

**Laser cutting** is a technology that uses a laser to cut materials, and is usually used in industrial manufacturing. Laser cutting works by directing the output of a high power laser, by computer, at the material to be cut. The material then either melts, burns, vaporizes away, or is blown away by a jet of gas, leaving an edge with a high quality surface finish. Industrial laser cutters are used to cut flat-sheet material as well as structural and piping materials. Some 6-axis lasers can perform cutting operations on parts that have been pre-formed by casting or machining."

-- Reference: Wikipedia.org

[150] "... Baalbek..."

"The great mystery of the ruins of Baalbek, and indeed one of the greatest mysteries of the ancient world, concerns the massive foundation stones beneath the Roman Temple of Jupiter. The courtyard of the Jupiter temple is situated upon a platform, called the Grand Terrace, which consists of a huge outer wall and a filling of massive stones. The lower courses of the outer wall are formed of huge, finely crafted and precisely positioned blocks. They range in size from thirty to thirty three feet in length, fourteen feet in height and ten feet in depth, and weigh approximately 450 tons each. Nine of these blocks are visible on the north side of the temple, nine on the south, and six on the west (others may exist but archaeological excavations have thus far not dug beneath all the sections of the Grand

Terrace). Above the six blocks on the western side are three even larger stones, called the Trilithon, whose weight exceeds 1000 tons each. These great stones vary in size between sixty-three and sixty-five feet in length, with a height of fourteen feet six inches and a depth of twelve feet.

Another even larger stone lies in a limestone quarry a quarter of a mile from the Baalbek complex. Weighing an estimated 1200 tons, it is sixty-nine feet by sixteen feet by thirteen feet ten inches, making it the single largest piece of stonework ever crafted in the world. Called the Hajar el Gouble, the Stone of the South, or the Hajar el Hibla, the Stone of the Pregnant Woman, it lays at a raised angle with the lowest part of its base still attached to the quarry rock as though it were almost ready to be cut free and transported to its presumed location next to the other stones of the Trilithon.

Why these stones are such an enigma to contemporary scientists, both engineers and archaeologists alike, is that their method of quarrying, transportation and precision placement is beyond the technological ability of any known ancient or modern builders. Various 'scholars', uncomfortable with the notion that ancient cultures might have developed knowledge superior to modern science, have decided that the massive Baalbek stones were laboriously dragged from the nearby quarries to the temple site. While carved images in the temples of Egypt and Mesopotamia do indeed give evidence of this method of block transportation - using ropes, wooden rollers and thousands of laborers - the dragged blocks are known to have been only 1/10th the size and weight of the Baalbek stones and to have been moved along flat surfaces with wide movement paths. The route to the site of Baalbek, however, is up hill, over rough and winding terrain, and there is no evidence whatsoever of a flat hauling surface having been created in ancient times.

Next there is the problem of how the mammoth blocks, once they were brought to the site, were lifted and precisely placed in position. It has been theorized that the stones were raised using a complex array of scaffolding, ramps and pulleys which was powered by large numbers of humans and animals working in unison. An historical example of this method has been suggested as the solution for the Baalbek enigma. The Renaissance architect Domenico Fontana, when erecting a 327-ton Egyptian obelisk in front of St Peter's Basilica in Rome, used 40 huge pulleys, which necessitated a combined force of 800 men and 140 horses. The area where this obelisk was erected, however, was a great open space that could easily accommodate all the lifting apparatus and the men and horses pulling on the ropes. No such space is available in the spatial context of how the Baalbek stones were placed. Hills slope away from where lifting apparatus would need to have been placed and no evidence has been found of a flat and structurally firm surface having been constructed (and then mysteriously removed after the lifting was done). Furthermore, not just one obelisk was erected but rather a series of giant stones were precisely put in place side-by-side. Due to the positioning of these stones, there is simply no conceivable place where a huge pulley apparatus could have been stationed."

References: (both of the following websites have excellent photos of the area)

http://www.sacredsites.com/middle_east/lebanon/baalbek.htm

http://www.bibliotecapleyades.net/esp_baalbek_1.htm

[181] "...The Domain took over the planet Venus..."

"The second-closest planet to the Sun, orbiting it every 224.7 Earth days. It is the brightest natural object in the night sky, except for the Moon, reaching an apparent magnitude of −4.6. Because Venus is an inferior planet, from Earth it never appears to venture far from the Sun: its elongation reaches a maximum of 47.8°. Venus reaches its maximum brightness shortly before sunrise or shortly after sunset, for which reason it is often called the Morning Star or the Evening Star.

Classified as a terrestrial planet, it is sometimes called Earth's "sister planet", for the two are similar in size, gravity, and bulk composition. Venus is covered with an opaque layer of highly reflective clouds of sulfuric acid, preventing its surface from being seen from space in visible light; this was a subject of great speculation until some of its secrets were revealed by planetary science in the twentieth century. **Venus has the densest atmosphere of all the terrestrial planets, consisting mostly of carbon dioxide,** as it has no carbon cycle to lock carbon back into rocks and surface features, nor organic life to absorb it in biomass. It has become so hot that the earth-like oceans the young Venus is believed to have possessed have totally evaporated, leaving a dusty dry desert scape with many slab-like rocks. The evaporated water vapor has dissociated and hydrogen has escaped into interplanetary space. **The atmospheric pressure at the planet's surface is 92 times that of the Earth,** the great majority of it carbon dioxide and other greenhouse gases.

Venus's surface has been mapped in detail only in the last 20 years; Project Magellan listed about a thousand meteor craters, a surprisingly low number compared to Earth. It shows evidence of being geologically very young with extensive volcanism, and the sulfur in the atmosphere is taken by some experts to show many of its volcanoes are still active today, but **it is an enigma as to why no evidence of lava flow accompanies any of the visible caldera.**"

As one of the brightest objects in the sky, **Venus** has been known since prehistoric times and as such has gained an entrenched position in human culture. The Babylonians named the planet Ishtar, **the personification of womanhood, and goddess of love.**

In western astrology, derived from its historical connotation with goddesses of femininity and love, Venus is held to influence those aspects of human life. In Indian Vedic astrology, Venus is known as Shukra, meaning "clear, pure" or "brightness, clearness" in Sanskrit.

-- Reference: Wikipedia.org

[152] "**... There are a few life forms on Earth that can endure an atmospheric environment like Venus...**"

"There are many different classes of **extremophiles**, each corresponding to the way its environmental niche. Many extremophiles fall under multiple categories. For example:

- Acidophile: An organism with an optimum pH level at or below pH 3.
- Alkaliphile: An organism with optimal growth at pH levels of 9 or above.
- Endolith: An organism that lives in microscopic spaces within rocks, such as pores between aggregate grains. These may also be called cryptoendoliths. This term also includes organisms populating fissures, aquifers, and faults filled with groundwater in the deep subsurface.
- Halophile: An organism requiring at least 2M of salt, NaCl, for growth.

- *Hyperthermophile: An organism that can thrive at temperatures between 80-121 °C, such as those found in hydrothermal systems.*
- *Hypolith: An organism that lives inside rocks in cold deserts.*
- *Lithoautotroph: An organism (usually bacteria) whose sole source of carbon is carbon dioxide and exergonic inorganic oxidation (chemolithotrophs) such as Nitrosomonas europaea. These organisms are capable of deriving energy from reduced mineral compounds like pyrites, and are active in geochemical cycling and the weathering of parent bedrock to form soil.*
- *Metalotolerant: capable of tolerating high levels of dissolved heavy metals in solution, such as copper, cadmium, arsenic, and zinc. Examples include Ferroplasma sp. and Ralstonia metallidurans.*
- *Oligotroph: An organism capable of growth in nutritionally limited environments.*
- *Osmophile: An organism capable of growth in environments with a high sugar concentration.*
- *Piezophile: An organism that lives optimally at high hydrostatic pressure. Common in the deep terrestrial subsurface, as well as in oceanic trenches.*
- *Polyextremophile: An organism that qualifies as an extremophiles under more than one category.*
- *Psychrophile/Cryophile: An organism that grows better at temperatures of 15 °C or lower. Common in cold soils, permafrost, polar ice, cold ocean water, and in/under alpine snowpack.*
- *Radioresistant: resistant to high levels of ionizing radiation, most commonly ultraviolet radiation but also includes organisms capable of resisting nuclear radiation.*
- *Thermophile: An organism that can thrive at temperatures between 60-80 °C.*
- *Xerophile: An organism that can grow in extremely dry, desiccating conditions. This type is exemplified by the soil microbes of the Atacama Desert.*

*Relative to the majority of the deep sea **extremophiles**, the areas around submarine hydrothermal vents are biologically more productive, often hosting complex communities fueled by the chemicals dissolved in the vent fluids, supporting diverse organisms, including giant tube worms, clams, and shrimp.*

*The water emerges from a hydrothermal vent at temperatures ranging up to 400°C, compared to a typical 2°C for the surrounding deep ocean water. The high pressure at these depths significantly expands the thermal range at which water remains liquid, and so the water doesn't boil. Water at a depth of 3,000 m and a temperature of 407°C becomes supercritical*

*One community has been discovered dubbed 'Eel City', which consists predominantly of eels. Though eels are not uncommon, as mentioned earlier invertebrates typically dominate hydrothermal vents. Eel City is located near Nafanua volcanic cone, American Samoa.*

*Other examples of the unique fauna who inhabit this ecosystem are a snail armored with scales made up of iron and organic materials, and the Pompeii worm (Alvinella Pompejana), which is **capable of withstanding temperatures up to 80°C (176°F). Over 300 new species have been discovered at hydrothermal vents.***

*Active hydrothermal vents are believed to exist on Jupiter's moon Europa, and ancient hydrothermal vents have been speculated to exist on Mars."*

-- Reference: Wikipedia.org

[153] "... asteroid belt..."

"The **asteroid belt** is the region of the Solar System located roughly between the orbits of the planets Mars and Jupiter. It is occupied by numerous irregularly shaped bodies called asteroids or minor plarnets. The asteroid belt region is also termed the **main belt** to distinguish it from other concentrations of minor planets within the Solar System, such as the Kuiper belt and scattered disk.

More than half the mass within the main belt is contained in the **four largest objects**: Ceres, 4 Vesta, 2 Pallas, and 10 Hygiea. All of these have mean diameters of more than 400 km, while Ceres, the main belt's only dwarf planet, is about 950 km in diameter. The remaining bodies range down to the size of a dust particle. **The asteroid material is so thinly distributed that multiple unmanned spacecraft have traversed it without incident.**"

-- Reference: Wikipedia.org

[154] "... Tiahuanaco..."

"Tiwanaku **monumental architecture** is characterized by large stones of exceptional workmanship. In contrast to the masonry style of the later Inca, **Tiwanaku stone architecture usually employs rectangular ashlar blocks laid in regular courses, and monumental structures were frequently fitted with elaborate drainage systems. Bronze or copper "double-T" clamps were often used to anchor large blocks in place. The stone used to build Tiwanaku was quarried and then transported 40 km or more to the city.** They were moved without the aid of the wheel, though much of the distance was over water.

The community grew to urban proportions (in antiquity) becoming an important regional power in the southern Andes. Satellite imaging was used recently to map the extent of fossilized suka kollus across the three primary valleys of Tiwanaku, arriving at population-carrying capacity estimates of anywhere between 285,000 and 1,482,000 people.

They worshipped many gods, and one of **the most important gods was Viracocha, the god of action, shaper of many worlds, and destroyer of many worlds. He created people, with two servants, on a great piece of rock.** Then he drew sections on the rock and sent his servants to name the tribes in those areas. In Tiwanaku he created the people out of rock and brought life to them through the earth. The Tiwanaku believed that **Viracocha created giants to move the massive stones that comprise much of their archeology,** but then grew unhappy with the giants and created a flood to destroy them."

-- Reference: Wikipedia.org

[155] "...Ollantaytambo..."

"Ollantaytambo is a town in southern Peru, located in the district of Ollantaytambo, province of Urubamba, Cusco region. It is approximately 60 km to the northwest of the city of Cusco, situated at an altitude of 2792 meters above sea level.

The city of Ollantaytambo is best known for its ruins, and for the spot where the Inca emperor Manco Inca was able to defeat the Spanish in a set-piece battle. **The finely cut rocks and plantation terraces were very large obstacles** for the Conquistadors to surpass, and the fortress was also used by Manco to conduct successful attacks on Francisco Pizarro and other Conquistadors who were based in Lima."

-- Reference: Wikipedia.org

[156] "... **Machupiccu** ..."

**Machu Picchu** (Quechua: Machu Picchu, "Old Peak") is a pre-Columbian Inca site located 2,400 meters (7,875 ft) above sea level. It is situated on a mountain ridge above the Urubamba Valley in Peru, which is 80 km (50 mi) northwest of Cuzco. Often referred to as "The Lost City of the Incas", Machu Picchu is probably the most familiar symbol of the Inca Empire.

One theory maintains that Machu Picchu was an Inca "llacta": a settlement built to control the economy of the conquered regions. It may also have been built as a prison for the selective few who had commited such henous crimes against the Inca society. Research conducted by scholars, such as John Rowe and Richard Burger, has convinced most archaeologists that rather than a defensive retreat, Machu Picchu was an estate of the Inca emperor, Pachacuti. In addition, Johan Reinhard presented evidence that the site was selected based on its position relative to sacred landscape features. One such example is its mountains, which are purported to be in alignment with key astronomical events.

Shamanic legends say that if you're a sensitive person and you rub your forehead against the world-famous **Intihuatana Stone** you will see the spirit world. The Intihuatana stone is one of the many ritual stones in South America. They are arranged so they point directly at the sun during the winter solstice. The Spanish did not find Machu Picchu until the 20th century so the Intihuatana Stone was not destroyed like many other ritual stones. It is also called "The Hitching Point of the Sun" because it was supposed to hold the sun in it's place. It is (as they said before) believed to be an astronomic clock built by the Incas."

-- Reference: Wikipedia.org

[157] "... **Pachacamac** ..."

"The temple of **Pachacamac** is an archaeological site 40 km southeast of Lima, Peru in the Valley of the Lurín River. It had at least one **pyramid**. They used Pachacamac as primarily a religious site for the veneration of the Pacha Kamaq creator god. The Ichma joined the Inca empire and Pachacamac became an important administrative center.

However the Inca maintained it as a religious shrine and allowed the Pachacamac priests to continue functioning independently of the Inca priesthood. This included the **oracle**, whom the Inca presumably consulted. The Inca built five additional buildings, including a **temple to the Sun** on the main square."

-- Reference: Wikipedia.org

[158] "... **an electronic, light-wave emitting stone cutter and carving tools**..."

"There are various laser cutting tools depending on the type of finished product that you prefer. Laser cutter routers that are computer-driven can cut each letter precisely, capturing every detail of the selected style. The said manufacturing systems are useful in cutting out symbols and logos in a cost effective manner.

Laser that is in a solid state uses one crystal rod with flat and parallel ends. Both ends have surfaces that have the ability to reflect. A light source that has high density and a flash tube surrounds the crystal.

When power is given by the network of pulse-forming, an intense light pulse called photon is released in one of the rod crystals. The light released is one wavelength and allows for minimum divergence.

A hundred percent of laser light is reflected on the rear mirror while thirty to fifty percent will pass through the mirror then to the shutter assembly to the angled mirror before going down through the lens and then to the work piece.

The laser light beam is not only coherent but also has high energy content. When it is focused on the surface, the laser light creates heat used for welding, drilling, and cutting.

The laser beam and the work piece is manipulated through the use of robotics. It can be adjusted to different sizes and heat intensity. The smaller laser is used for drilling, cutting, and welding while the larger machines are used in off giving heat."

-- Reference: http://ezinearticles.com/?Laser-Cutting-Tools&id=352889

[159] **"The "great" pyramid..."**

"A total of over 2,300,000 blocks of limestone and granite were used in its construction with the average block weighing 2.5 tons and none weighing less than 2 tons. The large blocks used in the ceiling of the King's Chamber weigh as much as 9 tons.

- Construction date (Estimated): 2589 B.C..
- Construction time (Estimated): 20 years.
- Total weight (Estimated): 6.5 million tons.
- The estimated total weight of the structure is 6.5 million tons!
- The base of the pyramid covers 13 acres, 568,500 square feet and the length of each side was originally 754 feet, but is now 745 feet.
- The original height was 481 feet tall, but is now only 449 feet.

The distance when Earth is closest to Sun (perihelion) is $147 \times 10^6$ km, which is translated into royal cubits $280 \times 10^9$, hinting at the height of the Great pyramid, 280 royal cubits.

The earth/moon relationship is the only one in our solar system that contains this unique golden section ratio that "squares the circle". Along with this is the phenomenon that the moon and the sun appear to be the same size, most clearly noticed during an eclipse. This too is true only from earth's vantage point...No other planet/moon relationship in our solar system can make this claim.

Although the problem of squaring the circle was proven mathematically impossible in the 19th century (as pi, being irrational, cannot be exactly measured), the Earth, the moon, and the Great Pyramid, are all coming about as close as you can get to the solution! If the base of the Great Pyramid is equated with the diameter of the earth, then the radius of the moon can be generated by subtracting the radius of the earth from the height of the pyramid.

The height of the Great Pyramid times 2π exactly equals the perimeter of the pyramid. This proportions result from elegant design of the pyramid with the height equal two diameters of a circle and the base equal to the circumference of the circle.

The **Pyramid of the Sun and the Great Pyramid of Egypt** are almost or very nearly equal to one another in base perimeter. The Pyramid of the Sun is "almost" half the height of the Great Pyramid. There is a slight difference. The Great Pyramid is 1.03 - times larger than the base of the Pyramid of the Sun. Conversely, the base of the Pyramid of the Sun is 97% of the Great Pyramid's base."

-- Reference: http://www.world-mysteries.com/mpl_2.htm

[160] "... **Pyramid texts.**"

"The Pyramid Texts are a collection of ancient Egyptian religious texts from the time of the Old Kingdom, mostly inscriptions on the walls of tombs in pyramids. They depict the Egyptian view of the afterlife, and the ascent into the sky of the divine Pharaoh after death. They were written upwards of five thousand years ago; thus, they are some of the oldest known writings in the world.

The Pyramid Texts are also the oldest collection of religious spells known to us from ancient Egypt. This collection forms the basis of much of the later religious theology and literature of ancient Egypt. The passages were eventually separated and categorized, as well as illustrated and eventually evolved into the Book of the Dead, or more properly, The Book of the Coming forth by Day.

It is difficult to date the Pyramid Texts. Their origins have aroused much speculation regarding their origin because they emerge, as a fully-fledged collection of mortuary texts, without any precedent in the archaeological record. The fact that the texts are made up of distinct utterances which do not have a strict narrative sequence linking them together has led scholars to believe that many of them were not composed specifically for the purpose of being inscribed in the pyramids but may have had earlier uses. In fact, spells such as Utterances 273-4, called the Cannibal Hymn, and which only appears in the Pyramids of Unas and Teti, refer to aspects of the funerary cult that seem to no longer been in practice at the time the pyramids were built.

Early analysts attempted to date the text as early as possible; even from the predynastic period. A very early dating of these texts remains a strong possibility, though today, scholars place the text's origins with the date of the monuments where they reside. In reality, we have very little idea of the date of their initial invention, perhaps other than the antiquated language employed."

-- Reference: http://www.crystalinks.com/pyramidtext.html

"The great pyramid was located precisely at the exact center of all of the land masses of Earth..."

*"The Great Pyramid (the Pyramid of Khufu, or Cheops in Greek) at Gizeh, Egypt, demonstrates the remarkable character of its placement on the face of the Earth. The Pyramid lies in the center of gravity of the continents. It also lies in the exact center of all the land area of the world, dividing the earth's land mass into approximately equal quarters.*

*The north-south axis (31 degrees east of Greenwich) is the longest land meridian, and the east-west axis (30 degrees north) is the longest land parallel on the globe. There is obviously only one place that these longest land-lines of the terrestrial earth can cross, and it is at the Great Pyramid!"*

-- Reference: http://www.world-mysteries.com/mpl_2.htm

[162] "...stars in the constellation of Orion's Belt (Ainitak), Sirius, Alpha Draconis and Beta Ursa Minor..."

*"The Hall of Truth in Light" (in the Great Pyramid) are an extension of the upward passage way (which) opens as a Grand Gallery. Other interior features include: a Great Step; a lower Queen's chamber; an upper King's chamber with an open tomb which was never used for burial; and, two passage ways which actually pinpoint Sirius and Ainitak in the "belt" of the Orion Constellation -- the other two precisely point to Thuban in the Draco Constellation which was the old North Star at the time of the Pyramid's supposed construction and the present North Star.*

-- Reference: http://www.geocities.com/regkeith/rkeith5a.htm

**Big Dipper Constellation** stars include:

Dubhe
Merak
Phecda
Megrez
Alioth
Mizar
Alkaid

**Alnitak** *is a double star system. Alnitak A is a blue O9.7Ib supergiant star about 15 times the diameter of the sun, at least 11,000 times more luminous than the sun.*

**Thuban** *is another name for the star is Adib from the Arabic Al Dhi'bah, "The Hyenas". A number of stars in the constellation of Draco. According to Allen, seamen were accustomed to call Thuban "The Dragon's Tail." Thuban is a white A0III giant having a luminosity about 260 times that of the sun. Spectral analysis indicates that Thuban has a companion star orbiting with a 51.4 day period.*

**Sirius** *is also known colloquially as the "Dog Star", reflecting its prominence in its constellation, Canis Major. It is the subject of more mythological and folkloric tales than any other star apart from the sun. The heliacal rising of Sirius marked the flooding of the Nile in Ancient Egypt and the 'Dog Days' of summer*

Sirius is the brightest star in the night sky with a visual apparent magnitude of −1.47, almost twice as bright as Canopus, the next brightest star. What appears as a single star to the naked eye is actually a binary star system, consisting of Sirius A, and a faint white dwarf companion of spectral type DA2, termed Sirius B.

Sirius is bright due to both its intrinsic luminosity and its closeness to the Sun. At a distance of 2.6 parsecs (8.6 light-years), the Sirius system is one of our near neighbors. Sirius A is about twice as massive as the Sun and has an absolute visual magnitude of 1.42. It is 25 times more luminous than the Sun.

Sirius is recorded in the earliest astronomical records, known in Ancient Egypt as Sopdet (Greek: Sothis). During the era of the Middle Kingdom, Egyptians based their calendar on the heliacal rising of Sirius, namely the day it becomes visible just before sunrise after moving far enough away from the glare of the sun. This occurred just before the annual flooding of the Nile and the summer solstice, after a 70 day absence from the skies. The hieroglyph for Sothis features a star and a triangle. Sothis was identified with the great goddess Isis who formed a part of a trinity with her husband Osiris and their son Horus, while the 70 day period symbolized the passing of Isis and Osiris though the duat (Egyptian underworld).

**North Star**, also known as the Pole Star, is the star that lies closest in the sky to the north celestial pole, and which appears directly overhead to an observer at the Earth's North Pole. The current North Star is Polaris, which lies about two-thirds of a degree from the pole at the end of the "handle" of the Little Dipper asterism in the constellation Ursa Minor. Polaris has a visual magnitude of 1.97 (second magnitude). (Some people mistakenly think that Polaris is the brightest star in the night sky. This title belongs to Sirius, and there are many others stars also brighter than Polaris.)

Due to the precession of the equinoxes the direction of the Earth's axis is very slowly but continuously changing, and as the projection of the Earth's axis moves around the celestial sphere over the millennia, the role of North Star passes from one star to another. Since the precession of the equinoxes is so slow, a single star typically holds that title for many centuries.

**In 3000 BC the faint star Thuban in the constellation Draco was the North Star.** At magnitude 3.67 (fourth magnitude) it is only one-fifth as bright as Polaris, the current North Star (situated 430 light-years away).

-- Reference: Wikipedia.org

[163] "...Pan, God of The Woods..."

-- Reference: For more detailed information about the IS-BE know as Pan, please read the book **"Pan, God of The Woods"** by Lawrence R. Spencer ( www.godofthewoods.com )

[164] " **The human pharaoh moved the Capital city of Egypt from Memphis to Heracleopolis".**

"Heracleopolis was the main city of Egypt during a turbulent time in our history, the First Intermediate Period. Details are not clear, but apparently when the VIth dynasty ended, the rulers who followed were too weak to rule the whole land. Akhtoy, the local nomarch, declared independence from Memphis, and when the last Memphite pharaoh died childless, he declared himself god-king of the Two Lands and founder of the IXth dynasty. All of Middle Egypt and part of the eastern Nile Delta submitted to Akhtoy's authority. Akhmin, in the 9th nome, became the southern boundary between those who supported Akhtoy and those who opposed him.

In Upper Egypt there were at least three governors who refused to acknowledge the new order: those of Thinis, Wast (Thebes) and Nekhen (Hierakonopolis). For a long time they fought among themselves, because chaos always reigns where there is no central authority. Finally one of them, Inyotef II of Wast, prevailed against the others; the nomarchs of Asyut now became the defenders of the dignity of the Heracleopolitan kings. The IXth dynasty was succeeded by the Xth at home, and for more than sixty years the line was held at Akhmin, despite frequent raids from both sides. Finally the grandson of Inyotef, Mentuhotep II, captured Asyut; once that happened he quickly marched downstream and overthrew the Xth dynasty. That marked the reunification of Egypt and the beginning of the Middle Kingdom. Heracleopolis was never as important afterwards, though it marked the site of a key fortress in the XXIInd dynasty, built by the second son of Osorkon II."

-- Reference: http://members.tripod.com/~Raseneb/Akhtoy.htm

[165] "... when Atlantis fell..."

"Plato's reference to Egypt as the source of the Atlantis myth, via Solon. The Egyptians called Atlantis Kepchu, which also happens to be their name for the people of Crete. It is speculated that survivors of the Minoan volcanic disaster asked Egypt for help, since they were the only other civilization with high culture at the time.

Plato described quarries on the island of Atlantis where "rocks of white, black, and red" were extracted from the hills and used to construct a great island city. The description matches the rocks found on Santorini.

The island-city of Atlantis was described as being laid out in a series of concentric circles of land and water, each one connected to the sea by a deep canal. Docks for a huge number of ships, and a causeway for unloading cargo of said ships, also was described. Unearthed frescos from the island have depicted Santorini with a configuration that can be interpreted in this way. It also shows a huge city on the island, theorized by archaeologists to represent the center of the caldera.

At Akrotiri there are multi-story buildings. This city may have had the earliest form of town planning (structured assembly of interconnecting roads and paths) ever discovered, again, with fresh running water and toilets in each house leading to a sewer system. Many such sites now have been unearthed, both on Crete and Santorini."

-- Reference: Wikipedia.org (See "Santorini")

[166] "... the Egyptians., who called "Atlantis" Kepchu, which also happens to be their name for the people of Crete."

"Minoan civilization disappeared suddenly, at the height of its wealth and power. This also was similar to Plato's description of the fate of the "Atlanteans". Scientists theorize that multiple tsunamis hit the island of Crete, circa 1500 BC, which came from the direction of the island of Santorini (then called Thera) about 100 miles from Crete.

265

Santorini is the site of a massive caldera with an island at its center. Vulcanologists have determined this ill-fated island was engulfed by the terrible ca. 1500 BC eruption and collapse of the Stroggili volcano there, which affected the entire eastern Mediterranean, as far away as the Near East—possibly the most powerful eruption in recorded history, ejecting approximately 30 km³ (7 cu miles) of magma, up to 36 km (23 miles) high. Volcanic events of this magnitude are known to generate tsunamis."

-- Reference: Wikipedia.org

[167] "... the exact geodetic center of Egypt..."

"Five years into the co-regency, Amenhotep IV changed his name to **Akhenaten** and left Thebes to establish a new Egyptian capital city, which he called Akhetaten (meaning the resting place or horizon of the Aten). The change in name indicated that he no longer considered himself to be the son of the god Amun, but of Aten. On the monuments marking the four corners of the new city, Akhenaten referred to the hateful words spoken about him and his forefathers by the priests of Amun. Obviously, he had hoped that the city of Akhetaten would be his resting place as well.

At the city of Akhetaten, the ancient religion of the Aten received a make-over. Aten temple design, ritual, and symbolism (by a falcon-headed man and a sun disc referred to as Re-Herakhty) derived originally from the traditional solar god Ra whose center of worship had been from very ancient times at Memphis and On (Heliopolis). By the end of the coregency, the falcon-man had been removed from the Aten's symbol. The Aten had in essence become a god without human or animal image. The disc of the sun was now considered to be the single physical representation of the invisible and eternal god, Ra, and a deity in its own right. (The sun disc was used later as a royal "lamelech" seal by the Kings of Judah). The cartouche of Akhenaten's god and heavenly father, the Aten, bore the name Imram. In the Bible, Moses is referred to as the son of Amram, the Hebrew equivalent.

The name of the Egyptian deity Aten transliterates into the Hebrew word Adon. Adon, which is translated by English Bibles as "the Lord" (and Adonai, translated as "my Lord") is used along with Jehovah (Yhwh) in the Bible as the exclusive personal names of God. Moreover, in ancient times, the name Jehovah (Yhwh) was written, but never spoken. Whenever the written name Jehovah (Yhwh) was to be read out loud, Adon (Aten) was voiced instead. The written form of Adon is infrequent, however, its limited usage is significant, especially in the first six books of the Bible (See under "LORD" in Strong's Exhaustive Concordance), where it is reserved for the following applications alone: Moses addresses God using the title Adon/Aten (Exodus 4:10,13; 5:22; 34:9; Numbers 14:17; Deuteronomy 3:23; 7:26; 10:17); Moses, himself, is addressed both by Aaron (Ex.32:22; Num.12:11) and by Joshua (Numbers 11:28) using the title Adon/Aten; and Joshua also addresses God using the title Adon/Aten (Joshua 5:14 b; 7:7). As mentioned above, there is an established relationship between the literature of the Egyptian 18th Dynasty and the Bible. Psalm 104 is an embellishment of the Hymn to the Aten which was found by archaeologists at the city of Akhetaten.

The religious reforms of Akhenaten included the rejection of traditional Egyptian magic and astrology associated with the cult of Amun, and the rejection of the cult of Osiris with its version of belief in eternal judgment and the afterlife as well. **The site chosen for the new capital of Egypt further demonstrated Akhenaten's desire for a new balance as it was located at the exact geodetic center of the country.**"

-- Reference: http://www.domainofman.com/ankhemmaat/moses.html

[168] "... the destruction of Troy as the finale of the Trojan War."

"In Greek mythology, the **Trojan War** was waged against the city of Troy by the Achaeans after Paris of Troy stole Helen from her husband Menelaus, the king of Sparta. The war is among the most important events in Greek mythology, and was narrated in many works of Greek literature, including the Iliad and the Odyssey by Homer. The Iliad relates a part of the last year of the siege of Troy, while the Odyssey describes the journey home of Odysseus, one of the Achaean leaders. Other parts of the war were told in a cycle of epic poems, which has only survived in fragments. Episodes from the war provided material for Greek tragedy and other works of Greek literature, and for Roman poets like Virgil and Ovid.

The war originated from a quarrel between the goddesses Athena, Hera and Aphrodite, after Eris, the goddess of strife and discord, gave them a golden apple, sometimes known as the Apple of Discord, marked "for the fairest". The goddesses went to Paris, who judged that Aphrodite, as the "fairest", should receive the apple. In exchange, Aphrodite made Helen, the most beautiful of all women, fall in love with Paris, who took her to Troy. Agamemnon, king of Mycenae and the brother of Helen's husband Menelaus, led an expedition of Achaean troops to Troy and besieged the city for ten years. After the deaths of many heroes, including the Achaeans Achilles and Ajax, and the Trojans Hector and Paris, the city fell to the ruse of the Trojan Horse. The Achaeans slaughtered the Trojans and desecrated the temples, thus earning the gods' wrath. Few of the Achaeans returned safely to their homes and many founded colonies in distant shores. The Romans later traced their origin to Aeneas, one of the Trojans, who was said to have led the surviving Trojans to Italy.

The Ancient Greeks thought the Trojan War was a historical event that had taken place in the 13th or 12th century BC, and believed that Troy was located in modern day Turkey near the Dardanelles. By modern times both the war and the city were widely believed to be non-historical. In 1870, however, the German archaeologist Heinrich Schliemann excavated a site in this area which he identified as Troy; this claim is now accepted by most scholars

The Trojan War derive from a specific historical conflict usually date it to the 12th or 11th centuries BC, often preferring the dates given by Eratosthenes, 1194–1184 BC, which roughly corresponds with archaeological evidence of a catastrophic burning of Troy."

-- Reference: Wikipedia.org

[169] "Homer, the blind Greek poet..."

"**Homer** (ancient Greek: Ὅμηρος, Homēros) was an ancient Greek (Ionian) epic poet, traditionally considered the author of the epic poems the Iliad and the Odyssey. No reliable biographical information about Homer survives from classical antiquity. The cardinal qualities of the style of Homer have been well articulated by Matthew Arnold: "the translator of Homer," he says, "should above all be penetrated by a sense of the four qualities of his author: that he is eminently rapid; that he is eminently plain and direct, both in the evolution of his thought and in the expression of it, that is, both in his syntax and in his words; that he is eminently plain and direct in the substance of his thought, that is, in his matter and ideas; and finally, that he is eminently noble".

The language used by Homer is an archaic version of Ionic Greek, with admixtures from certain other dialects, such as Aeolic Greek. It later served as the basis of Epic Greek, the language of epic poetry, typically in dactylic hexameter.

A number of traditions hold that he was blind (perhaps because, in the Aeolian dialect of Cyme, homēros bore this meaning) and that he was born on the island of Chios, at Smyrna or elsewhere in Ionia, where various cities vied in claiming him as one of their native sons. The characterization of Homer as a blind bard is supported by a possibly self-referential passage in the Odyssey in which a shipwrecked Odysseus listens to the tales of a blind bard named Demodocus while in the court of the Phaeacian king."

-- Reference: Wikipedia.org

[170] **"Solon, a wise man from Greece reported the existence of Atlantis.."**

"**Solon** was a famous Athenian statesman, lawmaker, and Lyric poet. The travel writer, Pausanias, listed Solon among the Seven Sages of the ancient world. Solon has acquired a place in history and in folklore through his efforts to legislate against political, economic and moral decline in archaic Athens. Some of his reforms failed in the short term, yet he is often credited with having laid the foundations for Athenian democracy.

After he had finished reforming the country, Solon traveled abroad. His first stop was Egypt. There he visited Heliopolis, where he discussed philosophy with an Egyptian expert on the subject, Psenophis. Subsequently, **at Sais, he visited Neith's temple and received from the priests there an account of the history of Atlantis. Solon wrote out this history as a poem, to which Plato subsequently made references in his dialogues Timaios and Critias.** Next Solon sailed to Cyprus, where he oversaw the construction of a new capital for a local king, in gratitude for which the king named it Soloi."

-- Reference: Wikipedia.org

[171] **" Zoroaster..."**

"**Zoroaster**, the prophet and poet sees the universe as the cosmic struggle between aša "truth" and druj "lie." The cardinal concept of aša - which is highly nuanced and only vaguely translatable - is at the foundation of all other Zoroastrian doctrine, including that of Ahura Mazda (who is aša), creation (that is aša), existence (that is aša) and Free Will, which is arguably Zoroaster's greatest contribution to religious philosophy. The purpose of humankind, like that of all other creation, is to sustain aša. For humankind, this occurs through active participation in life and the exercise of good thoughts, words and deeds.

The name Zoroaster was famous in classical antiquity, and a number of different Zoroasters - all described as having occult powers - appear in historiographic accounts.

In Pliny's Natural History, Zoroaster is said to have laughed on the day of his birth. He lived in the wilderness and enjoyed exploring it from a young age. Plutarch compares him with Lycurgus and Numa Pompilius (Numa, 4). Plutarch, drawing partly on Theopompus, speaks of Zoroaster in Isis and Osiris: In this work, the prophet is empowered by trust in his God and the protection of his allies. He faces outward opposition and unbelief, and inward doubt.

The works of Zoroaster had a significant influence on Greek philosophy and Roman philosophy. The ancient Greek writer Eudoxus of Cnidus and the Latin writer Pliny the Elder praised Zoroaster's philosophy as "the most famous and most useful." Plato learnt of

Zoroaster's philosophy through Eudoxus and incorporated some of it into his own Platonic realism. In the third century BC, however, Colotes accused Plato's The Republic of plagiarizing parts of (what is attributed to) Zoroaster's On Nature, such as the Myth of Er. Plato's contemporary, Heraclides Ponticus, wrote a text called Zoroaster based on Zoroaster's philosophy in order to express his disagreement with Plato on natural philosophy.

Zoroaster was mentioned by the nineteenth-century poet William Butler Yeats. His wife and he were said to have claimed to have contacted Zoroaster through "automatic writing."

The 2005 edition of the Oxford Dictionary of Philosophy places Zoroaster first in a chronology of philosophers."

-- Reference: Wikipedia.org

[172] "... an IS-BE called Ahura Mazda."

"**Ahura Mazda** (Ahura Mazdā) is the Avestan language name for a divinity exalted by Zoroaster as the one uncreated Creator, hence God. He is the nameless "Father Asura", that is, Varuna of the **Rigveda**. In this view, Zoroastrian mazda is the equivalent of the **Vedic** medhira, described in **Rigveda** 8.6.10 as the "(revealed) insight into the cosmic order".

Ahura Mazda is seen as the Ahura par excellence, superior to both \*vouruna and \*mitra, and the nameless "Father Asura" **of the Rigveda** and is a distinct divinity. The Zoroastrian faith is thus described by its adherents as Mazdayasna, the worship of Mazda. In the Avesta, "Ahura Mazda is the highest object of worship".

-- Reference: Wikipedia.org

[173] "Laozi, a philosopher who wrote a small book called "The Way"..."

"According to tradition, it was written around 6th century BC by the Taoist sage Laozi (or Lao Tzu, "Old Master"), a record-keeper at the Zhou Dynasty court, by whose name the text is known in China. **Tao Te Ching** is a Chinese classic text. Its name comes from the opening words of its two sections: 道 dào "**way**," and 德 dé "**virtue**".

This ancient book is also central in Chinese religion, not only for Taoism (Dàojiāo 道教) but Chinese Buddhism, which when first introduced into China was largely interpreted through the use of Taoist words and concepts. Many Chinese artists, including poets, painters, calligraphers, and even gardeners have used the Tao Te Ching as a source of inspiration. Its influence has also spread widely outside East Asia, aided by hundreds of translations into Western languages."

Tao is nameless. (Tao) goes beyond distinctions, and transcends language. **Laozi** describes a state of existence before time or space:

> "The Way that can be told of is not an unvarying way;
> The names that can be named are not unvarying names.
> It was from the Nameless that heaven and Earth sprang;
> The named is but the mother that rears the ten thousand creatures.
> Each after its kind."

269

*"The Spirit never dies.*
*It is the Mysterious Female.*
*The doorway of the Mysterious Female*
*Is the base from which Heaven and Earth sprang.*
*It is there within us, all the while;*
*Draw upon it as you will.*
*It never runs dry.*

*We put spokes together and call it a wheel;*
*But it is on the space where there is nothing that the value of the wheel depends.*
*We turn clay to make a vessel;*
*But it is on the space where there is nothing that the value of the vessel depends.*
*We pierce doors and windows to make a house;*
*And it is on these spaces where there is nothing that the value of the house depends.*
*Therefore just as we take advantage of what is,*
*we should recognize the value of what is not.*

*Knowing others is wisdom;*
*Knowing the self is enlightenment.*
*Mastering others requires force;*
*Mastering the self requires strength;*
*He who knows he has enough is rich.*
*Perseverance is a sign of will power.*
*He who stays where he is, endures.*
*To die but not to perish is to be eternally present."*

*Many believe the Tao Te Ching contains universal truths that have been independently recognized in other philosophies, both religious and secular."*

-- Reference: Wikipedia.org

[174] **"...Genesis..."**

*"Genesis (Greek: "birth", "origin") is the first book of the Bible of Judaism and of Christianity, and the first of five books of the Pentateuch or Torah.*

*"1 Now it came about, when men began to multiply on the face of the land, and daughters were born to them,*

*2 that the "sons of God" saw that the daughters of men were beautiful; and they took wives for themselves, whomever they chose.*

*3 Then Yaweh said, "My Spirit shall not strive with man forever, because he also is flesh; nevertheless his days shall be one hundred and twenty years."*

*4 The Nephilim were on the earth in those days, and also afterward, when the "sons of God" came in to the daughters of men, and they bore children to them. Those were the mighty men who were of old, men of renown.*

*5 Then Yaweh saw that the wickedness of man was great on the earth, and that every intent of the thoughts of his heart was only evil continually."*

-- Reference: http://bible.cc/genesis/6-4.htm

[175] **"... Omphalos stones..."**

*"An **omphalos** is an ancient religious stone artifact, or baetylusr. In Greek, the word omphalos means "navel" (compare the name of Queen Omphale). According to the ancient Greeks, Zeus sent out two eagles to fly across the world to meet at its center, the "navel" of the world. Omphalos stones used to denote this point were erected in several areas surrounding the Mediterranean Sea; the most famous of those was at the oracle in Delphi.*

*Most accounts locate the Omphalos in the temple adyton near the Pythia. The stone itself (which may have been a copy) has a carving of a knotted net covering its surface, and has a hollow centre, which widens towards its base*

*The Omphalos at Delphi came to be identified as the stone which Rhea wrapped in swaddling clothes, pretending it was Zeus. This was to deceive Cronus, his father, who swallowed his children so they could not grow up and depose him as he had deposed his own father, Uranus. **Omphalos stones were said to allow direct communication with "the gods".***

-- Reference: Wikipedia.org

[176] **"...Python, the serpent..."**

*"In Greek mythology **Python**, serpent, was the earth-dragon of Delphi, always represented in sculpture and vase-paintings as a serpent. She resided at the Delphic oracle, which existed in the cult center for her mother, Gaia, Earth, Pytho being the place name. The site was considered the center of the earth, represented by a stone, the omphalos or navel, which Python guarded. Pytho became the enemy of the later Olympian deity Apollo, who slew her and remade her former home and the oracle, the most famous in Classical Greece, as his own. Many pictures show the serpent Python guarding the **Omphalos**, the sacred navel-stone and mid-point of the earth, which stood in Apollo's temple".*

-- Reference: Wikipedia.org

[177] **"...Cyrus II of Persia..."**

**Cyrus the Great** *(c. 590 BC or 576 — August 529 BC or 530 BC), also known as **Cyrus II of Persia** and **Cyrus the Elder**, was a **Persian emperor**. He was the founder of the Persian Empire under the Achaemenid dynasty. The empire expanded under his rule, eventually conquering most of Southwest Asia and much of Central Asia, from Egypt and the Hellespont in the west to the Indus River in the east, to **create the largest state the world** had yet seen.*

*During his twenty-nine year reign, Cyrus fought against some of the greatest states of his time, including the Median Empire, the Lydian Empire, and the Neo-Babylonian Empire. Cyrus did not venture into Egypt, as he himself died in battle, fighting the Massagetae along the Syr Darya in August 530 BC. He was succeeded by his son, Cambyses II, who managed to conquer Egypt during his short rule.*

Beyond his nation, Cyrus left a lasting legacy on Jewish religion (through his Edict of Restoration), politics, and military strategy, as well as on both Eastern and Western civilization.

The only known example of his religious policy is his treatment of the Jews in Babylon. The Bible records that a remnant of the Jewish population returned to the Promised Land from Babylon, following an edict from Cyrus to rebuild the temple. This edict is fully reproduced in the Book of Ezra. **As a result of Cyrus' policies, the Jews honored him as a dignified and righteous king. He is the only Gentile to be designated as a messiah, a divinely-appointed king, in the Tanakh (Isaiah 45:1-6).**

Some contemporary Muslim scholars have suggested that the Qur'anic figure of Dhul-Qarnayn is Cyrus the Great. This theory was proposed by Sunni scholar Abul Kalam Azad and endorsed by Shi'a scholars Allameh Tabatabaei, in his Tafsir al-Mizan and Makarem Shirazi and Sunni scholar Abul Ala Maududi.

During his reign, Cyrus maintained control over a vast region of conquered kingdoms, achieved partly through retaining and expanding Median satrapies. **Cyrus' conquests began a new era in the age of empire building, where a vast superstate, comprising many dozens of countries, races, religions, and languages, were ruled under a single administration headed by a central government.**

In 1992, he was ranked #87 on Michael H. Hart's list of the most influential figures in history. On December 10, 2003, in her acceptance of the Nobel Peace Prize, Shirin Ebadi evoked Cyrus, saying:

**"I am an Iranian, a descendant of Cyrus the Great. This emperor proclaimed at the pinnacle of power 2,500 years ago that he 'would not reign over the people if they did not wish it.' He promised not to force any person to change his religion and faith and guaranteed freedom for all. The Charter of Cyrus the Great should be studied in the history of human rights."**

Many of the forefathers of the United States of America sought inspiration from Cyrus the Great through works such as Cyropaedia. Thomas Jefferson, for example, had two personal copies of the book, "which was a mandatory read for statesmen alongside Machiavelli's The Prince."

In a recent segment of **ABC's Nightline with Ted Koppel,** Ted Koppel mentioned Cyrus the Great, when he was talking about the new documentary film being made in his honor, and had this to say of him:

**"Cyrus the Great is genuinely one of history's towering figures. America's own founders such as Thomas Jefferson were influenced by Cyrus the Great in the field of Human Rights."**

-- Reference: Wikipedia.org

[178] **"... unique system of organization used by Cyrus II..."**

*"During his reign, Cyrus maintained control over a vast region of conquered kingdoms, achieved partly through retaining and expanding Median* **satrapies.** *Further* **organization of**

*newly conquered territories into provinces ruled by vassal kings called satraps, was continued by Cyrus' successor Darius the Great. Cyrus' empire demanded only tribute and conscripts from many parts of the realm.*

*Cyrus was distinguished equally as a statesman and as a soldier. By pursuing a policy of generosity instead of repression, and by favoring local religions, he was able to make his newly conquered subjects into enthusiastic supporters. Due in part to the political infrastructure he created, the Achaemenid empire endured long after his demise.*

*The rise of Persia under Cyrus's rule had a profound impact on the course of world history. Persian philosophy, literature and religion all played dominant roles in world events for the next millennia. Despite the Islamic conquest of Persia in the 7th century CE by the Islamic Caliphate (Arab Empire), Persia continued to exercise enormous influence in the Middle East during the Islamic Golden Age."*

-- Reference: Wikipedia.org

[179] "... tree of life...."

*"Trees of life appear in folklore, culture and fiction, often relating to immortality. These often hold cultural and religious significance to the peoples for whom they appear.*

*The Sumerian (or Persian) Tree of Life was represented by a series of nodes and criss-crossing lines. It was an important religious symbol among these peoples, often attended to by Eagle Headed Gods & Priests, or the King himself.*

- *In Chinese mythology a carving of a Tree of Life depicts a phoenix and a dragon - in Chinese mythology the dragon often represents immortality. There is also the Taoist story of a tree that produces a peach every three thousand years. The one who eats the fruit receives immortality.*
- *An archaeological discovery in the 1990s was of a sacrificial pit at Sanxingdui in Sechuan, China. Dating from about 1200 BCE, it contained 3 bronze trees, one of them 4 meters high. At the base was a dragon, and fruit hanging from the lower branches. At the top is a strange bird-like (phoenix) creature with claws. Also from Sechuan, from the late Han dynasty (c 25 - 220 CE) is another tree of life. The ceramic base is guarded by a horned beast with wings. The leaves of the tree are coins and people.*
- *In Egyptian mythology, in the Ennead system of Heliopolis, the first couple, apart from Shu & Tefnut (moisture & dryness) and Geb & Nuit (earth & sky), are Isis & Osiris. They were said to have emerged from the acacia tree of Saosis, which the Egyptians considered the tree of life, referring to it as the "tree in which life and death are enclosed".*
- *The Egyptian's Holy Sycamore also stood on the threshold of life and death, connecting the two worlds.*
- *In Germanic paganism, trees played a prominent role, appearing in various aspects of surviving texts and possibly in the name of gods.*
- *The tree of life appears in Norse religion as Yggdrasil, the world tree, a massive tree with extensive lore surrounding it. Perhaps related to the Yggdrasil, accounts have survived of Germanic Tribes honouring sacred trees within their societies.*
- *In Norse Mythology it is the golden apples from Iðunn's tree that provides immortality for the gods.*

- *The Tree of Life is mentioned in the Books of Genesis, in which it has the potential to grant immortality to Adam and Eve. (However, it is not immediately obvious, nor is it universally accepted, that the Book of Genesis account and the Book of Revelation account speak of the same Tree of Life.)*
- *A Tree of Life, in the form of ten interconnected nodes, is an important part of the Kabbalah. As such, it resembles the ten Sephirot.*
- *The Tree of Life appears in the Book of Mormon in a revelation to Lehi (see 1 Nephi 8:10-12). It is symbolic of the love of God (see 1 Nephi 11:21-23), and sometimes understood as salvation and post-mortal existence.*
- *Etz Chaim, Hebrew for "Tree of Life", is a common term used in Judaism. The expression, found in the Book of Proverbs, is figuratively applied to the Torah itself.*

- *Among pre-Columbian Mesoamerican cultures, the concept of "world trees" is a prevalent motif in Mesoamerican mythical cosmologies and iconography. World trees embodied the four cardinal directions, which represented also the fourfold nature of a central world tree, a symbolic axis mundi connecting the planes of the Underworld and the sky with that of the terrestrial world.*
- *Depictions of world trees, both in their directional and central aspects, are found in the art and mythological traditions of cultures such as the Maya, Aztec, Izapan, Mixtec, Olmec, and others, dating to at least the Mid/Late Formative periods of Mesoamerican chronology.*
- *Directional world trees are also associated with the four Year bearers in Mesoamerican calendars, and the directional colors and deities.*
- *World trees are frequently depicted with birds in their branches, and their roots extending into earth or water (sometimes atop a "water-monster", symbolic of the underworld).*
- *The central world tree has also been interpreted as a representation of the band of the Milky Way. Fragment of a bronze helmet from Urartu, with the "Tree of Life" depicted.*

- *In ancient Armrenia around 13th to 6th century BC, the Tree of Life was a religious symbol, drawn onto the exterior walls of fortresses and carved on the armour of warriors. The branches of the tree were equally divided on the right and left sides of the stem, with each branch having one leaf, and one leaf on the apex of the tree. Servants (some winged) stood on each side of the tree with one of their hands up as if they are taking care of it. This tree can be found on numerous Urartu artifacts, such as paintings on the walls of the Erebuni fortress in Yerevan, Armenia.*

- *The symbolism of the tree is mentioned in the 135th hymn of the 10th book of Rig-Veda, and in the 15th chapter of Bhagavad-gita (1-4).*
- *In the Japanese religion of Shinto, trees were marked with sacred paper symbolizing lightning bolts, as trees were thought to be sacred. This was propagated by the fact that after they passed (died), ancestors and animals were often portrayed as branches on the tree.*
- *The Book of One Thousand and One Nights has a story, 'The Tale of Buluqiya', in which the hero searches for immortality and finds a paradise with jewel-encrusted trees. Nearby is a Fountain of Youth guarded by Al-Khidr. Unable to defeat the guard, Buluqiya has to return empty-handed.*
- *The Epic of Gilgamesh is a similar quest for immortality. In Mesopotamian mythology, Etana searches for a 'plant of birth' to provide him with a son. This has a solid provenance of antiquity, being found in cylinder seals from Akkad (2390 - 2249 BCE).*

274

- One of the earliest forms of ancient Greek religion has its origins associated with tree cults.

*In mystical traditions of world religions, sacred texts are read for metaphorical content concerning the relationship between states of mind and the external experience of reality. As such, the tree is a manifestation/causal symbol - the Tree of Life representing the coveted state of eternal aliveness or fulfillment, not immortality of the body or soul. In such a state, physical death (which cannot be overcome) is nevertheless a choice, and direct experience of the perfect goodness/divine reality/god is not only possible, but ever present.*

*Once the ego (surface consciousness) experiences shame, having been tempted to absorb or believe in duality (such as eating of the Tree of Knowledge of Good and Evil), we are protected from living eternally in that limiting, fallen, experience by the cherubim guarding the gate of return to paradise. The cherubim are symbolic of the perfect knowledge of self or true nature, with the power of purification and return to being."*

-- Reference: Wikipedia.org

[180] "... the carvings show cone-shaped instruments, and electronic detection devices which are stylized as baskets or water buckets, being carried by eagle headed, winged beings...."

**EDITOR'S NOTE:** Excellent photographs of these can be viewed at the following website:

http://www.crystalinks.com/godswaterbuckets.html

[181] "... faravahar..."

*"The faravahar or farohar (transliteration varies) is one of the best-known symbols of Zoroastrianism.*

*The winged disc has a long history in the art and culture of the ancient Near and Middle East. Historically, the symbol is influenced by the "winged sun" hieroglyph appearing on Bronze Age royal seals. While the symbol is currently thought to represent a Fravashi (c. a guardian angel) and from which it derives its name, what it represented in the minds of those who adapted it from earlier Mesopotamian and Egyptian reliefs is unclear. Because the symbol first appears on royal inscriptions, it is also thought to represent the 'Divine Royal Glory' (khvarenah), or the Fravashi of the king, or represented the divine mandate that was the foundation of a king's authority.*

*This relationship between the name of the symbol and the class of divine entities reflects the current belief that the symbol represents a Fravashi. However, there is no physical description of the Fravashis in the Avesta and in Avestan the entities are grammatically feminine.*

*Prior to the reign of Darius I, the symbol did not have a human form above the wings. In present-day Zoroastrianism, the faravahar is said to be a reminder of one's purpose in life, which is to live in such a way that the soul progresses towards frasho-kereti, or union with Ahura Mazda."*

-- Reference: Wikipedia.org

"...Oannes..."

*"Oannes was the name given by the Babylonian writer Berossus in the 3rd century BC to a mythical being who taught mankind wisdom. Berossus describes Oannes as having the body of a fish but underneath the figure of a man. He is described as dwelling in the Persian Gulf, and rising out of the waters in the daytime and furnishing mankind instruction in writing, the arts and the various sciences.*

*Once thought to be based on the ancient Babylonian god Ea, it is now known that Oannes is in fact based on Uan (Adapa) - the first of the seven antediluvian sages or Abgallu (in Sumerian Ab=water, Gal=Great, Lu=man), who were sent by Ea to deliver the arts of civilization to mankind in ancient Sumerian mythology, at Eridu, the oldest city of Sumer."*

-- Reference: Wikipedia.org

[183] **"Some members of the lost Battalion have been found in the oceans inhabiting the bodies of dolphins or whales."**

Dolphins have long played a role in human culture. **Dolphins are common in Greek mythology** and there are many coins from the time which feature a man or boy riding on the back of a dolphin. The Ancient Greeks treated them with welcome; a ship spotting dolphins riding in their wake was considered a good omen for a smooth voyage. **Dolphins also seem to have been important to the Minoans, judging by artistic evidence from the ruined palace at Knossos.** In Hindu mythology, the Ganges River Dolphin is **associated with Ganga, the deity of the Ganges river.**

**Dolphins are often regarded as one of Earth's most intelligent animals,** though it is hard to say just how intelligent dolphins are, as **comparisons of species' relative intelligence are complicated by differences in sensory apparatus, response modes, and nature of cognition.** Furthermore, the difficulty and expense of doing experimental work with large aquatics means that some tests which could yield meaningful results still have not been carried out, or have been carried out with inadequate sample size and methodology. Dolphin behavior has been studied extensively by humans however, both in captivity and in the wild."

-- Reference: Wikipedia.org

[184] "... The Anunnaki..."

*"The **Anunnaki** are a group of Sumerian and Akkadian deities related to, and in some cases overlapping with, the **Annuna** (the 'Fifty Great Gods') and the **Igigi** (minor gods), meaning something to the effect of 'those of royal blood' or 'princely offspring' or "heaven and earth".*

*The Annunaki appear in the Babylonian creation myth, Enuma Elish. In the late version magnifying Marduk, after the creation of mankind, **Marduk divides the Anunnaki and assigns them to their proper stations, three hundred in heaven, three hundred on the earth. The Anunnaki were the High Council of the Gods, and Anu's companions. They were distributed through the Earth and the Underworld."*

-- Reference: Wikipedia.org

*"The **winged sun** is a **symbol associated with divinity, royalty and power** in the **Ancient Near East** (Egypt, Mesopotamia, Anatolia, and Persia). The symbol has also been found in the records of ancient cultures residing in various regions of **South America** as well as **Australia**.*

*In **Ancient Egypt**, the symbol is attested from the Old Kingdom (Sneferu, 26th century BC), often flanked on either side with a uraeus. In early Egyptian religion, the symbol Behedeti represented Horus of Edfu, later identified with Ra-Harachte. It is sometimes depicted on the neck of Apis, the bull of Ptah. As time passed (according to interpretation) all of the subordinated gods of Egypt were considered to be aspects of the sun god, including e.g. Khepri.*

*From roughly 2000 BC, the symbol spread to the **Levant** and to **Mesopotamia**. It appears in reliefs with **Assyrian** rulers and in Hieroglyphic **Anatolian** as a symbol for royalty, transcribed as literally, "his own self, the Sun". From ca. the 8th century BC, **it appears on Hebrew** seals, by now as a **generic symbol for "power"**. The symbol evolved into the **Faravahar** (the "visual aspect of Ahura Mazda") in Zoroastrian Persia."*

-- Reference: Wikipedia.org

186 "... he established a high standard of ethical, and humanitarian philosophy..."

*"Up to the time of the conquest of Media by **Cyrus the Great**, Median emperors ruled their conquered territories as provinces, through client kings and governors. **One of the keys to the Achaemenid success (as with most enduring great empires) was their open attitude to the culture and religion of the conquered people, so ironically the Persian culture was the one most affected as the Great King endeavored to melt elements from all his subjects into a new imperial style."*

-- Reference: Wikipedia.org

187 "... Teotihuacan..."

*"Several authors, including Zecharia Sitchin and Graham Hancock, have repeated each other's argument that there are major correspondences between the pyramids of Gizeh and those of Teotihuacan. The Pyramid of the Sun is 225m wide and 65 m high, constructed out of five successive layers of mud. Its ascent is via 242 stairs. The floor plan is rather close to that of the Pyramid of Khufu at Gizeh. The Pyramid of the Moon is much smaller: 42 m high and 150 m wide, yet its summit is as high as that of Sun, because it sits on the site's highest point. This feature can also be seen in Gizeh, where Khufu's and Khafre's pyramid reach an equal height, even though one is taller than the other.*

*The most obvious comparison, however, is that the layout of both the three pyramids at Gizeh and the three main structures of Teotihuacan represent the Belt of Orion. The Pyramid of the Moon compares with the smallest pyramid on the plateau, the Sun Pyramid with Khafre and the Temple of Quetzalcoatl, which has the largest ground plan, but never was built into a full pyramid, compares with that of Khufu.*
*Though there are individual differences, I would suggest that the same ingredients have been used, answering to the same general ground plan: to represent the Belt of Orion, which in ancient Egypt was the symbol of Horus (not Osiris as Adrian Gilbert and Robert Bauval have argued) and in the Mayan culture was part of the creation mythology. Local legends*

stated that the complex was built to transform men into gods. For sure, an "alien space station" could be an interpretation of that, but it is clear that the answer needs to be located in the domain of religion.

On May 17, ca. 150 AD, the Pleiades rose just before the Sun in the predawn skies. This synchronization, known as the heliacal rising of the Pleiades, only lasted approx. 100 year. It is now suggested that it was this event that was at the origin of Teotihuacan. The sun and the Pleiades are important in the religious rituals. The Sun-Pleiades zenith conjunction marked what is known as the New Fire ceremony. Bernardino de Sahugun's Aztec informants stated that the ceremony occurred at the end of every 52 year Calendar Round. The Aztecs and their predecessors had carefully observed the Pleiades, and on the expected night they were supposed to pass through the zenith, precisely at midnight, when the ceremony was performed."

-- Reference: http://www.philipcoppens.com/orionimage.html

[188] "... al-Hassan ibn-al-Sabbah..."

"The story is that al-Hassan ibn-al-Sabbah used hashish to enlist the aid of young men into his private army known as assassins (aschishin - or follower of Hassan). One of the primary sources for this information comes from the writings of Marco Polo who visited the area in 1273, almost 150 years after the reign of Al-Hassan.

There are many conflicting facts and sources for this information.

In the early 11th century, al-Hassan became the head of the Persian sect of the Ismailians, a rather obscure party of fanatics which gained local power under his guidance. In 1090, al-Hassan and his followers seized the castle of Alamut, in the province of Rudbar, which lies in the mountainous region south of the Caspian Sea. It was from this mountain home that he obtained evil celebrity among the Crusaders as "the old man of the mountains", and spread terror through the Mohammedan world.

In the account given by Marco Polo in "The Adventures [or Travels] of Marco Polo" it is told that "The Old Man kept at his court such boys of twelve years old as seemed to him destined to become courageous men. When the Old Man sent them into the garden in groups of four, ten or twenty, he gave them hashish to drink. They slept for three days, then they were carried sleeping into the garden where he had them awakened.

"When these young men woke, and found themselves in the garden with all these marvelous things, they truly believed themselves to be in paradise. And these damsels were always with them in songs and great entertainments; they; received everything they asked for, so that they would never have left that garden of their own will."

-- Reference: http://www.alamut.com/subj/ideologies/alamut/etymolAss.html

[189] "... Knights Templar..."

"The **Poor Fellow-Soldiers of Christ and of the Temple of Solomon** commonly known as the **Knights Templar** were among the most famous of the Western Christian military orders. The organization existed for approximately two centuries in the Middle Ages. It was founded in the aftermath of the First Crusade of 1096 to ensure the safety of the many Europeans who made the pilgrimage to Jerusalem after its conquest.

Around 1119, two veterans of the First Crusade, the French knight Hugues de Payens and his relative Godfrey de Saint-Omer, proposed the creation of a monastic order for the protection of the pilgrims. King Baldwin II of Jerusalem agreed to their request, and gave them space for a headquarters on the Temple Mount, in the captured Al Aqsa Mosque. The Temple Mount had a mystique, because it was above what was believed to be the ruins of the Temple of Solomon. The Crusaders therefore referred to the Al Aqsa Mosque as Solomon's Temple, and it was from this location that the Order took the name of Poor Knights of Christ and the Temple of Solomon, or "Templar" knights. The Order, with about nine knights, had few financial resources and relied on donations to survive. Their emblem was of two knights riding on a single horse, emphasizing the Order's poverty.

The Templars' impoverished status did not last long. They had a powerful advocate in Bernard of Clairvaux, a leading Church figure and a nephew of one of the founding knights. He spoke and wrote persuasively on their behalf, and in 1129 at the Council of Troyes, the Order was officially endorsed by the Church. With this formal blessing, the Templars became a favored charity across Europe, receiving money, land, businesses, and noble-born sons from families who were eager to help with the fight in the Holy Land. Another major benefit came in 1139, when Pope Innocent II's papal bull Omne Datum Optimum exempted the Order from obedience to local laws. This ruling meant **that the Templars could pass freely through all borders, were not required to pay any taxes, and were exempt from all authority except that of the Pope.**

With its clear mission and ample resources, the Order grew rapidly. Templars were often the advance force in key battles of the Crusades, as the knights on their heavily armed warhorses would set out to gallop full speed at the enemy, in an attempt to break opposition lines. One of their most famous victories was in 1177 during the Battle of Montgisard, where some 500 Templar knights helped to defeat Saladin's army of more than 26,000 soldiers.

Although the primary mission of the Order was military, **relatively few members were combatants. The others acted in support positions to assist the knights and to manage the financial infrastructure. The Templar Order, though its members were sworn to individual poverty, was given control of wealth beyond direct donations. A nobleman who was interested in participating in the Crusades might place all his assets under Templar management while he was away. Accumulating wealth** in this manner across Europe and the Outremer, **the Order in 1150 began generating letters of credit** for pilgrims journeying to the Holy Land: **pilgrims deposited their valuables with a local Templar preceptory before embarking**, received an encrypted document indicating the value of their deposit, then used that document upon arrival in the Holy Land to retrieve their funds. This innovative arrangement may have been the **first formal system to support the use of cheques**; it improved the safety of pilgrims by making them less attractive targets for thieves, and also contributed to the Templar coffers.

Based on this mix of donations and business dealing, **the Templar established financial networks across the whole of Christendom. They acquired large tracts of land, both in Europe and the Middle East**; they bought and managed farms and vineyards; they built churches and castles; they were involved in manufacturing, import and export; they had their own fleet of ships; and **at one point they even owned the entire island of Cyrprus. The Templar arguably qualifies as <u>the world's first multinational corporation</u>.**"

-- Reference: Wikipedia.org

[190] " **The Knights Templar were disbanded by King Philip IV of France, who was deeply in debt to the Order.**"

*"King Philip was already deeply in debt to the Templars from his war with the English and decided to seize upon the rumors for his own purposes. He began pressuring the Church to take action against the Order, as a way of freeing himself from his debts.*

*On Friday October 13, 1307 (a date linked with the origin of the Friday the 13th superstition), Philip ordered de Molay and scores of other French Templars to be simultaneously arrested. The Templars were charged with numerous heresies and tortured to extract false confessions of blasphemy. The confessions, despite having been obtained under duress, caused a scandal in Paris. After more bullying from Philip, Pope Clement then issued the bull Pastoralis Praeeminentiae on November 22, 1307, which instructed all Christian monarchs in Europe to arrest all Templars and seize their assets.*

*Pope Clement called for papal hearings to determine the Templars' guilt or innocence, and once freed of the Inquisitors' torture, many Templars recanted their confessions. Some had sufficient legal experience to defend themselves in the trials, but in 1310 Philip blocked this attempt, using the previously forced confessions to have dozens of Templars burned at the stake in Paris.*

*With the last of the Order's leaders gone, the remaining Templars around Europe were either arrested and tried under the Papal investigation (with virtually none convicted), absorbed into other military orders such as the Knights Hospitaller, or pensioned and allowed to live out their days peacefully. Some may have fled to other territories outside Papal control, such as excommunicated Scotland or to Switzerland.*

*It is estimated that at the Order's peak there were between 15,000 and 20,000 Templars, of whom about a tenth were actual knights."*

-- Reference: Wikipedia.org

[191] "**The Templars fled to Switzerland where they established an international banking system...**"

*"**Banking in Switzerland** is characterized by stability, **privacy and protection** of clients' assets and information. The country's **tradition of bank secrecy, which dates to the Middle Ages.***

*According to the CIA World Factbook, **Switzerland is "a major international financial centre vulnerable to the layering and integration stages of money laundering; despite significant legislation and reporting requirements, secrecy rules persist and nonresidents are permitted to conduct business through offshore entities and various intermediaries..."***

*In 1998, an international panel of historians released a study that claimed a **significant amount of gold had been stolen from Holocaust victims, as well as the treasuries of conquered countries, and deposited in the Swiss National Bank**. The panel found that, despite evidence of theft and wrongful acquisition of the gold, the SNB continued to accept* *the deposits. In 2000, a United States District Court judge approved a US$1.85 billion settlement between several Swiss banks and Holocaust victims."*

-- Reference: Wikipedia.org

[192] **"A primary influence of "Old Empire" operatives is on international bankers..."**

**EDITOR'S NOTE: The most famous example** of this kind of activity is **the "Bilderberg Conference"**. See the following reference to this organization from Wikipedia.org:

*"The **Bilderberg Group** or **Bilderberg conference** is an **unofficial** annual invitation-only conference of around 130 guests, most of **whom are persons of influence in the fields of business, media and politics**.*

***The elite group meets annually** at luxury hotels or resorts throughout the world — normally in Europe — and once every four years in the United States or Canada. It has an office in Leiden, South Holland, Netherlands. The 2007 conference took place from May 31 to June 3 at the Ritz-Carlton Hotel in Istanbul, Turkey.*

***Attendees of Bilderberg include central bankers**, **defense experts**, mass media press barons, government ministers, prime ministers, royalty, **international financiers** and political leaders from Europe and North America.*

***Some of the Western world's leading financiers** and foreign policy strategists **attend Bilderberg**. Donald Rumsfeld is an active Bilderberger, as is Peter Sutherland from Ireland, a former European Union commissioner and chairman of Goldman Sachs and of British Petroleum. Rumsfeld and Sutherland served together in 2000 on the board of the Swedish/Swiss engineering company ABB. Former **U.S. Deputy Defense Secretary** and former **World Bank head Paul Wolfowitz** is also a member. The group's current chairman is Etienne Davignon, the Belgian businessman and politician.*

*Critics say **the Bilderberg Group promotes the careers of politicians whose views are representative of the interests of multinational corporations**, at the expense of democracy.*

***The group's secrecy** and its connections to power elites has provided fodder for many who believe that the group is part of a conspiracy to create a New World Order.*

*Radio host Alex Jones promotes the theory that the group intends to dissolve the sovereignty of the United States and other countries into a supra-national structure similar to the European Union. Madrid-based author Daniel Estulin claims that the long-term purpose of Bilderberg is to "Build a One-World Empire". He states the group "is not the end but the means to a future One World Government". Another opponent of the group, Tony Gosling, has registered the domain name **Bilderberg.org**, largely **hosting material critical of Bilderberg.***

*Reporter Jonathan Duffy, writing in BBC News Online Magazine states "In the void created by such aloofness, an extraordinary conspiracy theory has grown up around the group that alleges the fate of the world is largely decided by Bilderberg."*

-- Reference: Wikipedia.org

[193] " A primary influence of "Old Empire" operatives on international bankers is to act as an unseen, non-combatant provocateur who covertly promote and finance weapons and warfare..."

(EDITOR'S NOTE: An excellent modern example of this activity has been documented in the World War II financing of Nazis by (Prescott Bush, Director of Union Banking Corp.) the patriarch of President George Bush and his son, President George W. Bush.:

*"On October 20, 1942, the U.S. government ordered the seizure of Nazi German banking operations in New York City that were being conducted by Prescott Bush, the father of former president George Herbert Walker Bush.*

*Harriman Bank was the main Wall Street connection for several German companies and the varied U.S. financial interests of Fritz Thyssen. Thyssen had been an early financial backer of the Nazi party until 1938, but by 1939 had fled Germany and was bitterly denouncing Hitler. He was later jailed by the Nazis for his opposition to the regime. Business transactions with Germany were not illegal when Hitler declared war on the United States on December 11, 1941, but, six days after the attack on Pearl Harbor, President Franklin Delano Roosevelt signed the Trading With the Enemy Act after it had been made public that U.S. companies were doing business with the declared enemy of the United States.*

*On October 20, 1942, the U.S. government ordered the seizure of German banking operations in New York City. Roosevelt's Alien Property Custodian, Leo T. Crowley, signed Vesting Order Number 248 seizing Bush's property under the Trading with the Enemy Act. The order cited only the Union Banking Corporation (UBC), of which **Bush was a director** and held one share, which had connections with a Dutch bank owned by Thyssen.*

***Fox News has reported that recently declassified material reveals** that the 4,000 Union Banking shares owned by the Dutch bank were registered in the names of the seven U.S. directors, according to a document signed by Homer Jones, chief of the division of investigation and research of the Office of Alien Property Custodian, a World War II-era agency. By 1941 Thyssen no longer had control over his banking empire, which was in the hands of the Nazi government.*

- *E. Roland Harriman – 3991 shares (**managed and under voting control of Prescott Bush**)*
- *Cornelis Lievense – 4 shares (He was the New York banker of the Nazi Party)*
- *Harold D. Pennington – 1 share (**Employed by Prescott Bush** at Brown Brothers Harriman)*
- *Ray Morris – 1 share (**a business partner of the Bush and Harriman families**)*
- *Prescott S. Bush – 1 share (director of UBC, which **was co-founded and sponsored by his father-in-law George Walker**; senior managing partner for E. Roland Harriman and Averell Harriman)*
- *H.J. Kouwenhoven – 1 share (organized UBC for Von Thyssen, managed UBC in Nazi occupied Netherlands)*
- *Johann G. Groeninger – 1 share (German Industrial Executive, a not unimportant member of the Nazi party)*

***Both E. Roland Harriman and Prescott Bush were members of Skull and Bones** as well as being members of the board of Brown Brothers Harriman & Co..*

The Harriman business interests seized under the act in October and November 1942 included:

- Union Banking Corporation (UBC) (for Thyssen and Brown Brothers Harriman). The President of UBC at that time was George Herbert Walker, Bush's father-in-law.
- Dutch-American Trading Corporation (with Harriman)
- the Seamless Steel Equipment Corporation (with Harriman)
- Silesian-American Corporation (this company was partially owned by a German entity; during the war the Germans tried to take full control of Silesian-American. In response to that, the American government seized German owned minority shares in the company, leaving the U.S. partners to carry on the business.)

The assets were held by the government for the duration of the war, then returned afterward. UBC was dissolved in 1951. **Bush was on the board of directors of UBC and held one share in the company. For it, he was reimbursed $1,500,000.(a huge amount of money at the time - but there is no documentary evidence to support this claim) These supposed assets were later used to launch Bush family investments in the Texas energy industry.**

Toby Rogers has claimed that Bush's connections to Silesian businesses (with Thyssen and Flick) make him complicit with the mining operations in Nazi-occupied Poland which used slave labor out of Oświęcim, where the Auschwitz concentration camp was later constructed.

**The New York Herald-Tribune referred to Thyssen as "Hitler's Angel" and mentioned Bush as an employee of the investment banking firm Thyssen used in the United States.** Some records in the National Archives, including the Harriman papers, document the continued relationship of Brown Brothers Harriman with Thyssen and some of his German investments up until his 1951 death. **Investigator John Loftus has said, "As a former federal prosecutor, I would make a case for Prescott Bush, his father-in-law (George Walker) and Averell Harriman [to be prosecuted] for giving aid and comfort to the enemy. They remained on the boards of these companies knowing that they were of financial benefit to the nation of Germany."**

**Two former slave laborers from Poland have filed suit in London against the government of the United States and the heirs of Prescott Bush in the amount of $40 billion.** A class-action lawsuit filed in the U.S. in 2001 was dismissed based on the principle of state sovereignty.

Prescott Bush connection to the Merchants of Death industry came from his father Samuel P. Bush who worked for Buckeye Steel Castings Company which manufactured railway parts for the railroad industry and barrels for guns and casings for shells for Remington Arms."

-- Reference: Wikipedia.org

There are also many well documented books which detail the relationship between **Swiss Banks the Nazi war machine:**

Germany and the Second World War: Volume VI: The Global War (Germany and the Second World War by Horst Boog, Werner Rahn, and Reinhard Stumpf

<u>**The complicity of the Swiss banks and government in funding the Nazi regime was known at the end of World War II.**</u> *Read the details on the following website: http://www.religioustolerance.org/holo_apol.htm*

<u>**"The Secret War Against the Jews, Unholy**</u> Trinity *(By Mark Aarons, John Loftus) tells one of the darkest tales of World War II. After the war had ended, fearing a surge of Soviet growth, the Papacy entered into an espionage alliance with British and American intelligence agents. Subsuming justice to the nascent Cold War ideology, these three powers ferreted Nazi criminals out of Europe so that they could be used in the supposedly greater fight against Communism. The Vatica's Nazi smuggling network was penetrated by Prince Anton Turkul, the great Soviet double agent who turned the operations into a sting for his masters in the Kremlin. Unholy Trinity exposes Turkul's "Red Nazi" operation for the first time and shows how Kim Philby, the infamous British-Soviet double agent, and his network were nearly sacrificed to preserve Turkul's Vatican operation. Exploring the Vatican's role in aiding Nazi criminals to escape punishment for their crimes, this book, originally published in 1991, first revealed the Vatican–Swiss bank connection to Nazi gold and documented the hidden links to Western investors in Nazi Germany. Since 1991, major revelations about the role of Swiss banks have confirmed Unholy Trinity's expose of the flight of the Nazi's stolen treasures; the new introduction and new final chapters, written by Aarons and Loftus for this edition, bring the book completely up to date and show how the media have missed the vital Vatican connection in the Swiss-bank story. Among other things, the authors demonstrate that U.S. and British code-breakers were fully aware of the Holocaust as early as 1941 but lied to the Western press; that the code-breakers bugged the Swiss banks and then buried secrets of Nazi gold transfers to protect U.S. intelligence chief Allen Dulles; and that the Australian, British, and Canadian governments are still waging a campaign to keep their citizens ignorant about the Nazi war criminals living among them. Covers all these topics and more, Unholy Trinity is the definitive history of a series of profoundly disturbing cover-ups involving the Holy See, Allen Dulles, the Swiss banks, and the remnants of the Third Reich."*

*-- Reference: http://books.google.com/books?id=HXxew8zc1GQC&vq=secret+war+funding,+Swiss+Banks &source=gbs_summary_s&cad=0*

*Otto Nathan (1893-1987) was an economist who taught at Princeton University (1933-35), New York University (1935-42), Vassar College (1942-44), and Howard University (1946-52). Dr. Nathan was a close friend of Albert Einstein for many years and was designated by Einstein as co-trustee of his literary estate with Helen Dukas. Otto Nathan was the author of the following books which detail the Swiss Banks involvement in WW II:*

> <u>**Nazi War Finance and Banking Our Economy in War**</u>. *Cambridge, Massachusetts: National Bureau of Economic Research, 1944. Paperback: ASIN B000J0VXBG.*

> <u>**The Nazi Economic System: Germany's Mobilization for War**</u>. *New York: Russell & Russell, 1971. Hardcover textbook: ISBN 0-846-21501-2, ISBN 978-0-84621-501-1"*

*-- Reference: Wikipedia.org*

[194] "...**Bloodletting**..."

"**Bloodletting** is one of the oldest medical practices, having been practiced among diverse ancient peoples, including the Mesopotamians, the Egyptians, the Greeks, the Mayans, and the Aztecs. In Greece, bloodletting was in use around the time of Hippocrates, who mentions bloodletting but in general relied on dietary techniques. Erasistratus, however, theorized that many diseases were caused by plethoras, or overabundances, in the blood, and advised that these plethoras be treated, initially, by exercise, sweating, reduced food intake, and vomiting. Herophilus advocated bloodletting. Archagathus, one of the first Greek physicians to practice in Rome, practiced bloodletting extensively and gained a most sanguinary reputation.

The popularity of bloodletting in Greece was reinforced by the ideas of Galen, after he discovered the veins and arteries were filled with blood, not air as was commonly believed at the time. There were two key concepts in his system of bloodletting. The first was that blood was created and then used up, it did not circulate and so it could 'stagnate' in the extremities. The second was that humoral balance was the basis of illness or health, the four humours being blood, phlegm, black bile, and yellow bile, relating to the four Greek classical elements of air, water, earth and fire. Galen believed that blood was the dominant humour and the one in most need of control. In order to balance the humours, a physician would either remove 'excess' blood (plethora) from the patient or give them an emetic to induce vomiting, or a diuretic to induce urination.

Bloodletting was especially popular in the young United States of America, where Benjamin Rush (a signatory of the Declaration of Independence) saw the state of the arteries as the key to disease, recommending levels of blood-letting that were high, even for the time. **George Washington was treated in this manner** following a horseback riding accident: almost 4 pounds (1.7 litres) of blood was withdrawn, **contributing to his death by throat infection in 1799.**"

-- Reference: Wikipedia.org

[195] "... you will find "evolution" mentioned in the ancient Vedic Hymns..."

"The Vedas are very exhaustive scriptures. Each Veda contains several sections and thousands of hymns. Some of the Vedic hymns, especially the hymns of the Rig Veda, are considered to be at least 6000-8000 years old.

**The Vedas** are believed to be revealed scriptures, because **they are considered to be divine in origin.** Since **they were not written by any human beings** but were only heard in deep meditative states, they are commonly referred as srutis or those that were heard."

-- Reference: http://www.hinduwebsite.com/vedicsection/vedichymns.asp

"The **Vedas** (Sanskrit véda वेद "knowledge") are a large corpus of texts originating in Ancient India. They form the oldest layer of Sanskrit literature and the oldest sacred texts of Hinduism. According to Hindu tradition, the Vedas are "not human compositions", being supposed to have been directly revealed, and thus are called śruti ("what is heard"). Vedic mantras are recited at Hindu prayers, religious functions and other auspicious occasions.

Philosophies and sects that developed in the Indian subcontinent have taken differing positions on the Vedas. Schools of Indian philosophy which cite the Vedas as their scriptural authority are classified as "orthodox" (āstika). Other traditions, notably Buddhism and Jainism, though they are (like the vedanta) similarly concerned with liberation did not regard *the Vedas as divine ordinances but rather human expositions of the sphere of higher spiritual knowledge, hence not sacrosanct."*

-- Reference: Wikipedia.org

[196] **"... the IS-BE who wrote a fictitious story one dark and stormy night..."**

*Frankenstein: or, The Modern Prometheus* is a novel written by the British author **Mary Shelley. Shelley wrote the novel when she was 18 years old.** The first edition was published anonymously in London in 1818. Shelley's name appears on the revised third edition, published in 1831. The title of the novel refers to a scientist, Victor Frankenstein, who learns how to create life and creates a being in the likeness of man, but larger than average and more powerful.

The story has had an influence across literature and popular culture and spawned a complete genre of horror stories and films. **It is arguably considered the first fully realized science fiction novel. The novel raises many issues that can be linked to today's society.**

**During the rainy summer of 1816, the "Year Without a Summer," the world was locked in a long cold volcanic winter caused by the eruption of Mount Tambora in 1815.** Mary Wollstonecraft Godwin, age 19, and her lover (and later husband) Percy Bysshe Shelley, visited Lord Byron at the Villa Diodati by Lake Geneva in Switzerland. The weather was consistently too cold and dreary that summer to enjoy the outdoor holiday activities they had planned, so **the group retired indoors until almost dawn talking about science and the supernatural.** After reading *Fantasmagoriana*, an anthology of German ghost stories, **they challenged one another to each compose a story of their own, the contest being won by whoever wrote the scariest tale.**

**Mary conceived an idea after she fell into a waking dream or nightmare during which she saw "the pale student of unhallowed arts kneeling beside the thing he had put together."** Byron managed to write just a fragment based on the vampire legends he heard while travelling the Balkans, and from this Polidori created *The Vampyre* (1819), the progenitor of the romantic vampire literary genre. Two legendary horror tales originated from this one circumstance.

Radu Florescu, in his book *In Search of Frankenstein*, argued that Mary and Percy Shelley visited Castle Frankenstein on their way to Switzerland, near Darmstadt along the Rhine, where a notorious alchemist named Konrad Dippel had experimented with human bodies."

-- Reference: Wikipedia.org

[197] **"...Grimm's Fairy Tales..."**

*"The world famous collection of German origin fairy tales Kinder- und Hausmärchen (KHM; English: Children's and Household Tales), commonly known as **Grimm's Fairy Tales**, was first published in 1812 by Jacob and Wilhelm Grimm, the Brothers Grimm. The brothers developed an interest in ancient fairy tales. They started to collect and write down tales that they alleged had been handed down for generations. On December 20, 1812 they published the first volume of the first edition, containing 86 stories; the second volume of 70 stories followed in 1814.*

The first volumes were much criticized because, although they were called "Children's Tales", they were not regarded as suitable for children, both for the scholarly information included and the subject matter. Many changes through the editions—such as turning the wicked mother of the first edition in Snow White and Hansel and Gretel to a stepmother, were probably made with an eye to such suitability. They removed sexual references, such as Rapunzel's betraying the prince by asking why her clothing no longer fit, and so revealing her pregnancy, but in many respects, violence, particularly when punishing villains, was increased.

The influence of these books was widespread. It ranks behind only the Bible and the works of William Shakespeare in sales. W. H. Auden praised it, during World War II, as one of the founding works of Western culture. The tales themselves have been put to many uses. The Nazis praised them as folkish tales showing children with sound racial instincts seeking racially pure marriage partners, and so strongly that the Allied forces warned against them. Writers about the Holocaust have combined the tales with their memoirs."

-- Reference: Wikipedia.org

[198] "...Hinduism..."

"Hinduism is often referred to as Sanātana Dharma, a Sanskrit phrase meaning "the eternal path" or "the eternal law".

Hinduism is the world's oldest major religion that is still practiced. Its earliest origins can be traced to the ancient Vedic civilization. A conglomerate of diverse beliefs and traditions, Hinduism has no single founder. It is the world's third largest religion following Christianity and Islam, with approximately a billion adherents, of whom about 905 million live in India and Nepal.

Hinduism is an extremely diverse religion. Although some tenets of the faith are accepted by most Hindus, scholars have found it difficult to identify any doctrines with universal acceptance among all denominations. Prominent themes in Hindu beliefs include Dharma (ethics/duties), Samsāra (The continuing cycle of birth, life, death and rebirth), Karma (action and subsequent reaction), Moksha (liberation from samsara), and the various Yogas (paths or practices).

Hinduism is a diverse system of thought with beliefs spanning monotheism, polytheism, panentheism, pantheism, monism and atheism. It is sometimes referred to as henotheistic (devotion to a single God while accepting the existence of other gods), but any such term is an oversimplification of the complexities and variations of belief.

Most Hindus believe that the spirit or soul—the true "self" of every person, called the ātman—is eternal."

-- Reference: Wikipedia.org

[199] "... Arcadia Regeneration Company".

"One of the birthplaces reported for Zeus is Mount Lycaeum in Arcadia. Lycaon, a cannibalistic Pelasgian king, was transformed into a werewolf by Zeus. Lycaon's daughter was Callisto. It was also said to have been the birthplace of Zeus' son, Hermes.

*Arcadia remained a rustic, secluded area, and its inhabitants became proverbial as primitive herdsmen leading simple pastoral unsophisticated yet happy lives, to the point that Arcadia may refer to some **imaginary idyllic paradise**.*

*The Latin phrase Et in Arcadia ego which is usually interpreted to mean "I am also in Arcadia" or **"I am even in Arcadia"** is an example of memento mori, a **cautionary reminder of the transitory nature of life and the inevitability of death**. The phrase is most often associated with a 1647 painting by Nicolas Poussin, also known as "The Arcadian Shepherds". In the painting the phrase appears as an inscription on a tomb discovered by youthful figures in classical garb. It has been suggested that the phrase is an anagram for the Latin phrase "I! Tego arcana Dei", which translates to **"Begone! I keep God's secrets."***

-- Reference: Wikipedia.org

[200] "... the majority of basic genetic material is common to all species..."

### "The Genetic Core of the Universal Ancestor

*J. Kirk Harris, Scott T. Kelley,[1] George B. Spiegelman,[3] and Norman R. Pace[1]*

[1] *Department of Molecular, Cellular and Developmental Biology, University of Colorado, Boulder, Colorado 80309-0347, USA;* [2] *Graduate Group in Microbiology, University of California, Berkeley, Berkeley, California 94720, USA;* [3] *Department of Microbiology and Immunology, University of British Columbia, Vancouver, British Columbia, Canada V6T 1Z3*

***Molecular analysis** of conserved sequences in the ribosomal RNAs **of modern organisms reveals a three-domain phylogeny that converges in a universal ancestor for all life**. We used the Clusters of Orthologous Groups database and information from published genomes to search for other universally conserved genes that have the same phylogenetic pattern as ribosomal RNA, and therefore constitute **the ancestral genetic core of cells**. **Our analyses identified a small set of genes that can be traced back to the universal ancestor and have coevolved since that time**.*

*As indicated by earlier studies, **almost all of these genes are involved with the transfer of genetic information**, and most of them directly interact with the ribosome. Other universal genes have either undergone lateral transfer in the past, or have diverged so much in sequence that their distant past could not be resolved. **The nature of the conserved genes suggests innovations that may have been essential to the divergence of the three domains of life**. The analysis also identified several genes of unknown function with phylogenies that track with the ribosomal RNA genes. The products of these genes are likely to play fundamental roles in cellular processes."*

-- Reference: http://www.genome.org/cgi/content/abstract/GR-6528v1?etoc

[201] "... biological engineers..."

*"**Biomedical engineering** is an application of engineering principles and design to challenges in human health and medicine. Bioengineering is related to Biological Engineering, the latter including applications of engineering principles to the full spectrum of living systems, from microbes and plants to ecosystems. Bioengineering exploits new developments in molecular biology, biochemistry, microbiology, and neurosciences as well*

as sensing, electronics, and imaging, and applies them to the design of medical devices, diagnostic equipment, biocompatible materials, and other important medical needs.

Bioengineering couples engineering expertise with knowledge in biological sciences such as genetics, molecular biology, protein chemistry, cytology, neurobiology, immunology, physiology, and pharmacology. Bioengineers work closely with, but are not limited to, medical doctors and other health professionals to develop technical solutions to current and emerging health concerns.

Bioengineering is not limited to the medical field. Bioengineers have the ability to exploit new opportunities and solve problems within the domain of complex systems. They have a great understanding of living systems as complex systems which can be applied to many fields including entrepreneurship."

-- Reference: Wikipedia.org

[202] "... Imperfections were worked out, modifications made and eventually the new animal was introduced into the actual planetary environment for final testing. "

"The basic ideals of **Eugenics** can be found from the beginnings of Western civilization. The philosophy was most famously expounded by Plato, who believed human reproduction should be monitored and controlled by the state. The basic eugenic principle from Plato's The Republic was, "The best men must have intercourse with the best women as frequently as possible, and the opposite is true of the very inferior.

However, Plato understood this form of government control would not be readily accepted, and proposed the truth be concealed from the public via a fixed lottery. Mates, in Plato's Republic, would be chosen by a "marriage number" in which the quality of the individual would be quantitatively analyzed, and persons of high numbers would be allowed to procreate with other persons of high numbers. In theory, this would lead to predictable results and the improvement of the human race. However, Plato acknowledged the failure of the "marriage number" since "gold soul" persons could still produce "bronze soul" children. This might have been one of the earliest attempts to mathematically analyze genetic inheritance, which was not perfected until the development of Mendelian genetics and the mapping of the human genome.

Other ancient civilizations, such as Rome and Sparta, practiced infanticide as a form of phenotypic selection. In Sparta, newborns were inspected by the city's elders, who decided the fate of the infant. If the child was deemed incapable of living, it was usually thrown from the Taygetus mountain. It was more common for girls than boys to be killed this way. Trials for babies which included bathing them in wine and exposing them to the elements. To Sparta, this would ensure only the strongest survived and procreated. Adolf Hitler considered Sparta to be the first "Völkisch State," and much like Ernst Haeckel before him, praised Sparta due to its primitive form of eugenics practice of selective infanticide policy which was applied on deformed children.

The 12 Tables of Roman Law, established early in the formation of the Roman Republic, stated in the fourth table that deformed children would be put to death. In addition, patriarchs in Roman society were given the right to "discard" infants at their discretion. This was often done by drowning undesired newborns in the Tiber River.

Sir Francis Galton initially developed the ideas of eugenics using social statistics. Sir Francis Galton systematized these ideas and practices according to new knowledge about the evolution of man and animals provided by the theory of his cousin Charles Darwin during the 1860s and 1870s. After reading Darwin's Origin of Species, Galton built upon Darwin's ideas whereby the mechanisms of natural selection were potentially thwarted by human civilization. He reasoned that, since many human societies sought to protect the underprivileged and weak, those societies were at odds with the natural selection responsible for extinction of the weakest; and only by changing these social policies could society be saved from a "reversion towards mediocrity," a phrase he first coined in statistics and which later changed to the now common "regression towards the mean."

-- Reference: Wikipedia.org

[203] "...**species**..."

"In biology, a **species** is one of the basic units of biological classification and a taxonomic rank. A species is often defined as a group of organisms capable of interbreeding and producing fertile offspring. While in many cases this definition is adequate, more precise or differing measures are often used, such as based on similarity of DNA or morphology. Presence of specific locally-adapted traits may further subdivide species into subspecies.

The commonly used names for plant and animal taxa sometimes correspond to species: for example, "lion," "walrus," and "Camphor tree," each refers to a species. In other cases common names do not: for example, "deer" refers to a family of 34 species, including Eld's Deer, Red Deer and Wapiti (Elk). The last two species were once considered a single species, illustrating how species boundaries may change with increased scientific knowledge.

Each species is placed within a single genus. This is a hypothesis that the species is more closely related to other species within its genus than to species of other genera. All species are given a binomial name consisting of the generic name and specific name (or specific epithet). For example, Pinus palustris (commonly known as the Longleaf Pine).

A usable definition of the word "species" and reliable methods of identifying particular species are essential for stating and testing biological theories and for measuring biodiversity. Traditionally, multiple examples of a proposed species must be studied for unifying characters before it can be regarded as a species. Extinct species known only from fossils are generally difficult to give precise taxonomic rankings to. A species which has been described scientifically can be referred to by its binomial names.

Nevertheless, as Charles Darwin remarked,

> 'I look at the term species as one arbitrarily given for the sake of convenience to a set of individuals closely resembling each other .... it does not essentially differ from the term variety, which is given to less distinct and more fluctuating forms. The term variety, again in comparison with mere individual difference, is also applied arbitrarily, and for mere convenience sake.'

Because of the difficulties with both defining and tallying the total numbers of different species in the world, **it is estimated that there are anywhere between 2 million and 100 million different species.**"

-- Reference: Wikipedia.org

**"...species of beetle..."**

*"Beetles are a group of insects which have the largest number of species. They are placed in the order Coleoptera, which means "sheathed wing" and contains more described species than in any other order in the animal kingdom, constituting about twenty-five percent of all known life-forms. Forty percent of all described insect species are beetles (about 350,000 species), and new species are frequently discovered. Estimates put the total number of species, described and undescribed, at between 5 and 8 million.*

*Beetles can be found in almost all habitats, but are not known to occur in the sea or in the polar regions. They interact with their ecosystems in several ways. They often feed on plants and fungi, break down animal and plant debris, and eat other invertebrates. Some species are prey of various animals including birds and mammals. Certain species are agricultural pests, such as the Colorado potato beetle Leptinotarsa decemlineata, the boll weevil Anthonomus grandis, the red flour beetle Tribolium castaneum, and the mungbean or cowpea beetle Callosobruchus maculatus, while other species of beetles are important controls of agricultural pests. For example, coccinellidae ("ladybirds" or "ladybugs") consume aphids, scale insects, thrips, and other plant-sucking insects that damage crops."*

-- Reference: Wikipedia.org

**"One species does not evolve to become another species, as the Earth textbooks indicate, without the intervention and manipulation of genetic material by an IS-BE."**

*"**Genetic engineering, recombinant DNA technology, genetic modification / manipulation (GM)** and **gene splicing** are terms applied to the direct manipulation of an organism's genes. Genetic engineering is not to be confused with traditional breeding where the organism's genes are manipulated indirectly. Genetic engineering uses the techniques of molecular cloning and transformation. Genetic engineering endeavors have found some success in improving crop technology, the manufacture of synthetic human insulin through the use of modified bacteria, the manufacture of erythropoietin in Chinese hamster ovary cells, and the production of new types of experimental mice such as the oncomouse (cancer mouse) for research.*

*Since a protein sequence is specified by a segment of DNA called a gene, novel versions of that protein can be produced by changing the DNA sequence of the gene. The companies that own the modified genome are able to patent it. In the case of basic crops, the companies gain control of foodstuffs, controlling food production on a large scale and reducing agrobiodiversity to a few varieties. The only apparent interest in promoting this tecnology appears to be purely economic, despite the claims of seed companies such as Monsanto and Novartis to solve the world food scarcity. It is now popularly understood that it is not the lack of food on a wholewide scale that is the main problem, but its distribution, aggravated by prohibitive tariffs by rich nations. Genetically modified crops do not reduce hunger. The majority of genetically crops are destined for animal food to meet the high demand for meat in developed countries. No genetic modification have yet to serve the needs of mankind despite all the promises in this direction.*

*However, even with regard to this technology's great potential, some people have raised concerns about the introduction of genetically engineered plants and animals into the environment and the potential dangers of human consumption of GM foods. They say that these organisms have the potential to spread their modified genes into native populations thereby disrupting natural ecosystems. This has already happened."*

-- Reference: Wikipedia.org

[206] **"...genetic manipulation of a species..."**

*"How much genetic variation is there? Historical debate:* **Classical school** *held that there was very little genetic variation, most individuals were homozygous for a "wild-type" allele. Rare heterozygous loci due to recurrent mutation; natural selection purges populations of their "load" of mutations.* **Balance school** *held that many loci will be heterozygous in natural populations and heterozygotes maintained by "balancing selection" (heterozygote advantage). Selection thus plays a role in maintaining variation.*

*How do we measure variation? To show that there is a genetic basis to a continuously varying character one can study 1)* **resemblance among relatives**: *look at the offspring of individuals from parents in different parts of the distribution; can estimate heritability (more later). 2)* **artificial selection**: *pigeons and dogs show that there is variation present; does not tell* **how much** *variation."*

-- Reference: http://biomed.brown.edu/Courses/BIO48/5.Geno.Pheno.HTML

[207] **"... Proteobacteria..."**

*"The* **Proteobacteria** *are a major group (phylum) of bacteria. They include a wide variety of pathogens, such as Escherichia, Salmonella, Vibrio, Helicobacter, and many other notable genera. Others are free-living, and include many of the bacteria responsible for nitrogen fixation. The group is defined primarily in terms of ribosomal RNA (rRNA) sequences, and is named for the Greek god Proteus (also the name of a bacterial genus within the Proteobacteria), who could change his shape, because of the great diversity of forms found in this group.*

*All Proteobacteria are Gram-negative, with an outer membrane mainly composed of lipopolysaccharides. Many move about using flagella, but some are non-motile or rely on bacterial gliding. The last include the myxobacteria, a unique group of bacteria that can aggregate to form multicellular fruiting bodies. There is also a wide variety in the types of metabolism. Most members are facultatively or obligately anaerobic and heterotrophic, but there are numerous exceptions. A variety of genera, which are not closely related to each other, convert energy from light through photosynthesis. These are called purple bacteria, referring to their mostly reddish pigmentation."*

-- Reference: Wikipedia.org

[208] **"...Phylum..."**

*"In biological taxonomy, a 'phylum' is a taxonomic rank at the level below Class and above Kingdom. "Phylum" is adopted from the Greek φυλαί phylai, the clan-based voting groups in Greek city-states."*

-- Reference: Wikipedia.org

"...Intensely hot blue star..."

"Blue stars are very hot and very luminous; in fact, most of their output is in the ultraviolet range. These are the rarest of all main sequence stars, constituting as few as 1 in 3,000,000 in the solar neighborhood. (Blue) stars shine with a power over a million times our Sun's output. *Examples: Zeta Orionis, Zeta Puppis, Lambda Orionis, Delta Orionis*"..

Reference: Wikipedia.org

"... responsible for coordinating creature production..."

**Editor"s Note:** For detailed information on the organization that controls **the World Congress of the Biotechnology Industry**, visit their website at **http://www.bio.org** .

Here is a statement from their website about who they are and what they do:

*"**BIO is the world's largest biotechnology organization**, providing advocacy, business development and communications services for **more than 1,150 members worldwide**. Our mission is to be the champion of biotechnology and the advocate for our member organizations—both large and small.*

*BIO members are involved in the research and development of innovative healthcare, agricultural, industrial and environmental biotechnology technologies. **Corporate members range from entrepreneurial companies developing a first product to Fortune 100 multinationals. We also represent state and regional biotech associations, service providers to the industry and academic centers**. Visit the **BIO Member Directory** to browse BIO members and Web site links as well as BIO state and international affiliates. "*

-- Reference: http://bio.org/aboutbio/

"... patent licenses for the biological engineering process   ..."

"A **biological patent** is a patent relating to an invention or discovery in biology.

The 1970's marked the first time when scientists patented methods on their biotechnological inventions with recombinant DNA. It wasn't until 1980 that patents for whole-scale living organisms was permitted. In Diamond v. Chakrabarty, **the Supreme Court overturned a previous precedent allowing the patentability of living matter.** The subject for this particular case was a bacterium that was specifically modified to help clean-up and degrade oil spills.

Since legal changes have occurred starting in 1980, there has been a general trend of patenting inventions on living matter. More knowledge and data has become available in recent years that have never before been available. However, for us to get to the point where it is making a significant difference in peoples' lives, a tidy sum of money needs to be invested. **Biotech and pharmaceutical companies in recent years have found out how lucrative biological research can be. These firms foster many research opportunities by funding made possible only through the private sector.**

Patents have provided an impetus for research to be pursued in that the end goal of money can be envisioned by companies with the funding cash. Especially during the genomic era, *more patents were issued. Companies and organizations like the University of California were patenting whole genomes.*

*In 1998, the U.S. Patent and Trademark Office (PTO) issued a broad patent claiming primate (including human) embryonic stem cells, entitled "Primate Embryonic Stem Cells" (Patent 5,843,780). On 13 March 2001, a second patent (6,200,806) was issued with the same title but focused on human embryonic stem cells.*

*Recently, there has been a slowdown and backlash against patenting biological material worldwide.*

*Some feel that the increase in patenting biological information leads to inefficiency in research. Many scientists are coming up against patent thickets, which are masses of information that they must obtain permission (and often pay large fees to utilize) before they can ever work with the information.*

*Michael Heller and Rebecca Eisenberg (2005) explain that there is a recent trend of patenting more and more steps along the research path. This creates a "tragedy of the anticommons," whereby "each upstream patent allows its owner to set up another tollbooth on the road to product development, adding to the cost and slowing the pace of downstream . . . innovation". A report shows that notwithstanding escalating funding, in the past half-decade biomedical innovation has slowed markedly. The number of drugs approved by the Food and Drug Administration has fallen below previous eras. The technologies approved, it continues, are less influential than previous innovations approved. The current trend of patenting what previously were thought of as basic science insights have raised the financial bar for other scientists wanting to use such insight. The overall trend of more patents may be slowing innovation.*

*However, others point out that patents are necessary for research. Without them, scientists would keep secret all discoveries for fear of colleagues and others stealing their ideas. There would also be little incentive for large-scale investments from the private sector.*

Reference: Wikipedia.org

[212] "..."cyclical stimulus-response generators".

*"Fixed Action Pattern (FAP) is an instinctive behavioral sequence that is indivisible and runs to completion. Fixed action patterns are invariant and are produced by a neural network known as the innate releasing mechanism in response to an external sensory stimulus known as a sign stimulus or releaser.*

*A mating dance may be used as an example. Many species of birds engage in a specific series of elaborate movements, usually by a brightly colored male. How well they perform the "dance" is then used by females of the species to judge their fitness as a potential mate. The key stimulus is typically the presence of the female.*

*Although fixed action patterns are most common in animals with simpler cognitive capabilities, humans also demonstrate fixed action patterns. For example, infants grasp strongly with their hands as a response to tactile stimulus."*

Reference: Wikipedia.org

[213] "...chemical-electrical trigger" mechanism..."

"A **taxis** (plural **taxes**) is an innate behavioural response by an organism to a stimulus. A taxis differs from a tropism (turning response, often growth towards or away from a stimulus) in that the organism has motility and demonstrates guided movement towards or away from the stimulus. It also differs from a kinesis, a non-directional change in activity in response to a stimulus that results in the illusion of directed motion due to different rates of activity depending on stimulus intensity.

For example, flagellate protozoans of the genus Euglena move towards a light source. Here the directional stimulus is light, and the orientation movement is towards the light. This reaction or behaviour is a positive one to light and specifically termed "positive phototaxis", since phototaxis is a response to a light stimulus, and the organism is moving towards the stimulus. If the organism moves away from the stimulus, then the taxis is negative. Many types of taxis have been identified and named using prefices to specify the stimulus that elicits the response. These include **anemotaxis** (stimulation by wind), **barotaxis** (pressure), **chemotaxis** (chemicals), **galvanotaxis** (electrical current), **geotaxis** (gravity), **hydrotaxis** (moisture), **phototaxis** (light), **rheotaxis** (fluid flow), **thermotaxis** (temperature changes) and **thigmotaxis** (physical contact).

**Chemotaxis** is a migratory response elicited by chemicals. Unicellular (e.g. protozoa) or multicellular (e.g. worms) organisms are targets of the substances. A concentration gradient of chemicals developed in a fluid phase guides the vectorial movement of responder cells or organisms.

**Electrotaxis is directional movement of motile cells in response to a electric field.** It has been suggested that by detecting and orientating themselves toward the electric fields. This notion is based on 1) the existence of measurable electric fields that naturally occur during wound healing, development and regeneration; and 2) **cells in cultures respond to applied electric fields by directional cell.**"

-- Reference: Wikipedia.org

[214] "... reproductive chemical-electrical impulses stimulated by testosterone or estrogen."

"**Testosterone** is a steroid hormone from the androgen group. In mammals, testosterone is primarily secreted in the testes of males and the ovaries of females, although small amounts are also secreted by the adrenal glands. It is the principal male sex hormone and an anabolic steroid.

The period of the early 1930's to the 1950's has been called "The Golden Age of Steroid Chemistry", and work during this period progressed quickly. Research in this golden age proved that this newly **synthesized compound — testosterone** — or rather family of compounds (for many derivatives were developed in the 1940's, 50's and 60's), was a potent multiplier of muscle, strength, and wellbeing

**In both men and women, testosterone plays a key role in health and well-being as well as in sexual functioning.**

*The human hormone testosterone is produced in greater amounts by males, and less by females. The **human hormone estrogen is produced in greater amounts by females**, and less by males.  On average, an **adult human male body produces about forty to sixty times more testosterone than an adult female body.***

*Testosterone causes the appearance of masculine traits (i.e deepening voice, pubic and facial hairs, muscular build, etc.) Like men, women rely on testosterone to maintain libido, bone density and muscle mass throughout their lives."*

-- Reference: Wikipedia.org

[215] **"The debilitating impact and addiction to the "sexual aesthetic-pain" electronic wave..."**

*"The term **Sexual addiction** is used to describe the behavior of a person who has an unusually intense sex drive or obsession with sex.  Sexual addiction, also called **sexual compulsion** is a form of psychological addiction.*

*The behavior of sex addicts is comparable to behavior of alcoholics and addicts, where sex functions like a drug. A common definition of alcoholism is that a person has a pathological relationship with this mood altering drug.  It provides a quick mood change, works every time and the user loses control over their compulsion. Like alcoholics, sex addicts' lives rotate around the constant desire for their "drug" of choice."*

-- Reference: Wikipedia.org

[216] **"...space craft of The Domain travel trillions of light-years in a single day..."** --

Using the Julian Calendar year (not Gregorian) of 365.25 days, or exactly 31,557,600 seconds, gives the light-year an exact value of 9,460,730,472,580,800 meters. ( A meter = 3.281 feet or 39.37 inches.)

The distance to the nearest star from Earth is 4.24 light years!

Distances measured in fractions of a light-year usually involve objects within a star system. Distances measured in light-years include distances between nearby stars, such as those in the same spiral arm or globular cluster.

One kilolight-year, abbreviated "kly", is one thousand light-years, or about 307 parsecs. Kilolight-years are typically used to measure distances between parts of a galaxy.

One megalight-year, abbreviated "Mly", is one million light-years, or about 306,600 parsecs. Megalight-years are typically used to measure distances between neighboring galaxies and galaxy clusters.

One gigalight-year, abbreviation "Gly", is one billion light-years — one of the largest distance measures used. One gigalight-year is about 306.6 million parsecs.

-- Reference: Wikipedia.org

[217] **"... a heavy gravity, nitrogen/oxygen atmosphere planet..."**

*"The Earth's atmosphere* is a layer of gases surrounding the planet Earth and retained by the Earth's gravity. It contains roughly (by molar content/volume) 78.08% nitrogen, 20.95% oxygen, 0.93% argon, 0.038% carbon dioxide, trace amounts of other gases, and a variable amount (average around 1%) of water vapor. This mixture of gases is commonly known as *air*. The atmosphere protects life on Earth by absorbing ultraviolet solar radiation and reducing temperature extremes between day and night.

There is no definite boundary between the atmosphere and outer space. It slowly becomes thinner and fades into space. Three quarters of the atmosphere's mass is within 11 km of the planetary surface. In the United States, people who travel above an altitude of 80.5 km (50 statute miles) are designated astronauts. An altitude of 120 km (~75 miles or 400,000 ft) marks the boundary where atmospheric effects become noticeable during re-entry. The Kármán line, at 100 km (62 miles or 328,000 ft), is also frequently regarded as the boundary between atmosphere and outer space.

**The atmosphere of Mars** is relatively thin, and the atmospheric pressure on the surface varies from around 30 Pa (0.03 kPa) on Olympus Mons's peak to over 1155 Pa (1.155 kPa) in the depths of Hellas Planitia, with a mean surface level pressure of 600 Pa (0.6 kPa), compared to Earth's 101.3 kPa. However, the scale height of the atmosphere is about 11 km, somewhat higher than Earth's 6 km. The atmosphere on Mars consists of 95% carbon dioxide, 3% nitrogen, 1.6% argon, and contains traces of oxygen, water, and methane. The atmosphere is quite dusty, giving the Martian sky a tawny color when seen from the surface; data from the Mars Exploration Rovers indicates the suspended dust particles are roughly 1.5 micrometres across.

**The atmosphere of Venus**, the second planet from the Sun, is much denser and hotter than that of Earth. The surface temperature and pressure on Venus are 740 K (467°C) and 93 bar, respectively. The Venusian atmosphere supports thick persistent clouds made of sulfuric acid, which make optical observations of the surface impossible. The information about surface features on Venus has been obtained exclusively by radar imaging conducted from the ground and Venera 15-16 and by Magellan space probes. The main atmosphereric gases on Venus are carbon dioxide and nitrogen, which make up 96.5% and 3.5% of all molecules. Other chemical compounds are present only in trace amounts.

The atmosphere of Venus is in state of a vigorous circulation and super-rotation. The whole atmosphere circles the planet in just four days (super-rotation), which is a short time compared with the sideral rotational period of 243 days. The winds supporting super-rotation blow as fast as 100 m/s. Near the poles of Venus anticyclonic structures called polar vortexes are located. In them the air moves downward. Each vortex is double eyed and shows a characteristic S-shaped pattern of clouds.

Only the ionosphere and thin induced magnetosphere separate venusian atmosphere from the space. They shield the atmosphere from the solar wind, which usually does not penetrate deep into it. However they are incapable of preventing the loss of water, which is continuously blown away by the solar wind through the induced magnetotail.

Despite the harsh conditions on the surface, at about a 50 km to 65 km level above the surface of the planet the atmospheric pressure and temperature is nearly the same as that of the Earth, making its upper atmosphere the most Earth-like area in the Solar System, even more so than the surface of Mars. Due to the similarity in pressure, temperature and the fact that breathable air (21% oxygen, 78% nitrogen) is a lifting gas on Venus in the same way that helium is a lifting gas on Earth."

-- Reference: Wikipedia.org

[218] "...Johannes Gutenberg..."

*"Johannes Gensfleisch zur Laden zum Gutenberg (c. 1400 – February 3, 1468) was a German goldsmith and printer, who is credited with inventing movable type printing in Europe (c. 1439) and mechanical printing globally. His major work, the Gutenberg Bible, also known as the 42-line bible, has been acclaimed for its high aesthetic and technical quality.*

*Although Gutenberg was financially unsuccessful in his lifetime, the printing technologies spread quickly, and news and books began to travel across Europe much faster than before. It fed the growing Renaissance, and since it greatly facilitated scientific publishing, it was a major catalyst for the later scientific revolution. Gutenberg is thought to have said: "Give me 26 soldiers of lead and I shall conquer the world."*

*Printing was also a factor in the Reformation: Martin Luther found that the 95 Theses, which he posted on the door of his church, were printed and circulated widely; subsequently he also issued broadsheets outlining his anti-indulgences position (ironically, indulgences were one of the first items Gutenberg had printed). The broadsheet evolved into newspapers and defined the mass media we know today."*

-- Reference: Wikipedia.org

[219] "...George Washington Carver..."

*"George Washington Carver (July 12, 1864 – January 5, 1943) was an American botanical researcher and agronomy educator who worked in agricultural extension at the Tuskegee Institute in Tuskegee, Alabama, teaching former slaves farming techniques for self-sufficiency.*
*George Washington Carver reputedly discovered three hundred uses for peanuts and hundreds more uses for soybeans, pecans and sweet potatoes. Among the listed items that he suggested to southern farmers to help them economically were adhesives, axle grease, bleach, buttermilk, chili sauce, fuel briquettes, ink, instant coffee, linoleum, mayonnaise, meat tenderizer, metal polish, paper, plastic, pavement, shaving cream, shoe polish, synthetic rubber, talcum powder and wood stain. Three patents (one for cosmetics, and two for paints and stains) were issued to George Washington Carver in the years 1925 to 1927; however, they were not commercially successful in the end. Aside from these patents and some recipes for food, he left no formulas or procedures for making his products. He did not keep a laboratory notebook.*

*Carver's most important accomplishments were in areas other than industrial products from peanuts, including agricultural extension education, improvement of racial relations, mentoring children, poetry, painting, religion, advocacy of sustainable agriculture and appreciation of plants and nature. He served as a valuable role model for African-Americans and an example of the importance of hard work, a positive attitude and a good education. His humility, humanitarianism, good nature, frugality and lack of economic materialism have also been widely admired.*

One of his most important roles was that the fame of his achievements and many talents undermined the widespread stereotype of the time that the black race was intellectually inferior to the white race. In 1941, "Time" magazine dubbed him a "Black Leonardo".

-- Reference: Wikipedia.org

[220] "...Jonas Salk..."

*"Jonas Edward Salk* (October 28, 1914 – June 23, 1995) was an American biologist and physician best known for the research and development of the first effective polio vaccine.

While being interviewed by Edward R. Murrow on "See It Now" in 1955, Salk was asked: "Who owns the patent on this vaccine?" Surprised by the question's assumption of the requirement of a profit-motive for his creation, he responded: "There is no patent. Could you patent the sun?"

-- Reference: Wikipedia.org

[221] "...Richard Trevithick..."

" *Richard Trevithick* (born April 13, 1771 in Cornwall - died April 22, 1833 in Kent) was an English inventor, mining engineer and builder of the first working railway steam locomotive."

-- Reference: Wikipedia.org

[222] "... Renaissance..."

The **Renaissance** (from French Renaissance, meaning "rebirth"; Italian: Rinascimento, from re- "again" and nascere "be born") was a cultural movement that spanned roughly the 14th through the 17th century, beginning in Italy in the late Middle Ages and later spreading to the rest of western Europe. It encompassed a revival of learning based on classical sources, the development of linear perspective in painting, and educational reform. The Renaissance saw developments in most intellectual pursuits, but is perhaps best known for its artistic aspect and the contributions of such polymaths as Leonardo da Vinci and Michelangelo, who have inspired the term "Renaissance men".

However, it was not until the nineteenth century that **the French word Renaissance achieved popularity in describing the cultural movement that began in the late 13th century**" (1200 AD - 1300 AD).

The term was first used retrospectively by the Italian artist and critic Giorgio Vasari (1511-1574) in his book The Lives of the Artists (published 1550). In the book Vasari was attempting to define what he described as a break with the barbarities of gothic art: the arts had fallen into decay with the collapse of the Roman Empire and only the Tuscan artists, **beginning with Cimabue (1240-1301) and Giotto (1267-1337) began to reverse this decline in the arts.** According to Vasari, antique art was central to the rebirth of Italian art.

During the 12th century in Europe, there was a radical change in the rate of new inventions and innovations in the ways of managing traditional means of production and economic growth. In less than a century, there were more inventions developed and applied usefully than in the previous thousand years of human history all over the globe. The period saw major technological advances, including the adoption or invention of printing, gunpowder, spectacles, a better clock, the astrolabe, and greatly improved ships. The latter two advances made possible the dawn of the Age of Exploration.

**Alfred Crosby described some of this technological revolution in The Measure of Reality : Quantification in Western Europe, 1250-1600 and other major historians of technology have also noted it.**

- The earliest written record of a windmill is from Yorkshire, England, dated 1185.
- Paper manufacture began in Italy around 1270.
- The spinning wheel was brought to Europe (probably from India) in the 13th century.
- The magnetic compass aided navigation, first reaching Europe some time in the late 12th century.
- Eyeglasses were invented in Italy in the late 1280s.
- The astrolabe returned to Europe via Islamic Spain.
- Leonardo of Pisa introduces Hindu-Arabic numerals to Europe with his book Liber Abaci in 1202.
- The West's oldest known depiction of a stern-mounted rudder can be found on church carvings dating to around 1180."

-- Reference: Wikipedia.org

[223] **"... explosions that were tested and used in the past two years on Earth have the potential to destroy all of life..."**

"A **doomsday device** is a hypothetical construction — usually a weapon — which could destroy all life on the Earth, or destroy the Earth itself (bringing "doomsday", a term used for the end of planet Earth).

Doomsday devices have been present in literature and art especially in the 20th century, when advances in science and technology allowed humans to imagine a definite and plausible way of actively destroying the world or all life on it (or at least human life). Many classics in the genre of science fiction take up the theme in this respect, especially The Purple Cloud (1901) by M. P. Shiel in which the accidental release of a gas kills all people on the planet.

After the advent of nuclear weapons, especially hydrogen bombs, they have usually been the dominant components of fictional doomsday devices. RAND strategist Herman Kahn proposed a "Doomsday Machine" in the 1950s which would consist of a computer linked to a stockpile of hydrogen bombs, programmed to detonate them all and bathe the planet in nuclear fallout at the signal of an impending nuclear attack from another nation. Such a scheme, fictional as it was, epitomized for many the extremes of the suicidal logic behind the strategy of mutually assured destruction, and it was famously parodied in the Stanley Kubrick film from 1964, Dr. Strangelove or: How I Learned to Stop Worrying and Love the Bomb. It is also a main topic of the movie Beneath the Planet of the Apes, in parallel with the species extermination theme. Most such models either rely on the fact that hydrogen bombs can be made arbitrarily large (see Teller-Ulam design) or that they can be "salted" with materials designed to create long-lasting and hazardous fallout (e.g.; a cobalt bomb).

There are many unconfirmed, anecdotal reports of a Soviet doomsday device involving a 200-megaton hydrogen bomb sheathed in (or, alternately, "salted" with) a highly radioactive material, usually said to be cobalt, of sufficient quantity to saturate the earth's atmosphere with deadly fallout should the device be detonated. Details regarding this device vary according to the source, but enough similarities in the dozens of different stories exist to suggest at least some basis in truth. According to various sources, at some point between 1967 and 1985, the device was designed but never constructed; built but never activated; built and activated, but dismantled at the end of the cold war; or designed and constructed in such a manner that it can never be de-activated, and is still in existence today. Tales of its location and means of operation are equally diverse: it was in an underground bunker west of Moscow, Siberia, the Ukraine, etc.; it was installed on a special rocket booster that would deliver it to the upper atmosphere upon activation; it was actually a series of bombs placed at intervals along the western border of the USSR; it was to be detonated upon command from the Kremlin, automatically by a special computer, a seismic trigger, or upon detection of incoming missiles. Many more versions exist, such as one with the device being permanently installed in the hold of an unmarked tramp freighter, steaming randomly from port to port in the North Sea."

-- Reference: Wikipedia.org

[224] "... paradigm..."

"Historian of science Thomas Kuhn gave this word its contemporary meaning when he adopted it to refer to the set of practices that define a scientific discipline during a particular period of time. Kuhn himself came to prefer the terms exemplar and normal science, which have more exact philosophical meanings. However, in his book The Structure of Scientific Revolutions Kuhn defines a scientific paradigm as:

- what is to be observed and scrutinized
- the kind of questions that are supposed to be asked and probed for answers in relation to this subject
- how these questions are to be structured
- how the results of scientific investigations should be interpreted

Alternatively, the Oxford English Dictionary defines paradigm as "a pattern or model, an exemplar."

-- Reference: Wikipedia.org

[225] "...Nicola Tesla..."

"Nikola Tesla (10 July 1856 – 7 January 1943) was an inventor, physicist, mechanical engineer, and electrical engineer. Born in Smiljan, Croatian Krajina, Military Frontier, he was an ethnic Serb subject of the Austrian Empire and later became an American citizen. Tesla is best known for his many revolutionary contributions to the discipline of electricity and magnetism in the late 19th and early 20th century. Tesla's patents and theoretical work formed the basis of modern alternating current electric power (AC) systems, including the polyphase power distribution systems and the AC motor, with which he helped usher in the Second Industrial Revolution. Contemporary biographers of Tesla have deemed him "the man who invented the twentieth century" and "the patron saint of modern electricity."
After his demonstration of wireless communication (radio) in 1893 and after being the victor in the "War of Currents", he was widely respected as America's greatest electrical engineer. Much of his early work pioneered modern electrical engineering and many of his discoveries were of groundbreaking importance. During this period, in the United States, Tesla's fame rivaled that of any other inventor or scientist in history or popular culture but due to his

eccentric personality and unbelievable and sometimes bizarre claims about possible scientific and technological developments, Tesla was ultimately ostracized and regarded as a "mad scientist". Never having put much focus on his finances, Tesla died impoverished at the age of 86.

Aside from his work on electromagnetism and engineering, **Tesla is said to have contributed in varying degrees to the establishment of robotics, remote control, radar and computer science, and to the expansion of ballistics, nuclear physics, and theoretical physics. In 1943, the Supreme Court of the United States credited him as being the inventor of the radio."**

He performed several experiments prior to Roentgen's discovery (including photographing the bones of his hand; later, he sent these images to Roentgen) but didn't make his findings widely known; much of his research was lost in the 5th Avenue lab fire of March 1895.

**A "world system" for "the transmission of electrical energy without wires"** that depends upon the electrical conductivity was proposed in which transmission in various natural mediums with current that passes between the two point are used to power devices. In a practical wireless energy transmission system using this principle, a high-power ultraviolet beam might be used to form a vertical ionized channel in the air directly above the transmitter-receiver stations. **The same concept is used in virtual lightning rods, the <u>electrolaser electroshock weapon</u>, and has been proposed for disabling vehicles.**

**Tesla demonstrated "the transmission of electrical energy without wires"** that depends upon electrical conductivity as early as 1891. The Tesla effect (named in honor of Tesla) is the archaic term for an application of this type of electrical conduction (that is, the movement of energy through space and matter; not just the production of voltage across a conductor)

Tesla also **<u>investigated harvesting energy that is present throughout space</u>**. He believed that it was just merely a question of time when men will succeed in attaching their machinery to the very wheelwork of nature, stating: Ere many generations pass, our machinery will be driven by a power obtainable at any point of the universe. —"Experiments With Alternate Currents Of High Potential And High Frequency" (February 1892)

Tesla began to theorize about electricity and magnetism's power to warp, or rather change, space and time and the procedure by which man could forcibly control this power. Near the end of his life, Tesla was fascinated with the idea of light as both a particle and a wave, a fundamental proposition already incorporated into quantum physics. This field of inquiry led to **the idea of creating a "wall of light" by manipulating electromagnetic waves in a certain pattern**. This mysterious wall of light would enable time, space, gravity and matter to be altered at will, and **engendered an array of Tesla proposals that seem to leap straight out of science fiction, including anti-gravity airships, teleportation, and time travel.**

The single strangest invention Tesla ever proposed was probably the **"thought photography" machine**. He reasoned that a thought formed in the mind created a corresponding image in the retina, and the electrical data of this neural transmission could be read and recorded in a machine. The stored information could then be processed through an artificial optic nerve and played back as visual patterns on a viewscreen.

Another of Tesla's theorized inventions is commonly referred to as **Tesla's Flying Machine**, which appears to resemble an **ion-propelled aircraft**. Tesla claimed that one of his life goals was to create **a flying machine that would run without the use of an airplane engine, wings, ailerons, propellers, or an onboard fuel source.** Initially, Tesla pondered about the idea of a flying craft that would fly using an electric motor powered by grounded base stations. As time progressed, Tesla suggested that perhaps such an aircraft could be run entirely electro-mechanically. **The theorized appearance would typically take the form of a cigar or saucer.**

In the Colorado Springs lab, **Tesla observed unusual signals that he later thought may have been evidence of extraterrestrial radio communications coming from Venus or Mars**. He noticed repetitive signals from his receiver which were substantially different from the signals he had noted from storms and earth noise. Specifically, he later recalled that the signals appeared in groups of one, two, three, and four clicks together. Tesla had mentioned before this event and many times after that **he thought his inventions could be used to talk with other planets**. There have even been claims that he invented a **"Teslascope"** for just such a purpose.

**"I hold that space cannot be curved, for the simple reason that it can have no properties. It might as well be said that God has properties.** He has not, but only attributes and these are of our own making. Of properties we can only speak when dealing with matter filling the space. To say that in the presence of large bodies space becomes curved is equivalent to stating that something can act upon nothing. I, for one, refuse to subscribe to such a view." -- New York Herald Tribune, September 11, 1932

**Tesla was critical of Einstein's relativity work, calling it :**

"...[a] magnificent mathematical garb which fascinates, dazzles and makes people blind to the underlying errors. The theory is like a beggar clothed in purple whom ignorant people take for a king..., its exponents are brilliant men but they are metaphysicists rather than scientists... " -- New York Times, July 11, 1935, p 23, c.8

"Nikola Tesla invented the 20th and 21st Century. A 'discoverer of new principles,' Tesla was the sole inventor of the alternating poly-phase current generators that light up every town in the world today. He was the original inventor of the radio, and placed his ideas in print and demonstrated them before the public 5 years before Marconi. By the turn of the century, he had discussed the feasibility of television; he created an atom smasher capable of evaporating rubies and diamonds; he built wireless neon lamps that gave off more light than today's conventional bulbs provide; he built precursors to the electron microscope, the laser and X-ray photographs. He sent his shadowgraphs to the **discoverer of X-rays in 1895 as** soon a Roentgen published his famous pictures. **Tesla also created Kirlian-like photographs 75 years before they became famous.** All of this took place before 1900!'

**Tesla, and <u>not Edison</u>, invented the poly-phase alternators that power our modern civilization;** and it was Tesla who was eventually awarded Marconi's wireless patents long after Tesla and Marconi were both dead. In all, Tesla contributed over 1200 patents, and we are currently using only some 200 of them. Near everyone remembers the Tesla Coil, but how many remember that he demonstrated wireless transmission of electric power prior to 1900?

When offered to share the Nobel Prize with Edison for their electrical inventions, Tesla turned the prestigious award down! Edison never received the Nobel Prize.

**Tesla is quoted as saying:**

*'In the dark I had the sense of a bat, and could detect the presence of an object at a distance of 12 feet away by a peculiar creepy sensation on the forehead...'*

*'In Budapest, I could hear the ticking of a watch with 3 rooms between me and the timepiece. A fly alighting on a table in the room would cause a dull thud in my ear. A carriage passing at a distance of a few miles fairly shook my whole body. The whistle of a locomotive 20 or 30 miles away made the bench or chair on which I sat vibrate so strongly that the pain was unbearable. The ground under my feet trembled continuously...'*

Tesla said in an 1892 lecture :

*'Ere many generations pass, our machinery will be driven by a power obtainable at any point of the universe. Throughout space there is energy. Is this energy static or kinetic? If static, our hopes are in vain; if kinetic - and this we know it is, for certain - then it is a mere question of time when men will succeed in attaching their machinery to the very wheelwork of nature.'*

-- Reference: http://www.world-mysteries.com/dougy.htm

[226]  **"... will be able to "reverse engineer" the technology..."**

*"After joining the Army in 1942, Philip Corso served in Army Intelligence in Europe. In 1945, Corso arranged for the safe passage of 10,000 Jewish WWII refugees out of Rome to Palestine. During the Korean War (1950-1953), Corso performed Intelligence duties under General Douglas MacArthur as Chief of the Special Projects branch of the Intelligence Division, Far East Command. One of his primary duties was to keep track of enemy prisoner of war (POW) camps in North Korea. Corso was in charge of investigating the estimated number of U.S. and other United Nations POWs held at each camp and their treatment. At later held congressional hearings of the Senate Select Committee on POW/MIA Affairs, Philip Corso would provide testimony that many hundreds of American POW's were abandoned at these camps.*

*Corso was on the staff of President Eisenhower's National Security Council for four years (1953-1957). In 1961, he became Chief of the Pentagon's Foreign Technology desk in Army Research and Development, working under Lt. Gen. Arthur Trudeau. When he left military intelligence in 1963, Corso became a key aide to Senator Strom Thurmond. In 1964, Corso was assigned to Warren Commission member Senator Richard Russell Jr. as an investigator into the assassination of John F. Kennedy.*

*Philip Corso relates in his book The Day After Roswell (co-author William J. Birnes) how he stewarded extraterrestrial artifacts recovered from a crash at Roswell, New Mexico in 1947.*

*According to Corso, the reverse engineering of these artifacts indirectly led to the development of accelerated particle beam devices, fiber optics, lasers, integrated circuit chips and Kevlar material.*

*In 1947, according to Corso, a covert government group (see Majestic 12) was assembled under the leadership of the first Director of Central Intelligence , Adm. Roscoe H. Hillenkoetter. Among its tasks was to collect all information on extraterrestrial spacecraft. The US administration simultaneously discounted the existence of flying saucers in the eyes of the public, Corso says. Corso further relates that the Strategic Defense Initiative (SDI), or*

*Star Wars, was meant to achieve the capability of killing the electronic guidance systems of incoming enemy warheads and disabling enemy spacecraft, including those of extraterrestrial origin."*

--- Reference: Wikipedia.org

[227] **"... attuned to the "neural network" of the craft."**

*"Traditionally, the term **Neural Networks** had been used to refer to a network or circuit of biological neurons. The modern usage of the term often refers to artificial neural networks, which are composed of artificial neurons or nodes. Thus the term 'Neural Network' has two distinct usages:*

> *1) **Biological neural networks** are made up of real biological neurons that are connected or functionally-related in the peripheral nervous system or the central nervous system. In the field of neuroscience, they are often identified as groups of neurons that perform a specific physiological function in laboratory analysis.*

> *2) **Artificial neural networks** are made up of interconnecting artificial neurons (programming constructs that mimic the properties of biological neurons). Artificial neural networks may either be used to gain an understanding of biological neural networks, or for solving artificial intelligence problems without necessarily creating a model of a real biological system."*

-- Reference: Wikipedia.org

[228] **"...microscopic wiring or fibers..."**

The **transistor was invented in 1947.** It was considered a revolution. Small, fast, reliable and effective, it quickly replaced the vacuum tube. Freed from the limitations of the vacuum tube, engineers finally could begin to realize the electrical constructions of their dreams.

It seems that the integrated circuit was destined to be invented. Two separate inventors, unaware of each other's activities, invented almost identical integrated circuits or ICs at nearly the same time.

Jack Kilby, an engineer with a background in ceramic-based silk screen circuit boards and transistor-based hearing aids, started working for Texas Instruments in 1958. A year earlier, research engineer Robert Noyce had co-founded the Fairchild Semiconductor Corporation. From 1958 to 1959, both electrical engineers were working on an answer to the same dilemma: how to make more of less.

Although the first integrated circuit was pretty crude and had some problems, the idea was groundbreaking. By making all the parts out of the same block of material and adding the metal needed to connect them as a layer on top of it, there was no more need for individual discrete components. No more wires and components had to be assembled manually. The circuits could be made smaller and the manufacturing process could be automated.

Jack Kilby (Texas Instruments) is probably most famous for his invention of the integrated circuit, for which he received the Nobel Prize in Physics in the year 2000. After his success with the integrated circuit Kilby stayed with Texas Instruments and, among other things, he led the team that invented the hand-held calculator.

Jack Kilby now holds patents on over sixty inventions and is also well known as the inventor of the portable calculator (1967). In 1970 he was awarded the National Medal of Science. Robert Noyce, with sixteen patents to his name, founded Intel, the company responsible for the invention of the microprocessor, in 1968. But for both men the invention of the integrated circuit stands historically as one of the most important innovations of mankind. Almost all modern products use chip technology.

-- Reference: Wikipedia.org

[229] "...wiring is used for light, sub-light and ultra-light spectrum detection and vision."

An **optical fiber** is a glass or plastic fiber designed to guide light along its length. **Fiber optics** is the overlap of applied science and engineering concerned with the design and application of optical fibers. Optical fibers are widely used in fiber-optic communication, which permits transmission over longer distances and at higher data rates than other forms of communications. **Fibers are used instead of metal wires** because signals travel along them with less loss, and they are immune to electromagnetic interference. Optical fibers are also used to form sensors, and in a variety of other applications.

In 1952, physicist Narinder Singh Kapany conducted experiments that led to the invention of optical fiber, based on Tyndall's earlier studies; **modern optical fibers**, where the glass fiber is coated with a transparent cladding to offer a more suitable refractive index, appeared later in the decade.

In 1991, the emerging field of photonic crystals led to the development of **photonic crystal fiber** (Science (2003), vol 299, page 358), which guides light by means of diffraction from a periodic structure, rather than total internal reflection. The first photonic crystal fibers became commercially available in 1996. Photonic crystal fibers can be designed to carry higher power than conventional fiber, and their wavelength dependent properties can be manipulated to improve their performance in certain applications."

-- Reference: Wikipedia.org

[230] "... fabrics of the interior of the craft..."

**"Technical textiles** is the term given to textile products manufactured for non aesthetic purposes, where function is the primary criterion. This is a large and growing sector and supports a vast array of other industries.

It has been heard that soon **textiles will be merged with electronics** in all areas. In future **wearable computers** would be launched, these will not be like advance wrist watches etc, they will contain IC s in fabric to develop fabric keyboards and other wearable computer devices. These types of products are known as **Interactive electronic textiles** (IET). Research to support IET development is being conducted in many universities. Growing consumer interest in mobile, electronic devises will initiate the demand for IET products.

**Technical textiles** include textile structures for **autmotive** applications, **medical** textiles (e.g. implants), **geotextiles** (reinforcement of embankments), **agrotextiles** (textiles for crop protection), **protective clothing** (e.g. **against heat and radiation** for fire figther clothing, against **molten metals** for welders, stab protection and **bulletproof** vests), **spacesuits** (astronauts)."

**Biotextiles** are structures composed of textile fibers designed for use in specific biological environments where their performance depends on biocompatibility and biostability with cells and biological fluids. Biotextiles include implantible devices such as surgical sutures, hernia repair fabrics, **arterial grafts, artificial skin** and **parts of artificial hearts.** <u>**They were first created 30 years ago**</u> *(1978) by Dr. Martin W. King, a professor in North Carolina State University's College of Textiles.*

**Medical textiles** are a broader group which also includes bandages, wound dressings, hospital linen, preventive clothing etc. Antiseptic biotextiles are textiles used in fighting against cutaneous bacterial proliferation. Zeolite and triclosan are at the present time the most used molecules. This original property allows to inhibits the development of odors or bacterial proliferation in the diabetic foot."

-- Reference: Wikipedia.org

[231] "... mechanisms for creating, amplifying and channeling light particles or waves as a form of energy."

In 1947, Willis E. Lamb and R. C. Retherford found apparent stimulated emission in hydrogen spectra and made the first demonstration of stimulated emission. In 1950, Alfred Kastler (Nobel Prize for Physics 1966) proposed the method of optical pumping.

The work of Schawlow and Townes, however, can be traced back to the 1940s and early 50s* and their interest in the field of microwave spectroscopy, which had emerged as a powerful tool for puzzling out the characteristics of a wide variety of molecules.

The invention of the laser, which stands for light amplification by stimulated emission of radiation, can be dated to 1958 with the publication of the scientific paper, *Infrared and Optical Masers*, by Arthur L. Schawlow, then a Bell Labs researcher, and Charles H. Townes, a consultant to Bell Labs. That paper, published in *Physical Review*, the journal of the American Physical Society, launched a new scientific field and opened the door to a multibillion-dollar industry.

Many different materials can be used as lasers. Some, like the ruby laser, emit short pulses of laser light. Others, like helium-neon gas lasers or liquid dye lasers emit a continuous beam of light.

*NOTE: According to the book, "The Day After Roswell", reports about microwave and light projecting components from the Roswell "flying disc", technology were "leaked" to Bell Laboratories through the Pentagon.

-- Reference: Wikipedia.org

[232] " There are as many universes as there are IS-BEs to imagine and perceive them, existing concurrently within it's own continuum."

The **multiverse** (or **meta-universe**) is the hypothetical set of multiple possible universes (including our universe) that together comprise all of reality. The different universes within the multiverse are sometimes called **parallel universes**. The structure of the multiverse, the nature of each universe within it and the relationship between the various constituent universes, depend on the specific multiverse hypothesis considered.

Multiverses have been hypothesized in cosmology, physics, astronomy, philosophy, theology, and fiction, particularly in science fiction and fantasy.

The specific term "multiverse," which was coined by William James, was popularized by science fiction author Michael Moorcock. In these contexts, parallel universes are also called "alternative universes," "quantum universes," "parallel worlds," "alternate realities," "alternative timelines," etc.

A multiverse of a somewhat different kind has been envisaged within the 11-dimensional extension of string theory known as M-theory. In M-theory our universe and others are created by collisions between membranes in an 11-dimensional space. This is unlike the universes in the "quantum multiverse".

The string landscape theory asserts that a different universe exists for each of the very large ensemble of solutions generated when ten dimensional string theory is reduced to the four-dimensional low-energy world we see.

"A common feature of all four multiverse levels is that the simplest and arguably most elegant theory involves parallel universes by default. To deny the existence of those universes, one needs to complicate the theory by adding experimentally unsupported processes and ad hoc postulates: finite space, wave function collapse and ontological asymmetry. Our judgment therefore comes down to which we find more wasteful and inelegant: many worlds or many words."

-- Reference: Wikipedia.org

[233] "...political, religious or economic expediency."

The common denominator of politics, religion and economics is that they are each based on vested interests. -- **The Editor**

**See the definition of "vested interest":**

"1) a survival or non-survival plan or agenda which has been "clothed" to make it seem like something other than what it actually is.

2) any person, group or entity which prevents or controls communication to serve their own purposes, (plans or agenda)."

-- Reference: English language Dictionary

[234] "... just before the Japanese attack on Pearl Harbor..."

"The **attack on Pearl Harbor** was a surprise attack against the United States' naval base at Pearl Harbor, Hawaii by the Japanese navy, at 0800 hours on the morning of Sunday, December 7, 1941, resulting in the United States becoming involved in World War II. Hostilities between the U.S. and Japan were expected by many observers, including President Roosevelt, who read a decrypted Japanese message (on December 1st, 1941) and told his assistant Harry Hopkins, "This means war."

At 03:42 Hawaiian Time, hours before commanding Admiral Chuichi Nagumo began launching strike aircraft, the minesweeper USS Condor spotted a midget submarine outside the harbor entrance and alerted destroyer USS Ward. Ward was initially unsuccessful in locating the target. Hours later, Ward fired America's first shots in the Pacific theater of WWII when she attacked and sank a midget submarine, perhaps the same one, at 06:37.

Closer to the moment of the attack, the attacking planes were detected and tracked as they approached by an Army radar installation being operated that morning as a mostly unofficial training exercise. The Opana Point radar station, operated by two enlisted men (Pvts. Lockard and Elliot) plotted the approaching force, and their relief team plotted them returning to the carriers. The initial radar returns were thought, by the ill-trained junior officer (Lt. Kermit A. Tyler) in charge at the barely operational warning information center at Pearl Harbor, to be a flight of American bombers expected from the mainland. In fact those bombers did arrive, from a somewhat different bearing in the middle of the attack.

Additionally, Japanese submarines were sighted and attacked (by USS Ward) outside the harbor entrance a few hours before the attack commenced, and at least one was sunk—all before the planes came within even radar range. This might have provided enough notice to disperse aircraft and fly off reconnaissance, except, yet again, reactions of the duty officers were tardy. It has been argued failure to follow up on DF bearings saved USS Enterprise. If she had been correctly directed, she might have run into the six carrier Japanese strike force.

After the attack, the search for the attack force was concentrated south of Pearl Harbor, continuing the confusion and ineffectiveness of the American response.

Another issue in the debate is the fact neither Admiral Kimmel nor General Short ever faced court martial. It is alleged this was to avoid disclosing information conspirators would not want to see made public. When asked, Kimmel replied, "Will historians know more later? Kimmel's reply to this was: ' ... I'll tell you what I believe. I think that most of the incriminating records have been destroyed. ... I doubt if the truth will ever emerge.' ..." It is equally, probably more, likely this was done to avoid disclosing the fact Japanese codes were being read, given there was a war on."

-- Reference: http://en.wikipedia.org/wiki/Pearl_Harbor_advance-knowledge_debate

[236] "...General Symington,"...

His first positions were chairman of the Surplus Property Board (1945), administrator of the Property Administration (1945–1946) and Assistant Secretary of War for Air (1946–1947). On September 18, 1947, the Office of the Secretary of the Air Force was created and Symington became the first Secretary. *Symington once formally requested a report from military sources regarding the possible existence of subterranean super humans.*

-- Reference: Wikipedia.org

[236] "...General Nathan Twining, ..."

He was named commander of the Air Materiel Command, and in 1947 he took over Alaskan Air Command. *In 1947, Twining was asked to study UFO reports*; he recommended that a formal study of the phenomenon take place; *Project Sign* was the result. When

Hoyt Vandenberg retired in mid-1953, Twining was selected as chief; during his tenure, massive retaliation based on airpower became the national strategy. In 1957, President Eisenhower appointed Twining chairman of the Joint Chiefs.

-- Reference: Wikipedia.org

[237] **"... General Jimmy Doolittle, ..."**

*"Soon after the attack on Pearl Harbor and the US entry into World War II, Doolittle was promoted to Lieutenant Colonel on January 2, 1942, and went to Headquarters Army Air Force to plan the first aerial raid on the Japanese homeland. He volunteered and received Gen. H.H. Arnold's approval to lead the attack of 16 B-25 medium bombers from the aircraft carrier USS Hornet, with targets in Tokyo, Kobe, Osaka, and Nagoya. It was the first and only combat mission of his military career.*

*Doolittle received the Medal of Honor, presented by President Franklin D. Roosevelt at the White House, for planning and leading the successful operation. The Doolittle Raid is viewed by historians as a major public-relations victory for the United States. Although the amount of damage done to Japanese war industry was minor, the raid showed the Japanese their homeland was not invulnerable.*

*Doolittle was portrayed by Spencer Tracy in the 1944 film Thirty Seconds Over Tokyo and by Alec Baldwin in the 2001 film Pearl Harbor, in which the Doolittle raid was depicted.*

*On May 10, 1946, Doolittle reverted to inactive reserve status and returned to Shell Oil as a vice president, and later as a director. He was the highest-ranking reserve officer to serve in the U.S. military in World War II."*

**EDITOR --**

**In March 1951, he was appointed a special assistant to the Air Force chief of staff, serving as a civilian in scientific matters which led to Air Force ballistic missile and space programs. (?!)**

*"He retired from Air Force duty on February 28, 1959 but* **continued to serve his country as** *Chairman of the Board of Space Technology Laboratories."*

-- Reference: Wikipedia.org

[238] **"...General Vandenberg..."**

*Lieutenant General Vandenberg was designated vice chief of staff of the Air Force on October 1, 1947, and promoted to the rank of General.*

-- Reference: Wikipedia.org

[239] **"... General Norstad..."**

*"On October 1, 1947, following the division of the War Department into the Departments of The Army and The Air Force, General Norstad was appointed deputy chief of staff for operations of the Air Force."*

**"... Charles Lindbergh was also in the office..."**

*"Charles Lindbergh gained sudden great international fame as the first pilot to fly solo across the Atlantic Ocean. He flew from Roosevelt Airfield in Garden City, New York, to Paris (Le Bourget Airport) on 20 May - 21 May 1927 in 33.5 hours. His plane was the single-engine aircraft, The Spirit of St. Louis.*

*Lindbergh's accomplishment won him the Orteig Prize; more significant than the prize money was the acclaim that resulted from his daring flight. A ticker-tape parade was held for him down 5th Avenue in New York City on 13 June 1927.*

*His public stature following this flight was such that he became an important voice on behalf of aviation activities, including the central committee of the National Advisory Committee for Aeronautics in the United States. The massive publicity surrounding him and his flight boosted the aircraft industry and made a skeptical public take air travel seriously. Lindbergh is recognized in aviation for demonstrating and charting polar air-routes, high altitude flying techniques, and increasing aircraft flying range by decreasing fuel consumption. These innovations are the basis of modern intercontinental air travel.*

*In his six months during WW II in the Pacific in 1944, Lindbergh took part in fighter bomber raids on Japanese positions, flying about 50 combat missions (as a civilian). The U.S. Marine and Army Air Force pilots who served with Lindbergh admired and respected him, praising his courage and defending his patriotism.*

*After World War II he lived quietly in Connecticut as a consultant both to the chief of staff of the U.S. Air Force and to Pan American World Airways. His 1953 book The Spirit of St. Louis, recounting his non-stop transatlantic flight, won the Pulitzer Prize in 1954.*

*Dwight D. Eisenhower restored Lindbergh's assignment with the Army Air Corps and made him a Brigadier General in 1954. In that year, he served on the Congressional advisory panel set up to establish the site of the United States Air Force Academy. In December 1968, he visited the crew of Apollo 8 on the eve of the first manned spaceflight to leave earth orbit.*

*From the 1960s on, Lindbergh became an advocate for the conservation of the natural world, campaigning to protect endangered species like humpback and blue whales, was instrumental in establishing protections for the "primitive" Filipino group the Tasaday and African tribes, and supporting the establishment of a national park. While studying the native flora and fauna of the Philippines, he also became involved in an effort to protect the Philippine eagle.*

**In his final years, Lindbergh became troubled that the world was out of balance with its natural environment; he stressed the need to regain that balance,** *and spoke against the introduction of supersonic airliners.*

**Lindbergh's speeches and writings later in life emphasized his love of both technology and nature, and a lifelong belief that "all the achievements of mankind have value only to the extent that they preserve and improve the quality of life."**

*In a 1967 Life magazine article, he said, "The human future depends on our ability to combine the knowledge of science with the wisdom of wildness."*

-- Reference: Wikipedia.org

[241] "...Dr. Wilcox..."

**Paul h. Wilcox, M. D.** The Traverse City State Hospital, Traverse City, Michigan.

**is the author of the following article, published in the American Journal of Psychiatry in August of 1947:**

**"A Review of Over 23,000 Treatments Using Unidirectional Currents**

*1. Forty percent of the most chronic patients showed significant improvement in ward behavior if adequately and repeatedly treated with suitable type of electroshock therapy. Relapses must be treated whenever they occur over months and years.*

*2. At least 60% of early cases, aged 60 or under, were rehabilitated within 1 year when adequately treated and 65% by the end of the second year after the start of treatment.*

*3. Adequate treatment means intensive treatment until the expected improvement has occurred and intensive treatment of relapses when they occur. No patient, otherwise suitable who still is not rehabilitated after 1 year, has had an adequate trial of treatment with less than 20 treatments.*

*4. An ideal therapy is one which achieves beneficial results without causing accumulating brain damage, thus permitting its use repeatedly for years if necessary.*

*5. This ideal is approached by the relatively low intensity 60-cycle pulsating direct current used in the treatment of the patients reviewed in this paper. This technique also has been accompanied by an exceptionally low percentage of skeletal complications."*

-- Reference: American Journal of Psychiatry 104:100-112, August 1947, doi: 10.1176/appi.ajp.104.2.100 © 1947 American Psychiatric Association

[242] "...Electroencephalograph..."

**Electroencephalography** (EEG) is the measurement of electrical activity produced by the brain as recorded from electrodes placed on the scalp. (EEG) is the measurement of electrical activity produced by the brain as recorded from electrodes placed on the scalp.

-- Reference: Wikipedia.org

[243] "...introduced himself as Mr. John Reid ..."

*"John Edward Reid, American criminologist developed a Polygraph in 1945 which was a scientific recording device designed to register a person's bodily responses to being questioned. Popularly known as a lie detector, the polygraph has been used chiefly in criminal investigations, although it is also used in employment and security screening*

practices. *Because no machine can unerringly recognize when a person is lying, the polygraph results are used in conjunction with other evidence, observations, and information. Emotional stress reflected by this test, for instance, need not be due to lying. On the other hand, a subject may be a pathological liar and therefore show no measurable bodily responses when giving false answers. Ordinary nervousness, individual physical or mental abnormalities, discomfort, excessive pretest interrogation, or indifference to a question also affect test accuracy. The polygraph can, however, provide a basis for an evaluation of whether or not the subject's answers are truthful. This test has also been helpful in exonerating innocent persons accused of crimes.*

*A polygraph is actually several instruments combined to simultaneously record changes in blood pressure, pulse, and respiration. The electrical conductivity of the skin's surface can also be measured—increased sweat-gland activity reduces the skin's ability to carry electrical current."*

-- Reference: Wikipedia.org

[244] "...lie detector testing..."

*"Dr. William Moulton Marston (May 9, 1893 – May 2, 1947) was an American psychologist, feminist theorist, inventor, and comic book author who created the character* **Wonder Woman***. Two strong women, his wife Elizabeth Holloway Marston and Olive Byrne, (who lived with the couple in a polyamorous relationship), served as exemplars for the character and greatly influenced her creation.*

*Dr. William Moulton Marston is credited as the creator of the systolic blood-pressure test used in an attempt to detect deception, which became one component of the modern polygraph. According to their son, Marston's wife, Elizabeth Holloway Marston, was also involved in the development of the systolic blood-pressure test: "According to Marston's son, it was his mother Elizabeth, Marston's wife, who suggested to him that 'When she got mad or excited, her blood pressure seemed to climb'. This would be the basis for Wonder Woman's* **Lasso of Truth.**

**The FBI considered William Moulton Marston,** *who invented the lie detector and created the comic book character Wonder Woman under the pseudonym Charles Moulton,* **to be a 'phony' and a 'crackpot.' He is alleged to have** <u>**misrepresented the result of a study he conducted**</u> *for the Gillette razor company in 1938, for which he reportedly received some $30,000, a handsome sum in those days.* **Despite these misgivings, the FBI today uses Marston's creation** *(the polygraph, not the Lasso of Truth)* **to guide investigations as well as to screen applicants and employees."**

-- Reference: Wikipedia.org

[245] "...truth serum..."

*"***Sodium thiopental***, better known as* **Sodium Pentothal** *(a trademark of Abbott Laboratories),* **thiopental, thiopentone sodium,** *or* **trapanal***, is a rapid-onset short-acting barbiturate general anaesthetic. It is an intravenous ultra-short-acting barbiturate. Sodium thiopental is a depressant and is sometimes used during interrogations - not to cause pain (in fact, it may have just the opposite effect), but to weaken the resolve of the subject and make him or her more compliant to pressure.*
*Thiopental is still used in some places as a truth serum. The barbiturates as a class decrease higher cortical brain functioning. Psychiatrists hypothesize that because lying is*

more complex than telling the truth, suppression of the higher cortical functions may lead to the uncovering of the "truth". However, the reliability of confessions made under thiopental is dubious; the drug tends to make subjects chatty and cooperative with interrogators, but a practiced liar or someone who has a false story firmly established would still be quite able to lie while under the influence of the drug."

-- Reference: Wikipedia.org

[246] "...the Witness Protection Program..."

"(also known as the **Witness Security Program**, or **WitSec**) was established under Title V of the Organized Crime Control Act of 1970, which in turn sets out the manner in which the U.S. Attorney General may provide for the relocation and protection of a witness or potential witness of the federal government, or for a state government in an official proceeding concerning organized crime or other serious offenses. See 18 U.S.C.A 3521 et. seq.

The Federal Government also gives grants to the states to enable them to provide similar services. The federal program is called WITSEC (the Federal Witness Protection Program) and was founded in the late 1960s by Gerald Shur when he was in the Organized Crime and Racketeering Section of the United States Department of Justice. Most witnesses are protected by the U.S. Marshals Service, while protection of incarcerated witnesses is the duty of the Federal Bureau of Prisons.

Normally, the witness is provided with a new name and location. Witnesses are encouraged to keep their first names and choose last names with the same initial. The U.S. Marshals Service provides new documentation, assists in finding housing and employment and provides a stipend until the witness gets on his or her feet, but the stipend can be discontinued if the U.S. Marshals Service feels that the witness is not making an aggressive effort to find a job. Witnesses are not to travel back to their hometowns or contact unprotected family members or former associates. Around 17 percent of protected witnesses that have committed a crime will commit another crime, compared to the almost 40 percent of parolees who return to crime. This has led to action by Congressional committees requiring WITSEC and other witness protection programs to notify local officials of a witness' transfer before relocating them.

Many states, including California, Illinois, and New York, have their own witness protection programs for crimes not covered by the federal program. The state-run programs provide less extensive protections than the federal program."

-- Reference: Wikipedia.org

[247] "... Suleiman the Magnificent..."

"**Suleiman I** (Ottoman Turkish: □□□□□ Sulaymān, Turkish: Süleyman; almost always Kanuni Sultan Süleyman in Turkish) (November 6, 1494 – September 5/6, 1566), was the tenth and longest-reigning Sultan of the Ottoman Empire, from 1520 to his death in 1566. He is known in the West as **Suleiman the Magnificent** and in the East, as **the Lawgiver** (in Turkish Kanuni; Arabic: □□□□□□□, al - Qānūnī), for his complete reconstruction of the Ottoman legal system. Suleiman became the pre-eminent monarch of 16th century Europe, presiding over the apex of the Ottoman Empire's military, political and economic power. Suleiman personally led Ottoman armies to conquer the Christian strongholds of Belgrade, Rhodes, and most of Hungary before his conquests were checked at the Siege of Vienna in

1529. He annexed most of the Middle East in his conflict with the Persians and large swathes of North Africa as far west as Algeria. Under his rule, the Ottoman fleet dominated the seas from the Mediterranean to the Indian Ocean.

At the helm of an expanding empire, Suleiman personally instituted legislative changes relating to society, education, taxation, and criminal law. His canonical law (or the Kanuns) fixed the form of the empire for centuries after his death. Not only was Suleiman a distinguished poet and goldsmith in his own right; he also became a great patron of culture, overseeing the golden age of the Ottoman Empire's artistic, literary and architectural development.

In a break with Ottoman tradition, Suleiman married a harem girl who became Hürrem Sultan, whose intrigues in the court and power over the Sultan have become as famous as Suleiman himself."

-- Reference: Wikipedia.org

[248] "... His assistant was a harem girl who rose up from slavery to become his wife..."

" According to late sixteenth century and early seventeenth century sources such as the Polish poet Samuel Twardowski, **she was born in the town which was then part of the Kingdom of Poland.** She was captured by Crimean Tatars during one of their frequent raids into this region and taken as a slave, probably first to the Crimean city of Kaffa, a major centre of the slave trade, then to Istanbul, and was selected for Süleyman's harem.

Suleiman was infatuated with Hurrem Sultan, a harem girl of Ruthenian origin. In the West foreign diplomats, taking notice of the palace gossip about her, called her "Russelazie" or **"Roxolana", referring to her Slavic origins**. The daughter of an Orthodox Ukrainian priest, she was captured and rose through the ranks of the Harem to become Suleiman's favorite. **Breaking with two centuries of Ottoman tradition, a former concubine had thus become the legal wife of the Sultan,** much to the astonishment of observers in the palace and the city. **He also allowed Hurrem Sultan to remain with him at court for the rest of her life, breaking another tradition**—that when imperial heirs came of age, they would be sent along with the imperial concubine who bore them to govern remote provinces of the Empire, never to return unless their progeny succeeded to the throne.

### Under his pen name, Muhibbi, Suleiman composed this poem for Roxolana:

"Throne of my lonely niche, my wealth, my love, my moonlight.
My most sincere friend, my confidant, my very existence, my Sultan, my one and only love.
The most beautiful among the beautiful...
My springtime, my merry faced love, my daytime, my sweetheart, laughing leaf...
My plants, my sweet, my rose, the one only who does not distress me in this world...
My Istanbul, my Caraman, the earth of my Anatolia
My Badakhshan, my Baghdad and Khorasan
My woman of the beautiful hair, my love of the slanted brow, my love of eyes full of mischief...
I'll sing your praises always
I, lover of the tormented heart, Muhibbi of the eyes full of tears, I am happy."

*Roxelana, as she is better known in Europe, is well-known both in modern Turkey and in the West, and is the subject of many artistic works. **She has inspired paintings, musical works (including Joseph Haydn's Symphony No. 63), an opera by Denys Sichynsky, a ballet, plays, and several novels.***"

*-- Reference: Wikipedia.org*

249 **"... Queen Elizabeth..."**

***Elizabeth I*** *(7 September 1533 – 24 March 1603) was Queen of England and Queen of Ireland from 17 November 1558 until her death. Sometimes called The Virgin Queen, Gloriana, The Faerie Queen or Good Queen Bess, Elizabeth was the fifth and last monarch of the Tudor dynasty. The daughter of Henry VIII, she was born a princess, but her mother, Anne Boleyn, was executed three years after her birth, and Elizabeth was declared illegitimate. Perhaps for that reason, her brother, Edward VI, cut her out of the succession. His will, however, was set aside, as it contravened the Third Succession Act of 1543, in which Elizabeth was named as successor provided that Mary I of England, Elizabeth's half-sister, should die without issue. In 1558, Elizabeth succeeded her half-sister, during whose reign she had been imprisoned for nearly a year on suspicion of supporting Protestant rebels.*

*Elizabeth set out to rule by good counsel. One of her first moves was to support the establishment of an English Protestant church, of which she became the Supreme Governor. This Elizabethan Religious Settlement held firm throughout her reign and later evolved into today's Church of England. It was expected that Elizabeth would marry, but despite several petitions from parliament, she never did. The reasons for this choice are unknown, and they have been much debated. As she grew older, **Elizabeth became famous for her virginity**, and a cult grew up around her which was celebrated in the portraits, pageants and literature of the day.*

***One of her mottos was*** *video et taceo: "I see, and say nothing".*

*This strategy, viewed with impatience by her counselors, often saved her from political and marital misalliances. Though Elizabeth was cautious in foreign affairs and only half-heartedly supported a number of ineffective, poorly resourced military campaigns in the Netherlands, France and Ireland, **the defeat of the Spanish armada in 1588 associated her name forever with what is popularly viewed as one of the greatest victories in British history**. Within twenty years of her death, she was being **celebrated as the ruler of a golden age**, an image that retains its hold on the English people. Elizabeth's reign is known as the Elizabethan era, famous above all for the flourishing of English drama, led by playwrights such as William Shakespeare and Christopher Marlowe."*

*-- Reference: Wikipedia.org*

250 **"... he was incarnated as Cecil Rhodes."**

***Cecil John Rhodes***, *(July 5, 1853 – March 26, 1902) was a British-born South African businessman, mining magnate, and politician. He was the founder of the diamond company De Beers, which today markets 60% of the world's rough diamonds and at one time marketed 90%. He was an ardent believer in colonialism and was the founder of the state of Rhodesia, which was named after him.*

Rhodes profited greatly from controlling Southern Africa's natural resources, the proceeds of which funded the Rhodes Scholarship upon his death. **Rhodes never married, pleading that "I have too much work on my hands"** and saying that he would not be a dutiful husband. **Queen Victoria reportedly asked him if he was a woman-hater**, which Rhodes denied insisting "How could I dislike a sex to which your Majesty belongs?"

**Rhodes famously declared:**

*"To think of these stars that you see overhead at night, these vast worlds which we can never reach. I would annex the planets if I could; I often think of that. It makes me sad to see them so clear and yet so far."*

-- Reference: Wikipedia.org

[251] **"... she was a Polish princess..."**

*"Princess Catherine Radziwill (March 30, 1858 - May 12, 1941) was a Polish princess from a famous Polish-Lithuanian aristocratic family called the Radziwills. She was born as Countess Ekaterina Adamovna Rzewuska. She married Prince Wilhelm Radziwill at age 15 and moved to Berlin to live with his family. It was speculated that she was the author of a book gossiping about the German Emperor William II and Berlin society in 1884 under the pen name Paul Vasili.*

*She stalked the English-born South African politician Cecil Rhodes and asked him to marry her, but he refused. She wrote a biography of Rhodes called "Cecil Rhodes: Man and Empire Maker".*

-- Reference: Wikipedia.org

[252] **"... One was named Kelly..."**

**William Kelly** (August 22, 1811 - February 11, 1888), born in Pittsburgh, Pennsylvania, was an American inventor. Kelly studied metallurgy at the Western University of Pennsylvania. Kelly started experimenting with his "air-boiling process," a process of blowing air up through molten iron to reduce the carbon content, in 1847. His initial goal was to reduce the amount of fuel required for iron and steel making, because of the immense amount of timber required to make the charcoal. He discovered that, contrary to the expectations of his iron workers, the injected air did not cool the molten iron, but instead combined with the carbon to cause the iron to boil and burn violently until the carbon was greatly reduced, **improving the quality of the iron or converting it to steel**. His experiments began in 1847. The same process was later **independently invented and patented by Henry Bessemer."**

-- Reference: Wikipedia.org

[253] **"...the other was Bessemer..."**

*"Sir Henry Bessemer (January 19, 1813 – March 15, 1898), English engineer and inventor.* Bessemer's name is chiefly known in connection with **the Bessemer process for the manufacturing of steel**. Patents of such obvious value did not escape criticism, and invalidity was freely urged against them on various grounds. But Bessemer was fortunate enough to maintain them intact without litigation, though he found it advisable to buy up the

317

*rights of one patentee, while in another case he was freed from anxiety by the patent being allowed to lapse in 1859 through non-payment of fees."*

-- Reference: Wikipedia.org

[254] " Another IS-BE who did this was Alexander Bell..."

*"As is sometimes common in scientific discoveries, simultaneous developments can occur, as evidenced by a number of inventors who were at work on the telephone.*

*Alexander Graham Bell (3 March 1847 – 2 August 1922) was an eminent scientist, inventor and innovator who is credited with the invention of the telephone. His father, grandfather and brother had all been associated with work on elocution and speech, and **both his mother and wife were deaf, profoundly influencing Bell's life's work**. His research on hearing and speech further **led him to experiment with hearing devices** that eventually culminated in Bell being **awarded the first U.S. patent for the invention of the telephone in 1876**.*

*In reflection, Bell considered his most famous invention an intrusion on his real work as a scientist and **refused to have a telephone in his study**."*

-- Reference: Wikipedia.org

[255] ..." It was invented by several others, including Elisha Gray."

*"**Elisha Gray** (August 2, 1835 – January 21, 1901) was an American electrical engineer and is best known for his development of a telephone prototype in 1876 in Highland Park, Illinois, U.S.A.. Mr. Elisha Gray, of Chicago also **devised a tone telegraph of this kind about the same time as Herr La Cour**. In this apparatus a vibrating steel reed interrupted the current, which at the other end of the line passed through an electromagnet and vibrated a matching steel reed near its poles. Gray's 'harmonic telegraph,' with the vibrating reeds, was used by the Western Union Telegraph Company. Since more than one set of vibrations — that is to say, more than one note — can be sent over the same wire simultaneously, the harmonic telegraph can be utilised as a 'multiplex' or many-ply telegraph, conveying several messages through the same wire at once; and these can either be read by the operator by the sound, or a permanent record can be made by the marks drawn on a ribbon of travelling paper by a Morse recorder. Bell's March 10, 1876 laboratory notebook entry describing his first successful experiment with the telephone.*

*Bell's patent application for the telephone was filed in the US patent office on February 14, 1876. **The usual story says that Bell got to the patent office an hour or two before his rival Elisha Gray**, and that Gray lost his rights to the telephone as a result.*

***According to Gray's account**, his patent caveat was taken to the US patent office a few hours before Bell's application, shortly after the patent office opened and remained near the bottom of the in-basket until that afternoon. Bell's application was filed shortly before noon on 14 February by Bell's lawyer who requested that the filing fee be entered immediately onto the cash receipts blotter and that Bell's application be taken to the examiner immediately. Late that afternoon, the fee for Gray's caveat was entered on the cash blotter and the caveat was not taken to the examiner until the following day. The fact that Bell's filing fee was recorded earlier than Gray's fee led to the story that Bell had arrived at the patent office earlier. Bell was in Boston on February 14 and did not know this was happening until he arrived in Washington on February 26. Whether Bell's application was filed before or* after Gray's caveat no longer mattered, because Gray abandoned his caveat, which opened the door to Bell being granted U.S. Patent 174,465_ for the telephone on 7 March 1876."

-- Reference: Wikipedia.org

## END OF FOOTNOTES

Books Written by

# Lawrence R . Spencer

## The Oz Factors
### The "Wizard of Oz" as an Analogy to the Mysteries of Life

( www.ozfactors.com )

## Pan - God of The Woods

( www.godofthewoods.com )

319

# The Big Bleep
## The Mystery of a Different Universe

( www.thebigbleep.com )

# ALIEN INTERVIEW

Based On Personal Notes and Interview Transcriptions Provided by :

## Matilda O'Donnell MacElroy

Editing and Supplemental Footnotes by:

## Lawrence R. Spencer

( Author of "The Oz Factors" )

# Alien Interview

Cover and book design by Lawrence R. Spencer

Printed in The United States of America
First Edition Printing: 2008


ISBN: 978-0-6152-0460-4